The Cambridge Companion to Monteverdi

Claudio Monteverdi is one of the most important figures of 'early' music, a composer whose music speaks powerfully and directly to modern audiences. This book provides an up-to-date and authoritative treatment of Monteverdi and his music, complementing Paolo Fabbri's standard biography of the composer. Written by leading specialists in the field, it is aimed at students, performers and music-lovers in general and adds significantly to our understanding of Monteverdi's music, his life and the contexts in which he worked. Chapters offering overviews of his output of sacred, secular and dramatic music are complemented by 'intermedi', in which contributors examine individual works, or sections of works in detail. The book draws extensively on Monteverdi's letters and includes a select discography/videography and a complete list of Monteverdi's works together with an index of first lines and titles.

The Cambridge Companion to

MONTEVERDI

. . . .

EDITED BY
John Whenham
and
Richard Wistreich

CAMBRIDGE
UNIVERSITY PRESS

CAMBRIDGE UNIVERSITY PRESS
Cambridge, New York, Melbourne, Madrid, Cape Town, Singapore, São Paulo, Delhi

Cambridge University Press
The Edinburgh Building, Cambridge CB2 8RU, UK

Published in the United States of America by Cambridge University Press, New York

www.cambridge.org
Information on this title: www.cambridge.org/9780521697989

First published 2007

Printed in the United Kingdom at the University Press, Cambridge

A catalogue record for this publication is available from the British Library

ISBN 978-0-521-87525-7 hardback
ISBN 978-0-521-69798-9 paperback

To Nigel Fortune and the memory of Denis Arnold

Contents

Illustrations

Contributors

Paola Besutti is Associate Professor in the Department of Communication Sciences at the University of Teramo and a member of the PhD Program on Musical Heritage at the University of Lecce. Since 2003 she has been editor of the *Rivista italiana di musicologia*. Her publications as author and editor include many articles on music and musical practice in late-Renaissance Mantua, among them *La corte musicale di Ferdinando Carlo Gonzaga ultimo duca di Mantova* (1989), *Claudio Monteverdi: Studi e prospettive* (1998) and *Quante erano le messe mantovane? Nuovi elementi e qualche precisazione su Palestrina e il repertorio musicale per S. Barbara* (2006).

Roger Bowers is Emeritus Reader in Medieval and Renaissance Music in the University of Cambridge. He has published articles on the history of Choral Institutions and of Musical Notation, and on English political, ecclesiastical and social history; one aspect of his work is represented by the articles collected in *English Church Polyphony: Singers and Sources from the 14th Century to the 17th* (1999).

Tim Carter was born in Sydney, Australia, in 1954 and studied at the Universities of Durham and Birmingham in the United Kingdom. Formerly at Royal Holloway and Bedford New College, University of London, he is now David G. Frey Distinguished Professor of Music at the University of North Carolina at Chapel Hill. He is the author and editor of numerous books on music in late Renaissance and early Baroque Italy, including *Monteverdi's Musical Theatre* (2002) and *The Cambridge History of Seventeenth-Century Music* (2005), and also of the Cambridge Opera Handbook on Mozart's *Le nozze di Figaro* (1987) and *'Oklahoma!' The Making of an American Musical* (2007).

Geoffrey Chew is Emeritus Professor of Music at Royal Holloway, University of London. His publications, as author, co-author and editor, have concerned a variety of fields, including Renaissance music, the music of eighteenth-century Austria and twentieth-century Czech music, and include the *New Grove* article on Monteverdi's works.

Suzanne G. Cusick is Associate Professor of Music at New York University and was the first Frederick Burkhardt Residential Fellow at the Villa I Tatti, the Harvard University Center for Italian Renaissance Studies (2001–2002). She has published extensively on gender and sexuality in relation to music, and has recently completed a monograph on the seventeenth-century Florentine singer-teacher-composer Francesca Caccini.

Iain Fenlon is Senior Tutor and Fellow of King's College and Professor of Historical Musicology at the University of Cambridge. He is the founding editor of *Early Music History* (1981–) and his many books and articles on Italian music and culture in the Reniassance include *Music and Patronage in Sixteenth-Century Mantua* (1980, 1982) and *Music and Culture in Late Renaissance Italy* (2000).

His major study of music and society in Renaissance Venice will be published shortly.

Jeffrey Kurtzman is Professor of Music at Washington University in St. Louis. He was the founder and first president of the Society for Seventeenth-Century Music. He has authored books, articles, and critical editions on Monteverdi and on Italian sacred music of the sixteenth and seventeenth centuries. Among these are *The Monteverdi Vespers of 1610: Music, Context, and Performance* (1999) and the ten-volume series *Seventeenth-century Italian Music for Vespers and Compline* (1995–2003). He is the general editor of the forthcoming *Opera omnia* of Alessandro Grandi, to be published by the American Institute of Musicology.

Massimo Ossi is Chair of the Department of Musicology at Indiana University. His research interests include early seventeenth-century Italian music theory and aesthetics, Italian lyric poetry, opera, and the Italian madrigal. He is general editor of *Music at the Courts of Italy*, past editor of the newsletter of the Society for Seventeenth-Century Music, and author of *Divining the Oracle: Aspects of Monteverdi's seconda prattica* (2003).

Anthony Pryer is a lecturer at Goldsmiths' College, University of London, where he directs the Masters' degree in historical musicology. Recently he has published on Mozart, Vivaldi and on the philosophy of music. He has been an elected member of the executive committee of the British Society of Aesthetics for the past six years, and is a trustee of the Accademia Monteverdiana.

Ellen Rosand is Professor of Music at Yale University, and the author of *Opera in Seventeenth-Century Venice: the Creation of a Genre* (1991) and *Monteverdi's Last Operas: a Venetian Trilogy* (2007). She has published essays on Barbara Strozzi, Monteverdi, Cavalli, Vivaldi, Handel, and music in sixteenth-century Venice.

Joachim Steinheuer is Akademischer Oberrat in Musicology at Ruprecht Karls-Universität, Heidelberg. His publications as author, co-author and editor include works on the secular vocal music of Tarquinio Merula, on Monteverdi reception in seventeenth-century Europe, a chapter on songs, canons and concert arias in the *Mozart Handbuch* and numerous contributions to the Encyclopedia *Die Musik in Geschichte und Gegenwart*.

John Whenham is Professor of Music History and Head of the Department of Music at the University of Birmingham. As author and editor he has published books on early seventeenth-century duets and dialogue settings, on Monteverdi's *Orfeo* and the Vespers of 1610. He has published articles on music at Venice and by Monteverdi's Venetian contemporaries Giovanni Rovetta and Martino Pesenti, and CD notes for the projected complete recordings of Monteverdi's madrigals by the Consort of Musicke and of his sacred music by The King's Consort.

Richard Wistreich is Senior Lecturer and Head of Performance at the International Centre for Music Studies at Newcastle University. He is a professional singer and co-founder of the ensemble Red Byrd. His book, *Warrior, Courtier, Singer: Giulio Cesare Brancaccio and the Performance of Identity in the Late Renaissance* was published in 2007.

Preface

It is now more than twenty years since the appearance of *The New Monteverdi Companion*, edited by Denis Arnold and Nigel Fortune, to whom this book is dedicated. During those years the re-evaluation of Monteverdi and his work by performers and historians alike has proceeded apace and shows no sign of abating. New generations of performers now work comfortably with the instruments of Monteverdi's day and continue to explore the types of vocal production with which he might have been familiar; and listeners can now experience a wide range of live and recorded interpretations of Monteverdi's music. More is known now about the context in which Monteverdi worked, and fresh questions have been asked about his musical output, not least those arising from the so-called 'New Musicology'. On his operas alone three new books have appeared within the last five years.

Monteverdi is now a familiar figure on the musical scene, and one whose music seems to speak directly and powerfully across the centuries to present-day audiences. Nevertheless, the world in which he worked was in many respects very different from our own, and the differences are themselves worth exploring. The present *Companion*, while centred on Monteverdi's music, seeks to place it in the context of the institutions for which Monteverdi worked and his intellectual, social and religious environment. It draws together many of the new strands of thought on the composer developed over the last twenty years and, indeed, adds to them. Monteverdi's own letters form a constant source of reference in the essays of this book, and we have all benefited from the availability not only of Éva Lax's edition of the Italian texts (Florence, 1994), but also of Denis Stevens's English translations (London, 1980, revised edn. Oxford, 1995); in order that readers can easily consult any of these editions, the letters are referred to in the text by date only, or by date and recipient if more than one letter survives from the same date.

Books in the *Cambridge Companion* series are aimed at the general reader, as well as students of music, and do not normally include detailed musical analyses. We felt, however, that when dealing with music of this early period, and with settings of Italian and Latin texts, students in particular might value some guidance on how to approach the study of individual works, or excerpts from works. We thus invited those of our contributors dealing with the larger *corpora* of Monteverdi's work to contribute short, analytical, *intermedi*, placed between the main chapters of the book, rather as musical *intermedi* were placed between the acts of spoken plays in the sixteenth and seventeenth centuries. In order to make it easy both to find individual works by Monteverdi and modern editions of them, the list of Monteverdi's works at the end of the book has been arranged in chronological order, rather than by type of work, and an index of titles and first lines also supplied. This also means that we have been able to include in a single sequence works that are now lost. Manuscripts and sacred *contrafacta* are also listed.

It remains to thank all our authors for their expert contributions to this book, and to Victoria Cooper, Rebecca Jones, Liz Davey and Michael Downes of Cambridge University Press for their support in seeing the book through the press.

John Whenham
Richard Wistreich

Chronology

1567	Monteverdi born in Cremona, then under Spanish control as part of the state of Milan. Baptised Claudio Zuan [Giovanni] Antonio Monteverdi on 15 May 1567 in the church of SS Nazaro e Celso, Cremona. He was the first of three children born to Baldassare Monteverdi, an apothecary, physician and surgeon, and Maddalena Zignani.
c.1576	Monteverdi's mother dies. His father remarries in this or the following year, and two further children are born to him and Giovanna Gadio.
1582	Claudio's *Sacrae cantiunculae*, a volume of three-voice motets, is published by Angelo Gardano at Venice, then the major centre of music publishing in Italy. The dedication was signed from Cremona, 1 August 1582, when Monteverdi was fifteen years old. On the title-page of this, and all his publications up to the Second Book of Madrigals (1590), Monteverdi describes himself as a pupil of Marc'Antonio Ingegneri, *maestro di cappella* of Cremona Cathedral.
1583	*Madrigali spirituali* for four voices published in Brescia by Vinzenzo Sabbio.
after 1583	Monteverdi's father marries Francesca Como following the death of his second wife.
1584	Monteverdi's first publication of secular music, *Canzonette* for three voices, published at Venice by Giacomo Vincenti and Ricciardo Amadino.
1587	Monteverdi, still only nineteen, publishes his First Book of five-part Madrigals, dedicated to Count Marco Verità of Verona, suggesting that he may have begun looking for employment outside Cremona.
1590	The Second Book of Madrigals is published by Angelo Gardano at Venice. The dedication is signed from Cremona, 1 January 1590, and addressed to Giacomo Ricardi, President of the Milanese senate. In it Monteverdi refers to himself as a player of the *vivuola*.

1590	Early in this year (see Chapter 4, note 1, below) Monteverdi is appointed as singer and instrumentalist (bowed strings and theorbo) to the *cappella* of Vincenzo Gonzaga, Duke of Mantua. Here he works under Giaches de Wert, one of Italy's most eminent composers, and alongside musicians such as Salamone Rossi, Benedetto Pallavicino and Giovanni Giacomo Gastoldi, who was choirmaster of Santa Barbara.
1592	The Third Book of Madrigals published and dedicated to the Duke of Mantua.
1595	June–November, travels with Vincenzo Gonzaga on a military expedition to Hungary as part of a *cappella* of eight – three priests and five singers.
1596	Wert dies on 6 May; succeeded as *maestro* of the duke's *cappella* by Benedetto Pallavicino.
1599	On 20 May marries Claudia Cattaneo, a court singer at Mantua, daughter of Giacomo Cattaneo, a string player. 7 June–15 October, travels with Duke Vincenzo to Spa in Flanders where he encounters the 'canto alla francese' (song in the French manner) which, his brother Giulio Cesare was to claim in 1607, he was the first to bring back to Italy.
1600	Giovanni Maria Artusi criticises works by Monteverdi in *L'Artusi, overo Delle imperfettioni della moderna musica* (The Artusi, or, On the Imperfections of Modern Music), Venice, 1600.
1601	His first son, Francesco Baldassare, born (baptised 27 August). 26 November, Pallavicino dies; in a letter of 28 November Monteverdi petitions the duke to appoint him *maestro* both of the chamber and of the church. He succeeds to the post of *maestro di cappella* in December.
1603	His daughter Leonora Camilla born (baptised 20 February). The Fourth Book of Madrigals published. On its title-page he styles himself *maestro della musica* of the duke. Artusi issues further criticism of Monteverdi's work in the *Seconda parte dell'Artusi*, Venice, 1603.
1604	His second son, Massimiliano Giacomo, born (baptised 10 May).
1605	Monteverdi's Fifth Book of Madrigals published – the first in which he includes madrigals with *basso continuo* accompaniment. It includes a statement in which Monteverdi responds to Artusi's criticisms and claims to be

	preparing a treatise entitled *Seconda pratica, overo Perfettione della moderna musica* (The Second Practice, or The Perfection of Modern Music). The treatise was never published.
1607	Monteverdi's first opera, *Orfeo*, performed on 24 February and repeated on 1 March. The *Scherzi musicali* for three voices, two violins and continuo published summer 1607. It includes a gloss by Giulio Cesare Monteverdi on the statement published in the Fifth Book. In this a distinction is drawn between the 'first practice . . . which turns on the perfection of the harmony' and the 'second practice . . . which makes the [words] the mistress of the harmony'. 10 September: his wife, Claudia, dies in Cremona; buried in S. Nazaro. 24 September: Monteverdi summoned back to Mantua to begin preparations for the celebrations attending the wedding of Francesco Gonzaga to Margherita of Savoy, scheduled for early 1608.
1608	After much delay the wedding celebrations take place in May and June. Monteverdi's contributions include the opera *Arianna*, the Prologue to *L'idropica* and the *Mascherata dell'ingrate*. By July he is seriously ill and retires to his father's house at Cremona. On 9 November his father petitions the duke either to restrict Monteverdi's work to church music or to release him from service. On 30 November, however, Monteverdi is summoned back to Mantua.
1610	The *Missa . . . ac Vesperae* published, perhaps with the intention of demonstrating Monteverdi's ability as a composer of church music and his fitness to be employed as a church musician. In October he travels to Rome to present the volume to its dedicatee, Pope Paul V.
1611	In his letter of 22 January Monteverdi mentions that his son Francesco is showing promise as a singer.
1612	8 February: Duke Vincenzo Gonzaga dies. He is succeeded by Duke Francesco who dismisses Claudio and Giulio Cesare from his service on 29 July. Claudio returns to Cremona.
1613	Auditioned for the post of *maestro di cappella* at S. Marco, Venice, 1 August 1613, performing a Mass by him which he had rehearsed at S. Giorgio Maggiore on the preceding days. 19 August: the Procurators of S. Marco approve his

	appointment, 'confirmed in this opinion . . . both by his works that are found in print and by those which . . . Their Most Illustrious Lordships have sought to hear to their complete satisfaction'. He travels to Venice to take up his position around 10 October.
1614	The Sixth Book of Madrigals published, preparation of which may have begun as early as 1610.
1616	The ballet *Tirsi e Clori* (published 1619) performed for Duke Ferdinando Gonzaga (crowned Duke of Mantua January 1616).
1617	His prologue to *La Maddalena* performed at Mantua for the wedding celebrations of Ferdinando Gonzaga and Caterina de' Medici (married 7 February 1617).
1619	His Seventh Book of Madrigals published, and dedicated to Caterina de' Medici. Monteverdi moves his son Francesco, now an able singer and, according to his father, in danger of being distracted from his study of jurisprudence, from Padua University to the University of Bologna, lodging him at the monastery of S. Maria dei Servi. Approached to return to Mantua. His reaction reflected in his letters of 8 and 13 March 1620.
1620	In early March the opera *Andromeda* and the ballet *Apollo* performed at Mantua. 13 June: attends a meeting of the *Accademia dei Floridi* held in his honour at S. Michele in Bosco, Bologna. 24 June: directs Vespers for the Feast of St John the Baptist, probably for the Florentine community at Venice and at SS Giovanni e Paolo (see Chapter 11, below). The occasion reported by Constantijn Huygens (see Chapter 14, below). 4 November: directs Vespers for the Feast of S. Carlo Borromeo for the Milanese community at Venice, probably at the church of S. Maria Gloriosa dei Frari. Francesco Monteverdi abandons his legal studies at Bologna to join the order of the Discalced Carmelite Fathers.
1621	25 May: directs music for the obsequies celebrated by the Florentine community at SS Giovanni e Paolo, Venice, for Grand Duke Cosimo II of Tuscany. His son Francesco sings the introductory '"O vos omnes attendite" . . . with the rest of the Introit'.
1622	18 January: contributes to *intermedi* performed at Mantua for the wedding celebrations of Eleonora Gonzaga and

	Emperor Ferdinand II. In letter of 26 February 1622 confirms that his son Massimiliano has been accepted to study medicine at Cardinal Montalto's college in Bologna.
1623	directs music for the state visit to Venice of the Duke and Duchess of Mantua (20–30 May) and publishes the monodic version of the *Lamento d'Arianna*.
after 1623	Denounced anonymously to the Venetian State Inquisitors for insulting the doge and the clergy and uttering treacherous support for the Holy Roman Emperor. The denunciation seems to have been ignored.
1624	The *Combattimento di Tancredi e Clorinda*, in which he introduces his new *genere concitato*, played at the Palazzo Dandolo (now the Danieli Hotel), Venice, home of Monteverdi's patron Girolamo Mocenigo.
1625	March: directs music for the private visit to Venice of Władisław Sigismund, heir to the throne of Poland.
1625–6	In a group of letters from 23 August 1625 to 28 March 1626 Monteverdi reveals his interest in alchemy. Enrolled in the Accademia dei Filomusi, Bologna.
1626	Early in the year Monteverdi's son Massimiliano graduates in medicine at Bologna. 15 June: a trio by Monteverdi sung at the Venetian state banquet for St Vitus' Day includes a refrain 'One cannot believe them because there is no faith there', which gives offence to the French ambassador. Late in the year Massimiliano Monteverdi imprisoned by the Inquisition for reading a prohibited book.
1627	May–September: Monteverdi works on the music for the comic opera *La finta pazza Licori*, to a libretto by Giulio Strozzi, for a proposed performance at Mantua. Project abandoned. 15 July: provides music for Georg Wilhelm, Elector of Brandenburg, then staying incognito at the house of the English ambassador.
1627–8	Commissioned to write music for the wedding celebrations at Parma in December 1628 for Duke Odoardo Farnese and Margherita de' Medici. Stays at Parma October–mid-December 1627, mid-January–March 1628 and December 1628. His work for Parma included a prologue and five *intermedi* for a performance of Torquato Tasso's *Aminta* and a tournament *Mercurio e Marte*. In a letter of 27 November 1627 to the Marquis Enzo Bentivoglio, Antonio Goretti wrote of Monteverdi: 'Signor Claudio composes only in the

morning and the evening: during the afternoon he does not wish to do anything at all ... It is true that the labour is great, and tedious; but still, he is a man who likes to talk things over in company at great length (and about this I make it a rule to take the opportunity away from him during working hours).' 8 April 1628: his sonnet cycle for two voices, *I cinque fratelli*, is performed at a banquet at the Arsenale, Venice, to honour the state visit of the Grand Duke of Tuscany.

1630   16 April: his first opera for Venice, *Proserpina rapita*, commissioned by Girolamo Mocenigo, is performed in the upper solar of Palazzo Dandolo (now the Danieli Hotel), Venice, as part of wedding festivities for Giustiniana Mocenigo and Lorenzo Giustiniani.

1630–1   The imperial troops who sacked Mantua in July 1630 bring an epidemic of plague which sweeps through northern Italy. The illness is brought to Venice by a diplomatic mission headed by Count Alessandro Striggio, Monteverdi's Mantuan confidant and librettist of his *Orfeo*. The plague kills nearly fifty thousand in Venice alone, and in Bergamo, Alessandro Grandi, who had been Monteverdi's assistant at S. Marco, is another victim. The Venetians vow to found a church in honour of the Blessed Virgin to seek her intercession. The foundation stone of Santa Maria della Salute (St Mary of Health) is laid on 1 April 1631, and on 21 November a solemn Mass of Thanksgiving held in S. Marco, with music by Monteverdi.

1631   9 March: admitted by Patriarch Giovanni Tiepolo to the clerical tonsure and the four minor orders in the chapel of the patriarchal palace at S. Pietro di Castello, Venice.

1632   10 April: Monteverdi ordained sub-deacon by Monsignor Sebastiano Querini at the church of S. Maurizio, Venice. 13 April: ordained deacon by Monsignor Querini at the church of Santa Maria del Giglio, and on 16 April, at the same church (which is also called S. Maria Zobenigo), ordained priest. He was, however, aggregated to the clergy of Cremona, and clearly had the intention of retiring there. The Venetian music publisher Bartolomeo Magni issues a volume of *Scherzi musicali* by Monteverdi that he has collected.

1635	3 and 4 November: directs music for the Feast of S. Carlo Borromeo at the church of S. Maria Gloriosa dei Frari for the Milanese community at Venice.
1636	May have responded to the celebrations in honour of the coronation of Ferdinand III as Holy Roman Emperor in December with the *ballo* 'Volgendo il ciel' and possibly the revised *Ballo delle ingrate*, both published in 1638.
1637–1638	Provides music for Giulio and Barbara Strozzi's *Accademia degli Unisoni*.
1638	The Eighth Book of Madrigals – *Madrigali guerrieri ed amorosi* – published, with a preface in which he explains the genesis of his *genere concitato*. The volume is dedicated to the Holy Roman Emperor Ferdinand III.
Carnival 1639–40	*Arianna* revived at the Teatro San Moisé, Venice.
1640	Before 22 February: *Il ritorno d'Ulisse* premiered, probably at the Teatro SS Giovanni e Paolo, Venice.
Carnival 1640–1	*Le nozze d'Enea e Lavinia* premiered, probably at the Teatro SS Giovanni e Paolo, Venice.
1641	7 February: the ballet *Vittoria d'Amore* performed at Piacenza to celebrate the birth of the seventh child of Duke Odoardo Farnese. The *Selva morale e spirituale* published at Venice and dedicated to Eleanora Gonzaga, widow of the Holy Roman Emperor Ferdinand II.
1643	*L'incoronazione di Poppea* performed at the Teatro SS Giovanni e Paolo. 29 November: dies in Venice and is buried in Santa Maria Gloriosa dei Frari in the chapel of the Milanesi. His funeral is commemorated in the *Fiori poetici raccolti nel funerale del molto illustre e molto reverendo signor Claudio Monteverdi*, ed. Giovan Battista Marinoni and published at Venice in 1644.

1 Approaching Monteverdi: his cultures and ours

ANTHONY PRYER

In an anonymous letter, written just two years before Monteverdi died, and printed with the libretto of his opera *Le nozze d'Enea con Lavinia*, the author recommends the composer to the audience and imagines the fate of his music in the far-distant future:

> Enjoy the music of the never-enough-praised Monteverdi, born to the world so as to rule over the emotions of others ... this truly great man ... known in far-flung parts and wherever music is known, will be sighed for in future ages at least as far as they can be consoled by his most noble compositions, which are set to last as long as they can resist the ravages of time.[1]

The future predicted in this letter seems substantially to have come true. Centuries after his death Monteverdi's works continue to be appreciated in far-flung parts of the world, they continue to console us, and we still think of Monteverdi as a great musical figure. As for the ravages of time, over three hundred of his works have managed to survive[2] together with one hundred and twenty-seven of his letters[3] and numerous other documents directly relevant to his life and times.

The mere fact of the survival of many of Monteverdi's compositions would be remarkable, but his music has also accomplished something else: it has reached out to exert a formidable influence on the imaginations of many recent composers. Numerous adaptations and arrangements of his works have appeared over the past hundred years (those by D'Indy, Orff, Respighi, Hindemith, Maderna and Henze are only the most famous), and his musical procedures have shown a remarkable capacity to insinuate themselves almost seamlessly into the creative fabric of our modern musical languages. This can be seen, for example, in works as contrasted as Strauss's 1935 opera *Die schweigsame Frau* (where a section of *Poppea* is transformed into material for a singing lesson in Act III), the jazz piece by the American composer Harold Shapero entitled, in honour of Monteverdi's name, *On Green Mountain* (1957), and the recent compositions by the English composer John Woolrich (*Favola in Musica*, *Ulysses Awakes*, *Ariadne Laments*) where fragments of Monteverdi's works are transliterated into a post-modern idiom.

To these musical signs of assimilation and integration one might add examples from other fields. For example, Monteverdi has featured in literary works both as a subject for discussion amongst the protagonists (as in *Il fuoco*, 1898, by the Italian novelist Gabriele D'Annunzio), and as a participating character (in *Masque of the Gonzagas*, 1999, by the British writer Clare Colvin). Moreover, both he and his works perform a notable role in the constant play of allusions to be found in *La Carte postale* (1980), a study of the exchange of messages between past and present by the French philosopher Jacques Derrida.[4] It is precisely this ability to form part of the easy currency of shared reference and communication, without the need for self-conscious explanation, that most sociologists and anthropologists would take as a clear sign of 'belonging' to a culture, and in that sense Monteverdi belongs to ours – as well as his own.

But the constructive link between identity and culture is potent, and it would be very difficult for a person to become deeply embedded in more than one culture and remain unchanged.[5] If we are really concerned to approach Monteverdi a little more closely then we have to begin by understanding something of the grids of meaning from our own culture that we have thrown across his (rather different) social practices and attitudes. The notion of 'cultural meaning' is itself of relatively modern origin and academic analyses of it are still ongoing. In the brief space of this chapter, we can merely pick out some particularly established and influential interpretations of the term 'culture' – those connected with national identity, the art world, popular interests, and technology and progress – and investigate how these recent perspectives may have transformed (or even obscured) Monteverdi's practices in our modern retelling of them.

Cultural perspectives

Modern conceptions of culture mostly have their roots in the revolutionary account of the topic developed by the eighteenth-century German philosopher Johann Gottfried Herder. In his *On German Character and Art* (1773) he established the highly influential notion of the 'Volksgeist' – the spirit of the people – which, he claimed, unified and underpinned the history, destiny, and attitudes of a nation. He also distinguished between 'Culture' and 'Civilisation', the former comprising the spirit that holds a society together in a distinctive way, and the latter being a veneer of technology and social practices that may be shared across many societies.

The German Romantics and, after them, the early anthropologists, took from Herder his central idea that culture was the defining essence of a nation – the same thought that persuades some to think of Monteverdi as an essentially Italian musician, with all that that might entail. Others of a more classical persuasion, such as the pioneering German educationalist Wilhelm von Humbolt, borrowed from Herder an interest in culture as the supposed fiefdom of an educated elite who produced 'improving' works which were assumed to require intellect and study for their meaningful appreciation. Out of this tradition comes the view of Monteverdi as a creator of original, cultivated art music in the written, western tradition. As for 'popular culture', Herder himself famously published some early collections of folksongs (1778–9), but the use of the term as indicating a concern with the widely shared interests and tastes of the common populus, and acting in some senses in opposition to so-called 'elite' cultures, gained a firm foothold in the 1960s among sociologists and those concerned with the academic discipline of 'cultural studies'. Little has been said about Monteverdi from this perspective, though there is some scope for discussing the influence on his works of the 'popular' music of his time (whatever Monteverdi and his contemporaries might have construed by such a term).

Finally, we come to 'civilisation' and its associations with technology, urban society and industrialisation. This perspective (or, rather, this antithesis to culture as Herder saw it) – with its interest in the depersonalised functions of human beings, the operations of the market place, and technological innovation as a sign of progress – has attracted a good deal of analysis and negative criticism from theorists, particularly those of the twentieth-century Frankfurt School such as Adorno, Benjamin and Horkheimer. From these viewpoints we may learn something about Monteverdi's music as an economic commodity (then and now), about the uneasy tensions he felt between his functional roles (as courtier and servant) and his special gifts as an individual, and also about the nature of his innovations in musical technology (new instruments and notational devices) and the mechanics and devices of musical expression. What follows is a brief account of these modern ways of construing Monteverdi as a 'cultural phenomenon', together with comments on some of their consequences for his realistic survival in our imaginations.

Monteverdi as an Italian: national cultures and nationalism

To have called Monteverdi an 'Italian' composer in the seventeenth century would not have been inappropriate even though Italy (as a country) did not become politically unified (as a state) until 1861. 'Italy' was the place where the 'nation' of Italians lived and where they spoke, more or less, a common language and shared a history – but they did not yet share a central, guiding legislature nor a corporate political autonomy, both of which are key ingredients of statehood. These distinctions between country, nation and state are important because they help to explain the allegiances and antagonisms that arise in the lives of communities and individuals.

In Monteverdi's time citizens of the country of Italy were subject to at least two levels of statehood. The first came from the local 'city-states', most of which were ruled by dynastic families such as the Medici (Florence), the Gonzagas (Mantua), the Farnese (in Parma and Piacenza) and the Este family (in Ferrara and Modena). Monteverdi, at first as an instrument of Gonzaga influence, and later in his own right as a famous composer, wrote works for many of these families. Interestingly, there seems to have been a complete absence of commissions from the Medici for pieces to be performed in Florence, though in 1614 Francesco de' Medici asked to borrow the score of *Arianna*,[6] and Monteverdi hints at an invitation to go to Florence in a letter of 20 January 1617. Complicated rivalries and hierarchies may lie behind this situation.

The second level of state control in Italy came from the Holy Roman Emperors (the Habsburgs) based in Vienna and Innsbruck. They were, at least nominally, the military defenders of the Pope and the Catholic Church, and they intervened regularly in the affairs of Italy. Monteverdi himself gives a small example of this in a letter to Alessandro Striggio of 10 September 1627, where he tells us that his problems over a church benefice could be solved 'at once by means of an order from Her Majesty the Empress to the Governor of Milan or to the Cardinal of Cremona'. His connections with the Habsburgs are demonstrated by the dedication of his Eighth Book of Madrigals to Emperor Ferdinand III, and his *Selva morale* collection of sacred music to the Empress Eleonora (formerly a Gonzaga princess).

Additionally, a portrait of Monteverdi now in Innsbruck (Fig. 1.1(a)) may have some direct connection with the Habsburg court. It is apparently a copy of a picture now in Vienna[7] but, rather oddly for a copy, someone has made an incomplete and slightly incompetent attempt to add musical notation to the book held by Monteverdi. This music, even as it stands, is intriguingly very close to a section in the sole surviving manuscript source of his opera *Il ritorno d'Ulisse* – the point in scene 7 of the final act where Giunone (Juno) sings the words 'Gran Giove' (Great Jove) (Figs. 1.1(b) and (c)).[8] The 'G' for the character of Giunone is particularly clear in the painting. The Holy Roman Emperor and Empress were often allegorised as Jove and Juno, as we can see from the *intermedi* composed by Monteverdi for the wedding of Eleonora and Ferdinand II in 1622,[9] and from a ceiling painting in the Sala dei Giganti in the Palazzo Te in Mantua. The Innsbruck portrait seems also to be attempting to make

Fig. 1.1a Portrait of Monteverdi, after Bernardo Strozzi

this link. It may be significant, too, that, in the final act of *Il ritorno d'Ulisse* (at least in the version as we now have it), the Imperial Eagle is made to sweep across the stage, which may indicate a connection with the Habsburgs for the opera itself.

The Imperial family and the Gonzagas have received much attention in our usual approaches to Monteverdi, but the influence of Spain, cutting across our modern comfortable style-and-place organisation of his life (Cremona, Mantua, Venice), requires a special effort to bring into

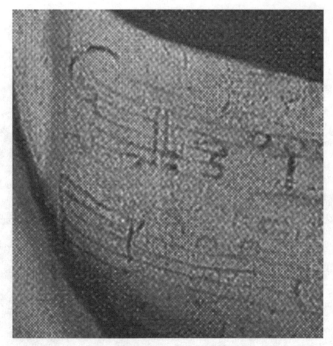

Fig. 1.1b Detail of music in Fig. 1.1a

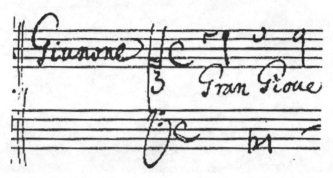

Fig. 1.1c Detail from Vienna manuscript of *Il ritorno d'Ulisse in patria*

focus. Spain, through the Spanish branch of the Imperial Habsburg family, controlled both the Kingdom of Naples in the South and Milan and its territories in the North. Monteverdi's birthplace, Cremona, lay in the territory of Milan, which was a Spanish possession, and so, in effect, he was born a Spanish citizen. His father organised the Spanish census in Cremona in 1576,[10] and the Monteverdi family showed a strong preference for imperial names, whether of ancient Roman origin (Claudio and his brother Giulio Cesare), or of the Habsburgs (Monteverdi's son Massimiliano was named after the Holy Roman Emperor at the time of his birth). When Monteverdi died he was buried in a chapel of the Frari church in Venice reserved for Milanese citizens, since, as a 'foreigner', he was not allowed to be interred in S. Marco. Perhaps we should not be surprised that a document survives in which Monteverdi is accused of making traitorous remarks about the Republic of Venice, allegedly hoping that it would one day be 'subjugated to the King of Spain' and that the 'Imperial Eagle' would rule there.[11] In Mantua there was a steady flow of musicians with connections to Spanish Naples (for example, Giaches de Wert, Adriana Basile, and the guitarist Pedro Guiterrez), as well as Southern poets (Tasso, Marino), and Duke Ferdinando Gonzaga was said to speak Spanish with as much facility as Italian.[12]

The effects of these Spanish cultural connections on Monteverdi's music have yet to be fully studied. It is clearly relevant to this perspective, for example, that *Fumia la pastorella* in his First Book of Madrigals (1587) is apparently in praise of a Neapolitan gentlewoman, and that several manuscript copies of Monteverdi's works survive in Naples – those for 'Voglio di vita uscir' (SV337), a Gloria for eight voices (SV307), and one of the scores of *Poppea* (SV308). There is also a work for Spanish guitar published in Rome in 1637 which is probably an arrangement of a dance by Monteverdi (the 'Ballo del Monte Verde', SVA1), and seems to reflect southern traditions.

These overlapping notions of statehood and nationhood in Monteverdi's life cannot be related in any simple way to our more modern concept of 'nationalism'. This last term does not just imply a sense of attachment to a nation, which Monteverdi might well have had, and which we should properly call 'patriotism'. It also involves a conscious 'ideology of attachment' which tends to suggest that deep spiritual and racial causes lie behind the special characteristics of a nation, that their individual members inescapably exemplify those attributes, and that, under certain conditions, those same individuals have self-denying responsibilities in the service of the nation's prestige and destiny.[13]

Nationalism has now been around for some two hundred years, but it has undergone various changes in interpretation and implementation. These changes are not reflected very clearly in the story of the reception of Monteverdi's compositions simply because most of his works were not recovered until a fairly late stage of nationalism, that of Italian Fascism in the 1920s and 30s: Malipiero's complete edition dates from 1926–42. However, one interesting exception to this (there are others) concerns the modern rediscovery of Monteverdi's lament from his opera *Arianna* (1608).

In the early phase, nationalist historians were most concerned to gather documents relevant to the history of a nation and to codify and preserve them. This approach was carefully theorised by the German historian Leopold von Ranke in the early nineteenth century: he argued that the historian should be objective, that facts should have primacy over theories, and that the past should be understood in its own terms.

The earliest modern references to Arianna's lament show some signs of reflecting these principles. Esteban de Arteaga, in his history of Italian opera of 1783, carefully notes the importance of *Arianna* for the Italian tradition (he talks of its influence on Pergolesi), and quotes verbatim six lines of text from the lament, beginning not with the opening words but with 'O Teseo, O Teseo mio / Se tu sapessi, oh Dio!' from the middle of the second section.[14] Carl Winterfeld, in his 1834 work on Giovanni Gabrieli and his times, provides some of the music, replicating the clefs and the bare bass-and-voice of the original notation.[15] His edition is without the addition of expression and dynamic markings, and like Arteaga he gives only a tiny fragment of the work, since he reproduces only the opening section of the lament. This incompleteness was reme-died first by the German musicologist Emil Vogel in his pioneering and extraordinarily professional study of Monteverdi published in 1887.[16] Vogel's completion of the music was replicated in Angelo Solerti's history of early seventeenth-century opera issued in 1904.[17] Both Vogel and Solerti retained the original clefs and the bare notation, but neither of these 'objec-tive' historians was quite able to resist subtly re-barring the piece so as to make it conform to 'logical' accentuation and regular divisions of the beat. In their scholarly endeavours the 'scientific' understanding of music took precedence over mere antiquarianism.

In the late nineteenth century in Italy, in parallel to the reconstruc-tive work of Vogel and Solerti, another kind of nationalism was gain-ing ground, one based not just (or even) on the responsible recovery of national documents, but rather on the demonstration that there were unifying, distinctive and prestigious national characteristics, and that their 'innateness' was proved by their continuous existence throughout the history of the nation.

An interesting demonstration of this principle can be seen in Alessandro Parisotti's famous version of Monteverdi's lament in the second volume of his collection called *Arie antiche* (1890). Parisotti provides only the opening section (in which truncated version it was frequently performed in recitals up to the 1950s), though he knew about the rest since he tells us that lament was complete in the manuscript source in Florence he had used for his publication. To make the piece palatable to his contemporaries, he pro-vided modern clefs, a slightly over-chromaticised piano accompaniment, and 'expressive' articulation and dynamic markings (from *piano* to *forte*). No phrase marks were added to the voice part, but they are everywhere in the accompaniment, evoking what Parisotti apparently considered to be the lyrical flow of the music.

In the 1890s the question of the distinctive musical identity of Italy rested very strongly on the achievements of Giuseppe Verdi and the claims of Italian opera as against those of Wagner and the German tradition. This is exactly the argument that plays such an important part in Gabriele D'Annunzio's 1898 novel *Il fuoco* mentioned earlier. In that novel Monteverdi is invoked as a proto-lyricist, the possessor of an 'heroic soul, purely Italian in essence'. At a crucial moment towards the end of Part I of the book, it is precisely a performance of Arianna's lament that awakens the protagonists to a continuous line of expressive beauty and drama that links the past to the present and the future.[18] Once this trans-cultural view of the lyrical 'essence' of Monteverdi's music became accepted, its 'objective' historical integrity was in jeopardy – the supposed 'long line' of the melody became as important as the localised moments of rhetorical intensity, and the concentration on emotional expression seemed to justify a link between past and future based on a notion of 'trans-historical humanness'. This viewpoint also, incidentally, established a still discernible bias (with some notable exceptions) towards an interest in Monteverdi's secular, rather than his sacred, music.

Respighi's arrangement of Arianna's lament in 1909 was one of the more extreme manifestations of these tendencies. Its heavy orchestration, extra chromaticism and complete re-ordering of the sections so as to begin with Arianna yearning directly for Teseo by name, now allowed the piece to proceed rather like a *verismo* aria. This trend towards lyrical intensification can also be seen in Pietro Floridia's edition of 1923.[19] Unlike Parisotti, he added lyrical phrase marks to the vocal line, and drove up the dynamics to *fortissimo*, while adding *affrettando* and *ritenuto molto* to the expression marks. When Malipiero came to publish the work in the complete edition (Volume XI in 1930), he supplied some very subdued dynamic marks (mostly *piano* with one moment of *forte*), which seem, if one is to add such marks at all, curiously over-cautious. After all, from the accounts we have of vocal performances in Monteverdi's time (including *Arianna*) they could sometimes be what we might want to call melodramatic, though usually within the confines of a chamber-music environment.[20] Malipiero's subdued dynamic markings seem to have been his way of controlling the perceived excesses of his own contemporary performers – his 'inauthentic' notation was perhaps designed to manipulate the singers into rendering scaled-down, more 'authentic' performances. The clash of cultures between Monteverdi's music, Malipiero's scholarly traditions and the performance practices of the early twentieth century can be read off the pages of that first complete edition.

Monteverdi as a composer: artistic cultures and popular cultures

Monteverdi was valued as a composer in the seventeenth century, and so he still is in the modern world. Moreover, the reasons behind these two judgements seem, at first glance, to be reassuringly similar. In the seventeenth century Monteverdi was praised for the 'variety of his compositions', for their 'musical way of moving some particular emotion in the breasts of men' (both remarks from Matteo Caberloti),[21] and for his ability to outshine his contemporaries as the sun does the moon (so described in a letter published with the scenario of the opera *Ulisse Errante*, 1644).[22] The implied criteria here of diversity of output, artistic power and comparative worth are ones with which we might easily agree today – and which seem to have engendered his popularity within the present early music field. Moreover, it is clear that his creative abilities inflected the decision-making processes in his appointments. For example, in the dedication to his Fifth Book of Madrigals (1605) he tells us that it was his compositions, welcomed with 'singular favour', that had led to his heading the musical establishment at Mantua. Similarly, when the Procurators of S. Marco appointed him *maestro di cappella* in August 1613, their official acceptance commended him as a 'most outstanding individual' whose 'quality and virtue' was evidenced by his 'works which are found in print' as much as by the way he directed performances.[23]

Once employed, however, Monteverdi seems to have been a performer, director and servant first, and a composer only second.[24] At first glance, that functionary aspect to his work may not seem to distinguish him radically from the modern world in which composers also find themselves working under contract. However, our contract law is underpinned by an important modern moral precept – that a contract can only be undertaken by an autonomous agent who, by acting voluntarily and with full knowledge of the implications, thereby creates the conditions of his or her obligations. These modern ideas are derived partly from political notions of a social contract between free citizens as developed by Rousseau in the eighteenth century. It is doubtful that Monteverdi's situation matched those conditions of freedom, since he seems to have felt an inescapable obligation towards the Gonzagas even after he left Mantua, and at one point cryptically remarks that the duke was responsible for his marriage.[25] Furthermore, the unpredictability of his patrons never really allowed him to know the implications of his commissions. The Gonzagas, for their part, were concerned with what seemed to them to be issues concerning the natural order of things: hierarchy, respect and the obedience of functionaries. When Francesco became duke he wrote to his brother on 6 July 1612 revealing that he had made secret plans to dismiss the Monteverdi brothers 'when they least expect it' in order to 'take revenge for my reputation', and this notwithstanding the fact that 'Monteverdi is the subject that he is'.[26] Music at court was primarily a means to an end, part of a wider ceremonial or political purpose, and therefore it had to be supplied at all costs. 'Art for art's sake' (an aesthetic slogan invented in 1818 by the French philosopher Vincent Cousin) was not yet on the agenda in any direct sense.

One hundred and fifty years after Monteverdi's death many ideas on art and also, crucially, the specialness of the artist – genius, originality, taste, imagination – were brought brilliantly into focus in the writings of the philosopher Immanuel Kant. Some of Kant's clarifications do not matter so much for our purposes since they merely crystallise ideas that had been around for some time. For example, none of Monteverdi's contemporaries called him a genius[27] in precisely those terms (the word – or its equivalent in any language – perhaps first appears in relation to a composer in the Preface to Purcell's *Orpheus Britannicus* of 1698), but we ourselves should not hesitate to do so. What we do need to be cautious about is seeing Monteverdi as a genius on the Beethovenian model (which, in any case, does not quite fit Beethoven) – transcending social constraints, capturing the spirit of the times, and acting as a musical revolutionary. The implication here is that there is an important distinction to be made between 'having genius' (which could be said of many early composers), and 'being a genius' as a special kind of iconic presence in the cultural firmament (a concept which some assert only emerges in the age of Beethoven).

Again, Monteverdi is one of the earliest composers for whom we are tempted to associate the steps in his musical development with three rather neat geographical locations – Cremona (1567–90), Mantua (1590–1612)[28] and Venice (1613–43) – and link them to his early, middle and late styles on the nineteenth-century 'progressive trajectory' model established for Bach (Weimar, Cöthen, Leipzig), Mozart (Salzburg, Italy, Vienna), and other composers. Those who do not quite fit the style–place development model seem to have a harder time fixing themselves in our historical consciousness, no matter how talented. Among Monteverdi's contemporaries, Luca Marenzio and Sigismondo d'India may particularly have fallen into this historiographical trap, as is evidenced by their rather poor showing in the present performing and recording arenas.

Other concepts that we need to treat with caution in relation to Monteverdi and his worlds are those of 'authorship' and 'originality'. It is a strong part of our modern culture to be concerned with the identifiable and comprehensively controlling authorship of works of art. This principle has clearly played an uneasy role in the recent debate that has surrounded the possibility that sections of *L'incoronazione di Poppea* (1643) (and especially its 'culminating' final duet) might not be by Monteverdi.[29] A complicating factor here is that we simply cannot read off the pages of a score the day-to-day collaborations, cross-borrowings and hasty adaptations that might well have been a normal part of getting the music ready for an operatic performance. But that kind of confusion is doubtless reflected in practices in the modern theatre as well, and does not represent a difference of compositional approach. More historically divisive is the Renaissance and Baroque tendency to imitate, emulate and pay homage to colleagues through the medium of quotation – and then subtly to rework their musical material in a newly creative way. Such practices can be seen, for example, in Monteverdi's setting of 'Zefiro torna' from his Sixth Book of Madrigals (1614) where the second half of the piece openly displays its reliance on Marenzio's setting of the text, only then to transform the latter's notes into music derived from the Messenger's scene in Monteverdi's own *Orfeo*.[30]

Even more obstructive to our approach to Monteverdi as an autonomous composer and artist, are the many confluences and interactions in his time between the improvised and composed, and the oral and written, cultures of music. For example, standard bass patterns such as the *passamezzo antico*, the *ruggiero*, the *romanesca*, probably derived from improvisational practices, underpinned many 'composed' works in the written repertory from this period. A case in point is Monteverdi's own 'Dolci miei sospiri' from his *Scherzi musicali* (1607) where a *passamezzo antico* bass, together with the usual harmonisation (see the scheme in Ex. 1.1), appears in lightly decorated form as the opening instrumental section.

A more complex and intriguing interaction can be seen in 'Monteverdi's' aria, 'Possente spirto' from his opera *Orfeo* (1607). If we strip away from this piece the instrumental interludes and concentrate only on the vocal episodes, it becomes clear that these sections are also based on the *passamezzo antico* scheme (compare Ex. 1.2 with the lowest stave of Ex. 1.1).[31] Moreover, Monteverdi famously provided in his score two forms of the vocal line, commonly referred to as the 'plain' and 'decorated' versions, but we can now see that the 'plain' version is itself already a decorated instance of the traditional scheme. Even more curious is the fact that the decorated and plain versions (together with their bass lines), taken line by line alternately, reveal a remarkable closeness to another aria, 'Qual trascorrendo', composed seven years earlier by Giulio Caccini for his opera *Il rapimento di Cefalo*, and published in his collection, *Le nuove musiche* (see the comparison in Ex. 1.3). That aria, as Caccini tells us, was sung by none other than the tenor Francesco Rasi, who has long been known to have performed in *Orfeo*, and the identification of this connection

Ex. 1.1 A standard harmonisation of the *passamezzo antico* bass

Ex. 1.2 The relation between the *passamezzo antico* and the plain version of Monteverdi's 'Possente spirto'

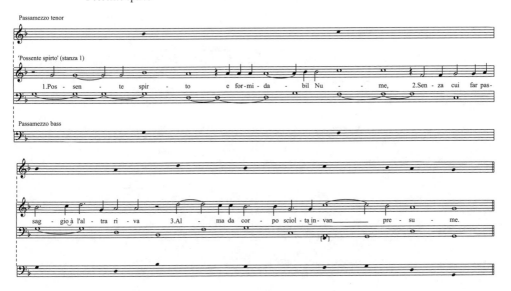

Ex. 1.3 The relation between Caccini's 'Qual trascorrendo' (1600) and Monteverdi's 'Possente spirto' (1607)

between the arias now confirms his exact role. Despite the very close correlation between the two arias Monteverdi seems to claim 'Possente spirto' as his own in a letter of 9 December 1616 when he tells us '*Arianna* led me to a just lament, and *Orfeo* to a righteous prayer'. It may be that Monteverdi was implying, not ownership of the skeletal aria scheme, but rather the 'novelty' or 'invention' of his grand adaptation and its effects – novelty and invention are qualities that are mentioned often in his writings. A word that he seems never to have used, however, is 'originality' (*origina-lità*) – that quality of being creatively absolutely unique – and neither does the word occur in Italian dictionaries contemporary with Monteverdi.[32]

Although we think of Monteverdi as a 'serious' composer, there can be little doubt that he must have come into contact with what we would now call the popular cultures of his time.[33] The music of those cultures is rather hard to track down, and one reason for this is that it is usually impossible to know whether a given piece is genuinely popular in origin, or only by destination (composed by a professional for popular consumption), or perhaps only by parody (as an aristocratic conceit). To find genuinely popular songs in Monteverdi's output one would need to begin by looking for melodies that also turn up in other pieces, but where the second work seems to have no direct connection with his composition. A promising example of this type is the tune that opens 'Di far sempre gioire' in Monteverdi's posthumous Ninth Book of Madrigals (1651). It shows an interesting relation to that of a keyboard 'Balletto' by Bernardo Storace, who worked in Sicily,[34] and may also be further evidence of southern, Spanish influence on Monteverdi's output.

To apply the term 'popular' to a style of music says nothing, of course, about how widespread, frequently performed, or enthusiastically received any works displaying such attributes might be. If, for example, we are to judge popularity by the number of times Monteverdi's editions of secular music were re-issued in his lifetime, then apparently ('apparently', because complex factors need to be taken into account) the least popular were his two collections of *Scherzi musicali* – perhaps prime examples of music 'popular' by artful parody – and the most was his Fifth Book of Madrigals. On the other hand, the Florentine Severo Bonini, writing *c.*1650, tells us of *Arianna* that 'there has been no house which, having harpsichords or theorbos therein, did not have its lament'.[35] If by that Bonini meant the operatic version for solo voice (rather than the madrigal adaptation in the Sixth Book of Madrigals), then he is referring to something that was printed in 1623 and never again in Monteverdi's lifetime. We do know that print runs for music probably ranged between two hundred and five hundred copies,[36] and that manuscript copies were made from prints (four survive for Arianna's lament), but the sparse remains over time make it very difficult to know how much penetration there was of the potential market for these publications.

As for Monteverdi's market competition with other Renaissance composers, that is extremely difficult to judge. Certainly in his own day he cannot have competed with Palestrina (a generation earlier) who had at least forty publications to his credit, most of them in an essentially choral format without the need for instruments. Moreover, Palestrina could rely on his connections with Rome and the entire institutional network of the Catholic Church. His music never really died out, and it was given a strong boost in the nineteenth century through the interests of the

Caecilian movement and the formation of choral societies. Indeed, although Monteverdi's revival really began with the work of Emil Vogel, even Vogel developed his interest in early Italian music after working on a complete edition of Palestrina as an assistant to Franz Haberl in the 1880s. Today, if we are to judge from internet sales, more printed music by Palestrina (reflecting his institutional hold on church music) than by Monteverdi seems to be sold, but there is more demand for recordings of the latter than the former (perhaps reflecting the varied and secular nature of much of his output).[37] Within the performing world, Monteverdi has clearly dominated the public, media-attractive venues, while Palestrina has quietly inhabited the vast network of religious assemblies and vocal societies whose many 'concerts' go unreported and whose performers are often amateurs in the best sense. Our notions of 'popularity' here are not simply statistical, but are strongly inflected by the social prestige associated with the performance occasion.

Although the Monteverdi revival began off the back of Palestrina, the cultural uses of their music quickly diverged. The enduring genre of opera ensured that Monteverdi, as its first great composer, would attract attention from European and American opera houses, with their attendant star singers and conductors. Moreover, even his church music is frequently ceremonial and festive, with a cross-over into secular styles founded on soloistic display: we should not be surprised that it was the 1610 Vespers that provided the content for the first BBC Promenade Concert devoted to Monteverdi in 1967. Other factors in the relative success of Monteverdi and Palestrina are more subtle. First, both have found a supportive place in levels secondary to public recognition – scholarship and education. But whereas Palestrina's 'regular' counterpoint has performed mainly a didactic role for musicians, Monteverdi's controversies with his contemporaries have made him seem a kindred spirit in modern culture, a view displayed vividly in the title of Leo Schrade's 1950 study, *Monteverdi: Creator of Modern Music*. Second, Palestrina's vast output militates against anything like a complete recording of his music, whereas Monteverdi's oeuvre is sufficiently compact to invite comprehensive attempts at discrete genres: madrigals, operas and church music. Third, the Rome of Palestrina does not quite have the imaginative cachet of the Venice of Monteverdi, which has been constructed by whole literatures of effusive (rather than reverent) commentary, from writers such as Ruskin, Henry James, Thomas Mann and many more – the sense of place and context acts much more strongly for Monteverdi than it does for Palestrina, irrespective of how accurate the association between place and particular works might be. Clearly, the two composers are differently distributed in both the performing and listening cultures, though what either achievement says about 'popularity' as an indication of artistic prestige, rather than frequency of performance, is impossible to measure.

What is clear is that, speaking of cultural society as a whole, both composers are minority interests and always were. In Monteverdi's day, fifteen hundred copies was a typical press run for books of general interest, but music collections might only be produced in a tenth of those numbers.[38] Today, one of Monteverdi's highest-selling discs is John Eliot Gardiner's recording of *Orfeo* which, since being issued in 1989, has sold seventy thousand copies, five and a half thousand of them in the United Kingdom.[39] In terms of 'popularity' those figures should be compared with Nigel Kennedy's recording of Vivaldi's *Four Seasons*, also issued in 1989, which has sold over two million copies 'worldwide' (that is, mostly in Europe, Australia, Japan and the USA, but not in Muslim countries, for example).[40] In classical music 'popularity' is always a sub-cultural, rather than a cultural, concept.

Monteverdi and the history of culture: progress and civilisation

In sociological terms, Monteverdi was a composer living in urban centres that had already undergone a 'civilising process'.[41] The warrior nobility of the medieval period had largely been replaced by a courtly nobility with new standards of decorum and repugnance. In terms of human happiness this was certainly some kind of advance – the perennial needs for food, shelter and security were now met more effectively than in the past; a change that it would be right to call progress. In Italian science and technology, too, there were signs of advance, particularly in medicine and anatomy. In Rome in 1603 Galileo helped to found the Accademia dei Lincei, the first scientific academy ever established, and the influence of the 'new science' was everywhere. Even Monteverdi was addressed as a 'Great Professor of Chemistry' in a poem by Paolo Piazza in the commemorative volume *Fiori Poetici*, published after his death.[42] This was probably on account of his interest in alchemy as demonstrated in his letter of 23 August 1625; not all Renaissance science was 'progressive' in the modern sense.[43]

Whatever the uses might be of the concept of progress in the sciences and technologies of civilisation, its application to art and artistic culture produces at least two kinds of problem. The first is that progress can only be said to take place in circumstances where needs remain the same but they come to be met more efficiently or ingeniously. That test of continuity of need is very difficult to satisfy in relation to artistic culture. For example, Monteverdi may have increased the expressive devices available to notated music (through his *seconda pratica*, his use of the violin to mirror and match the new flexibility of vocal writing, his attempts to notate new metrical and rhythmic relationships, and so on), but without a deeper justification as to why his and future generations should prefer a greater (and continually similar) emotionalism in their music, those innovations cannot be simplistically equated with progress – indeed they might be seen as a distracting indulgence. Just such a view can be found, for example, in Theodor Adorno's essay 'Music and New Music', written in 1960, in which he decries the listening habits of the public which 'enable them to deal with everything from Monteverdi to Strauss' but 'do not give them access to Schoenberg, Webern or Boulez'.[44]

Written into the sub-text of Adorno's remark is the second danger of the transfer of ideas from technology and science to the arts – the notion of 'progressivism'. This is not simply the thought that things change and can get better, but rather that progress is necessary and desirable, that cultures form a continuum of development, and that any true artists should actively seek change so as to play their part in that continuum. In so doing they would be bound (so the theory goes) to view their innovations not merely as alternatives to current practices, but as replacements of them. These ideas of course are not unknown in our contemporary representations of Monteverdi, and Adorno does not hesitate to place him at the beginning of what he sees as the still normative (if outmoded) tradition of experiencing and using music for emotive purposes.

Just exactly what Monteverdi and his contemporaries might have made of these complexities of modern historiographical and cultural theory it is difficult to say.[45] We do have the evidence of Secondo Lancellotti, a monk from Perugia, who tells us that in 1623 he met Monteverdi who 'said to me I don't know what against the conservatives, but because I did not write it down, all has vanished',[46] and Monteverdi himself states in a letter of 23 October 1633 that 'I would rather be moderately praised for the new style than greatly praised for the ordinary'. But neither of these reports demonstrates that he wanted to be a modernist in our contemporary sense (by disposing completely of the *prima pratica* or the *stile antico*), even if he did feel frustration at the resistance to any new ideas developing alongside traditional ones. And in a discussion of church and theatre styles (letter of 9 January 1620) he seems to be saying that he saw the two traditions as equal ingredients of his compositional palette; as the situation changed, he needed one or the other 'to become familiar again', otherwise 'I shall have to send mere notes rather than something appropriate.' Finding music that would be appropriate for changing cultural circumstances seems to have been Monteverdi's method, rather than trying to force the culture to respond only to his new kind of music. This suggests that, if we need to characterise Monteverdi in historical terms, then the model of evolution rather than revolution might better reflect his achievements. After all, there can be 'evolutionaries' of genius as well as 'revolutionaries', though our modern culture tends to deify the latter rather than the former in those peculiar rituals of ancestor worship which it calls 'the writing of history'.

2 Musical sources

TIM CARTER

Monteverdi's music might seem to be relatively straightforward in terms of its surviving sources, given that the vast majority of it seems to have been printed during his lifetime. The main exceptions are the late Venetian operas surviving in manuscript, for reasons that will become clear. However, scholars have tended to assume that once print became a standard, and standardised, medium of musical transmission, at least by the 1540s, manuscripts increasingly gained a secondary status. They were still of use in local or individual circumstances – either for practice or presentation – or in the case of music for limited consumption or for particular instrumental repertories (often those not using mensural notation). But these sources and their contents remained marginalised from a mainstream that was more and more defined by printed musical texts. The *Census-Catalogue of Manuscript Sources of Polyphonic Music* compiled by the Musicological Archives for Renaissance Manuscript Studies at the University of Illinois (1979–88) stops at 1550, and the efforts to deal with later manuscripts on the part of the *Répertoire international des sources musicales* (*RISM*) have been famously problematic, though *RISM* completed its catalogue of printed music by individual composers, 1500–1800, in 1981. Further, print is presumed somehow to grant the musical object some kind of permanence, and also some kind of status as a 'work' that therefore can be inserted (or not) into a canon, and into its place in music history.

Monteverdi's own publishing strategies clearly demonstrate his awareness of the power of print to establish, market and preserve his works, and therefore, in some sense, himself. His first publications worked their way carefully up the scale of three-voice motets (1582), four-voice spiritual madrigals (1583), and three-voice canzonettas (1584), until, at age twenty, he felt confident enough to make the standard entrance to the rank of 'serious' composers by way of a first book of five-voice madrigals (1587). From his Third Book on, he maintained (like many younger Mantuan composers) a regular relationship with the Venetian printer Ricciardo Amadino until the mid-1610s (when Amadino appears to have gone into some manner of retirement), shifting to the Gardano press (run by Bartolomeo Magni) for the Seventh Book and then switching between Magni and the other main Venetian press run by Alessandro Vincenti.

[20]

Presumably all these printers benefited from the relationship. Monteverdi also often used prints in one of two conventional ways. On the one hand, they could mark professional advancement, as with the Third Book of Madrigals of 1592 following his appointment to the Gonzaga court in Mantua, or the Fourth of 1603 after his promotion to the position of Duke Vincenzo's *maestro della musica* (although Monteverdi had intended it to come out sooner and to dedicate it to Duke Alfonso II d'Este of Ferrara). On the other hand, prints were a means of seeking employment, such as the Second Book of 1590 dedicated to Giacomo Ricardi in Milan, and, perhaps, the 1610 *Missa . . . ac vesperae* dedicated to Pope Paul V. Other prints, while seemingly less tied to particular circumstances, still served particular purposes: the Fifth Book (1605) and *Scherzi musicali* (1607) to assert the premises of the *seconda pratica*; the Seventh Book (1619) to take advantage of the arrival in Mantua of Caterina de' Medici, the new duchess; and the Eighth Book (1638) and the *Selva morale e spirituale* (1641) to cement the composer's emerging relationship with the Habsburgs. Indeed, the entire Artusi–Monteverdi controversy was conducted very publicly in print, and may even have been fuelled by two competing printers (Amadino for Monteverdi, and Giacomo Vincenti, who published Artusi), while Monteverdi's locating of the *prima* and *seconda pratica* in particular historical circumstances is also a sign of emerging print cultures.[1] So, too, is his increasingly careful notation of performance parameters (embellishment, instrumental scoring, etc.) within his music, fixing in stone (or at least, in printer's ink) what might previously have been left to the performer's imagination.[2]

Monteverdi's printed output was significant in terms of the number of first editions – seventeen, plus various pieces in anthologies – and still larger if one takes second and subsequent editions into account: for example, the Fifth Book of Madrigals (1605) was reissued by Amadino in 1606, 1608, 1610, 1611, 1613 and 1615, in Antwerp by the Phalèse press in 1615 and 1643, and by Magni in Venice in 1620. These reissues are commonly called 'reprints', but they are not so, strictly speaking. In letterpress printing (as distinct from engraving), individual pieces of type are assembled and then locked into a forme, the forme is impressed upon however many sheets of paper are required, the forme is then unlocked, and the type is broken down into its separate pieces and boxed for future use. Type is not left standing for any length of time such that reprinting, in the literal sense, is possible. Second or subsequent editions needed to be reset from scratch, and although the typesetter might follow the first edition closely in terms of layout, the result will still be different.

This may just seem like bibliographical nitpicking, though several obvious points follow. A second or subsequent edition need not have the same content as the first edition, and even if it does, it will almost always have variants to a degree dependent on the attention paid by the typesetter to his source – it is rare that a typesetter (or a manuscript copyist) can or will reproduce a source with total accuracy – or on alterations to the source (or the presentation of new sources) for type-setting. Significant differences between editions may be identified on a title page in some formula such as 'newly revised and reprinted', or 'third impression, updated by the composer', but the absence of such formulas does not imply the absence of difference. This has been a problem for Monteverdi scholarship, at least until fairly recently.

For all his considerable merits as a pioneering editor of Monteverdi's music, Gian Francesco Malipiero tended to take a casual approach to his choice of which edition of a given musical print to follow: he often seems to have adopted the one to which he had easiest access (for example, in a nearby library), regardless of its date. Thus he fell victim to inadequacies in sources that were sometimes quite distant from the composer, and he made no apparent effort to compare editions. As an example of the consequences, however, the first and second editions of the Fifth Book of Madrigals (1605, 1606) contain significant differences. The improvements – if they are – in the second must have been made, or at least sanctioned, by the composer on the basis of his dissatisfaction with Amadino's initial work.[3] Any modern critical edition should list and explicate these differences, at least in terms of evaluating their contribu-tion to a 'best text' (and what if the 1606 changes were not sanctioned by Monteverdi after all?).

Even within the typesetting and printing of a single edition, changes may be introduced by way of stop-press corrections, when the typesetter, or a proofreader, identifies an error, stops the press, unlocks the forme and rearranges the type, relocks the forme, and resumes the print run. Depending on the seriousness of the error, or the conscientiousness of the printer, sheets printed prior to the stop-press correction may or may not be removed from the reckoning, and thus may still be present in some surviving copies. The process may also be repeated several times during the print run. This creates another bibliographical caveat: a single 'edition' can survive in one or more different 'states' depending on the extent of corrections made by stopping the press, or by some later addition (paste-overs, manuscript annotations, etc.). This further leads to a standard bibliographical axiom: not all copies of a single printed edition will necessarily be the same.

While most scholars have tended to learn the lesson of multiple editions, and thus would not repeat Malipiero's mistake, fewer have realised the consequences of this second, more specific axiom.[4] Thus editors of Monteverdi's Fifth Book would now tend to want to see a copy of each edition proximate to the composer, although they might not bother travelling to libraries in Oxford, Gdańsk, Ghent or Wolfenbüttel to see the Phalèse edition of 1615 (but they should). However, they probably would not trouble to see every single surviving copy of the 1605 edition (in Augsburg, Berlin, Bologna, Ferrara, Kassel, London and Verona). This could, of course, be a mistake: these copies may present different states, and without close examination of all of them, there is no guarantee which is better than which. A simple object lesson is provided by Wolfgang Osthoff's preface to the facsimile of the 1609 edition of *Orfeo*, which reproduces the copy in the Biblioteca Estense in Modena.[5] However, Osthoff appears to have prepared his critical commentary (listing errors and oddities in the print) from a close examination of a different copy (probably the one in the Biblioteca Nazionale Centrale, Florence). He may have thought he was looking at the same thing, but he was not. Osthoff's commentary is thorough indeed, and is indispensable to anyone using the facsimile. However, of the two hundred or so errors that he lists, fifty-four were in fact resolved by corrections clearly present in the Modena copy. In these cases, therefore, Osthoff proposes emendations where they had already been made by the typesetter.

While two hundred or so errors in a single print might seem a high number, *Orfeo* was a highly complex typographical endeavour because of its relatively new score format – it was also a large edition (104 printed pages) – and most of the mistakes are fairly minor and can be corrected easily, if not automatically, by an editor or performer. The stop-press corrections are also, for the most part, commonsensical, and could have been spotted by a competent proofreader (who need not have been the composer). However, the *Orfeo* edition contains other interesting issues. Page 76 of the score (in all copies), three pages into Act IV, has a rather strange verbal annotation against a short passage of music assigned to 'Un spirito del coro': 'Un tono più alto'. This could mean one of three things depending on how one reads 'tono' and 'alto': the Spirit should sing 'louder'; his music should be transposed 'up a tone'; or it should be placed 'in a higher mode'. If it means 'louder,' then it is an instruction to the performer similar to the dynamic markings (e.g., *forte*) that were starting to appear in some scores in this period, though there are no other such instructions on dynamics in *Orfeo*. If the annotation means to transpose the passage (either up a tone or into a higher mode), then it still addresses performance, but it may instead have been an instruction to the printer ('print this up a tone'), or it may have been an addition that someone made to the original score of *Orfeo* because of a need arising out of specific performance circumstances (the original singer could not sing the passage at pitch, or something happened to cause a change of singers). In these cases, the printer was probably not meant to print the instruction, but should either have acted upon it (printing the passage up a tone), or ignored it. However, typesetters tend to set what is put in front of them: they do not have the time – nor always the expertise – to make significant editorial decisions. I have argued elsewhere that this annotation arose from a specific, unanticipated, circumstance: the revision of the ending of *Orfeo* to include the descent of Apollo, and Orfeo's apotheosis. Because of the revision, the allocation of roles needed to be revised to allow a singer to play Apollo: therefore the tenor who sang 'Un spirito del coro' was removed from Act IV, and his music reallocated, so that he had time to change costume and mount the stage machine that would provide his descent in the middle of Act V.[6]

This leads to my third, and perhaps most intriguing, bibliographical axiom: a print will reproduce (with varying degrees of accuracy) the materials presented to the typesetter. These materials, the so-called *Stichvorlagen*, may be printed (when a typesetter is producing a second or subsequent edition), or may be a manuscript that the composer (or someone else) has prepared for printing. As a result, although we have almost no manuscripts of Monteverdi's music stemming directly from the composer, his first editions reproduce manuscripts that must have existed at some stage, traces of which can still be found in the prints. Thus in the case of our transposing Spirit in *Orfeo*, someone – be it Monteverdi or a continuo player – annotated the manuscript score that someone – be it Monteverdi or his nominee – eventually submitted to the printer for typesetting. As this example suggests, such ghostly echoes of the *Stichvorlage* tend to be identifiable only when something is wrong or otherwise odd within a print. However, in the case of all of Monteverdi's musical editions, we can reasonably ask about their sources, and about how the nature of those sources might have influenced the format and content of the print. And we can plausibly construct a *stemma* of these sources that, while hypothetical (the sources are lost), may well be revealing.

For example, the 1610 *Missa ... ac vesperae* was published in a customary format of seven part-books, labelled Cantus, Altus, Tenor and Bassus (containing soprano, alto, tenor and bass parts) plus Quintus, Sextus and Septimus (i.e., Fifth, Sixth and Seventh). There is in addition a *Bassus generalis* part-book for the organ or other continuo instrument(s) that sometimes contains the pieces in *partitura* (a form of short score) and sometimes just has the basso continuo line. In the case of

the Vespers, the seven part-books contain the vocal and (upper) instrumental parts, the former according to a logical, and consistent scheme
(the second tenor part in the Quintus part-book, the second soprano in
the Sextus). However, the instrumental parts migrate: for example, the
two violin parts are in the Cantus and Sextus part-books for the Response
'Domine ad adiuvandum', in the Sextus and Altus in the *Sonata sopra*
'*Sancta Maria, ora pro nobis*', and in the Bassus and Quintus for the large
Magnificat (there are similar variations in the disposition of the various
cornett and trombone parts for individual pieces). It is not clear whether
this is by accident or design, and if the latter, whether the design is simply
the printer's so as to use the available number of pages in each part-book
in the most efficient manner. However, it is also possible that this shifting
arrangement of the voice and instrument parts reflects the *Stichvorlagen*,
and therefore (although it is a leap) the disposition of the original
performers performing from the manuscript part-books that comprised
them; thus these performers (vocalists and instrumentalists) positioned
themselves differently in different pieces.[7] While this might seem far-
fetched, other aspects of the layout of the 1610 Vespers suggest that
Monteverdi (or his editor, or his printer) was aware of such practical
issues: all the echo passages (of which there are a number in the Vespers)
are notated both in the part-books and in the *Bassus generalis*, meaning
that they could, in principle, be done from various locations, including
the organ loft (separate from the main body of the performers, if it was)
assuming that the organist used the *Bassus generalis* for performance. Of
course, these various scenarios collapse if the original or intended performers were to copy out additional parts, or even just perform from
memory. However, merely asking the question raises important issues
about the practical requirements of performance materials that were
subsequently transferred to print. And Monteverdi was nothing if not a
practical composer.

We have not yet securely identified an occasion for which Monteverdi
might have composed (and directed a performance of) the 1610 Vespers,
whether as a whole or in its constituent parts. Certainly, *Orfeo* was
performed for the first time on 24 February 1607, and vestiges of that
performance remain in the 1609 print, not least in the rubrics that explain
how, say, a given instrumental passage *fu sonato* ('was played', in the past
tense). However, the questions remain why *Orfeo* took two years to
appear in print, and indeed, why it was published at all (and then reissued
in 1615). Although a number of early operas were printed – including
Peri's *Euridice* (1601) and Marco da Gagliano's *Dafne* (1608) – and even
reissued (*Euridice* in 1607), it is hard to see what broader purpose was
served thereby, save as a simple act of self-promotion on the one hand, or

commemoration on the other: these scores cannot have had a broader market within the book trade save for their curiosity value. The 1609 edition of *Orfeo* certainly appears to anticipate future performances – Monteverdi also gives rubrics explaining how a given instrumental passage should be played (*si suona*) – but there cannot have been enough of them to justify, or recoup, the cost of printing. The case of the composer's lost *Arianna* is much more logical from this perspective, however frustrating it might be for modern scholars.

We do not know how much of Monteverdi's music is lost because it never reached the press, for whatever reason. Clearly a number of theatrical works have disappeared, including the operas *Andromeda* (Mantua, performed between 1 and 3 March 1620), *Proserpina rapita* (Venice, 16 April 1630), and *Le nozze d'Enea e Lavinia* (Venice, Carnival 1640–1), for which librettos survive.[8] His letters also refer to secular and sacred music that cannot always be matched to surviving works,[9] and one assumes that he wrote more sacred works for S. Marco and other Venetian institutions than were eventually published in the *Selva morale e spirituale* and the posthumous *Messa . . . et salmi* (1650). It is surprising, however, how little of Monteverdi's unprinted music survives in manuscripts. He seems to have been fairly protective of his works, keeping a master copy of those for which he envisaged some future performance and allowing further copies to be made only in special circumstances. Some of these master copies presumably found their way into the posthumous prints (the Ninth Book of Madrigals of 1651 and the *Messa . . . et salmi*), though they were thin pickings. The rest seem to have been kept too much under tight control to survive his death and the subsequent distribution of his estate.

Arianna is both typical and atypical. Monteverdi set Ottavio Rinuccini's *tragedia in musica* for the festivities celebrating the wedding of Prince Francesco Gonzaga and Margherita of Savoy in May–June 1608 (it was performed on 28 May). Work on these festivities, for which Monteverdi also provided the prologue for Guarini's play *L'idropica* (2 June) and the *Mascherata dell'ingrate* (4 June), drove the composer to exhaustion and precipitated a crisis in his relations with the Mantuan court, from which he sought dismissal in December. *Arianna* was also ill-starred because the intended singer of the title role, Monteverdi's pupil Caterina Martinelli, died of smallpox in early March 1608; she was replaced by the renowned singer-actress Virginia Andreini, for whom the part may have been rewritten and expanded. Monteverdi's disenchantment with the 1608 festivities – also caused by the greater favour granted the Florentine composer Marco da Gagliano – seems to have made him disinclined to do anything with the music, at least immediately. The *Mascherata dell'ingrate* was published only thirty years later, as the *Ballo delle ingrate*, in a revised form (for Vienna) in the Eighth Book of Madrigals, the *Madrigali guerrieri, et amorosi* (1638). *Arianna* was not published at all, though Monteverdi had the score with him in Venice in 1620, when he gave it to a copyist to produce materials for an intended performance in Mantua (which never came to fruition);[10] and he revived it at the Teatro S. Moisè, Venice, in Carnival 1639–40 as he made his grand entrance into Venetian 'public' opera.

Some restriction may have been placed on the circulation of the 1608 music by the Gonzagas, either because they wished to keep it private or because they were unwilling to finance its printing. But *Arianna* would, in principle, have been no less worthy of publication than *Orfeo* – assuming that Monteverdi had materials in a state fit to send to a printer (he may not have) – not least because the fame of its lament was already being noised abroad, in part as a result of Federico Follino's extravagant account of how it moved the audience (or at least, its female members) to tears.[11] Similarly, the opera somehow stayed in the mind: in December 1613, Prince Francesco de' Medici asked Cardinal Ferdinando Gonzaga for a copy (it is not clear that he ever got one). However, when Monteverdi published the lament, in his Sixth Book of Madrigals (1614), he did so in the rather odd format of a five-voice arrangement (perhaps made in 1610), which suited the purpose of the book but not so much the dramatic style of the piece.[12] By now, however, the cat was coming out of the bag. Copies of the lament were starting to circulate in manuscript: at least four survive in Florence (Biblioteca Nazionale Centrale, B. R. 238 (Magl. XIX.114)); London (British Library, Add. MS 30491, copied by or for Luigi Rossi, perhaps in 1617); Modena (Biblioteca Estense MS Mus. G.239), Venice (Biblioteca del Conservatorio di Musica Benedetto Marcello, Fondo Fausto Torrefranca MS 28600; copied by Francesco Maria Fucci). Their variants suggest their derivation from a still more complex nexus of other manuscript sources, perhaps mixed in with some manner of oral transmission.[13]

Certain oddities in the libretto of *Arianna*, including its non-adherence to the canonical five-part division (by acts or by choruses) required of a 'tragedy', suggest that the lament may have been a late insertion, perhaps specifically at the request of Virginia Andreini who, as a leading actress of her day, may well have wanted more than was typically provided for female operatic characters in this period.[14] One assumes, too, that Andreini kept the lament in her suitcase as she toured northern Italy and abroad, pulling it out for special performances; presumably this was at least one source of the surviving manuscripts (or at least, of their sources). This may also (but it is pure speculation) have

been the route by which it reached the music printers Michel'Angelo Fei
and Rinaldo Ruuli in Orvieto, near Rome, who included the lament as a
monody in their anthology *Il maggio fiorito: arie, sonetti, e madrigali, à
1.2.3. de diversi autori*, published in 1623. In that same year, Monteverdi
seems himself to have given in, allowing (one assumes) the Venetian
printer Bartolomeo Magni to issue the piece in a small volume that
forcefully claimed authorship of it on the title page: *Lamento d'Arianna
del Signor Claudio Monteverde maestro di cappella della Serenissima
Republica. Et con due lettere amorose in genere rapresentativo* (the two
lettere amorose had already been published in the Seventh Book of
1619).[15] Monteverdi later included a sacred contrafactum, as a *Pianto
della Madonna*, in the *Selva morale e spirituale*.[16] The fame of the piece
lived on: the Florentine theorist Giovanni Battista Doni praised it highly
in the 1630s – although he gave more credit to Rinuccini than to
Monteverdi – while in the early 1650s, another Florentine, Severo
Bonini, said that there was no musical household in Italy that did not
have a copy.

The *Lamento d'Arianna* had become somewhat detached from the
opera even in Monteverdi's mind at least by 1620 (if not 1614), when
he provided a separate manuscript of it for Mantua independent of the
rest of the score currently at the copyist's.[17] Presumably, there would have
been even less purpose in publishing the entire opera now than in 1608,
and the downturn in the music-printing trade from the late 1610s
onwards would have discouraged it still more. With only a few Roman
exceptions – Filippo Vitali's *Aretusa* (1620), Domenico Mazzocchi's *La
catena d'Adone* (1626) and Stefano Landi's *Sant'Alessio* (1634) – operas
were too specific in terms of their occasion and their performance
requirements (and performers) to warrant the luxury of commercial, or
even vanity, printing. Not a single Venetian opera through the rest of the
century was printed, and Monteverdi's two surviving late dramatic works,
Il ritorno d'Ulisse in patria and *L'incoronazione di Poppea*, are only
in manuscripts somewhat distanced from the composer, the former
now in Vienna (Österreichische Nationalbibliothek, MS 18763), and the
latter in two sources from the early 1650s in Venice (Biblioteca Nazionale
Marciana, MS 9963 (It. IV.439)) and Naples (Biblioteca del Conservatorio di Musica S. Pietro a Majella, MS Rari 6.4.1). The single copy of *Il
ritorno d'Ulisse*, which has some gaps, leaves editors and performers with
little choice of a performance text; the two copies of *L'incoronazione di
Poppea* pose significant problems and challenges in terms of their priority
and preferences.[18]

Yet the question remains of just what Monteverdi did when he decided
to print something that had been sitting in his bottom drawer for some

time. The *Ballo delle ingrate* as published in 1638 has textual revisions to suit a performance (real or intended) in Vienna in the mid-1630s, and at least some of its music (particularly for Plutone) seems unlikely to come from 1608. Another work in the *Madrigali guerrieri, et amorosi* provides even more intriguing problems. The *Combattimento di Tancredi e Clorinda* was first performed at an evening's entertainment arranged by Monteverdi's Venetian patron Girolamo Mocenigo in Carnival 1624. A copy seems to have been made available to the German composer Heinrich Schütz on his second visit to Venice in 1628–9; Schütz may have been the source of the German version of the Testo part now in the Bibliotheca Musashino Academia Musicae, Tokyo (no shelfmark). Monteverdi then seems to have prepared manuscript materials for trans-mission to Vienna as part of his campaign to woo the Habsburgs; following the pattern of *Arianna* in 1620, he would have sent his master copy (with or without subsequent annotations) to a musical copyist. He then used these materials, or further copies thereof, for the inclusion of the piece in the Eighth Book.

The vocal and instrumental parts of the *Combattimento* are distributed across the *Canto primo*, *Alto secondo*, *Tenore primo* and *secondo*, and *Basso secondo* part-books (five of eight) in the *Madrigali guerrieri, et amorosi*, and the piece is also presented in full score in the *Basso continuo* part-book. However, there are significant differences between the piece as presented in the part-books and in the score. On the whole, the part-books preserve better musical readings: in the central 'Notte' stanza – an interlude in the battle where Testo apostrophises the glory to be gained by Tancredi and Clorinda in their heroic conflict – Testo's part concludes with a more elaborate cadential embellishment and also has other improvements on the score. However, the score presents a much better literary reading of the text: Monteverdi tended to be careless at times in his treatment of Tasso's poetry, misreading words, distorting the syntax, and even destroying the regular poetic scheme of the *ottava rima* stanzas, and in the score, someone has tried to correct matters where correction was possible. Moreover, the orthographies of the text underlay differ quite markedly between the part-books and the score, with those in the part-books closer to what we know of Monteverdi's preferences from his letters, while those in the score appear to be by another hand. On the assumption (see above) that typesetters reproduced what they had in front of them (the *Stichvorlagen*), these orthographical differences seem to reflect particular scribal mannerisms, and it becomes clear that the manuscripts for the part-books and for the score come from different branches of the (hypothetical) *stemma* of the sources for the *Combattimento*. Furthermore, the evidence leans at least potentially towards the notion that the part-books somehow stem from Monteverdi's original manuscript parts, with amendments made therein in the course of preparing the first performance, whereas the score reproduces a later manuscript copy of Monteverdi's original manuscript score (or some such), in which performance amendments were not included (they were not needed there given that they did not alter the overall musical fabric). In this later copy, someone, almost certainly not the composer but maybe his printer, tried to correct Monteverdi's (mis)treatment of the text.

Such speculative stemmatics may seem far-fetched, again, but they are a logical outcome of the kinds of source-based issues raised here. They also reveal just how much is still to be done in terms of examining the printed and manuscript sources of Monteverdi's music, and of understanding their origins and their purpose. And while such nit-picking approaches might seem to represent musicological positivism run riot, in fact, the questions they seek to address are fundamental to the performance, analysis and historical understanding of music that is not quite as straightforward as we might care to assume.

3 A model musical education: Monteverdi's early works

GEOFFREY CHEW

It is not easy to trace Monteverdi's musical apprenticeship reliably, for the facts are scanty. In his published volumes up to the Second Book of Madrigals (1590) he merely describes himself as the 'disciple' (*discepolo*) of the composer Marcantonio Ingegneri, *maestro di cappella* of Cremona Cathedral; later, he looks back to Ingegneri as a respected composer of the old school. But many of his works, up to and beyond the Second Book, are modelled on works by composers of his own and earlier generations, sometimes well outside the range of Ingegneri's musical language, and he seems also to have used modelling to alter and renew musical style in general. The music of these early books, and of their models, thus represents the only surviving evidence of Monteverdi's musical education; and the latter can, therefore, be traced only through musical analysis.

At this period, the use of models was prompted by rhetorical and educational principles. And so Monteverdi's early compositions may support three hypothetical reconstructions: first, of some aspects of his musical education (perhaps under Ingegneri's guidance, if it was Ingegneri who had the generosity to recommend the young composer to imitate most of the available models, old and new); second, of some of the processes by which musical style evolved at this period; and third, perhaps the most important, of some of the aesthetic implied by Monteverdi's works.

Renaissance 'imitation'

Renaissance writers on rhetoric, following principles established by ancient writers, recommended authors (and occasionally, by extension, composers) to 'imitate' models: in late antiquity Quintilian outlined an educational programme in which 'authors worthy of our study' give us our 'stock of words, the variety of our figures [that is, rhetorical embellishments] and our methods of composition ... For there can be no doubt that in art no small portion of our task lies in imitation.'[1] Although the concept is fuzzy, the term 'imitation' in this sense entered musicological literature in the 1980s as a more adequate replacement for 'parody', a term used before that to refer to polyphonic reworkings of pre-existing compositions.[2]

In a classic exposition, G. W. Pigman recognised three 'classes' and three 'versions' of Renaissance imitation.[3] These were drawn from Bartolomeo Ricci, *De imitatione* (1541), though no Renaissance writer (even Ricci) differentiated between them systematically. The 'classes', not mutually exclusive, are recommended strategies for authors: 'transformative', where the model is to be altered in quotation, 'eristic' (that is, competitive), where the model is to be corrected or surpassed, and 'dissimulative', where the identity of the model is to be concealed. (The last of these classes signals the difficulty of matching compositions with specific models at times, even when they exist.)

The 'versions' are 'following', 'imitation' and 'emulation', and classify the practical manifestations of imitation. They intersect with the 'classes' but are not coterminous with them:

> *Following*, or nontransformative imitation, is the gathering or borrowing of phrases, sentences, passages which amounts to a transcription of the model(s) into the text ... In an *imitation* [distinguished from 'following' by belonging to the transformative class] the differences between text and model are at least as pronounced as the resemblances ... Critical reflection on or correction of the model distinguishes *emulation* or eristic imitation from (transformative) imitation, and this criticism is often grounded in an awareness of the historical distance between present and past.[4] [my italics]

This paragraph (unfortunately, but inevitably, complex) well illustrates Renaissance thinking on originality and plagiarism. 'Following', the least sophisticated form of imitation, virtually invites plagiarism – an adherence to models much closer than that we would be likely to find acceptable today; but originality, grounded in the realisation that models are dead and gone and need to be superseded, was a real aim of the higher forms, 'imitation' and 'emulation'.

The relationship between compositions and their models might be measured in terms of Harold Bloom's 'anxiety of influence', in which artistic value is proportionate to the strength of poets to overcome influences, 'with the persistence to wrestle with their strong predecessors, even to the death'.[5] The metaphor depicting intertextuality as a banner in a heroic mortal combat, in which poets subject their strong predecessors to wilful misreading (Bloom calls it 'misprision') as their only means of becoming strong themselves, has been potent in literary criticism and also in music theory, where it has been adapted most fully by Kevin Korsyn and Joseph Straus.[6] But Renaissance imitation legitimately included 'following', which to Bloom, as to modern thought generally, would represent capitulation and fatal weakness. Imitation provides an alternative mythology, especially for its own period, in which antagonistic competition between predecessor and successor is only one of a number of alternative metaphors, and in which stylistic renewal often depends on the loss of the precursor. As Thomas Greene remarked, in the most satisfactory full-scale discussion of this topic known to me, 'In Harold Bloom's terms, the problem of the precursor is that he is not lost and not dead, thus not available for resurrection ... Between the precursor and follower, no discontinuity can intervene, since for Bloom discontinuity would be freedom.'[7]

For music, the practical aspects of modelling in the Renaissance are sparsely documented, especially in Italy, though Zacconi suggested, a little later in Monteverdi's lifetime, that young composers should transcribe pieces in score, leaving empty staves below the copies for variations of the original to be entered.[8] But a careful acceptance of Pigman's classifications of imitation and their implications may cast light on Monteverdi's handling of models, and also on the historical awareness that he developed during and beyond his apprenticeship, and so the discussion here will focus on his use of models during the 1580s.

The *Sacrae cantiunculae* (1582)

The *Sacrae cantiunculae*, modest three-voice settings of sacred texts, were the young composer's first publication. Denis Arnold thought them merely run-of-the-mill.[9] One might speculate that Monteverdi was here learning his craft through non-transformative 'following', though models are not yet known for most of them. One, however – 'Quam pulchra es' – is unmistakably based on an extraordinarily archaic model: a piece with the same text by Costanzo Festa, first published in 1521.[10] Leo Schrade, who drew attention to the connection, knew Festa's piece as a three-voice motet, and thought there was a third, four-voice motet related to it; in fact, the two are the same piece with or without an old-fashioned alto.[11] The three-voice version was first published in 1543 by Gardane (the publishing house also responsible for Monteverdi's *Sacrae cantiunculae*), and the four-voice version then disappeared until its republication in the twentieth century.[12] Gardane's collection went through later editions, any of which may have been Monteverdi's source.

This piece offers valuable clues concerning Monteverdi's technique of imitation at the beginning of his career, which may be followed by comparing the settings in the two pieces of the phrase 'Quam pulchra es

Ex. 3.1 C. Festa, 'Quam pulchra es', bars 1–11, with contrapuntal reduction (text omitted except at imitative entries)

et quam decora' (repeated and extended for 'Quam pulchra es, amica mea'). Ex. 3.1 shows this section in Festa's piece (quoting bars 1–22 in Seay's modern edition, in the older four-voice version[13]), which elaborates two distinct but related contrapuntal patterns. The first, in bars 1–6, comprises a two-bar motif reminiscent of a ground-bass, elaborated through diminution, inserted rests and so on. The motif makes successive 'fugal' entries easily possible at the unison and the octave, but is independent of them; and although the two-voice model does not require suspended dissonances, these too can be superimposed on it, creating small-scale cadences on F or A. Then the upper voice of bars 1–2 is transferred into the bass to produce the pattern of bars 7–9. None of this essentially modifies the pattern with which the composition begins. This contrapuntal pattern may be termed 'introductory'; the second is 'cadential', at bars 9–11, and again at bars 20–22: here the two-bar pattern is extended motivically with a three-bar diatonic 5–4–3–2 line in the upper voice, producing a half-cadence.

Monteverdi borrows significant pitch and rhythm configurations from the original for the same text. Though he alters the basic introductory pattern

Ex. 3.2 Monteverdi, 'Quam pulchra es', bars 1–11, with contrapuntal reduction (text omitted except at beginnings of phrases)

at the outset, making it one of consecutive thirds (see Ex. 3.2), his *imitatio* is not transformative: he follows Festa in varying this pattern, first heard in full here at bars 3–4, by inverting it at bars 7–8, and then proceeding to the cadential pattern, here generated by a 3–2–1 upper-voice diatonic descent, at bars 10–11.

Throughout both pieces, similar comparisons could be made; even when greater scope is allowed later by Festa and hence also Monteverdi to word-painting, the design of both remains clear and schematic. This may explain why Festa's piece seemed an attractive model in the 1580s, and also why it appealed two centuries later to Charles Burney, who commented that it was, 'in the church style of the times, a model of elegance, simplicity, and pure harmony; the subjects of imitation are as modern, and the parts sing as well, as if it was a production of the present [eighteenth] century.'[14] For Leo Schrade, however, this piece represented an antiquated Netherlandish 'flow of melismata without phrases or caesurae', and he thought Monteverdi had conferred on it a modern 'clarity by means of the well-designed contours of the individual phrases' and their symmetrical motivic construction.[15] According to Schrade's analysis, summarised in Ex. 3.3, there are four melodic motifs (*a*, *b*, *c* and *d*) elaborated in the upper voices of Monteverdi's piece. For Schrade, these motifs and phrases have an autonomous logic like that of Beethoven: *a* is a

Ex. 3.3 Leo Schrade's account of the motivic (thematic) structure of Monteverdi's 'Quam pulchra es', bars 1–11

'group of tones ... crystallized into a motif which proceeds according to its own power'. And he sees the motifs *a*, *b*, *c* and *d* as constituents of larger-scale motifs, *A* and *A'*, also interrelated by organic development. The three staves of Ex. 3.3 show the successive stages of Schrade's reduction. Ultimately he thinks the whole piece is generated by the organic manipulation of a single melodic fragment. His reading of the piece through thematic development (rather than through the elaboration of contrapuntal models), and with a sense of history, is charming. But his implication that it exemplifies *emulatio* rather than 'following', and a turn towards modernity, seems wrong. Only two aspects of Monteverdi's piece might be thought more modern than Festa's: the three-voice texture, which itself goes no further than Gardane's published version of Festa's piece, and the slight emphasis at the outset on thirds between the upper voices. Otherwise, Monteverdi's procedure seems no different from that current for many decades in Italy.

The *Canzonettas* (1584)

With the early set of *Canzonette a tre voci* (1584), Monteverdi embraced secular vocal polyphony, and imitated up-to-date models, for the first but by no means the last time in his career.[16] The canzonetta was the most modern genre available in the 1580s, and, as Ruth DeFord has shown, Orazio Vecchi was largely responsible for its popularity.[17] Monteverdi borrowed some of the verse, probably written by Vecchi himself, from Vecchi's First Book of Canzonettas of 1578 or 1579.[18] More important, he also drew specific models for musical imitation from Vecchi's book, and enlarged the transformative scope of his imitation. In canzonettas, the

Ex. 3.4 Comparison of structure for text 'Contate i miei dolori' in Vecchi's and Monteverdi's settings of 'Canzonette d'Amore' (Vecchi, bars 6–9; Monteverdi, bars 5–8)

Italian vernacular verse shapes the music decisively. At this date canzonettas were still settings of traditional seven- and eleven-syllable verse, with little melismatic writing, and with a cadence, or at least a rhythmic caesura, at the end of every phrase. So musical phrases comprise seven or eleven notes, occasionally extended with short melismas, especially at cadences, and they are more uniform than those of the *Sacrae cantiunculae*.

Nos. 2 and 4 in Monteverdi's collection may be considered here, both with texts by Vecchi and both modelled on four-voice canzonettas from Vecchi's First Book, though they are themselves three-voice pieces. No. 2, 'Canzonette d'amore', is the simpler: each of its short lines is set syllabically, like those of the model, and each phrase is cadential. Musically, its relationship with its model is closest in the refrain ending each stanza; the respective settings of the line 'Contate i miei dolori' are illustrated in Ex. 3.4. Monteverdi borrows Vecchi's imitative subject (slightly varied), the pitches at which voices enter, the rhythmic structure and the melodic contour. He departs from his original, as in the *Sacrae cantiunculae*, by replacing notes with others a third distant, introducing new cadential goals at phrase ends and reworking the underlying contrapuntal models (shown here on single staves below each reduction). But his technique is now more radical. He replaces Vecchi's G *mollis* tonal type (G final, flat signature) with a D *mollis* one of higher tessitura (D final, flat signature). Vecchi has a 3–2–1 diatonic descent (5–4–3 if one takes into account the overall G tonality) leading into the cadence on B-flat; Monteverdi uses the same pitches for the cadential descent, but extends and reinterprets them

Ex. 3.5 Vecchi, 'Raggi, dov'è'l mio bene', bars 1–5

Ex. 3.6 Monteverdi, 'Raggi, dov'è'l mio bene', bars 1–10

as a 5–4–3–2 pattern leading into a Phrygian cadence on D, with an
underlying pattern of consecutive fifths harmonising a diatonic descending tetrachord.

No. 4, 'Raggi, dov'è il mio bene', is more melismatic, but nevertheless
apparently based on the syllabic setting by Vecchi of the same text.
Vecchi's original is dominated by an overall 5–4–3–2–1 progression in
the upper voice – in other words, by a unified tonal plan – whose general
nature can be illustrated from the scheme of the first five bars, which
summarise it in advance (Ex. 3.5). Monteverdi makes use of Vecchi's
opening melody and the basic diatonic cadential descent (Ex. 3.6). But he
turns the C *durum* tonal type (C final, no key signature) into a G *mollis*
tonal type (G final, flat signature), and adds a rapidly ascending scale as a
new countersubject, perhaps a reference to the 'rays' ('raggi') of the text,
which starts before the borrowed material, together with 'fugal' entries,
based on Vecchi's opening phrase, at the unison.[19] (Vecchi himself

quoted the new countersubject in 'Raggi, dov'è il mio male', a further witty *risposta* in words and music to his own and Monteverdi's canzonettas, in his Fourth Book of Canzonettas of 1590.) Monteverdi thus transforms Vecchi's opening phrase into an introductory contrapuntal model of two bars, repeated several times before Vecchi's second phrase becomes the basis for a cadential model. This is a good example of transformative imitation, in which an adherence to the model is used to produce novel structures.

It is a commonplace that the 'cadential' contrapuntal models favoured in canzonettas, described here, and their goal-directedness, contributed significantly to Monteverdi's new tonal language in the late sixteenth century, and that this was first evidenced in this collection. One might be tempted to relate them, and the high tessitura resulting from the high clefs (*chiavette*) mostly found in these pieces, to the contemporary notion of 'air' (*aria*), denoting a desirable up-to-date quality, except that that notion is so vague that a technical definition is hardly possible.[20] But the adoption of a consciously modern style must have implied a new historical self-awareness. Even though Monteverdi's new style does not go beyond Vecchi's, here he had learnt a self-awareness that would soon allow him to transcend his models.

The First and Second Books of Madrigals (1587, 1590)

Monteverdi's First and Second Books of Madrigals launched the composer on a genre that would occupy him for many years. The persistence in them of *imitatio* of diverse styles has sometimes been thought to suggest that Monteverdi had not yet found his voice as a composer; Glenn Watkins and Thomasin LaMay, indeed, argue that Monteverdi abandoned imitation after the Second Book, once he had become independent of models.[21] Their argument depends on the false assumption that the products of *imitatio* must be settings of the same texts as the models; but, more important, *imitatio* is not something one would expect a Renaissance composer to put away as a childish thing. The notions of 'independence' and a composer's 'voice' imply an anachronistic aesthetic at a period in which variety of musical treatment was valued at least as highly as the authenticity of a composer's utterance.

Identifiable models in the First Book include Luca Marenzio's 'A che tormi il ben mio' (1584) for Monteverdi's setting of the same text, Luzzasco Luzzaschi's 'Gratie ad amor' (1582) for the end of Monteverdi's 'Baci soavi e cari', and Ingegneri's 'Ardo sì, ma non t'amo' and its *seconda parte* for the first two of the madrigal cycle at the end of the volume.[22] Marenzio's is an example of what Alfred Einstein loosely termed the 'canzonetta-madrigal' – the madrigal infused with the airy canzonetta style, prominent in Monteverdi's First Book. None of these madrigals needs to be discussed here in detail.

In the Second Book, however, the *imitatio* is far-reaching, and the collection assumes a much more consciously historical stance than any hitherto, despite the allegation by Watkins and LaMay that 'there are only two pieces in the *Libro II* which are imitative: Camillo Cortellini's "Tutte le bocche belle" served as a structural model for Monteverdi's madrigal; and Pallavicino's "Crudel, perché mi fuggi" provided an interesting reference for Monteverdi's setting of the poem.'[23] Indeed, the collection assumes a much more consciously historical stance than any hitherto. It begins with a setting of a modern text ('Non si levav'ancor l'alba novella' by Tasso), and ends with a setting of Pietro Bembo's 'Cantai un tempo, e se fu dolce il canto', a piece in an archaic musical style, probably that of Cipriano de Rore.[24] Despite the disparity in style, there seem no grounds for drawing inferences about the relative dates of these madrigals: Monteverdi need not invariably have assumed the most modern compositional voice possible. Rather, the note of nostalgia in the selection of 'Cantai un tempo' as the parting text for a madrigal volume seems to suggest not only that the collection as a whole has traversed a great distance between past and present styles, but also that the supersession of the outdated style confers loss as well as gain. The authorial (or editorial) voice of the Renaissance can lay claim to a rich historical self-awareness.

Discussion here will be confined to 'Non si levav'ancor l'alba novella'. 'Ecco mormorar l'onde', perhaps the greatest masterpiece of the Second Book, will be reserved for fuller analysis in the following 'Intermedio'. Both these works exemplify new compositional methods devised by Monteverdi for longer-range formal planning in his music. But they also show that the mastery that was the objective of rhetorical *emulatio* combines past with present, demonstrating (in Nancy Struever's words) both 'a command of past techniques which possess continuous sanctions' and a 'sensitivity to the unique demands of the present situation', thus providing a 'model of continuity in change'.[25] Pieces that remain close to their models may paradoxically be those offering the greatest scope for stylistic change; this may cast light on the emergence of early Baroque style in general. In the present discussion I have ignored the extent to which polyphonic textures give way to homophonic ones in this repertory, but Monterosso Vacchelli discusses the role of the Second Book in this development.[26]

'Non si levav'ancor l'alba novella' is modelled on Marenzio's 'Non vidi mai dopo notturna pioggia' (the fifth stanza of No. 127 of Petrarch's *Canzoniere*, 'In quella parte dove Amor mi sprona'), that begins his First

Ex. 3.7 Fauxbourdon progression in Marenzio, 'Non vidi mai dopo notturna pioggia', bars 34–43, with contrapuntal reduction illustrating fauxbourdon progression

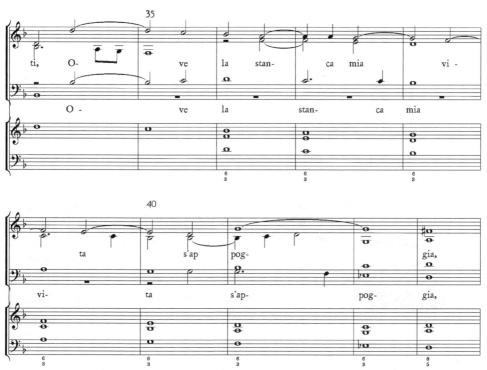

Book of Madrigals for four voices of 1585 (there is also an incidental resemblance in the opening bars to 'Raggi, dov'è il mio bene' from Monteverdi's own canzonettas, mentioned above).[27] Tasso's verse for Monteverdi's setting appears also to have been modelled on the Petrarch stanza, whose nine eleven-syllable lines also depict a striking nocturnal landscape.

In his setting, Marenzio treats each line more or less syllabically as a single musical phrase, usually occupying five or six bars but sometimes as few as three. One phrase (bars 34–43) is uniquely extended to ten bars, and concludes the first half of the setting, with an important division at a 'Phrygian' cadence in bar 43. Although superficially 'fugal' in texture (the alto and bass entering late) it is constructed from a simple homophonic pattern of alternating 5–3 and 6–3 sonorities which itself elaborates a fauxbourdon pattern of successive 6–3s, harmonising a diatonic scale in the top voice descending evenly through an octave from the initial d'' to the d' an octave lower, with which it concludes (see Ex. 3.7). Largely because of its clear goal-progression and central position, it strongly articulates the musical form of the piece.

Ex. 3.8 Monteverdi, 'Non si levava ancor l'alba novella', bars 62–72, with contrapuntal reduction

At the outset of his *prima pars*, Monteverdi adopts the same invertible counterpoint for his first eleven-syllable line as Marenzio, omitting the first bar of Marenzio's six-bar unit, using the resulting five-bar unit three times instead of Marenzio's twice, and reorganising the cadences to suggest a D tonal type even though, like Marenzio's, this piece is in a G *mollis* tonal type. Nearly all Monteverdi's phrases are drawn from the model, and the allusions are often underlined with correspondences between key words in Tasso and Petrarch: for example, the passage where Monteverdi sets 'Ma fiammeggiava l'amorosa stella' reuses Marenzio's passage for 'E fiammeggiar fra la rugiada e 'l gielo'.

In text and music, the resemblances provide striking reminiscences of specific turns of phrase, item by item through the piece. There are, however, two significant differences between the two texts, with musical consequences. First, Tasso's text has both seven- and eleven-syllable lines, necessitating some shorter phrases in Monteverdi's setting, which are not easily accommodated to the model; second, Tasso's text is as a whole far longer than Petrarch's, and Monteverdi must therefore repeat and elaborate material if he is to remain faithful to the model.

Both these points may be illustrated in Monteverdi's use of bars 34–43 of the Marenzio madrigal, quoted above. First, he probably alludes to them for the line 'Gl'augelli al novo lume', bars 20–4. These bars feature the retarded rhythms of the Marenzio passage, and some of the same characteristic pitches, but set only seven syllables. So the phrase falls not through an octave but through a major third, into a cadence on B-flat at bar 24 (see Ex. 3.8).

Then there is Monteverdi's setting of the seven-syllable line 'Ne le accoglienze estreme', more obviously based on Marenzio's bars 34–43, illustrated above in Ex. 3.7 and occupying a similar central formal position, though now after, rather than before, the midpoint. The 'fugal' entries exceptionally lengthen the phrase to eleven bars, permitting the model to be followed closely in rhythm and durations. But even though

Ex. 3.9 Monteverdi, 'Non si levava ancor l'alba novella', bars 62–72

the upper voices retain the octave descent and the final Phrygian cadence on D, the fauxbourdon structure is entirely effaced, since the bass line is here largely independent of the descending octave scale (see Ex. 3.9).

The implications for formal construction of long descending lines are not carried through as fully in this madrigal as in 'Ecco mormorar l'onde', but there is a further remarkable formal innovation in this madrigal, not borrowed from Marenzio: the opening phrase is repeated at the end of the *prima parte*. This novel, if simple, method of cementing musical unity through formal repetition has been seen by writers at least since Leichtentritt (1909–10) as anticipating the Baroque da capo aria. Leichtentritt cited precedents for the form, which he related to ternary *Liedform*, in motets by Lassus, Jacobus Gallus and Banchieri; Monterosso Vacchelli has pointed out another precedent in Ingegneri.[28] Wherever the idea came from, it is highly significant that Monteverdi should tolerate, in the 'serious' madrigal repertory, formal devices hitherto confined to 'lighter' genres.

Generally, this piece is a real *tour de force* of Renaissance imitation, and well deserves its prominent position at the beginning of a book of madrigals with a clear sense of history. The Second Book as a whole, too, is a classic in its own right, offering a microcosm of the musical education that Monteverdi had absorbed through the 1580s, one that had given him a sense of musical history that prepared him well for defending himself against Artusi's future accusations of compositional incompetence. Moreover, these early works supply a perspective from which to assess Monteverdi's recourse to modelling later in his career – for example, in the echoes of Marenzio and others to be found in the organisation, and the individual pieces, of the Fifth Book (1605).

INTERMEDIO I

'Ecco mormorar l'onde' (1590)

GEOFFREY CHEW

'Ecco mormorar l'onde', deservedly the best-known madrigal of Monteverdi's Second Book (1590), occupies a centrally important place within that volume; it represents a particularly rich version of *imitatio* (see Chapter 3, above), and established durable new models for musical form and tonal organisation. Anna Maria Monterosso Vacchelli has suggested that it is also the central madrigal of an interrelated group of three, 'Mentr'io mirava fiso', 'Ecco mormorar l'onde' and 'Dolcemente dormiva la mia Clori' (Nos. 12, 13 and 14 in the Second Book), together projecting the most modern aspect of the volume. (These are their numbers in the first edition, not in the less reliable later editions, nor in Malipiero's Collected Edition.)[1]

Essential models for modern style in the Second Book include Marenzio, already identified in Chapter 3, above, and the Eighth Book of Madrigals for five voices (1586) of Giaches de Wert, a friend of Tasso, who supplied most of Monteverdi's texts for this volume.[2] 'Ecco mormorar l'onde' interweaves two sharply different models from Wert's Eighth Book, 'Io non son però morto' and 'Vezzosi augelli';[3] both have been identified hitherto, but only in isolation from one another.

Carl Dahlhaus identified 'Io non son però morto' as a model for 'Ecco mormorar l'onde', and listed common features: 'the "monodic" declamation of the first line [of the verse], from whose repeated notes it is only the melodic accent on the penultimate syllable that stands out; the rhythmic pattern 3 + 3 + 2, conflicting with the "beat"; the imitative answer to the *dux* [main subject] in the tenor by a *comes* [fugal answer] in parallel thirds; the canzonetta rhythm of the second line, which on the one hand counterpoints the first line with strong contrast, and on the other clarifies its rhythm in emphasizing that it comprises an irregular rhythm 3 + 3 + 2 [across the modern barlines ("Ec-co **mor**-mo-rar **l'on-de**")], rather than a regular 3 + 3 + 3'.[4] These features are all illustrated in Ex. I.1. In addition to these similarities, the text of Wert's madrigal will resonate, for those who recognise the allusion, as having suddenly become a playful reference to *imitatio* itself – the breathing of new life into a dead model:

Ex. I.1 Opening of Monteverdi's 'Ecco mormorar l'onde' compared with that of Wert's 'Io non son però morto'

Io non son però morto,	But I am not dead,
anzi ritorno in vita . . .	instead I return to life . . .

The melodic phrases from Wert's madrigal not only have new life breathed into them by Monteverdi, but are carefully chosen to match their new context. The static, monodic initial phrase depicting 'death' in 'Io non son però morto' perfectly suits the 'murmuring' of 'Ecco mormorar l'onde' (Behold! The waves murmur), and both lines comprise seven syllables; the playful canzonetta-style countersubject, introduced almost simultaneously with the main subject, fits the 'trembling' of the new text as well as it does the 'return to life' of the original.[5] The monotone declamation also recalls the initial gesture of 'Vezzosi augelli', where the texts of precursor and successor are connected straightforwardly without irony. Both depict similar landscapes, both include the key verb 'mormorar', and both are intoned on a C and then a low bass F (compare Ex. I.1, above, with Ex. I.2). The *imitatio* in 'Ecco mormorar', as in earlier works, involves adherence to models but radical reinterpretations of them. Ex. I.1, bars 3–5, shows Monteverdi preserving the literal note names of Wert's two-voice *comes* in 'Io non son però morto' (beginning with the F♯–A third), but quoting them, with an F natural replacing the F sharp, within a quite different F *mollis* tonal type (F final, low clefs, flat signature: a low-pitched 'F major', in modern terms) rather than the G *mollis* of 'Io non son' ('G minor', with G final, low clefs and flat signature). Notes within the figuration are also replaced by others a third distant.

Ex. I.2 Opening of Wert's 'Vezzosi augelli' (bars 1–5)

If 'Dolcemente dormiva' is a genuine further intertext of 'Ecco mormorar', its opening monodic declamation may constitute a remoter variation on the same model, extended to eleven syllables rather than seven, and pitched an octave higher, since the tonal type (though still with G final and flat signature) now involves high clefs (*chiavette*). But the correspondences are not traditional, and though Monterosso Vacchelli calls the three madrigals an 'ideal triptych', they are not a madrigal cycle (a setting, in successive madrigals unified in tonal type, of separate sections of a single poem).[6]

Whatever the similarities, 'Io non son però morto' does not adequately account for the cadential and tonal structure of 'Ecco mormorar l'onde'. For this Monteverdi apparently drew on 'Vezzosi augelli', already mentioned, which has been favoured as the sole model for the piece in literature in English.[7] As Gary Tomlinson wrote,

> The textual similarities inspired a musical relationship as well. The tonal type of Wert's work is identical to that of Monteverdi's, and 'Vezzosi augelli' also steadfastly adheres to its F tonic, cadencing only twice, in passing, on C. It opens with the same monotonal murmuring in the lower voices as 'Ecco mormorar'...'Vezzosi augelli' also provides a model for...a prominent use of villanella [i.e. canzonetta] texture and frequent E-flat inflections of the 'F-major' tonality.[8]

The canzonetta texture, including its 'E-flat inflections', is reflected in Wert's simple cadential contrapuntal model (Ex. I.3) combining a

Ex. I.3 Basic cadential model in Wert, 'Vezzosi augelli', bars 1–2

neighbour-note 5–6–5 figure and a diatonic upper-voice 5–4–3–2 descent into a half-close on the second degree of the scale, or a 5–4–3–2–1 descent into a full close on the first, with the fourth degree of the scale harmonised each time with a flattened leading-note (anachronistically, '♭VII') in the bass. Wert's piece seems throughout to be in an uncomplicated F major, despite the E-flat triads, because there are no cadences on A, which might have been expected in an F-final piece of the period, but there are cadences on C (as at bar 24), resembling passing modulations to a tonal dominant; these seven bars provide a model for the way in which the relationship between 'tonic' and 'dominant' colours the tonality of the whole piece (Ex. I.4).

At bars 7–12 of 'Ecco mormorar', the E-flat inflection seen in bar 2 (originally of Wert's madrigal) colours a harmonisation of the upper-voice descent to the cadence with lightly concealed consecutive fifths (see Ex. I.5). Within the canzonetta-style trio texture these may represent a written-out version of improvisational practice; to quote Dahlhaus, 'The consecutive 5–3s do not recall villanella technique ... so much as *contrappunto alla mente*, counterpoint improvised over a cantus firmus in the bass ... The false consecutives and irregular dissonances, which were unavoidable in improvisation, appear to have been perceived as a piquancy [*Reiz*].'[9] When the same text occurs in bars 21–6, the first seven notes of the upper-voice figure, 5–6–5–4–3–2–1, appear in the bass, generating a chord progression, V–vi–V–IV–iii–ii–I, to use anachronistic terminology, before another perfect cadence. Consecutive parallel triads are again strongly projected (Ex. I.6).

Monteverdi uses and extends this cadential model, beyond anything in either of Wert's pieces, for the final rhyming couplet of the work:

| L'aura è tua messaggiera, e tu de l'aura | The breeze is your messenger, and you hers, |
| ch'ogni arso cor ristaura. | who revives every parched heart. |

Ex. I.4 Interrelation of cadences in Wert, 'Vezzosi augelli', bars 20–26

A long, undecorated stepwise descent, from a B-flat to the F an octave and a half below, begins in the bass at bar 72 after a rhythmic caesura, setting each of the eleven syllables of the first of those two lines, one each bar (see Ex. I.7).[10] The steady unfolding of the diatonic scale in the bass gives the passage and the text it sets a purposeful inevitability. 'L'aura',

Ex. I.5 Monteverdi, 'Ecco mormorar l'onde', structure underlying bars 7–12

Ex. I.6 Monteverdi, 'Ecco mormorar l'onde', structure underlying bars 20–26

key to this ideal pastoral landscape, is not only 'the breeze', but also a girl (like those in canzonetta texts), here the Ferrarese singer Laura Peverara, Tasso's dedicatee. Each bass note supports a 5–3 triad, before a series of suspended dissonances in the progression to the final cadence (bars 85–92), perhaps echoing the ending of 'Io non son però morto'. The passage provides a fine example of the 'epigrammatic' structures towards the ends of madrigals, featuring descending parallel fifths and octaves, which are ultimately drawn from cadential models in canzonettas of the 1580s, and produce tonal closure and, no doubt, *meraviglia* ('wonder': an aesthetic objective of the period).

Such structures (Monteverdi's 'trademark', as Leichtentritt wrote a century ago) also appear in the Second Book near the beginning of 'Dolcemente dormiva', in 'Non son in queste rive', and, briefly, in 'Tutte le bocche belle'.[11] Later, they occur in such very different contexts as 'Io mi son giovinetta' in the Third Book (1592), some of the instrumental ritornellos in *Orfeo*, and the celebrated ending of the *seconda parte* of 'Or che 'l ciel e la terra' in the Eighth Book (1638). The influence of the

Ex. I.7 Monteverdi, 'Ecco mormorar l'onde', structure underlying bars 72–84

canzonetta extends also to musical form. Dahlhaus (while warning against facile recourse to alphabetic schemes) argues that most of 'Ecco mormorar l'onde' before the peroration comprises a four-section form derived from the canzonetta:

> Around 1590, a formal scheme like A^1-A^2-B-A^3, on which bars 1–55 in 'Ecco mormorar' are based, was very unusual (A^1: 1–12; A^2: 12–26; B: 27–39; A^3: 43–55). It is not that 'architectural' principles were totally alien

to the building of musical form, but they were generally restricted to simple
text settings in the 'humble style' . . . If the early 'progress' of the madrigal
had depended on an 'ennobling' through borrowing from the motet, its
later progress depended on its being 'degraded' by borrowing from song
forms.[12]

The process was to go much further in the seventeenth century, especially
after the introduction of new verse structures in arias and canzonettas,
and instrumental voices in polyphonic madrigals. Here Monteverdi
merely underlines the formal structure with caesuras in the structure
and with stylistic differentiation[13] – things previously avoided, but
newly prominent in seventeenth-century genres.

In summary, Monteverdi brilliantly interweaves two very different
models into a single seamless garment in this madrigal. And through a
close adherence to those models he paradoxically derives entirely new
forms, at least one of which, the affective peroration, was to provide a
durable model for the future. In Dahlhaus's closing words:

> The energy with which Monteverdi assembled the various elements into a
> single work, and with which he made the inner connection palpable
> between 'architectural' form, contrasting three-voice textures, 'logical'
> development of motives and tonal organization, is just as astonishing as the
> sure touch with which he put together this compositional material for
> expressing the individuality of a Tasso text. The stylistic avant-gardism of
> the most modern madrigal of the 1590 collection, and the aesthetic per-
> fection of the work, share a common origin.[14]

4 Monteverdi at Mantua, 1590–1612

ROGER BOWERS

Music at the Ducal Court of Mantua in 1590

Early in 1590, the most probable date at which Monteverdi entered the employment of Vincenzo Gonzaga, Duke of Mantua,[1] the Palazzo Ducale offered an environment wherein music was cultivated under three distinct identities. One was the duke's personal *cappella* of clergy and choir, maintained within his entourage to discharge his obligations as the orthodox and dutiful master of a great Christian household. It has long been considered that Monteverdi's engagement at the Gonzaga court was exclusively as a secular musician, but a new appraisal of the documentary evidence indicates that this is rather a misapprehension. He was recruited to the central musical department of the household, the *cappella* (chapel). Whatever that term was to come to mean in future times, in Counter-Reformation Mantua under the devout dukes Guglielmo and Vincenzo it could only maintain its historic signification as the household department to which the duke committed the ordering both of his personal daily devotions and of those conducted in his name. Thus, in 1589 the staff of his *cappella* comprehended personnel both sacerdotal and musical: a principal chaplain, four priests (of whom three were also fully qualified as singers), a *maestro di cappella* (the director of music, since 1565 the composer Giaches de Wert), and ten adult male singers.[2]

The principal function of the *cappella* was to conduct the most important services of divine worship according to the liturgical books of the Roman Catholic Church. Within the palace, therefore, there had to be locations wherein the clergy and choir of the *cappella* assembled (probably daily) to perform High Mass and the greater services of the Office (principally matins, prime and vespers). A remark made by a contemporary annalist identifies the church of S. Croce in Corte, standing within the Corte Vecchia of the palace and dating from *c.*1425, as the established locale for much of the *cappella*'s observance.[3] As crudely drawn on a plan of 1628 this appears to have been a building of modest but adequate size, extending to three western bays and an eastern limb separated by a 'crossing' supporting a tower and spire (Fig. 4.1). It appears that the church was not newly built in *c.*1425, but had been fashioned out of the southern flank of the pre-existing building known as Magna Domus. The prominence of

Fig. 4.1 Gabriele Bertazzolo, Pianta prospettiva di Mantova (1628), showing location 179, S. Croce in Corte

the spire, seen in a painting of the Mantuan skyline of *c.*1615 (Fig. 4.2), corroborates the church's substantial dimensions. No other depictions are known. In 1627/8 S. Croce was still a working church, but at some point thereafter was deconsecrated and turned into store-rooms; between 1763 and 1773 its ecclesiastical character was obliterated utterly by its conversion into part of the domestic suite now known as the 'Stanze dell'Imperatrice'.[4]

Fig. 4.2 Detail from Francesco Borgani, 'St Francis intercedes for the cessation of an epidemic', *c.*1615, showing, immediately above the saint's hand, the tower and spire of S. Croce in Corte, Mantua

In 1576 an ecclesiastical Visitor noted that in the immediate vicinity of the church there lay also a separate private oratory of the duke, likewise dedicated to the Holy Cross.[5] Its fragmentary remains, lying to the south of the church and now embedded within the eastern range of the court-yard, have lately been identified as those of the church itself.[6] However, in reality this was a structure far too small to have accommodated the grand liturgical occasions known to have been conducted within S. Croce church.

It was the duty of the duke's *cappella* to conduct divine service not at large in the city but only in a physical proximity to his person sufficiently close to enable him to be in attendance at any time he liked, a purpose which by its location and dimensions S. Croce was perfectly fitted to fulfil. In no sense, moreover, was S. Croce rendered redundant by the comple-tion of the basilica of S. Barbara in 1566, which was established to fulfil purposes entirely different. Thus the report of 1576 noted that in S. Croce High Mass was celebrated when the duke was hosting local princes or foreign magnates, a function which, as the relevant department of his household, it was the duty of the priests and singers of his *cappella* to discharge. Further, on every day of liturgical solemnity ten or twelve friars came from the city to serve the church, observing first and second Vespers, Mass, and the Office of the day.[7] Their engagement to assist in the plainsong gave scope for the *cappella* to concentrate on the polyphonic

music of the greater services. Since there was never any general congrega-
tion, S. Croce sufficed to accommodate even the elaborate performance
style likely to have been undertaken on grand occasions following the
accession of Vincenzo (1587), enhanced with the concerted polyphony of
voices and instruments.

Suitable for observances on a more intimate scale was a second chapel,
of which the room within the Corte Vecchia now known as the 'Sala della
Crocefissione' probably once was part.[8] Apparently this was the normal
locale for the duke's attendance at daily mass performed by his *cappella*.
Here stood 'an organ wonderfully made, of a breadth of four yards [*braccia*]
or thereabouts, of a height of two yards or thereabouts, in which almost
every kind of music is heard to be sounded . . . wonderful both to see and to
hear'.[9] Contemporary documents preserve numerous references to the
duties of the *maestro di cappella* 'in both chamber and church';[10] evidently
it was primarily in S. Croce and the Corte Vecchia chapel that those 'in the
church' were conducted.

Most of the chapel staff served in a double capacity, furnishing also a
substantial component of the chamber ensemble of singers and instrumentalists by whom the duke and his guests were entertained either with
secular music or with edifying sacred chamber music. The singers were
expected to possess voices satisfactory in the distinct repertories both of
salon and of church and chapel.[11]

The third musical entity was the collegiate basilica of S. Barbara.[12]
Utterly separate from the ducal household and court, wholly self-sufficient
on its independent endowment, this had been created during the 1560s by
Duke Guglielmo for the same primary reason as that for which every great
corporate church existed: *ad augmentacionem cultus divini* (for the increase
of divine worship). Its choir consisted of up to sixty of its sixty-one members,
supreme among whose duties was an observance of the sacred liturgy,
especially of its plainsong chant, that was discharged continuously and in
a manner as perfect as human management could make it. By creating this
foundation Guglielmo was matching exactly the doubled provision for
liturgical observance undertaken by fellow sovereigns and aristocrats at
their capital palaces. Thus respectively within the Louvre (Paris) and Windsor
Castle (England), the self-sufficient collegiate choirs of the Sainte Chapelle
and St George's Chapel conducted service continuously in their magnificent churches, whilst elsewhere, within the palace's domestic apartments,
a chapel smaller but no less lavish served simultaneously as locale for
services sung by the members of the Chapelle Royale of the king of
France and Chapel Royal of the king of England, when resident. With
such arrangements, the Duke of Mantua's S. Barbara and S. Croce offered
an exact parallel.

There was nothing to stop the priests, clerks and boys of S. Barbara endeavouring to perform polyphony in such relatively undemanding styles as those composed to Guglielmo's special order by Wert and Palestrina. However, the sole means for the performance of more elaborate polyphony on festivals was furnished by the somewhat grudging provision of the music of professional singers engaged *ad hoc* from outside the foundation, consisting of a Master of the Singers, professional singers in unspecified number, and an organ-player.[13] For this purpose, Guglielmo sometimes lent the musicians of his own *cappella*. However, since 1588 the basilica had been employing its own team of up to eight singers and an organist under Giovanni Giacomo Gastoldi as *maestro*.[14] Consequently, by 1590 there existed within the palace compound not one *cappella* but two, each entirely independent of the other: that of the ducal household under Wert, and that of S. Barbara under Gastoldi.

1590–1601: the rank-and-file musician

Within the *cappella*, Monteverdi was appointed to be an instrumentalist (bowed strings and theorbo), composer and singer,[15] and within two years of his admission he was already, at twelve and a half *scudi* per month, the highest-paid member of the *musici* after Wert himself.[16] There was much that he was qualified to contribute to the burgeoning artistic environment of chapel and salon. In particular, youthful sojourns in the court of Ferrara had introduced Vincenzo to avant-garde developments particularly in secular music, which he now wished his own musicians to emulate. He had already begun to augment the character of music-making at his court by admitting to his salon musicians eight further employees – the Jews Salamone and Europa Rossi (respectively violin and voice) and Isacchino della Profeta (solo voice and lute), and five members of the Pelizzari family, including the singers Isabetta and Lucia. Vincenzo's introduction of adult female singers has been convincingly identified as a wish to replicate in Mantua the *concerto delle dame* which had been a prominent feature of the courtly musical life he had encountered in Ferrara.[17] Indeed, Vincenzo's desire to augment the domestic duties of his *cappella* was pervasive; although Monteverdi was appointed to one of the ten established places for *cantori*, the text of his dedication of the Third Book of Madrigals (1592) to the duke indicates that it was primarily for his virtuosity as a string-player that he had been engaged, to which his role as a singer, mentioned but once in surviving records, appears to have been rather subordinate.[18] Further, in 1598 the young virtuoso tenor Francesco Rasi was induced to accept permanently a position as a singer in Vincenzo's court. He remained on the Gonzaga payroll for the rest of his career,[19] so introducing at Mantua not only the promotion of performance by star soloists, but also the opportunity to compose monody for them to deliver.

Little is known of Monteverdi's first ten years as a Gonzaga household employee. In May 1596 the office of *maestro di cappella* became vacant on the death of Wert; although he expressed an interest, Monteverdi saw the post conferred upon his colleague Benedetto Pallavicino. On 20 May 1599, at the age of thirty-two, he was married in Mantua to Claudia Cattaneo, singer, and daughter of Giacomo, a string-player in Vincenzo's service. Among his jobs was composition, both of liturgical music for the ducal chapels and of secular and sacred chamber music for the salon. In 1592 he published his Third Book of Madrigals for five voices, dedicated to Vincenzo, and from 1594 he began to contribute compositions to anthology volumes collected by others. However, little of his sacred music from this period has survived.

Between 1590 and 1601 there were mounted at court numerous events to which a prominent contribution was made by the corps of musicians, including the production in 1598 of Guarini's pastoral verse-drama *Il pastor fido*,[20] mounted to mark the passage through Mantua of Margareta of Habsburg, bride-to-be of Philip III of Spain. Vincenzo provided sumptuous barges for the royal party's passage along the River Po, and banquets 'accompanied with devine Musicke'. The play itself generated great astonishment, not least for the music of voices and instruments performed as *intermedi* between the acts: 'most rare musicke of many partes, with divers instruments, accompanied with angelical & delicate voices, insomuch that it seemed rather a divine, than humane thing'.[21]

Monteverdi was caught up in Vincenzo's youthfully restless urge to travel, most particularly his military expedition to Hungary in 1595. To order his devotions Vincenzo was accompanied by a small but fully functional *cappella*, including – as well as a portable organ – a staff of eight. Principal chaplain was Don Federico Follino, with one further priest; there were six singers, including Monteverdi as *maestro di cappella*,[22] whose work was both sacred and secular. On each day Mass was celebrated four or five times in Vincenzo's quarters, while on days of solemnity he offered also a musically elaborate service of Vespers, executed by the clergy, singers and organ. As well as their surplices and music for Mass and Vespers the singers took with them a secular repertory, and on numerous occasions the army commander, Matthias, Archduke of Austria, secured their services for his own entertainment.

In 1599 Monteverdi accompanied Vincenzo on a venture to Flanders, and his brother Giulio Cesare was later to claim that there Claudio became acquainted with the style of the *canto alla francese*, applicable 'now for motet texts, now madrigals, now canzonettas and arias'; and he asked rhetorically 'Who before him brought it back to Italy...? Who before him began to apply it to Latin texts and to those in the vernacular tongue?'.[23] This passage usefully confirms that as well as madrigals the composition of motets and other Latin-texted pieces figured routinely among Monteverdi's duties at this period, though the exact meaning of the term *canto alla francese* is not immediately evident.

Monteverdi's reluctance to publish after 1592 any newly composed secular music may well have been generated by a sense of caution arising from his embarkation upon certain means for achieving a heightened degree of sensitivity and responsiveness in word-setting. His resort to the calculated exploitation of elements of contrapuntal licence, introducing dissonance unconventionally prepared and resolved, duly attracted the attention of Giovanni Maria Artusi, a respected if conservative theorist.[24] Apparently towards the end of 1598 he encountered Monteverdi's settings of 'Cruda Amarilli', and of 'Anima mia, perdona' and its second part, 'Che se tu se' il cor mio', and was unfavourably struck by a number of instances of unconventional dissonance usage, by certain melodic intervals which he considered ungracious in line and resistant to analysis, and by inconsistencies in modal usage and identification.

'Full of amity and civility', he attempted to open a correspondence with Monteverdi. The latter, however, was no theorist; rather, in his name response was made by someone who proceeded to correspond anonymously with Artusi under the *nom-de-guerre* 'L'Ottuso Accademico' (whose true identity has never been established). Early in 1599 Artusi received from L'Ottuso a defence of the relevant aspects of Monteverdi's compositional practice. He did not deny but acknowledged the commission of departures into innovation and novelty; however, he reported that these were conscious and intentional, and insisted that they could not be considered irrational but were supported by reason. Three more letters followed; Artusi was given no satisfaction and chose to pursue the issue further by adverting to it in the course of his next major publication, *L'Artusi, overo Delle imperfettioni della moderna musica ragionamenti dui* (Two discourses concerning the imperfections of recent music) of November 1600. He tendered a critique of certain practices of a contemporary composer, offering actual musical excerpts. However, by leaving them unattributed he made clear that his animadversion was to certain trends in modern music in general, rather than to Monteverdi personally. Artusi's critique was not necessarily unfair, since into the mouth of one of the disputants, however timid and easily dissuaded, he put possible defences for these innovations. His conclusions, however, remained assertively condemnatory. It appears unlikely that at this stage Monteverdi lost very much sleep over this unsought controversy. Nevertheless, the appearance of the escutcheon of Artusi's patron Cardinal Arigoni on the title page did advise him that the Curia might not appreciate favourably the propagation of the characteristics of 'la moderna musica' into the music of the church.

On 26 November 1601 Pallavicino died, and the post of *maestro di cappella* within the ducal household again fell vacant. Presenting himself as duty-bound by his loyalty so to seek the enhanced opportunity to serve his master that this promotion would bring, Monteverdi humbly requested appointment to the job (letter of 28 November 1601). He sought it in respect of both the secular and the ecclesiastical aspects of its functions, going out of his way to emphasise the manner in which his interest lay primarily in the latter. He described the post as 'the position now vacant in this branch of the Church', and pointed out to the duke the manner in which such promotion would afford him 'yet greater opportunity for showing himself to your most refined taste as of some worth in motets and masses'. Further, he indicated obliquely that his real desire was to exercise, in addition, a defining influence over the conduct of sacred music in the basilica of S. Barbara, explicitly requesting appointment to the job as it had been exercised not by Pallavicino but by his predecessor Wert. Pallavicino had been simply *maestro* of the household *cappella*, whose duties were performed in the salon and church of the ducal household.[25] In requesting appointment to the job as Wert had exercised it, Monteverdi was seeking rather more.

Wert had never occupied any formal office at S. Barbara at any time.[26] However, from his position as *maestro di cappella* of the ducal household he had, prior to Gastoldi's appointment in 1588, exercised a determining influence over music-making at the basilica, and had composed polyphony for the non-professional musicians of its internal chorus.[27] On occasions he had even undertaken the job of ad hoc *Magister Cantorum*, directing a group of singers from the duke's *cappella*.[28] Thus, when Monteverdi explicitly sought to be engaged as Wert had exercised the post, he was seeking appointment to responsibilities which extended also to Wert's initially pervasive influence over the music of S. Barbara. Perhaps this is not surprising. Monteverdi was very devout, even to the extent of obtaining ordination as priest in his later years, and much in his career is consistent with a supposition that within his profession it was the Church and its music that always held the greatest appeal. In this wish he was to be disappointed. Vincenzo duly did appoint Monteverdi, probably

during December 1601, but only to be *maestro di cappella* of his household. His monthly stipend was increased from twelve and a half *scudi* per
month to twenty-five – but was promptly reduced to twenty when he
declined to look after Francesco Campagnolo, an adolescent tenor (letter
of 2 December 1608).

1601–6: master of the *cappella*, servant of the duke

In December 1601 Monteverdi succeeded to an office now of some
complexity. He was *maestro* of the ducal *cappella* of four chaplains and
ten singers (including, from 1604, his brother Giulio Cesare), and was
manager of the same body of musicians when they performed chamber
music, secular and sacred, in the ducal salon. In this latter context the
cappella was now augmented with the talents of further performers,
including Francesco Rasi, the three lady sopranos (Monteverdi's wife
Claudia now was probably the third, with Lucia and Isabetta Pelizzari),
and three string-players, including Salamone Rossi. It is, therefore,
understandable that he considered his job to be not simply *maestro di
cappella* but *maestro della musica* of the duke, as he described himself
in 1603 and 1605 on the title pages of the Fourth and Fifth Books of
madrigals.[29]

His duties, however, were about to become yet more demanding.
Vincenzo certainly appreciated the glamour and esteem which the promotion of music brought to his court, and was zealous in keeping abreast of all
contemporary manifestations of musical innovation and enterprise. By
1605, when a correspondent remarked that 'I understand that Your
Highness is reforming your vocal and instrumental personnel,'[30] the job
was in fact well on the way to completion. By the end of 1601 the adolescent Campagnolo was being groomed as a second star tenor (letter of
2 December 1608), and was added to the payroll from June 1604. Another
virtuoso singer caught young was the soprano Caterina Martinelli; born in
Rome in 1589 or 1590, she was brought to Mantua in summer 1603 at the age
of thirteen.[31] Within months she was performing solo song to the duke's
acknowledged satisfaction, and her singing became one of the principal
ornaments of the Gonzaga court. Other specialist singers attracted during
this recruiting drive up to the end of 1605 included Pandolfo del Grande
(tenor), Giulio Cardi (castrato), Eleuterio Buosio (voice-type unknown),
Henrico Vilardi (voice-type unknown), and Giovanni Battista Sacchi (castrato). The Gonzagas kept virtuosi such as these content through the liberal-
ity with which licence was given to them to accept the many invitations they
received to perform elsewhere.

Further, between 1602 and 1604 the string band was increased from three players to an ensemble of eight, run as a self-contained unit under the direction of Salamone Rossi. Other virtuosi recorded at this time include Lucrezia Urbana (harp and voice); Giovanni Maria Lugaro (voice, chittarone, spinet, harp, and 'viola'); Giovanni Leite, primarily an organist; and Pasquino Bernardino Grassi (keyboard). Among wind players, the principal of the ensemble was Giulio Cesare Bianchi (cornett), a close associate of Monteverdi who joined the duke's employment in 1602. Others were Giovanni Domenico Arriemi, trombone, and Giovanni Srofenaur, trombone and clarino trumpet.[32] These three, however, constituted less than a serviceable wind ensemble, and it seems likely that among the other instrumentalists there were some who also were expert on wind. Overall, between the beginning of 1602 and about the middle of 1605 Monteverdi found himself presiding over an expansion by Vincenzo of his musical establishment (excluding the priests of the chapel) which almost doubled its numbers, from eighteen to some thirty-five.

After a silence of eleven years, he published in 1603 his Fourth Book of Madrigals. Into this he may be understood to have put the best of his secular work to date for the Gonzaga court, though it was appreciated no less by the *cognoscenti* of Ferrara, to whom the book was dedicated. This book included two items which had furnished Artusi with examples of 'moderna musica' condemned in his critique of 1600, and now he was provoked into revisiting his earlier animadversions. He published later in 1603 his *Seconda parte dell'Artusi*, in which he both printed his earlier exchange of correspondence with L'Ottuso Accademico and found further condemnatory remarks to make. The intellectual fuel for his animadversions was much the same as before, and Monteverdi was not much concerned; he did decide to draft a response, but never completed it.

By 1605 Monteverdi was in charge of a resource very serviceable for making music of all kinds, and naturally Vincenzo was at pains to find means for putting it conspicuously to constructive use. Soon, therefore, Monteverdi found himself under siege from Vincenzo's newly prolific demands for composition. Thus 'Duo seraphim', a *sacer concentus* (sacred concerto) on a text celebrating the Holy Trinity and realisable by the duke's three tenors (Rasi, Campagnolo, del Grande), probably was composed for the thanksgiving conducted in the church of Holy Trinity, Mantua, on 29 December 1605 for the recent beatification of Luigi Gonzaga.

However, it was Vincenzo's requirements for the conspicuous exposure of his much-enhanced musical resources in large secular spectacle that made the greatest demands on Monteverdi. Carnival in February 1604 was marked by the performance of some theatrical comedy, distinguished by spectacular *intermedi* and tournaments, *balli* and music.[33] In December he reported on progress on compositions lately commanded by the duke, including four instrumental dances for a ballet, but took the opportunity also to report that he was beginning to find his creative powers attenuated by recent overwork; he hoped that the duke would never again burden him 'either with so much to do at once, or in so short a time' (letter of December 1604).

Nevertheless, Vincenzo did little to abate his demands. In the foreword to his Fifth Book (1605), Monteverdi regretted his inability to offer any defence against Artusi, 'because, being in the service of His Most Serene Highness, I am not the master of so much time as would now be necessary'. Giulio Cesare took up similar cudgels in 1607, explaining how Claudio had responsibility for managing within the ducal court not only the music of both church and chamber, but also 'other extraordinary services, for, being in the service of a great prince, he finds the greater part of his time taken up now with tournaments, now with ballets, now with comedies and various *concerti*, and lastly in the playing of the two *viole bastarde*'.

Monteverdi saw his Third Book of Madrigals reissued again in 1604, and the Fourth Book in 1605. The Fifth Book was published in 1605. Like the Fourth (1603), its contents apparently include a significant number of pieces composed in the 1590s; Monteverdi noted in the course of the dedication that Vincenzo had enjoyed hearing them in his chambers in performances from manuscript, on the strength of which it had pleased him to honour the composer with promotion (in December 1601) 'to custody over your most noble music'.[34] However, this book also includes items fully engaging the enlarged vocal ensemble, the string band and other instrumental resources available to him since 1602, in adventurous and evocative scorings. It also included pieces from which Artusi had drawn other examples of allegedly uncouth 'moderna musica', and Monteverdi printed a note 'To the Studious Reader',[35] asking him not to be surprised that he was printing these madrigals without having first replied to Artusi's objections to some momentary details within them. In order to show that in his composition of music he was neither gauche nor maladroit he had indeed written a suitable reply, which when revised he would publish under the title *Seconda Pratica, overo Perfettione Della Moderna Musica*.

For Monteverdi his evocative term *seconda pratica* had a special significance. Artusi had claimed that the 'moderns' 'call absurd the things composed in [the conventional] style, and would have it that theirs is the true method of composition ... They mock those who hold otherwise.'[36] This misrepresented Monteverdi completely. Rather, he saw the traditional and the modern not as opposed, but as complementary. His way of composition was neither better nor poorer than the conventional, and in no sense the sole legitimate method; rather, it was simply a 'Second Practice', standing alongside and of equal validity with the 'First'.[37]

The substantial influx of professional musicians under his responsibility was now affording Monteverdi outstanding opportunities both for composition and for performance. However, Vincenzo's manner of implementation brought also several drawbacks, of which the most corrosive was the division, in May 1604, of the overall corps of musicians into two separate bodies, one enjoying a level of appreciation conspicuously denied to the other.[38] Thus, in 1605, in a record of remuneration paid directly out of the Treasury, the heading *Cantori* comprehended none but the eleven vocal stars of the salon. Indeed, to Vincenzo even his *maestro della musica* did not qualify for inclusion among the élite; although this document overall lists no fewer than 349 members of his household staff, of neither Monteverdi nor the rank-and-file singers of the *cappella* is there any sign.[39] Evidently they were no longer paid by standard Treasury procedures, but had been relegated to some other more peripheral means of remuneration – which in fact failed to work at all.

Thus Monteverdi was obliged to accept that his job was thenceforth of not the first tier of recognition, but the second. He was merely the employee and journeyman who worked behind the scenes to prepare the music. Composing the notes for the star performers to sing, moreover, was merely what his regular salary was for – if, under the new dispensation, he could obtain it. On 27 October 1604 he was reduced to writing to Vincenzo, to explain that neither he, nor his wife Claudia, nor his father-in-law Giacomo, had been able to raise from the Treasury any of their expected salaries. He himself appears to have obtained satisfaction; although he was to complain bitterly in the future of the inadequacy of his monthly stipend of twenty scudi (letter of 2 December 1608), there have at least survived no further complaints that he was unable even to obtain it. However, Claudia and her father did not achieve similar assurance until November 1606.[40]

Thus, for over four and a half years between May 1604 and January 1609 Monteverdi found himself persistently among those disadvantaged by Vincenzo's consistent lionising of his star singers, and by his incapacity to appreciate the contributions made by everyone else – not least, by his principal house composer. Eventually, this degree of unmindful disregard and inconsideration was to lead to an epic confrontation.

1606–9: exploitation and confrontation

At some point, probably in 1606, there occurred to Vincenzo's son and heir, Prince Francesco, the idea of emulating recent enterprise at Florence in mounting an opera. Since about the middle of 1605 his father's corps of musicians had extended to the necessary resources and Vincenzo was presently persuaded so to allow their use during Carnival 1607. Francesco was to promote the opera in his role as titular President of the Academy of the Invaghiti of Mantua; the libretto was to be written by Alessandro Striggio, a member of the Academy, and the music by Monteverdi.[41] Insofar as fundamentally it required the availability of one virtuoso tenor but no corresponding female star soprano, a handful of other named roles mostly for high voices, and a competent and versatile chorus primarily of lower male voices, the mythological story of Orpheus was chosen to be the opera's subject, clearly because its plot could so readily be manipulated to match the court's musical resources as they stood in 1606.

Rehearsals began early in 1607, though Francesco suddenly found himself unexpectedly with a gap to fill; the substantial pool of women's voices available when the opera was first planned had evidently evaporated. Fortunately for Monteverdi, finding a top-quality soprano at short notice was considered no job for a mere director of music; he merely watched as the Gonzaga affinity was sprung into action. On the pretext that 'here we have few sopranos, and they little good', Francesco recruited from the Medici the youthful *soprano castrato* Giovanni Gualberto Magli, who eventually sang the roles of Musica, the Messenger and Proserpina. Magli learnt most of his music in the space of a week; Francesco applauded the feat, characteristically according all the credit to the singer and overlooking entirely the contribution of the musical director whose expertise in coaching had procured so satisfactory a result in so brief a time. *Orfeo* was first performed on 24 February 1607, and gave satisfaction so universal that Vincenzo ordered a second performance for 1 March (the day *after* Ash Wednesday!), 'before all the ladies of the city'. He then planned yet a third, evidently for the holiday period following Easter Sunday, 15 April, which may have been the occasion for which Monteverdi composed the opera's alternative ending. This performance may very well have materialised, since it was not until 30 April that Francesco finally sent Magli back to Florence.[42]

In July 1607 Monteverdi published the *Scherzi musicali a tre voci*, dedicated to Prince Francesco. The music had been composed since 1599 for performance in Francesco's chambers, and was brought to the press by Monteverdi's brother Giulio Cesare. In conveying compositions in strophic form for a vocal trio of two sopranos and bass, with ritornellos for instruments *à* 3, the music reflected the modesty of the prince's resources; it was, nevertheless, the earliest publication to associate voices and instruments in this particular way.

Giulio Cesare took this opportunity to offer a further instalment of the controversy over the *seconda pratica*. Claudio's Fifth Book (1605) had provoked a contribution (its text now lost) from one Antonio Braccino da Todi (apparently a pseudonym of Artusi himself). In response, Giulio Cesare reprinted Monteverdi's note 'To the Studious Reader' from the Fifth Book, heavily glossed with further comment of his own.[43] He pointed out that *seconda pratica* usages were not the invention of Claudio, but were of earlier introduction; he insisted that the *seconda pratica* neither superseded nor demoted the *prima pratica*, but complemented it. Inevitably, in the wake of *Orfeo*, Giulio Cesare's defence was actually as much of monody as of Claudio's madrigal style. In 1608 Braccino returned to the debate, but had little substantial to add. From neither brother did it elicit any response, and all the primary parties appear to have been content to consider the controversy unresolved, but now exhausted.

In summer 1607 Monteverdi was with his wife and children in Cremona, composing music to two sonnets sent to him by the duke.[44] Also during 1607 he saw all his first four books of madrigals reprinted, and in August he visited Milan, where Aquilino Coppini was converting some of his madrigals into spiritual settings by the editorial substitution of devotional texts in Latin.[45] It was in Cremona that, on 10 September 1607, his wife Claudia died. She was accorded the honour of a cathedral funeral, and afterwards was buried in the churchyard of S. Nazaro.

Monteverdi was given little time to grieve. Early in 1608 Prince Francesco was due to marry Margherita of Savoy in Turin, and the couple's spectacular reception on return to their new home in Mantua was already being planned. Monteverdi received the commiserations and condolences of both friends and court, and an exhortation to return to duty at Mantua immediately. By 9 October he had complied, and was instructed to write the music for a pastoral opera, as a centrepiece of the celebratory programme. Its libretto, the work of Rinuccini, was to tell the mythological story of Ariadne (Arianna) and Theseus. Monteverdi composed intensively from October onward. In the event, however, the wedding was postponed to 17 February 1608, and no celebrations welcoming the couple's return could take place during Lent. On 2 March Monteverdi was reported almost to have completed the composition of *Arianna*;[46] more than once in later years he was to recall, without pleasure, the enormous effort it cost him.

He was kept busy during Carnival, when Caterina Martinelli performed the character of Venus in Marco da Gagliano's opera *Dafne* as her first dramatic starring role. It was also her last: on 7 March she died of smallpox. To secure a replacement for her in the role of Arianna, the Gonzaga connections were again exploited to the full. Monteverdi was but little consulted, and by 14 March the services not of a professional singer but of a singing actress, Virginia Andreini, were procured.[47] For Monteverdi there was no relief. The postponement of the reception in Mantua simply provided an opportunity for the procurement of yet further musical spectacle. His share was the composition of one of six *intermedi* for performance between the acts of Guarini's comedy *L'idropica*, and the *Mascherata dell'ingrate*, a texted dance entertainment of some thirty-five minutes' duration eventually revised and published in 1638 as the *Ballo delle ingrate*. He was later to reckon that for the 1608 celebrations he set to music some fifteen hundred lines of poetry (letter of 2 December 1608).

Francesco and his bride arrived in Mantua on 24 May, and *Arianna* was performed on 28 May. Rinuccini's libretto remains but, with the exception of his setting of Arianna's lament 'Lasciatemi morire', Monteverdi's music is lost. The Modenese ambassador approved greatly of Rasi's singing of Theseus, while Virginia Andreini's presentation of Arianna impressed him even more. Of the castrati and other singers, however, he thought rather little.[48] On 2 June Guarini's play *L'Idropica* was performed, with the *intermedi* and the music composed to accompany them. Monteverdi's music has not survived, though clearly it was a substantial piece, set for instruments and seven singers. Mantua having still no female soprano of solo calibre, the principal role was performed by the imported singer Angiola Zanibelli. On 4 June Monteverdi presented his sung *scena* with dance the *Mascherata dell' ingrate*.

Over two years Monteverdi had composed, rehearsed and presented two substantial operas, had composed an elaborate prologue and a complete *ballo*, had undertaken all the routine work of a *maestro di cappella* in a sovereign household, and had lost his wife. The effect was to reduce him to exhaustion. In July 1608 he retired to Cremona and appears to have entertained no appetite or even inclination to return to his duties in Mantua. Overwork had rendered him genuinely ill, and momentarily he was beginning to formulate a strategy for transferring to a different source of employment under Vincenzo's ultimate patronage, both less stressful and better paid.

During November his father Baldassare wrote to both Vincenzo and Duchess Eleonora.[49] He reported Claudio's illness, and offered his diagnosis of the underlying causes: overwork and poverty. He then suggested tactfully that Vincenzo implement the award of a perpetual pension promised to Claudio apparently at the time of the 1608 festivities. Secondly, he asked the duke to grant to Claudio an honourable discharge from his service. Alternatively, and without embarking upon detail, he suggested, in effect, that Claudio might be transferred to the office of *maestro di cappella* at S. Barbara.

By this date Gastoldi probably was already known to be suffering from the illness of which within two months he was to die. A vacancy was impending, and Baldassare suggested that if the duke 'commands only that he [Claudio] serve in the church, that he will do'. His observation that such a promotion would assure to Claudio receipt of four hundred *scudi* per year, plus a hundred and fifty as extras, makes clear that the church to which he was making reference was that of S. Barbara. Most probably, this transfer was what Claudio really sought as his route of escape from the Gonzaga court. On 30 November 1608 Claudio received his reply from the palace: a peremptory summons from the ducal counsellor Chieppio to return as soon as possible to Mantua and there to resume and perform his duties. A second letter let him know that he was required to begin composing a ballet for Carnival 1609.[50]

Monteverdi snapped. His response, incandescent with indignation and rage, conveyed a spectacularly bitter tirade of anger and grievance (letter of 2 December 1608). He assured Chieppio that if the duke's purpose in summoning him to Mantua was to require him to compose yet more large-scale theatrical music, it would certainly be the death of him. It is especially noticeable that it was this distaste for the prospect of composing yet more opera that came to mind foremost among his many grievances. He further let Chieppio know that if the duke's purpose in sending for him was to grant him rewards and favours, then the duke could keep them. In nineteen years of consecutive service he had received the duke's favour many times, and on every single occasion the benefit had come with a detriment by which it was far outweighed, leaving him worse off than he was before. Another source of grievance was the manner in which he was being denied by poverty the opportunity to fulfil his own and others' perceptions of his duty to his offspring. He also complained of denial of that public recognition of his worth by his prince that would in turn bring him respect and authority within the community, with all the material advantage that would accrue. Moreover, following the death of his wife Vincenzo had resolved to order that thenceforth he receive a monthly allowance equivalent to Claudia's lost salary. However, the duke had then reneged, leaving him convinced that he had been shamefully tricked.

Monteverdi resorted to open mutiny. His response was not to pack his bags and meekly take the high road to Mantua, as ordered, but defiantly to remain precisely where he was, in Cremona. Indeed, he implored Chieppio's support in obtaining from the duke his immediate and honourable dismissal. For only one purpose would he come to Mantua, and that was to receive his discharge from Gonzaga service.

The outcome was a not dishonourable compromise. At S. Barbara Gastoldi died and was succeeded by Stefano Nascimbeni; evidently

Vincenzo had no intention of surrendering Monteverdi's services to anyone. Rather, on 19 January 1609, he fulfilled his pledge to grant the pension long promised, and couched the text of the award in terms calculated to mollify every one of Monteverdi's outraged sensibilities. It fully acknowledged the value of his services; moreover, its sum of a hundred *scudi* per year was granted in perpetuity, so conferring a source of wealth to be left in due course to his sons and descendants. Vincenzo further authorised an increase in his annual salary, from twenty to twenty-five *scudi* per month, representing exactly a restitution of the sum first promised to Monteverdi in December 1601.[51] It appears likely that this sum was deputed thenceforth to be drawn directly on the Treasury, so conferring on Monteverdi restoration at last of his elevated status among the élite membership of the duke's musicians.

He returned to his post at Mantua. The *contretemps* was over, and there was not a little in which he could both draw satisfaction and find promise of future relief. Even so, the duke had not capitulated completely. What he gave was no more than that which at one time or another had actually been promised, and he permitted Monteverdi no leave to transfer to S. Barbara. On the other hand, he did yield in one substantial particular: never again did he burden Monteverdi with a call to compose an opera. And in this respect, perhaps, Monteverdi's gain has been posterity's loss.

1609–12: achievement and apprehension

The three years following this resolution of differences appear to have been relatively calm. In autumn 1608 Monteverdi had been refusing to leave Cremona to return to court; on 24 August 1609 he wrote to Striggio, now one of Vincenzo's four principal counsellors, looking forward to bringing some recent compositions to Mantua 'because I want to be back in service shortly' (letter of 24 August 1609). Nevertheless, the straitness of his basic salary, and the continuing inconsiderateness of the Gonzagas in failing ever to amplify it with recognition and reward for individual pieces of work well done, continued to rankle. Indeed, there were many elements within his working conditions with which Monteverdi was, and remained, profoundly dissatisfied, and the memory of them long remained with him. Thus, in rebuffing in 1620 an approach to lure him back, he pointedly gave a list of all the things he most liked about working in Venice, so yielding a very clear insight into the nature of the grievances still afflicting him in Mantua even after 1609. These concerned pay and security of tenure, but predominantly the prevailing failure deferentially to invest him with the level of respectful and responsible autonomy appropriate to himself and to his office (letter of 13 March 1620). Indeed, given the frequency with which his madrigals, despite their music's elevated character and technical challenge, were now having to be reissued to meet demand, and given the likely repute of the work for his prince as yet unpublished, by 1609 Monteverdi could be satisfied that at the age of forty-one he was achieving recognition as among Italy's most accomplished living composers.

At court Vincenzo was particularly keen to maintain his ensemble of around ten virtuoso singers. Characteristically, recruitment at this level was considered no job for a mere *maestro di cappella*, and Monteverdi found himself uninvolved; it was the duke's recruiting agents who filled the vacancy for a star soprano by the engagement in June 1610 of Adriana Basile. Full documentation is lacking, but it appears that the musical establishment remained some thirty-five in number. Several of his letters of this period show Monteverdi fulfilling the routine work of a *maestro di cappella*. He was empowered at least to hear any singer who happened to be nominated for appointment to membership of the *cappella*, and to advise the duke of the candidate's suitability for engagement. Thus in June 1610 he auditioned a 'certain contralto' and, in October 1611 he was instructed to audition in Cremona and report upon two men considered suitable for appointment as a *basso da camera*.[52]

Meanwhile, for Monteverdi, there emerged during 1609 a particular source of residual anxiety that could not be overlooked. In November Prince Francesco was due to take up appointment as governor of Vincenzo's distant duchy of Monferrato, for which capacity there was now formed about him a complete seigneurial household, including a self-contained *cappella* of musicians under its own *maestro*. Following Vincenzo's death, therefore, Monteverdi's career would rest entirely on the whim of the new duke, who would determine whether to re-engage his services, or to discard them in order to promote his existing *maestro*. Few of the Gonzaga lords had ever made old bones, and in 1609 Vincenzo was already forty-seven. Necessarily Monteverdi began to contemplate the future.

While keeping all his options open, he was particularly eager to nurse the cultivation of a favourable relationship with Francesco, wishing Striggio in August 1609 to convey to him 'the great desire I have in my heart to prove what a very devoted and very humble servant I am' (letter of 24 August 1609). He responded with particular alacrity to a request from Francesco to investigate the possibility of his augmenting his household by the employment of a troupe of five wind-players (letter of 10 September 1609), and also to a request, conveyed by Striggio, for information about one Galeazzo Sirena, a composer and organist whom in 1609 Francesco was contemplating appointing as an inaugural member of his *cappella*. In fact, Monteverdi did not believe Sirena to be well suited to such employment, and Sirena himself found the idea of serving Francesco entirely unappealing. However, Monteverdi did not wish to disoblige the prince, so he duly tendered a sketch of this man, as eloquent in description as sharp in characterisation, and reported that he had told Sirena to go away and think about it a little more (letter of 10 September 1609).

Sirena's subsequent enquiry whether Francesco wanted him to serve actually in the office of *maestro di cappella* provoked Monteverdi into anxious agitation. He asked Striggio to discover both Francesco's intentions for the direction of his new *cappella* now in 1609, and his expectations for its direction when he succeeded as duke. Despite all the favour shown to him by Francesco over recent years, and despite all his obsequious service, Monteverdi's impression of Francesco thus appears to have been of an unpredictable man, little given either to warmth of appreciation of the worth of those who had done him service, or to any sense of constructive gratitude. Striggio's response (if any) does not survive. Probably it was shortly after these exchanges that Francesco, paying no further attention to Sirena, appointed as his *maestro di cappella* Monteverdi's brother, Giulio Cesare. Such a move can only have increased Claudio's apprehensions by many orders of magnitude. When Francesco succeeded as duke, the musician against whom he would be in competition for appointment as *maestro di cappella* to the new ruler would be his own brother.

A letter of 26 March 1611 reveals his continuing concern to cultivate Francesco's favour, recommending a wind-player to fill a vacancy among his instrumentalists. Moreover, though he may not have been composing opera any longer, he was certainly composing for the church service, and sent to Francesco some recent pieces, including a setting of the psalm 'Dixit Dominus', a motet for the Virgin Mary and 'a little motet for two voices' for the Elevation at Mass. He also undertook to send two recent madrigals and anything else that he thought Francesco would find to his taste.

However, he was writing on the eve of Palm Sunday, and he advised that he would not be able to send this extra music until after Holy Week was over – and this remark is very illuminating for the light it casts upon the nature of Monteverdi's current duties as *maestro di cappella*. Any purely secular musician would have had little to do at so penitential a time. Monteverdi, however, had duties so onerous that he could attend immediately to no other business. For any professional *cappella*, Palm Sunday initiated all the elaborate ceremonies and music of Holy Week and it is evident that he was disabled from being of any further immediate service to Francesco because his duties in S. Croce rendered this the busiest and most taxing week of the year.

Thus, from 1609 Monteverdi was beginning to make concerted plans for his future career, and sought to ensure for himself fame for composition beyond the bounds set merely by the secular madrigal. His first resort, in 1609, was the publication of *Orfeo*, as public advertisement of his mastery of the new operatic form, prefaced by a dutifully respectful dedication to Francesco as its begetter. His next project was the issue of a representative volume of his sacred music. There is no reason to believe other than that he had been composing music for the liturgical service ever since 1590. Of this he had so far published none at all – probably because the music was of such scale and complexity, requiring such a wealth of executive resources, that it could not generate a sufficiency of potential purchasers in Italy or anywhere else. It was, therefore, not for the satisfaction of any market but as a methodical and representative showcase of his talents that he planned his album of sacred music, so yielding a volume quite unlike any other of its time: the Mass, Vespers and 'motets' of the Blessed Virgin of 1610.

The Mass, for six voices with basso continuo for organ, was conceived on an especially expansive scale, and would have been particularly suitable for performance in S. Croce at High Mass on such occasions as the reception of foreign princes and other guests of high rank described in the Visitation Report of 1576. The contents of the Vespers were laid out as if for a notional service, conducted, in principle, according to the strict liturgical order of First Vespers on principal Marian feasts in the Tridentine Rite (the authorised rite, observed in the Gonzaga household chapel just as in most of Catholic Europe). Many times during twenty years of ducal employment Monteverdi would have participated in such a service, sung and played in grand style by himself and his colleagues in the household church of S. Croce. The Vespers of 1610 appears to offer an idealised and somewhat inflated vision of such an occasion, inauthentically but opportunistically incorporating five domestic motets and kindred pieces intruded into slots following the psalms, of which each slot during any genuine service was conventionally occupied only by a small-scale polyphonic substitute for the suppressed repeat of the plainsong antiphon.

By 1 September, the date appended to the text of dedication to Pope Paul V, the completion of printing was imminent, but Monteverdi was oddly secretive about his actual journey to the Vatican, evidently giving to both Francesco and Vincenzo a date for his travel much further into the future than that on which he actually planned to arrive.[53] Clearly he had in mind the pursuit of some prior and clandestine business of his own, to be conducted before anyone associated with his Gonzaga employers knew he was there. He arrived on 3 October and found accommodation in an inn; but whatever his purpose, it was frustrated three days later when he was seen and recognised by a servant of Vincenzo's second son Prince Ferdinando (now Cardinal and resident in Rome), who insisted that Monteverdi accept accommodation in Ferdinando's palace. He had little choice but to comply, and doubtless now went about only the business he was expected to be conducting in Rome.

His known business there, all at the Curia, was twofold. Probably he did secure his audience with the Pope; there still survives an isolated copy of the Altus part-book of the 1610 publication with a cover bearing the coat of arms of Paul V, which may be a remnant from the very set presented by the composer.[54] His other business was to seek for his elder son Francesco collation to some small sinecure benefice, the income from which would serve to meet the cost of the training for the priesthood which Claudio wished to provide for him at some seminary in Rome. He was unsuccessful (letter of 28 December 1610); nevertheless, this episode demonstrates clearly the pious character of Monteverdi's household, and his pervasive devotion to the Church of which he wished his elder son to become a priest.

We can only speculate concerning Monteverdi's clandestine business in Rome. However, it seems significant that the dedication of his 1610 publication to Paul V concluded with expression of his desire that 'I may be able to serve both God, and the Blessed Virgin, and You'. It is entirely possible that his intention was to seek out the possibility of future employment by the Pope in Rome, in either the Cappella Sistina or Cappella Giulia. If so, he was to be disappointed; no offer came.

In summer 1610 Monteverdi had been intending to complete the showcase of his compositional talent by preparing a volume of his recent secular chamber music. Eventually this was published as the Sixth Book of Madrigals in 1614; evidently, however, it contains work composed during his last seven years at Mantua. Meanwhile, the popularity of his madrigals was reaching new heights; the Fifth Book was reprinted in 1610, and in 1611 all of the Third, Fourth and Fifth Books.

1612: crisis and dismissal

On 18 February 1612 Vincenzo died. Because of foreign preoccupations the cultivation of music was not among Duke Francesco's most immediate priorities; his sole known initiative was an interest in procuring conventional singing boys for the *cappella*.[55] Giulio Cesare was now *maestro* in Francesco's ducal household, and Claudio *maestro* of the waning household of the late duke, due for final disbandment in probably six months' time. At first Francesco apparently amalgamated the personnel of the two *cappelle*, with Giulio Cesare informally deferring as *maestro* to his much more distinguished brother. In the long run, however, not all Vincenzo's musicians could be retained, and only one Monteverdi could be *maestro*.

On 8 June Francesco released a number of Vincenzo's musicians, among whom were Bassano Cassola and Giulio Cesare Bianchi; the long-serving G. B. Marinone also now left. Others became restive, their resolve only sharpened by a general sense of disappointment at the current absence of musical enterprise at court. Adriana Basile was dissatisfied, and the castrato G. B. Sacchi outraged Francesco by fleeing the court without leave, sending word from Florence that he had no wish to return. Those dismissed in June included Monteverdi's oldest colleagues, and more than likely his oldest friends, and his response can readily be diagnosed: if all his friends were going, so was he. The report of 8 June continued: 'and perhaps also Signor Claudio Monteverdi, who with many entreaties is requesting licence, in whose place his brother will serve'.[56]

The brothers clearly had their own agenda, and a guess may be made at its content. At S. Barbara there was understood to be an impending vacancy in the post of *maestro di cappella*, Nascimbeni having apparently proved unsuccessful.[57] Francesco had two *maestri di cappella*, and only one long-term job. One simple solution presented itself: Giulio Cesare would remain *maestro* in Francesco's household, while Claudio moved to S. Barbara. Francesco's ultimate response is readily explicable if it be understood that the brothers were already making clandestine approaches to his advisers with such a scheme. To Francesco, it represented yet a further instance of the perpetration by mere musicians of all but *lèse-majesté*. He of all men knew the worth of Claudio in comparison to that of his brother, and was hardly likely to view favourably any proposal to surrender the abler brother and retain the services only of the less distinguished.

On 6 July, in a letter to Ferdinando, Francesco presented himself as wounded by disloyalty and disrespect on the part of servants upon whom he and his family had long bestowed their generous favour; he was prepared to be vengeful in his proposals for making appropriately lordly response, planning peremptorily to dismiss both brothers. He continued: 'do not marvel that, Monteverdi being the subject he is, I should condescend to deprive myself of him; for if you knew with what intent of gain and with what self-interest he and his brother are dealing with me, you would grant me every reason'.[58]

On 29 July 1612 Francesco dismissed Giulio Cesare from his own household service, and from the service of the court his brother Claudio.[59] Thus it was only from a distance that in August Claudio would have heard of the removal also of Nascimbeni, and of his replacement at S. Barbara by Amante Franzoni.[60] And as he was resentfully to recall in 1615, after over twenty-one years' service for the Gonzaga dukes he departed with so little thanks that all he had in his purse was twenty-five *scudi*, the single month's pay with which his employment there was terminated (letter of 6 November 1615).

5 Spaces for music in late Renaissance Mantua

PAOLA BESUTTI

Precise identification and detailed knowledge of the spaces, both indoor (rooms, theatres, churches) and outdoor (gardens, courtyards, public squares, towers) in which individual musical works or whole repertories were performed, or for which they were conceived, should be essential for study of the production, composition and performance of music in any age. The realisation of this objective, however, often turns out to be impossible because of gaps in documentation or remodelling of the places concerned. The presence in this *Companion* of a contribution specifically devoted to the spaces in which Monteverdi's music was heard, and for which he composed during his employment at Mantua, demonstrates how such an approach, once only vaguely acknowledged, has in recent years become a recognised methodology. Monteverdi himself, speaking of the madrigals in his Fifth Book (1605), reminded its dedicatee, Duke Vincenzo Gonzaga, of the many times in which he had heard them 'in his royal chamber' before they were published, as if himself to spur us on to this final, interdisciplinary frontier of musicological research.

An investigation of the relationship between music and spaces for music during Monteverdi's Mantuan years runs into various problems. The configuration of the Gonzaga palace today consists of numerous buildings added over the centuries to the original medieval nucleus, which faces on to the Piazza Sordello (formerly the Piazza San Pietro). Various individual buildings have been joined together to form inner courtyards, gardens, galleries and elevated walkways, resulting in the complex structure of a palace 'in the form of a city' (Baldassare Castiglione) which is still visible today, albeit partially demolished and rearranged. Though the more important architectural works are usually well documented, many lesser works have left traces so faint as to be unreadable. It is from the reign of Duke Guglielmo Gonzaga that we begin to have a clear vision of the intensive use of court locations for music and spectacle, and Guglielmo was the real instigator of the reorganisation of the constituent spaces of the Gonzaga palace; thus he will be frequently mentioned in the following pages.

When Monteverdi arrived at Mantua, there existed in the court and the city a multiplicity of places used more or less frequently for music; in order to keep this discussion within reasonable bounds, then, only those locations will be discussed that have a well-documented link to Monteverdi or for which a conjectural link can reasonably be sustained.

'Every Friday evening music is performed in the Hall of Mirrors'

Although it was Monteverdi's talents as a string player that particularly recommended him to Duke Vincenzo Gonzaga, he described his precocious publication of madrigals of 1592 as 'fruits', rather than the more ephemeral 'flowers' of performing (dedication to the Third Book), indicating that he had also applied himself immediately to the composition of chamber music. Trying to identify the places where such music was performed is usually a difficult task. Music was practically a daily activity at a court where the arts were considered vehicles of pleasure and an effective means of communication; chamber music, save in exceptional cases, was not documented, just as in the case of many routine dances, or the performances of the court comedians. In Monteverdi's case, however, a small window on to this activity is opened by some well-known letters of his. Thus, he wrote on 28 December 1610 to Cardinal Ferdinando Gonzaga at Rome:

> Dear Sir, make me worthy of one of them [an *aria*] so that I may undeceive her [Adriana Basile] with this proof, at which point I pray you also to give Signor Santi [Orlandi] the task of sending me the cantata with accompaniment for two arch-lutes promised me by Your Eminence, so that I can let His Highness hear it one Friday evening in the Hall of Mirrors.

And thus, a few weeks later (22 January 1611), after having thanked the cardinal for two madrigals received from him:

> Every Friday evening music is performed in the Hall of Mirrors . . . On a similar splendid occasion I shall have the theorbos played by the *casalaschi* [the brothers Orazio and Giovanni Battista Rubini, perhaps from Casalmaggiore, rather than Casale as Denis Stevens suggested], to the accompaniment of the wooden organ (which is extremely sweet), and in this way Signora Adriana and Don Giovanni Battista [Sacchi] will sing the extremely beautiful madrigal 'Ahi, che morire mi sento', and the other madrigal to the organ alone.

Fig. 5.1 Mantua, Palazzo Ducale: the Hall of Mirrors at the time of its rediscovery

These phrases of Monteverdi's, reconsidered together with architectural and artistic sources, led in 1998 to the incredible rediscovery of the Hall of Mirrors (Sala degli Specchi or dello Specchio) (Fig. 5.1), which until then had been rendered unrecognisable by later restructuring and a partial collapse of the roof,[1] and above all by the confusion with another Hall of Mirrors – the 'Logion Serato' (the great enclosed *loggia*), a picture gallery[2] resulting from the transformation of a *loggia* of the early seventeenth century, which only became known as the 'Hall of Mirrors' much later (1779).[3]

The construction of the Hall of Mirrors mentioned by Monteverdi, the only one that will be considered from here onwards, dates from the years 1582–5 when the duke-composer Guglielmo Gonzaga,[4] then more than forty years of age, commissioned a new apartment from the architect Bernardino Facciotto, leaving to his son Vincenzo the more sumptuous Stanze di Troia (Trojan Rooms).[5] A comparative study of Facciotto's plans, the rediscovered space and fragments of the walls left in layers of the floor during the restructuring, allowed a preliminary virtual reconstruction of the Hall of Mirrors (Fig. 5.2) on the basis of which the difficult work of restoration proceeded.

The space has an irregular geometry (Fig. 5.3) with an area of around 150 square metres (the sides measure 20.29 metres; 14.72 metres; 14.88 metres; and 3.88 metres) and a maximum height of seven metres. The room had, in fact, a trapezoidal, or rather, a truncated triangular

Fig. 5.2 Mantua, Palazzo Ducale: Virtual reconstruction of the Hall of Mirrors

shape; the problem of roofing it was solved boldly by giving it an umbrella-like structure composed of twenty 'sails', each one corresponding to a frescoed lunette portraying *putti* playing (fifteen of these have been rediscovered and attributed to Giovan Battista Giacarelli). The canopy, decorated with vegetable motifs, was constructed from light materials (wood and cane) and the mirrors were perhaps placed at the apex of this eccentric ceiling or on the inside of the parietal *boiseries* in a way analogous to other rooms of the same period (at Sabbioneta and Fontanellato, for example), bringing the mirrors to the centre of the ceiling and on the short walls. The decoration of landscapes and rosy skies, for the panels situated under the lunettes, completed the idea of an environment hinting at the original structure of a loggia and a winter garden. Such allusive reference to bright open spaces, in a place used during the long, dark, winter months, must have made a great effect on guests, who, as though crossing an enchanted forest, reached it from the Hanging Garden (Giardino Pensile) and the Fauns' Corridor (Corridoio dei Fauni); the duke was able to use his own entrance from the vestibule positioned along the lesser of the short sides.[6] Conviction hardens, therefore, that within the living complex created by Guglielmo the Hall of Mirrors took on the function of a place used predominantly for the performance of secular music for, at most, a select group of listeners. In his new apartments Guglielmo could enjoy within the radius of just a few metres a secluded study, a loggetta where he could eat in the open air with a view on to S. Barbara, a room for private music (the Hall of Mirrors) and finally, on the other side, a large dining room (the Refectory, now the

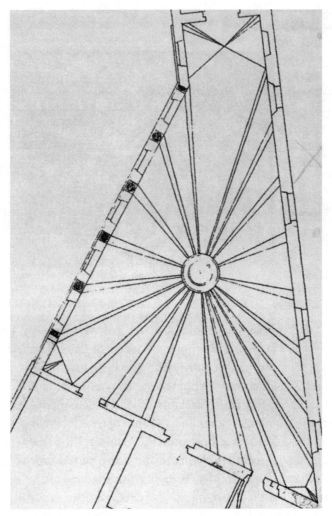

Fig. 5.3 Bernardino Facciotto, Plan of the Hall of Mirrors

Rivers Room (Sala dei Fiumi)); a perfect arrangement in which the spaces for enjoying and making music represented the beating heart, but which seems also to recall other similar examples like the Palazzo S. Croce in Rome, in which a Hall of Mirrors opens on to a hanging garden.

This evocative hypothesis of a living complex focused on rooms for music finds final support in the decoration of the walls of the room and of its neighbouring environment. It seems, in fact, that in the small vestibule that afforded the duke private access to the Hall of Mirrors ('passetto per andar nelli camarini della Sala dei Specchi') there was located a large painting, 'The Nine Muses in the Heavens' (1575–9), by Jacopo Tintoretto (Fig. 5.4), which has a curious figurative programme.[7] It depicts the nine muses mostly engaged in tuning musical instruments

Fig. 5.4 Jacopo Tintoretto, Le nove muse in aera

or in other activities preceding a genuine performance.[8] Supposing that the purchaser was Guglielmo, the subject was a fortunate one: Apollo with the muses of classical ancestry, rediscovered and revived in the humanistic age in the courts of Ferrara, Mantua[9] and Urbino, seems to have become an allegory of good government; here it would find new clothes in which might be seen the political programme and life of the duke-composer. And compared to the iconographical plans of other princely rooms of the humanist–Renaissance era, the Bacchanals and games of the *putti*, represented in the twenty *lunettes* (Fig. 5.5), hinting at the Bacchanals of Andrea Mantegna, find a meaningful equivalent in the decorations of the Sala degli Angeli of the ducal palace in Urbino, a room not far from the private place in which is located another well-known depiction of Apollo with the muses as musicians.[10]

Following the reign of Guglielmo there were no further important innovations in the creation of spaces assigned to music in the ducal palace at Mantua. Although explicit testimony on the use of the Hall of Mirrors for music dates only from the Monteverdi era, around thirty years after its construction, it seems likely, as was argued above, that this was the purpose for which Guglielmo had planned and used it and that this was maintained by his successor, Duke Vincenzo, with whom the palace remained substantially unchanged, as also did its traditional usages. We might consider, moreover, that the Hall of Mirrors was particularly appropriate for the pastimes described by Monteverdi. Its dimensions were suitable for the 'reserved' character of those weekly musical

Fig. 5.5 Mantua, Palazzo Ducale: One of the small frescos in the Hall of Mirrors

gatherings and compatible with such mundane matters as heating, provided during the winter months by a large stove whose remains were found
during restoration work. However, in spite of systematic documentary
study undertaken at Mantua during the last decade, the only evidence so
far discovered on the use of the room for music is threefold: the famous
partial trial of Rinuccini and Monteverdi's *Arianna* (14 March 1608)
during which Virginia Andreini performed those parts of the opera that
she had learned during the preceding six days,[11] and the two performances of madrigals on Friday evenings during the winter of 1610–11
mentioned in Monteverdi's letters.

From these last we learn of the presence in the Hall of Mirrors of a
highly-praised *organo di legno* (organ with wooden pipes) of which recent
research, though not definitive, has furnished some traces. Guglielmo
probably planned from the beginning to equip the Hall of Mirrors with an
organ, and it may have been for this that he negotiated at Venice in 1586,
in competition with the doge, the purchase of an important house organ of
German manufacture meticulously described by the intermediary.[12] The
date of the negotiation is noteworthy since it coincides with the end of
the work on the Hall of Mirrors itself. The high price demanded by the
builder – too far from the figure offered by the duke – very probably put paid
to the purchase. However, it may be that just such a German organ was
located subsequently in the Hall of Mirrors. It is known that during the years
of Vincenzo's reign a German-built positive organ existed in court, perhaps
acquired by him during his journey to Augsburg in 1591. This can be
deduced from an order for payment, for 'a box to be made [in Innsbruck]

for the *organo di legno* during his return.[13] The instrument was much loved by him, so much so that he sent it for repairs in 1602 to its unknown builder in the city of Augsburg. Monteverdi's praise for the organ in the Hall of Mirrors leads us to suppose that he was dealing with a particularly note-worthy and beloved instrument of the duke's and that he may indeed have been referring to the organ from Augsburg. For the sake of completeness it should be noted that Vincenzo acquired another organ from Venice in 1605, but about this at the moment there is no other information.[14]

Although later documentation on the use of the Hall of Mirrors for music is lacking, it seems likely that it retained its established function under Duke Ferdinando; in the years immediately following the sack of the palace and city of Mantua in 1630–1 it was instead used as a treasury and furnished with cupboards.[15] After its partial collapse it was re-covered with a simple truss-roof and divided into two floors, the lower of which was subdivided into five rooms, used as the offices of the Scalcheria from at least 1735 and by an engraver from 1934. After its rediscovery in 1998, the so-called 'Carbonati Apartment' was demolished, together with the intermediate floor, the lunettes were restored together with the wall panels, and a terracotta floor laid whose tiles and layout corresponded to the original. In the last few months, for demonstration purposes, the canopy of curved sails has been partially reconstructed in a light white material on an aluminium structure (Fig. 5.6). Compared, therefore, with the almost 'archaeological' look that the room had at the moment of its rediscovery, it now closely resembles its original state. The work of restoration is not, however, complete: a substantial body of eighteenth-century building work is still wedged in the room, blocking it; this cannot at the moment be demolished since it houses the staircase of a private apartment adjoining the palace. Only when alternative access to this apartment is arranged will it be possible to restore the Hall of Mirrors at least to its original dimensions. The Hall, still not included on the usual tourist itinerary, is often open for visiting and has occasionally accom-modated musical performances.

The Hall of *Orfeo* and other 'royal chambers'

In the very recent past, the history of the Hall of Mirrors, the only Mantuan musical location explicitly mentioned by Monteverdi, has, through a series of misunderstandings, intersected with one of the unre-solved mysteries of the Gonzaga palace – identification of the room that accommodated the first, academic, performance of *Orfeo* on 24 February 1607. A notice bearing the inscription 'Every Friday evening music is

Fig. 5.6 Mantua, Palazzo Ducale: The Hall of Mirrors today with, on the left, the mass of building work still not demolished

made in the Hall of Mirrors', painted on the door-jamb of the 'Logion Serato', has created in the popular and tourist tradition not only the false idea that it was here that Monteverdi's music was performed, but also the false notion that this was the location of the performance of *Orfeo*, thus multiplying the error conveyed by the notice. The rediscovery of the Hall of Mirrors of the Monteverdi era has led some to think that the performance of *Orfeo* might have taken place there. This hypothesis can be firmly excluded, both because of the narrowness of the place and because in Monteverdi's time it was commonly called the 'Hall of Mirrors' and would thus have been described as this by those who spoke of the performance. However, as we know, there is only one letter describing the location of *Orfeo*, and that places it in a less distinctive room vaguely defined as a room in the 'apartment used by the Most Serene Lady of Ferrara' ('partimento [appartamento] che godeva Madama Serenissima di Ferrara'),[16] that is the apartment assigned to Margherita Gonzaga, widow of Duke Alfonso II d'Este after her return to Mantua in 1598 and before she retired to the Convent of Sant'Orsola. This room has not yet been identified with certainty.

Any investigation of this question encounters methodological problems analogous to those that we saw in relation to identifying the Hall of Mirrors: given the continual alterations to the palace and its living quarters, any memory of the location and characteristics of this apartment have been lost. However, while no definitive document has been found, indirect evidence leads to the hypothesis that it was situated in the Corte Vecchia on the ground floor in the vicinity of the chapel of S. Croce under the existing Sala del Pisanello.[17] This may be the same apartment occupied in 1621 by Caterina de' Medici, wife of Ferdinando Gonzaga.[18] The name of these apartments had a certain persistence since an inventory of Gonzaga property of 1665 still speaks of an 'apartment of the Most Serene Lady' which included some small rooms (*camerini*) facing the Piazza San Pietro (now the Piazza Sordello) and a 'gallery'.[19] This last space, which by definition refers to dimensions adequate for a theatrical performance restricted to an academic meeting, is not at the moment identifiable because it may subsequently have been subdivided into smaller servants' quarters. What is so far known about the 'partimento di Madama Serenissima' induces us also to exclude other hypotheses formulated in recent years regarding the Sala di Manto and the Refectory (now the Sala dei Fiumi), both of which must be excluded since they can certainly not be ascribed to the said 'apartment'; and finally the Sala Imperiale, situated on the ground floor near the Chapel of S. Croce must be excluded since it is too small for the purpose.[20]

Following an analogous (and entirely conjectural) train of thought, it is likely that the room in which *Orfeo* was performed had dimensions of at least two hundred square metres, an elongated rectangular plan and a vaulted ceiling. Very probably it was equipped for the occasion with a simple raised platform with wings, of the kind erected for the plays of the palace comedians. A basic construction of this kind could house a central element depicting the two required scenes (pastoral and infernal) as well as the group of musicians, in part hidden by the wings and in part visible on the stage or at its feet. The papers of the Gonzaga Scalcheria, the office designated to oversee the domestic management of the court (food, furnishings, linen, etc.) show that the ducal drapery contained curtaining, fabrics and various materials that were used for the preparation of rooms on the occasion of festive, theatrical and musical entertainments.[21]

Beyond what it is possible to document today, Monteverdi's music must certainly have been heard in many other 'Royal chambers', among which should be mentioned as a highly probable location the room in Duke Vincenzo's apartments defined in the inventories of the picture collection as the 'room where dances are held' (adjacent to the present Sala degli Arcieri). A painted panel over a doorway showing a concert scene (bought as a Titian, but now attributed to Padovanino) confirms this as a customary destination for musical entertainments and dance. It is not difficult to imagine that Monteverdi's *Scherzi* and his other dance music were often heard there.

Scenes narrow, august and ephemeral

The operatic representation of *Orfeo* was ordered by the hereditary prince Francesco Gonzaga as a carnival entertainment for 'our academy' (the Academy of the Invaghiti).[22] As a kind of chamber theatre it offered an up-to-date alternative to the play with *intermedi* that his father Vincenzo had had performed on the previous evening 'in the *usual* theatre and with *customary* magnificence'.[23] The duke, having been present at, and enjoyed his son's opera, organised a repeat performance on 1 March 'for all the ladies of the city',[24] presumably in the same location as before, to judge by the short time between the two performances. A third performance was projected as an offering to Duke Carlo Emanuele of Savoy, whose visit was expected, but then cancelled;[25] it is likely that for so important a guest the performance would have been prepared not on a narrow ('angusta'), but on an 'august' (augusta) stage,[26] that is the 'usual theatre' already mentioned, equipping it of course with more traditional and striking scenic devices, such as for the Apollonian finale with its *deus ex machina*.

The Mantuan court possessed a court theatre ('scena di corte', 'scena di Castello', 'teatro grande'), planned by Giovan Battista Bertani and constructed between 1549 and 1561 in the lee of the Corte Nuova on one side of what was to become the Prato di Castello (now the Piazza Castello) (Figs. 5.7a and 5.7b). Among the oldest permanent theatres in Italy, it featured high tiers of seats in a semicircle, a slightly inclined stage with a permanent scene, both painted and in relief, representing a city, and a large 'orchestra' for tournaments.[27] Burned down in a fire of 1588 that also destroyed the armoury and the collection of standards and trophies that had adorned its walls and occupied the space underneath the tiers of seats, it was immediately reconstructed on the same site to a design of Ippolito Andreasi, with interventions by Anton Maria Viani and completed in 1598.[28] In Monteverdi's time the theatre was situated on the

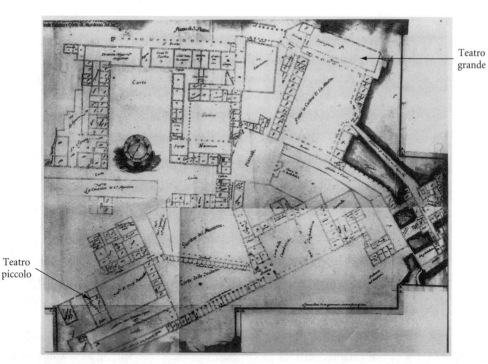

Fig. 5.7a Ludovico Checchi, Plan of the ducal palace, Mantua, 1743, showing the position of its theatres: No. 159 Teatro grande; No. 105 Teatro piccolo

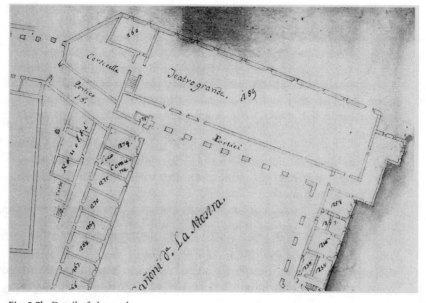

Fig. 5.7b Detail of above plan

ground floor and featured many windows, tiered seats and, very probably, boxes; on the walls there were portraits of twelve princes (four *capitani*, four marquises and four dukes, Vincenzo among them) painted in gouache; the stage was of considerable depth; the stage area was brightly lit, unlike the public area; the ceiling was painted to represent a sky with clouds; the entrance was through a large doorway.[29] The theatre possessed, moreover, one of the oldest raisable curtains, with paintings of Manto and Virgil, certainly used on the occasion of the performances of *L'idropica* and the *Mascherata dell'ingrate* (1608).[30]

Though it is uncertain whether a repeat performance of *Orfeo* was played in this theatre, many other compositions of Monteverdi must have been heard there, among which the following are documented: the prologue (Manto) in the play *L'idropica* by Battista Guarini (2 June 1608), a spectacle which lasted in total seven hours, with eight changes of scene; the *Mascherata dell'ingrate*, on a libretto by Ottavio Rinuccini (4 June 1608); the lost *intermedio* and *licenza* to Ercole Marliani's play *Le tre costanti* (18 January 1621).[31] Many other of Monteverdi's compositions with theatrical associations were probably played there: his madrigals for the various repeats of Guarini's *favola pastorale*, *Il pastor fido* (Carnival, June, September, 22 November 1598; and 1600); a *ballo* (*Endimione*), perhaps as an *intermedio* to the play *Accesi de amor*, played by the Jewish comedians in Carnival 1604–5;[32] and who knows how many others hidden under the recurrent general title of 'musiche per intermedi' in the Mantuan chronicles for almost every carnival.

The placing of instrumentalists in this theatrical space was changeable, offering various solutions from one show to another. From the scarce documentation that we have of them, for example, we know that on the occasion of the performances of *Il pastor fido* and *L'idropica* the instruments were hidden behind the scenes, providing the *concerti* that accompanied the changes of scene; during the *intermedi* the musicians with their instruments could instead have appeared on the scene in various places – on stage, under the stage, in the sky. On the occasion of the *Mascherata dell'ingrate* the musicians were placed in view on a structure on the left-hand side of the stage between the stage itself and the public, opposite another similar structure reserved for the 'Gentleman of the Ambassadors'.[33]

As an instance of a different conception of festive theatrical genre – different from the play with *intermedi* – the performance of the *tragedia in musica*, *Arianna* (28 May 1608), on a text by Rinuccini, did not take place in the Teatro Grande, but in a temporary theatre constructed specifically to house this inaugural spectacle of the great festivities for the marriage of Francesco Gonzaga to Margherita of Savoy.[34] Capable of housing several thousand spectators (the chroniclers differ as to whether four or six thousand),[35] it required a very large space which, by a process of elimination, may be identified as the Cortile della Mostra (today the Cortile della Cavallerizza). No hall in the palace, not even the great Sala di Manto, could have accommodated so large a public – the Cortile d'Onore was not available, since it was given over to the great tournament;[36] nor could it have been the Prato del Castello across which the sumptuous nuptial procession progressed. We know, too, that on several other occasions the Cortile della Mostra had been covered with awnings painted to look like the sky and thus transformed into a temporary theatre. On the occasion of *Arianna* the instrumentalists seem to have been partly hidden – that is, 'behind the scenes', which were dominated by the much-praised effect of the sea.[37]

In the time of Monteverdi there existed at court (probably since 1594) another theatre, commissioned by Duke Vincenzo, who was notoriously inclined to the world of actors and acting. Called the 'sena pubblica', or the 'teatro piccolo di corte', or the 'usual room of the comedians' ('stanza solita dei comedianti'), and equipped in the modern style with boxes, it may have been the work of Antonio Maria Viani. It was built at the end of the 'Contrada del Zuccaro' (now the Via Teatro Vecchio) and in the Florentine fashion, connected directly to the court by means of corridors and covered passages.[38] Plays put on by comedians were most frequently staged there, but given the continual intersection between theatre and music the latter may well also have been performed there, including works by Monteverdi of which we now know nothing.

Thus, though there is no explicit testimony to link Monteverdi's name to the many other places at court and in the city in which, during the years of his Mantuan service, there were festive theatrical events (all those forms of public spectacle that fall under the general headings of tournaments, jousts, quintains and 'barriere'), the lakes, the Cortile della Mostra, the Piazza S. Pietro, the courtyard of the Palazzo Te, the main street, the courtyard of the Corte Vecchia (now the Piazza Pallone) were their frequent location, at least from the time of the wedding celebrations of Guglielmo Gonzaga and Eleonora of Austria (1561); these were forms of more or less elaborate spectacle in which music played a part, under various headings, from the simple beating of drums with the blaring of pipes and small trumpets to more structured 'concerts' of voices and instruments.[39]

Of the two permanent court theatres existing at the time of Monteverdi only the facades remain today; the space once given over to the Teatro Grande is now given over to the Archaeological Museum, and the small court theatre now houses a mechanical workshop.

The Palatine Basilica of S. Barbara and other sacred spaces

Although little evidence survives of Monteverdi's activity as a composer of sacred music at Mantua, there are musical and documentary traces that show that his compositions were performed in sacred spaces both inside and outside the Gonzaga court.[40]

The Gonzaga's sacred jewel was the Palatine Basilica of S. Barbara, a collegiate church with its own liturgy and with a repertory of plainsong specifically reformed for its use,[41] with an extraordinary repertory of polyphonic music,[42] and with an important musical *cappella* to whose musical direction Monteverdi aspired as relief from the heavy loads placed on him by his responsibility for all the court's secular music. During the Monteverdi period the *cappella* was actually directed by Giovanni Giacomo Gastoldi (from 1588 to 1609, the year of his death), by Antonio Taroni (for three months in 1609) and by Stefano Nascimbeni (from 1609 to August 1612).[43] The only musician who in those years had for a while responsibility for all the Gonzaga music, both sacred and secular, at S. Barbara and at court, was Giaches de Wert; from the beginning of Duke Vincenzo's reign in 1587 and the enlargement of court music, the roles were separated and entrusted to different musicians.

S. Barbara, not merely a chapel, but an important sacred building, and autonomous despite being within the palace grounds, was built in 1561–2 and almost immediately enlarged, between 1563 and 1566, to a plan of Giovan Battista Bertani.[44] Its highly regarded organ, by the Brescian builder Graziadio Antegnati, dates from 1565, from the last stages of the construction of the basilica; it is positioned on the balcony built on the right wall of the choir and decorated with doors painted by Fermo Ghisoni.[45] The church's bell dates from slightly later; its manufacture by Venetian masters was followed closely by Guglielmo Gonzaga, who wanted from it a 'sweet voice' and a specific pitch (c sol fa ut, corresponding to the present c').[46]

In this large basilica (some sixty metres long), with its unique nave with six side chapels, there are clearly distinguishable spaces for clergy, instrumentalists and professional musicians: a choir reserved for the clerics appointed to sing plainsong, placed, after the enlargement of the church, in the apse behind the altar; a large choir loft for the professional musicians located above the entrance (its dimensions are ten metres wide by six metres deep); an organ with its own balcony (nine metres long by one metre deep) placed opposite another small choir loft of the same dimensions with the addition of a recess three and a half metres deep (Fig. 5.8). Each choir loft affords an extraordinarily clear view of all the other places designated for music and the organist could oversee

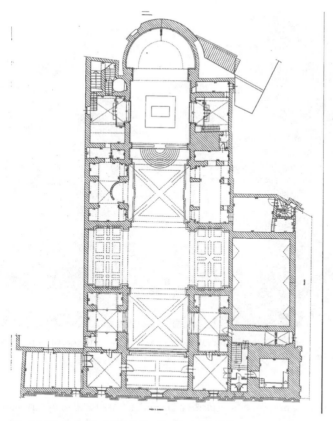

Fig. 5.8 Mantua, Plan of Palatine Basilica of S. Barbara

everything with ease, including the area for the liturgical celebration. A well-constructed system of entrances allowed the dukes, and also the singers and organist, to reach the zones reserved for them directly from court. The few testimonies that survive on the quality of the music performed for daily and extraordinary services allow us to guess how the possibilities offered by the mixing of fixed or moveable sound across the carefully gauged distances between the various spaces might have been intensively exploited:[47] this is confirmed by the uncommon regard of Duke Guglielmo for musical forms playing on the alternation between monody and polyphony, and, in the age of Dukes Vincenzo and Ferdinando, the flowering of musical liturgies in the form of elaborate projects of an almost theatrical kind. If we can only hypothesise that many of the movements in Monteverdi's 1610 volume of church music might have been conceived for this basilica, the hymn 'Ave maris stella' at least can be shown to have been composed on the reformed plainsong in use there.[48] The lengthy work of restoring S. Barbara and its organ is now

Fig. 5.9 Mantua, Palatine Basilica Palatina of S. Barbara on the eve of its re-opening, July 2006

complete, and since September 2006 the basilica has again been ready for use, mainly for concerts, but also, on special occasions, for religious services (Fig. 5.9).

While the Palatine Basilica, with its artistic riches, with its rare collection of relics,[49] and with its numerous chapter, was the representative church for the court, there also existed in the palace another palatine church of smaller dimensions (perhaps little more than thirty square metres): S. Croce in Corte,[50] not to be confused either with the oratory of S. Croce (S. Maria del Melone), the seat of a confraternity situated in the present-day Via Cavour and now recognisable only from its facade (it is now given over to commercial activity), nor another church of S. Croce situated in a completely different part of the city. S. Croce in Corte was located on the ground floor in the Corte Vecchia, with an entrance from the courtyard nowadays called the Cortile di S. Croce; built in the fifteenth century in gothic style and furnished with a high bell-tower grafted directly on to its roof, it was subdivided into two levels (the lower and upper churches). This little church was restructured in 1580 according to the wishes of Guglielmo Gonzaga, Eleonora and Caterina de' Medici, and much of it remained in the eighteenth century until it was rendered completely unrecognisable (today it houses rooms for temporary exhibitions). Besides S. Croce, there existed other chapels for private devotions within the palace: a chapel in the Corte

Vecchia (Palazzo Capitano) situated on the first floor close to the present-day Sala del Pisanello; and two small old chapels in the Castello S. Giorgio. In Monteverdi's time the church of S. Croce was certainly in use, as also were the oratory situated above it and Vincenzo Gonzaga's own small chapel, but it is difficult to know which of the other private chapels were still in use; given the presence at court of portable organs, however, we cannot exclude the idea that music might occasionally have been made in these, too.[51]

The dukes also extended direct influence over the cathedral of S. Pietro, which was developed from 1545, gaining its present aspect by 1599. It had been endowed with a permanent musical *cappella* with its own *maestro* from 1511.[52] Musical activity there, supported by the Gonzagas, took place in the chapel of S. Maria de' Voti (now 'dell'Incoronata'), constructed between 1480 and 1482 to honour a miraculous image of the Virgin, and endowed with an important series of codices of plainsong[53] and an organ (from at least 1491; it was replaced by a larger instrument in 1517); today the organ is located in the right wing of the transept, fronted symmetrically by a choir loft. The cathedral, which has an attractive internal space, subdivided into five by its nave and aisles, with a flat roof and a frescoed dome with angel musicians,[54] was connected to the court through a vestibule and walkway. It is likely that on the most solemn occasions, works by Monteverdi were heard here, though at present none is documented.

A significant explicit testimony of 26 May 1611, the Feast of the 'Sensa' (i.e., the Ascension)[55] records the performance of Vespers music by Monteverdi in the city's other imposing basilica, S. Andrea, built to a plan of Leon Battista Alberti and begun in 1472, the year of his death and also of the suppression of the associated Benedictine monastery and the elevation of its church to collegiate status. Our knowledge of its musical life is fragmentary.[56] We know that its first organ (in existence from at least 1387) was replaced by a new instrument and an organist appointed in the sixteenth century; today the organ is located in the right wing of the transept, with a choir loft placed in front of it. Although many splendid ceremonies may have taken place there it is not certain that it possessed a permanent *cappella*; rather, it seems likely that on special occasions music was provided by musicians of the duke and of the cathedral. The remarkable size of the church, increased visually by its structure as a single nave with effects of light and shade caused by a system of larger and smaller chapels at the sides, and with its wooden roof, lead one to hypothesise the necessity of a large musical body to obtain satisfactory results.

Finally, of the more than sixty other churches that existed in Mantua in the early seventeenth century, many had sporadic or regular contacts with the Gonzaga court, which was usually ready to lend its musicians to celebrate special occasions in a worthy manner. Careful re-examination of Mantuan history may well come to show the possible involvement of Monteverdi.

In the Jesuit church Santissima Trinità the motet 'Duo seraphim' (published 1610) may have been sung on the occasion in 1605 of the installation of the celebrated painting by Peter Paul Rubens depicting Vincenzo Gonzaga and his family adoring the Holy Trinity; the church, constructed at the same time as the Jesuits' religious house (1597) in the present-day Via Roberto Ardigò, is occupied today by the holdings of the State Archive and can be recognised only by its facade, though even this is remodelled, and inside through some fragments of stucco and fresco.

The reaffirmation at Mantua of the cult of the Virgin Mary in 1611 may have been the occasion for the performance of Marian musical works in various of the city churches. The church of the Capuchin fathers, which was closed as such and rededicated as the church of the Immaculate Conception on 24 March 1611, is now lost.[57] Destroyed by bombing during the Second World War, it was originally located close to the church of S. Gervasio in an area now occupied by the local health authority. In 1611, too, the medieval church of S. Francesco (1304) hosted the revival of the Company of the Immaculate Conception, placed under the protection of Cardinal Ferdinando Gonzaga. Closely tied to the Gonzaga family, who placed in it their own mausoleum, the church was rich in works of art and furnished with an organ,[58] but it was sacked by Napoleon's troops, turned into an arsenal in 1811 and bombed in 1944. Today it has been completely rebuilt and it is difficult to imagine what it must have looked like in the seventeenth century. In both these locations works by Monteverdi that now survive in the 1610 volume may have been performed, and may even have been commissioned for use there; but on this, for the moment, the documents are silent.

6 The Mantuan madrigals and the *Scherzi musicali*

MASSIMO OSSI

When Monteverdi arrived in Mantua, he stepped from the provincial Cremonese environment into one of the most cosmopolitan and artistically ambitious courts of northern Italy.[1] Under the Gonzagas' rule, Mantua had been for over a century an important commercial centre, and its financial resources had fuelled the patronage goals – musical, artistic, and literary – of a succession of rulers: in the first decades of the sixteenth century the Marquis Francesco and his wife, Isabella d'Este, established a permanent musical chapel and through their court composers, Marco Cara and Bartolomeo Tromboncino, cultivated the development of such Italian vernacular forms as the *frottola*; Duke Federico II and in particular his brother, Cardinal Ercole, enhanced the sacred *cappella*; Guglielmo, himself a competent composer, built the basilica of Santa Barbara and as a strongly religious ruler fostered primarily sacred music, employing such composers as Alessandro Striggio, Giovanni Giacomo Gastoldi, Giaches de Wert, and Benedetto Pallavicino, as well as maintaining a correspondence with Palestrina, whom he tried to hire and from whom he sought advice on his own compositions; and Monteverdi's direct employer, Vincenzo I, sought to make Mantuan music competitive in its forward-looking style with that of the Ferrarese court under Alfonso II d'Este, encouraging the composition of secular works by Wert, Pallavicino and Monteverdi himself.

The court also enjoyed a long-standing tradition of theatrical music, reaching back to the days of G. P. della Viola (1486 *La representatione di Phebo e Phetonte*) and Atlante Migliorotti (who composed the music for the revival of Poliziano's *Orfeo*, staged and sung throughout, in 1491).[2] In the 1590s this was about to reach its peak, first with the preparations for a production of Battista Guarini's *Il pastor fido* (negotiations for its performance began in 1590 and the play, with extensive music, was finally produced in 1598), and later with Monteverdi's own operas *Orfeo* (1607) and *Arianna* (1608). Mantuan theatrical circles, which focused locally on the activities of Jewish actors and dancing masters, also included such prominent itinerant companies as the Compagnia degli Uniti, Francesco Andreini's troupe – a connection that eventually brought Virginia Andreini to Mantua to perform the title role in Monteverdi's *Arianna*.[3]

The theatre at Sabbioneta, designed by Vincenzo Scamozzi (1588–90), housed spoken plays (presumably with incidental music) on a stage intended to reproduce those of classical Greece and Rome in imitation of Palladio's Teatro Olimpico in Vicenza, and Gonzaga architects included Leon Battista Alberti, Giulio Romano and Anton Maria Viani, all of whom had important international careers.[4] Allied with theatrical music and with the latest trends in secular vocal music was the presence of important literary figures: Mantua could boast of having been the birthplace of Virgil, and among its Renaissance poets was the court secretary and poet Alessandro Striggio Jr (the librettist of Monteverdi's *Orfeo*); the court also hosted such visitors as Torquato Tasso, Battista Guarini, Gabriello Chiabrera and Ottavio Rinuccini, all of whom were there between the 1580s and 1610. Finally, Mantua enjoyed a long and distinguished tradition of patronage in the visual arts as well, reaching back at least to Mantegna at the end of the fifteenth century and continuing through the sixteenth century with Giovanni Bellini, Titian, Giulio Romano (whose frescoes in the Palazzo Te are perhaps the best-known symbol of Gonzaga artistic patronage in the sixteenth century), Correggio, Tintoretto and Rubens.

By all accounts, Mantua was an important crossroads on the European artistic and intellectual map, and Monteverdi must have been exhilarated and perhaps overwhelmed by the sudden immersion in such a high-powered milieu. Not that he was unprepared for it: it is clear from the dedications of his first two books of madrigals that under Ingegneri's tutelage he had been groomed to aspire to this kind of employment. Nonetheless, the change in his pattern of production after his arrival at the Gonzaga court, which is evident in both the slower rate at which his publications appeared and in their contents, suggests that Monteverdi was deeply affected by his new circumstances. The importance given to Monteverdi's potential as composer at the time when he was hired into the Gonzagas' service is not clear: historical hindsight places probably a greater weight on it than it may have had at the time, and in focusing on Monteverdi the composer we tend to overlook his broader musical personality as performer, administrator and thinker. The duke's musical establishment already numbered several important and productive composers, and it is likely that what was really needed was a good singer and string-player.

Arguably, four books of madrigals belong to Monteverdi's Mantuan period: the Third, which appeared in 1592 and represents his first publication as a member of the Gonzaga court; the Fourth (1603) and the Fifth (1605), published close together and linked with the public dispute ignited by the theorist Giovanni Maria Artusi over aesthetic and theoretical issues; and the Sixth (1614), which appeared only after Monteverdi's move to Venice, but which bears very close ties to Mantua in both musical content and context. In addition, the Mantuan years also saw the publication of the first volume of *Scherzi musicali* (in 1607, but probably composed as early as the turn of the century[5]), a collection of three-voiced canzonettas with instrumental ritornellos setting the then-fashionable poetry of Gabriello Chiabrera. The gaps in this series are immediately apparent, and cannot be easily filled in by taking into account pieces preserved outside Monteverdi's main publications, since only five compositions, four canzonettas and one madrigal, were published in contemporary anthologies (in 1594 and 1597), and the single manuscript source from this period (I-BRq L. IV. 99) mainly preserves re-texted versions of pieces found in the 1607 *Scherzi*.[6] Thanks to Artusi's criticisms of a group of compositions by Monteverdi performed in 1597, we can add to the total of works securely known to have been written in the 1590s a group of six madrigals that Monteverdi eventually published in the Fourth and Fifth Books.[7] Not many pieces for a period of some eleven years, especially when compared to the output of his *maestro di cappella*, Wert, and his older colleague, Pallavicino, each of whom, in the span of the 1590s, produced two volumes of madrigals (Wert died in 1596).

It is of course impossible to be sure what Monteverdi's activities were like during a period for which no archival evidence and no compositions survive to fill the void, and any discussions of the eleven-year hiatus between publications have to remain highly conjectural. It seems likely that, having been hired into the court's *cappella*, Monteverdi simply had little opportunity to compose and publish new music, and that following an initial flush of productivity after being hired, he found himself busy enough with other duties that assembling a new madrigal book after 1592 would have required more time and energy than he had available. His apparent drop in productivity after the Third Book, however, may also have been due to major new aesthetic challenges that originated in the court's intense literary, theatrical and musical activities, as well as in musical developments in centres outside Mantua.

First among these challenges must surely have been the need to adapt to his new working conditions, and in particular to Wert's influence on his style and poetic choices. The Third Book of Madrigals (1592) is regarded as having been written in Wert's shadow, felt particularly in Monteverdi's choice of texts by Tasso, whose lyric poetry already permeated the Second Book (1590) but is entirely absent from the Third, being replaced by two major cycles of *ottave* from the *Gerusalemme liberata*.[8] This new interest in classically inspired epic poetry, along with an austere focus on homorhythmic, declamatory textures reflects Tasso's own ideas regarding the proper expressive language of the madrigal, which he expounded in his dialogue *La cavaletta*. As Tomlinson has argued, it also follows Wert's own extensive cultivation of a heroic style devoted to epic poetry going back to his *Primo libro de' madrigali a quattro voci* (1561). Wert's influence, felt in Monteverdi's own heroic style, remained strong and provides the platform upon which Monteverdi eventually constructed the recitative style of Arianna's lament; it is also felt very clearly in the settings of texts from Guarini's *Pastor fido* in the Fifth Book (1605).[9]

The other major new poetic voice in the Third Book is Guarini's, which accounts for about half the contents: although Guarini's poetry had appeared sporadically in both Monteverdi's First and Second Books, it is in the Third that Monteverdi seriously confronts it and develops a language specifically intended to set it to music. Unlike the *ottave* from *Gerusalemme liberata*, Guarini's lyric poetry is treated more contrapuntally, and Monteverdi begins to lean more in the direction of the epigrammatic style of the Fourth (1603) and Fifth Books of Madrigals. There is also a tendency to incorporate the lighter idioms of the canzonetta-madrigal, with its lighter textures and dance-like rhythms.[10]

Both Tasso and Guarini moved in and out of the Mantuan court in the early 1590s: Tasso actually lived there during 1591–3, and during the same period Guarini visited the court in conjunction with the attempts being made to produce his pastoral *tragicommedia*, *Il pastor fido*. The extent of their contact with Monteverdi may have been minor, given his status as a junior member of the *cappella*, but it seems legitimate to assume that he was able at least to observe them at close quarters and that the discussions that must have taken place around their presence provided him with lessons he was quick to absorb.

It is thus likely that the strong focus on theatrical music, and specifically on Guarini's play, may well have taken up a great deal of Monteverdi's time and energy – whether he participated as singer, instrumentalist, or composer in the on-again, off-again efforts to produce the work we cannot be sure, but the issues raised by the use of music in the theatre must have provided a second area of new problems and ideas for Monteverdi to confront. Certainly the organisation of his Fifth Book of Madrigals strongly suggests that Monteverdi absorbed the play's themes and characters quite deeply and that he sought a musical language appropriate to their portrayal.[11] These experiences also seem to have served him well as he later embarked on his first operatic projects, *Orfeo* (1607) and *Arianna* (1608).

Third, Monteverdi must have been aware of the growing importance of solo singing and of the new developments in virtuoso vocal ornamentation that were driving fashion in Florence, Ferrara and Mantua itself.

Although he arrived in Mantua after the court had travelled to Florence for the wedding celebrations of Grand Duke Ferdinando de' Medici and Christine of Lorraine in 1589, he was likely aware of the musical and dramatic impact of the *intermedi* performed in conjunction with Girolamo Bargagli's play *La pellegrina*, which included monodic contributions by Francesco (?Giulio) Caccini and others.[12] Moreover, although the Ferrarese *concerto delle dame* had ceased its activities by the 1590s, its influence continued to be felt not only among composers such as Luca Marenzio, Carlo Gesualdo, Luzzasco Luzzaschi and others, but also in 'copy-cat' ensembles such as Mantua's own Pellizzari family, which Vincenzo Gonzaga hired in 1588 in imitation of his Ferrarese brother-in-law's ensemble.[13]

Finally, if the scant information provided by Artusi's account of the events that led to his criticisms of Monteverdi's music can be taken as evidence of the existence of a circle of progressive composers in the region of Mantua and Ferrara, then it seems plausible that Monteverdi, during the 1590s, had established himself among them. On Artusi's evidence we can name Luzzaschi among those in attendance, and Antonio Goretti, the host of the musical evening during which the theorist heard Monteverdi's music; in addition, in 1594–6, Gesualdo was a presence there, and in the first half of the decade Wert, who might have introduced Monteverdi to Ferrarese circles as well.[14] Certainly, on the strength of Monteverdi's preface to the Fourth Book of Madrigals, we know that Duke Alfonso II d'Este liked his works and that Monteverdi had promised to send him a group of madrigals– presumably the core of the collection– before the duke's death in 1597. To the Ferrarese composers we might add Monteverdi's Mantuan colleagues Benedetto Pallavicino, who in spite of a generally conservative style seems to have absorbed some of the more expressive aspects of the younger generation, and Giovanni Giacomo Gastoldi, who contributed to the *Pastor fido* music a setting of the *giuoco della cieca* ('game of blind man's bluff') from Act III and whose *balletti* form part of the background for Monteverdi's own *Scherzi musicali* – a collection that plays an important part in Monteverdi's response to Artusi.[15] In addition to the composers who were active around Monteverdi's home turf, we can also include those whose music was known to the composer and his colleagues, and who are listed as comrades-in-arms by Giulio Cesare Monteverdi in the 'Dichiarazione' of 1607: Rore, the elder statesman and inspiration, and Caccini, Cavalieri, Alfonso Fontanelli, Tomaso Pecci and others.

The existence of a circle of self-consciously 'modernist' composers, most likely centred around the music-obsessed Duke Alfonso's Ferrarese court, helps to explain the sudden and vehement attack published by Artusi in 1600. In particular, Monteverdi's pointed insistence in the prefatory 'Lettera' of the Fifth Book, on his paternity of the term 'seconda pratica', and Artusi's cavalier treatment of it, as well as his reference to musicians who sought to explain their practice by drawing on classical theories, suggests that in the years before 1597–8, when the evening at Goretti's house took place, there had already been widespread talk of new theories and new approaches to composition, and that Monteverdi was a participant in this conversation, possibly even one of its most prominent contributors, but by no means the only one to advocate a new way of doing things. From nearby Bologna, Artusi had very likely been following this conversation, and may well have participated in it himself: he clearly understood both sides of the argument in a way that suggests he had been steeped in it for some time, knew the cast of characters, and had heard (and seen) a lot of the music he was criticising.

If the controversy with Artusi seems to define Monteverdi's historical position, it also seems to have been about stylistic developments that, by 1600, Monteverdi had already outgrown.[16] This appears to be the message of the *Scherzi musicali*, to which Giulio Cesare Monteverdi appended his 'Dichiarazione': Claudio's reputation as an innovator rested on his introduction of new ideas and new styles, and the *Scherzi* – as unlike the madrigals critiqued by Artusi as any compositions might be – were evidence of his forward momentum, music written just as Artusi was finishing and issuing his criticisms. If anything, the *Scherzi* represented a whole new approach to text-setting, driven by rhythm more than by text expression and based on Chiabrera's new poetic aesthetic, which was as foreign to the Petrarchan aesthetic of the madrigal as Monteverdi's three-voice settings were to Renaissance polyphony. Moreover, it was the *Scherzi* – not madrigals like 'Cruda Amarilli' – that pointed the way to the future: they provided a structural model on which Monteverdi based the forms of his first operatic essay, *Orfeo*, and they remained part of his vocabulary throughout the remainder of his career.[17]

With his canzonetta texts, Chiabrera signalled a departure from the Petrarchan and Bembist aesthetic of the sixteenth-century madrigal towards a lighter, more direct form of poetry based on clearly expressed, common sentiments and a flexible, rhythmically oriented prosody. In this, he self-consciously followed French poets like Pierre de Ronsard, whose works he openly admired. He was, moreover, strongly influenced by the notion of singability: poetry should be composed so that it may be set to music, and he held up as a model the canzonettas of Giulio Caccini composed to his own verses.[18] To the madrigal's clever *concetti*, couched in self-contained single epigrammatic stanzas of *endecasillabi* and *settenari* flexibly linked by an ad hoc rhyme scheme, he juxtaposed strophic poems of strictly rhyming verses consisting of six to eight syllables each. For Monteverdi, the emphasis on metre provided a kind of freedom that the madrigal did not: the canzonettas offer little opportunity for specific word-painting, and are characterised by syncopations and cross-accentuations of word stresses, as well as by primarily syllabic declamation, sometimes enhanced by pairs of quavers on a single syllable. Moreover, because the versification emphasises short recurrent metric groups, much of the melodic writing in these pieces relies on brief rhythmic modules that are repeated, expanded and rearranged as needed. It is no coincidence that Giulio Cesare Monteverdi, drawing on Chiabrera's popularity in Mantua around 1600, was able to ally his brother with the poet's new French-inspired poetic ideas: 'The *canto alla francese* in the modern manner ... who before him [used it] before he brought it back from the baths at Spa in 1599?'[19]

'Damigella tutta bella' presents many of the characteristics of the *Scherzi*. Chiabrera's poem consists of six strophes, each containing six lines arranged in the pattern a–a–B–c–c–B, where lower cases indicate four-syllable *quaternario* lines and upper case *ottonari* (eight-syllable lines). The subject matter is extremely simple: an anacreontic drinking song, it exhorts a pretty serving maid to keep wine (described as a dew distilled from rubies and topaz) flowing to drown the poet's amorous sorrow. This is the general tone of the canzonettas in the rest of the volume, most of which deal with vaguely pastoral settings and pretty girls, flowers, and the occasional thorn that torments lovers.

Damigella	Young maid,
Tutta bella	Pretty all over,
Versa versa quel bel vino	Keep that wine flowing:
Fa che cada	Let it fall,
La rugiada	That dew
Distillata di rubino	Distilled from rubies.

Monteverdi sets the poem in an ambiguous triple metre (C 3/2, oscillating between simple 3 and compound 6); he emphasises the main accentuation of each verse – in the *quaternari* only one accent is possible, whereas the *ottonari* have two – and also draws attention to the internal rhymes set up by the accented syllables, 'gel', 'bel', and 'ver'; 'ver' and 'vi'; 'vi' and 'bi'; and 'ca', 'gia', and 'la'. Moreover, the bars of 6/8 introduce cross-accentuations that keep the verse-derived rhythm from becoming too stodgy. The melodic structure also emphasises the short–short–long–short metre of the poetry, essentially alternating only two rhythmic cells throughout (Ex. 6.1).

Ex. 6.1 Top line of 'Damigella tutta bella' showing its two main cells

The melodic and metric regularity of the setting strongly evokes the dance, and indeed there are clear dance connections between the *Scherzi* and musical practices at Mantua and Ferrara.[20] Dancing played an important role at court, most likely in imitation of the focus on dance at Ferrara where the court cultivated dancing and maintained an ensemble of dancing ladies similar to the singing ensemble of the duke.[21] At Mantua, Gastoldi may also have provided music for courtly dancing, with his famous *balletti*, which share some rhythmic characteristics with Monteverdi's *Scherzi*. And Monteverdi's particular attention to the instrumental component of the *Scherzi* also suggests a dance context: he specifically called for violins, which were emerging as important virtuoso instruments, having long been the dancing master's tool; the formal scheme for the canzonettas, which pitted the full vocal and instrumental ensemble for the outer strophes against the ad hoc use of solo voices for the internal ones, resembled a dancing scheme he described in a letter of 1604 in which solo dancers emerged from the larger group in a series of rotating solo 'stanzas';[22] and the music itself seems perfectly designed not to distract from the dance, being homorhythmic, repetitive, and therefore predictable, keeping to a very straightforward harmonic language grounded in its main tonal centre of G. The instrumental ritornellos, which are somewhat more complex than the vocal writing, provide a steady alternation of timbre and musical content that lends itself easily to choreography.

The Fourth and Fifth Books of Madrigals represent two very different worlds, and were likely planned by Monteverdi at the same time with the intention of making a sharp distinction between them.[23] As Gary Tomlinson has argued, the Fourth can be seen as representing several layers of Monteverdi's development in the 1590s – thus filling in the gap of those years with a few more works – beginning with pieces in the style of the Third Book and leading up to the madrigals heard by Artusi in 1597.[24] Consequently, the range of techniques present in the collection is very broad, from the extreme contrapuntal complexity of the closing madrigal, 'Piagne e sospira', which is based on six motifs presented in constantly changing combinations during the first eighty-seven bars, to the canzonetta-madrigal textures of the pair 'Io mi son giovinetta' and 'Quell'augellin che canta', to the pithy expression of the epigrammatic

'Anima del cor mio', and the Caccini-inspired declamatory style (notated, exceptionally, as *falsobordone*) of 'Sfogava con le stelle'.[25] Contrapuntal variety and dissonance are important expressive tools throughout the volume, especially in such works as 'Ah dolente partita' and the erotically charged setting of Maurizio Moro's 'Sì ch'io vorrei morire', one of Monteverdi's most overtly sexual madrigals. In spite of the presence of one of the madrigals criticised by Artusi, 'Anima mia perdona' and its *seconda parte*, 'Che se tu se' il cor mio', the overall conception of the Fourth Book as an anthology of disparate works is firmly rooted in the sixteenth century and is closer to the Third than to the Fifth Book.[26]

The Fifth Book, whose core works are also among those chastised in *L'Artusi*, moves well beyond the Fourth, not only because it includes compositions in the new *concertato* style, requiring not only an obbligato basso continuo and in the last work a *sinfonia* as well, but also, and more importantly, in the dramatic logic of the Book. The pieces within it are grouped into two parts; first, the *a cappella* madrigals, which focus on the two main plots of *Pastor fido* (Amarilli–Mirtillo and Silvio–Dorinda), representing them in their characteristic moments and psychological states: Amarilli and Mirtillo fixed in their mutual love and alienation and Silvio and Dorinda at the moment of epiphany, when Silvio, having wounded Dorinda nearly to death, realises his love for her. The second group consists of the *concertato* madrigals, but their separation from the rest is not based on instrumentation alone – they set a group of disparate lyric poems, which Monteverdi gathers to form a concise history of a love affair seen from the point of view of the lover who hesitantly and resignedly abandons himself to it. 'Questi vaghi concenti', the final work, comments on both cycles, summarising their affective vicissitudes.[27]

The unified narrative theme that governs the organisation of the Fifth Book does not prevent Monteverdi from employing a variety of textures and styles. The opening pair, 'Cruda Amarilli' and 'O Mirtillo', are perhaps the most contrapuntally complex works in the volume, and the most harmonically daring, as well. Both drew Artusi's censure – 'Cruda Amarilli' for several examples of unprepared and improperly resolved dissonances, and 'O Mirtillo' for improper modal mixture.[28] The cycle of five madrigals that makes up the dialogue between Silvio and Dorinda, as well as the three-section 'Ch'io t'ami' cycle that follows, provide a stark contrast to the opening pair, employing instead largely the kind of declamatory homophony that Monteverdi learned from Wert. The effect of these madrigals is quite stark and recitative-like, and they have been linked to the language that Monteverdi eventually distilled into the recitatives for *Orfeo* and for Arianna's lament.[29]

The madrigals with basso continuo, on the other hand, are for the most part quite florid. It is remarkable that in these works Monteverdi makes very little use of actual monody and that when he does, he approaches it rather timidly. Surely he was aware of Caccini's monodies – his indebtedness to the Florentine composer's 'Sfogava con le stelle' leaves no doubt of it – and yet he never embraced the genre wholeheartedly. Only in the Seventh Book, which appeared in 1619, did he include one madrigal setting for solo voice ('Con che soavità', which is hardly typical of the genre); his other pieces for one voice and continuo are either theatrically oriented (the strophic variations of 'Tempro la cetra', the *Lettera amorosa* and *Partenza amorosa*, the lone extract from *Arianna* (1623)) or are canzonettas like 'Eri già tutta mia', 'Maledetto sia l'aspetto', and 'Quel sguardo sdegnosetto' (all 1632). His most eloquent early essay in the solo madrigal genre is to be found in *Orfeo*: 'Rosa del ciel' in Act I can stand on its own and bears comparison with any of Caccini's madrigals in *Le nuove musiche*. It is fair to say that counterpoint – perhaps ironically in light of Artusi's criticisms – remained the bedrock of Monteverdi's compositional art to the end of his career.

In the Fifth Book, soloistic writing means largely highly florid duets such as are found in 'Ahi, come a un vago sol cortese giro' and 'E così a poco a poco' – highly ornamented but essentially polyphonic. Solo passages do appear, most prominently in 'Amor, se giusto sei' and in 'Troppo ben può questo tiranno Amore', but pleasing as they are, they lack a clear motivation, especially as the voices supplant one another in presenting the first-person text. To apply a concept Monteverdi would cite only a few years later when discussing *Arianna*, they lack verisimilitude and appear motivated more by the desire to vary the texture than by the inherent dramatic needs of the text. More effective in these terms is the solo voice in '"T'amo mia vita" la mia cara vita', which Monteverdi uses to 'personify' the remembered voice of the beloved, obsessively recalled by the narrator – who is embodied by the three lower voices, in a similar effect to the one he would later employ for the narrating and commenting chorus in the famous *Lamento della ninfa*. In '"T'amo mia vita"' Monteverdi takes his cue from Guarini's repetition of the poem's opening words, '"T'amo mia vita"', in the last line, to impose a refrain-like structure on the poem that is both dramatically and musically driven (Ex. 6.2). By the Sixth Book (1614), all hesitancy in writing for the solo voice has vanished, and although the continuo madrigals in that collection are very similar in conception to those of the Fifth, the monodic style is fully integrated into the ensemble madrigal.

Structurally, the continuo madrigals of the Fifth Book also point the way for developments that Monteverdi expands and solidifies in *Orfeo* and later works. Symmetrical structures, such as the refrains of '"T'amo mia vita"' and the repetitions of 'Troppo ben può' are so obvious as to

Ex. 6.2

have prompted comparisons to later Baroque forms – concerto, trio sonata, and ritornello.[30] Without going quite so far, other techniques, such as the incipient strophic bass of 'Ahi, come a un vago sol cortese giro' (see Intermedio II, below, Ex. II.1) and 'Amor se giusto sei' (Ex. 6.3) hint at Monteverdi's later use of this as an organisational principle without, however, being worked out to its full extent – in both pieces such techniques appear sporadically, and are abandoned part way through. Again, in the Sixth Book strophic basses will return as an important feature of the continuo madrigals, where they will be more rigorously worked out in such works as 'A Dio Florida bella' and 'Misero Alceo'.

As Monteverdi reflected on it some thirty years later, the *seconda pratica* had never really been about dissonance treatment, which in retrospect was only a means to an end – text expression – that quickly became subordinated to a still larger aim, that of expressing the affective subtext of human psychology. The core of the compositional problems he sought to solve, first within individual madrigals, then across the span of entire books, and eventually in operas, Monteverdi later described as the 'via naturale all'immitatione' – the 'natural means of imitating human emotion'. If Monteverdi linked his realisation of the real problem to the composition of Arianna's lament, the foundation of his awareness of it and of the new language he developed in that work had already been laid in the Fifth Book of Madrigals, which was steeped in the *Pastor fido* experiences of the 1590s.

Ex. 6.3

Arianna's lament provides a link connecting the Sixth Book of Madrigals, published in Venice without a dedication, with the Mantuan court. As Giovanni Battista Doni tells the story, Monteverdi was persuaded by 'a Venetian gentleman' to arrange the lament for an ensemble of voices, and this – the earliest version of the lament officially published by Monteverdi – appears in the Sixth Book as one of two multi-sectional laments around which the volume is organised.[31] The other, the *sestina amorosa*, *Lagrime d'amante al sepolcro dell'amata* on a text by the Mantuan courtier Scipione Agnelli, commemorates the singer Caterina Martinelli, who had come to the Mantuan court from Florence as one of the duke's favourite singers. She was Monteverdi's pupil, in whose care she was placed and in whose household she lived; the role of Arianna was originally conceived for her, but she died during the rehearsal period in 1608, and the part was eventually assigned to the *commedia* actress Virginia Andreini – presumably rewritten to reflect her particular talent. The lament's legendary success in moving the audience may well have derived from Andreini's renowned acting ability, and the remarkably flexible declamatory language Monteverdi was able to create (after considerable effort and experimentation, as he recalled thirty years later) seems indeed more suited for a consummate actress than for a singer (and even today it is least effective when 'sung', beauty of tone and lyricism being obstacles to its expressive power). Perhaps that may have been the silver lining in what was, for both composer and duke (he is the 'amante' who does the lamenting), a deeply felt loss. For Monteverdi, Caterina's death was compounded by that of his wife, Claudia, who had died earlier in autumn 1607, and coming on top of the stress of producing the music for the wedding festivities, it plunged him into a crisis that continued for over a year and eventually, exacerbated by his feeling of not having been rewarded adequately for his efforts, led to his departure from Mantua. Monteverdi's setting, briefly quoting from Arianna's lament, neatly summarises the significance of the *sestina* while providing an effective connecting element between the two laments.[32]

The Sixth Book, like the Fifth, mixes *a cappella* and *concertato* madrigals. As in the Fifth, the two types help to establish a structure for the volume as a whole, but in the Sixth the plan is more complex. The book divides into two roughly symmetrical halves, each of which begins with one of the multi-part laments followed by a sonnet by Petrarch ('Zefiro torna e 'l bel tempo rimena', and 'Ohimé il bel viso, ohimé il soave sguardo'), also set *a cappella*, and then a group of continuo madrigals. The pattern in each half, then, repeats that of the Fifth Book (*a cappella*, then continuo madrigals, and finally a larger-scale work with mixed forces), though in place of the narrative logic of the preceding volume, the Sixth deals generally with themes of loss, headlined by the two laments, and juxtaposes sonnets by Petrarch (a rarity for Monteverdi) and Giambattista Marino – two polar extremes, the latter of whom may be seen as representing the end of the Petrarchan Renaissance tradition, which is thus neatly summarised in Monteverdi's choices. The last piece, 'Presso a un fiume tranquillo' is a grand closing dialogue for seven voices, much as 'Questi vaghi concenti' had been in the Fifth Book, but in this case it breaks with the preceding pieces in setting a *canzonetta* by Marino – a recently introduced and self-consciously popularising genre that, lacking the pedigree, formal stiffness, and rhetorical aims of the sonnet, recalls Monteverdi's pointed use of the *Scherzi musicali* to respond to Artusi's criticisms of his contrapuntal skills.

Quite apart from its aesthetic merit, which was already questioned in the seventeenth century, the polyphonic version of Arianna's lament provides an object lesson in the close relationship between monodic recitative and counterpoint – the solo vocal line of the 'original' lament (if it can be so considered, given that what Monteverdi published in 1623 was likely only a skeleton of the version heard from the stage in Mantua) proves quite malleable in being adapted to the ensemble version.[33] What it loses in interpretative flexibility it gains in the richness of the counterpoint, though it also lacks the expressive power attributed to the instrumental arrangement that accompanied Virginia Andreini's performance. Tomlinson has suggested that the 'viole et violini' that supported the voice so expressively from their off-stage position might have resembled at times the ensemble vocal version, providing a 'quasi-contrapuntal' accompaniment, though it is also possible to look at the extraordinary instrumental writing in 'Con che soavità' from the Seventh Book (1619) to see how an ensemble of strings and continuo might have been deployed to follow even the most flexible of vocal parts.[34]

Perhaps the most extraordinary pieces of the Sixth Book are the two Petrarch settings, not only because they are Monteverdi's first of only six attempts at setting the fourteenth-century master's poetry (two are in the *Madrigali guerrieri, et amorosi* (1638), and two in the *Selva morale* (1641)), but also because they provide some stunning musical moments.[35] The *concertato* madrigals expand on the techniques Monteverdi had already used in those of the Fifth Book, and clearly benefit from the formal structures he developed in larger works such as *Orfeo*, *Arianna*, the *Mascherata dell'ingrate*, and the *Vespers* of 1610, as well as from a more refined approach to writing for solo voices. The use of strophic variations, which was incipient in such pieces as 'Ahi, come a un vago sol' and 'Amor, se giusto', is now fully developed and forms the backbone of such works as 'Misero Alceo, dal caro albergo fore' and 'A Dio, Florida bella, il cor piagato'. Formally closed designs, such as the narrative opening and closing sections of 'Misero Alceo' serve to provide both tonal and structural boundaries for the madrigals, which become miniature dramatic scenes.

Finally, the works Monteverdi produced beginning at the turn of the century show evidence of his expanding interest in true *concertato* writing that uses obbligato instrumental parts in addition to the *basso continuo*. Mantua was a centre of violin playing (for example the composer and virtuoso Salamone Rossi was active there).[36] As early as the *Scherzi musicali* Monteverdi prescribed not only the doubling of vocal parts by the violins that play the ritornellos, but also the insertion, within the sung strophes, of brief passages for instruments alone. The presence of a *sinfonia* to introduce and punctuate 'Questi vaghi concenti' in the Fifth Book reflects a tradition of instrumental ensemble introductions that goes back at least to the 1580s and improvised ritornellos can be traced back to the lute accompaniments of *frottolas*; they were part and parcel of the guitarist's repertory. The specificity with which Monteverdi treats the instrumentation of the *Scherzi musicali*, however, was something entirely new in published music and found ready employment in the extensive and highly varied use of instruments in *Orfeo*. Monteverdi continued to expand his use of instruments in his later madrigal books as well as in theatrical and semi-theatrical pieces such as the *Combattimento di Tancredi e Clorinda* (Carnival 1624, but published in the *Madrigali guerrieri, et amorosi* of 1638). In this aspect of composition, Monteverdi clearly benefited from his early experiences as a member of the Mantuan instrumental ensemble: not only did he have a strong inclination towards using instruments, but he was also sensitive to the effects of sonority and timbre that could be obtained by combining them with the human voice.[37] From a purely structural point of view, he took the convention of largely ad hoc, improvised insertion of instrumental elements into vocal music and turned it to advantage as an integral part of the compositional process, thus laying the foundation not only for his own, but others' development of a true *concertato* style.

Monteverdi's compositions from the Mantuan period strongly suggest that throughout his twenty or so years there his compositional techniques and aesthetics were in a constant state of transition. The intellectual, literary and aesthetic cross-currents to which he was exposed as a member of the court propelled the trajectory that took him a long way from the promising but malleable young composer he was in 1590. His development during these formative years must have been aided by his ability to absorb and internalise new ideas and especially new sounds and virtuoso techniques, to which he was exposed as a member of vocal and instrumental ensembles. By the time he was ready to leave the court in 1609–12, he had become established as a leading figure of the new aesthetic movement away from Renaissance conceptions of the relationship between text and music. The madrigals of the Fifth and Sixth Books, and even more so the canzonettas of the *Scherzi musicali*, point the way towards a new conception of music as not merely subservient to the imperatives of textual meaning, but as equal partner in the creation of new meanings both explicit and implicit in the text. It was a shift of which Monteverdi himself may have been only partially aware, but which gathered momentum very quickly after the turn of the century, as the powerful pull towards a theatrical conception of music, first felt in the *Pastor fido* madrigals and made overtly manifest in the early operas, spread to other musical genres.

INTERMEDIO II

'Ahi, come a un vago sol cortese giro' (1605)

MASSIMO OSSI

This is the opening piece of the cycle of five continuo madrigals that Monteverdi placed at the end of the Fifth Book. As I argued in the preceding chapter, these madrigals, all but one of which are taken from Battista Guarini's *Rime*, are arranged to form a kind of narrative. Beginning with 'Ahi, come a un vago sol' we are introduced to the opening stages of an amorous infatuation – brought on by the glance of a woman's beautiful eyes – into which the poet allows himself to be drawn in spite of his better judgement. His ambivalent attitude is made clear in this poem, in which he laments that 'it does no good to hide' even if, because he has been in love before, he knows that he will be hurt again. In the next poem, 'Troppo ben può questo tiranno Amore', his ambivalence is the focus, as fear and temptation compete, but by the third madrigal, 'Amor, se giusto sei', it is clear that the lover has given in, and he begs Love to be just and make his beloved as receptive to him as he is to her. By the fourth poem – '"T'amo, mia vita"', la mia cara vita' – he wallows in the sound of his beloved's words ('I love you, my life'), and in the fifth – 'E così a poco a poco' – he is consumed by the affair, 'like a moth to the flame', conscious that to try to put out the blaze merely makes it worse. Certain images, like the arrow that pierces the heart, the eyes that wound, and the burning pain of love, recur in several of the poems, reinforcing the thematic link provided by the narrative with the return of specific words and phrases. It should be noted that these poems were not written as a group, but that Monteverdi chose them precisely because they share certain common traits and develop a single narrative thread.

This is the text of Monteverdi's madrigal:

Ahi, come a un vago sol cortese giro	Alas, just as it was from the lovely single gentle glance
De due begli occhi, ond'io	of two beautiful eyes that I
Soffersi il primo, e dolce stral d'Amore,	suffered my first sweet arrow of love,
Pien d'un nuovo desio,	now, full of a new desire,
Sì pronto a sospirar, torna il mio core!	my heart is once again ready to sigh!

Lasso, non val ascondersi ch'omai	Wretch, there is no point in taking cover, for
Conosco i segni, che'l mio cor m'addita	I know the signs that my heart points out
De l'antica ferita,	of the ancient wound,
Ed è gran tempo pur che la saldai:	and it has been a long time since I healed it:
Ah, che piaga d'amor non sana mai!	alas, for love's wound never heals!

It is cast in a typical sixteenth-century genre called 'madrigale'. This was a flexible form that freely mixed eleven-syllable (*endecasillabi*) and seven-syllable (*settenari*) lines in a single strophe, which might range in length from as few as five lines to as many as fifteen or so. *Madrigali* had no prescribed rhyme scheme or other formal requirements, though many ended with a couplet, often of *endecasillabi*, that expressed the essence of the poem in a pithy statement (the *concetto* or conceit). 'Ahi, come a un vago sol cortese giro' comprises ten lines, in the pattern AbCbCDEeDD (*endecasillabi* are here represented by upper case, *settenari* by lower-case letters). The poem's syntactical structure agrees with the organisation of the rhyming pattern: the first five lines form a single clause, which may be considered the premise of the argument: 'how quickly my heart returns to that which had hurt it'. The second half of the poem also forms a single syntactical unit, leading up to the *concetto*, here expressed in a single line, 'Alas, for love's wound never heals!'. Both halves of the poem feature prominent enjambements, where a syntactical unit begun on one line continues into the next, as in lines 1 into 2 and 2 into 3, and again at 5 into 6 and 6 into 7; this creates tension between the form of the poem (its rhymes and verse structure) and its content.

Monteverdi's musical setting works both with Guarini's poem and against it. The overall scheme emphasises the two larger units of five lines each.

Line	Rhyme	Bars	Cadence	Ensemble
1	A	1–5	———	QT
2	b	5–6	———	
3	C	7–12	———	
4	b	12–14	———	
5	C	15–23	D	
[10]	*Refrain*	24–32	D	SAB
6	D	33–8	———	QT
7	E	39–41	[D, weak]	
8	e	41–5	G	
[10]	*Refrain*	46–51	A	SAB
9	D	52–5	———	QT
[10]	*Refrain twice*	56–61, 62–73	D (61), A (73)	QT, then Tutti
9	D	74–7	———	
10	D *Refrain*	78–91	D	Tutti

The first section (bars 1–23) is given entirely to the duet between Tenor and Quinto (also a tenor). It is tonally closed, ending on a highly ornamented cadence to D at bar 23. The second half of the poem emphasises different vocal combinations – a trio (S, A, B); the tenor duet of the first part; and the entire five-voice ensemble. Moreover, it takes the *concetto* 'Ahi, che piaga d'amor non sana mai' and turns it into a refrain that occurs four times, twice as a trio and twice for the full ensemble. In this way, Monteverdi violates the form and the sense of the poem: the *concetto*, which was introduced as the concluding moral of the story, now appears prematurely out of logical sequence. But treating it as a refrain makes strong musical logic – its repetition creates formal clarity out of what would otherwise be a long declarative sentence similar to the first twenty-three bars, and its progressively heavier and more repetitive statement (see the immediate repetitions at bars 62–73) makes for a strong conclusion. If the formal integrity of the poem suffers, its underlying rhetoric does not, however: the tonally stable refrain lends an air of inevitability to the repeated statement, and the urgency of its repeated 'misplacement' underscores the pained resignation of the speaker.

The schematic treatment of this poem, using blocks of different voice combinations and a refrain to create formal and rhetorical clarity, is a new element in Monteverdi's madrigals.[1] The presence of a continuo instrument makes certain extended textures possible – the long declamatory duets, for example – and thus helps in creating the various elements that make up the contrasting blocks; beyond that, it seems to encourage a kind of purely musical formal experimentation that can be seen throughout these five continuo madrigals.

One purely musical element, directly tied to the instrumental bass, is the use of repeating bass lines to delineate musical or textual sections; this is the earliest example I am aware of in Monteverdi's works of the 'strophic variation' bass – a repeating bass line over which the vocal parts are varied. In later strophic variation songs, by Monteverdi and others, every strophe uses the same bass line (sometimes with rhythmic modifications, but with the same pitch sequence) while the upper parts are new each time (see for example the duet 'Ohimé, dov'è il mio ben, dov'è il mio core?' from the Seventh Book (1619), or the Prologue to *Orfeo*, 'Dal mio Permesso amato', both of which are built on this principle). At the beginning of 'Ahi, come a un vago sol', the bass articulates a sequence of pitches (bars 1–7, ending on A as V of D); this is then repeated nearly verbatim, albeit with some minor rhythmic changes, in bars 8–15, ending on C-sharp (again as a first inversion of V of D); the pattern then starts again in bar 15, but is abandoned at bar 18 to establish the dominant pedal that cadences on D in bar 23 (Ex. II.1).

Ex. II.1

What is the point of this repeating bass? It coincides with the verse structure: the first statement supports the first pair of lines and the second lines 3 and 4; the third, partial, statement suggests a continuation of the thought, but Monteverdi breaks it just as Guarini turns to his conclusion ('torna il mio core' – my heart turns back again). Given the declamatory nature of the upper parts, the repeating bass provides an underlying logic for the first section. The repeating nature of the bass itself is well masked: the vocal parts overlap its conclusion each time, so their sectional nature does not appear to be governed by it. In fact, the listener is far more aware of the smaller, declarative, units of the duet, and is very likely not to notice the rigorous musical logic that supports them.

The bass also makes possible the extremely florid writing of the upper parts. Vocal duets and trios, made popular by vocal ensembles like the *concerto delle dame* at Ferrara and its imitators elsewhere, made use of extensive ornamentation largely derived from the practice of improvised divisions that was common in the sixteenth century. The ornaments Monteverdi notates in 'Ahi, come a un vago sol' are inspired, instead, by Caccini's new style, which often relies on dotted-note figures and irregular groupings of rhythmic values. Moreover, in 'Ahi, come a un vago sol', as in many of Monteverdi's works, the ornaments are written out, not left to the improvisational skill of the performer: this is a matter of practicality in a duet, but Monteverdi often does this in solo vocal lines as well, making it clear that the singer is not to improvise other ornaments – see for example the instructions for the passage that begins 'Notte' in the *Combattimento di Tancredi e Clorinda* in the Eighth Book of Madrigals (1638). The ornamentation is used in a way similar to typical sixteenth-century madrigalisms: words like 'giro' (turn), 'stral[e]' (arrow), 'core' (heart), and 'lasso' (wretch) are treated appropriately – we might argue that Monteverdi integrates ornamentation into compositional practice, using it as building-blocks for melody rather than as something imposed on to it.

Finally, Monteverdi's treatment of the duets, particularly in the first half of the madrigal, is carefully controlled to emphasise the importance of the text. Each of the five phrases (bars 1–5; 5–6; 7–12; 12–13; 15–23) presents a logical unit of the text; the two short phrases isolate key concepts (beautiful eyes, and the heart's new desire). Emphasis derives from where the composer places his caesuras and texture changes. In the longer phrases, the voices are treated imitatively – this will be the basic language of Monteverdi's duets to the end of his career – and quite expansively in the ornamented sections. The shorter phrases consist of block declamation, as for the all-important 'De due belli occhi' (of two beautiful eyes) and 'Pien d'un novo desio' (filled with renewed desire), which are isolated as if they were being regarded with wonder by the speaker. This pattern, in which imitative phrases alternate with paired declamation, is maintained in the second part as well, as is evident in bars 33–45; Monteverdi likes symmetrical concepts, especially when they do not result in slavish, obvious symmetry, because they establish a foundational logic on which to construct larger musical structures without sacrificing the flexibility that expressive text-setting requires.

The first twenty-three bars are filled with the erotic tension of new sexual desire and romantic ardour, but contrast the passionate 'Sì pronto a sospirar' with the dirge-like choral declamation of 'Ah, che piaga d'amor', which brings the sensuous vocal displays to a stop. After this wet blanket of a refrain makes its appearance, even the duetting tenors abandon their exaggerated ornamentation: 'lasso' (alas) and 'antica ferita' (ancient wound) lack the verve of 'giro', and for good reason. Rushing imitation gives way to recitative-like block declamation, and the refrain leaves no doubt what it all means, pointless though the warning turns out to be.

The harmonic language of 'Ahi, come a un vago sol' is considerably pared down from that of earlier *a cappella* madrigals. The continuo line articulates a series of circle-of-fifths progressions: D–G–C–F–C–F–C–A (as third of a diminished chord on F-sharp leading to) E–A (as V of D). The central tonal reference is to D throughout the madrigal, with secondary cadences to G (bar 45) and A (bars 51 and 73); Monteverdi plays with D both as transposed Mixolydian (or major), with written C-sharps and F-sharps, and as transposed Aeolian (or minor), with prominent F harmonies and B-flats within phrases that ultimately resolve to D (as in the refrain, 'Ah, che piaga d'amor non sana mai' at bars 24–32). The two aspects of D coincide with the speaker's ambivalent emotions: the Mixolydian form of D pervades the whole of the first twenty-three bars (but notice the strategically placed B-flat at the words 'torna il mio core' (my heart turns back again) in bars 17–18!), and the Aeolian is felt more clearly in the second part. The 'illegal' dissonances that so troubled Artusi are difficult to find in this piece: in bar 5 the G-sharp in the Quinto, dissonant against the A in the bass, does not resolve properly – it is followed by the B in bar 6, a skip away, though it 'sounds' properly in the Tenor part; for the rest of the piece there is nothing to which to take exception.

Should one consider this work within the framework of the *seconda pratica*, or is the concept even applicable in this case? The question is unavoidable, given that Monteverdi chose to respond to Artusi's criticisms for the first time in the famous 'Lettera' that introduces this book, using the term *seconda pratica* to describe his new approach to composition. And yet this madrigal is quite different from 'Cruda Amarilli' or 'O Mirtillo': its language is not as flagrantly dissonant, nor as contrapuntally complex, and the formal scheme Monteverdi adopts is alien to the genre, at least as he had pursued it up to this point, and perhaps seems to run counter to the notion that the text governs all aspects of the musical setting. But considering the *seconda pratica* in larger terms – beyond dissonance treatment and as a new way of conceiving the relationship between text and music, in which the composer is free to manipulate both for the sake of a particular reading, then it seems clear that 'Ahi, come a un vago sol' represents a new way of doing things. This madrigal was written well after the works chastised by Artusi, and probably after Monteverdi had composed the works later published as the *Scherzi musicali*. It shows the composer working with a variety of musical elements, including some that are newly acquired – basso continuo, ornamentation after the new monodic style, recitative-like declamation, musical devices like the strophic bass, large-scale formal elements like refrains and text repetitions – in the interest of exploring the inner dynamics of the allure and trepidation of the nascent love affair into which the poem's persona is about to plunge. The first person is still expressed by a corporate 'I', and there is no identification between singer and character, but the aim here is not simply to match the music to individual words, as we find in the Renaissance madrigal: Monteverdi's aim is to reach deeper into the inner workings of the poem. Within the conventions – or limitations – of the ensemble madrigal, he does so with remarkable subtlety, and produces a setting that breathes the air of the stage: Monteverdi here approaches what he called 'la via naturale all'immitatione' – the natural means of imitating human emotions.

7 *Orfeo* (1607)

JOACHIM STEINHEUER

The myth of early opera

Early opera is often regarded as a completely new genre, created *ex nihilo* by a small circle of theorists and musicians in Florence and Rome as a conscious attempt to reinvent Ancient Greek tragedy which, some believed in the later sixteenth century, was sung throughout. Although this view has been justifiably criticised on a number of occasions,[1] it still tends to be the prevalent model for the rise of opera even in recent encyclopaedias and textbooks.

However, none of the dramatic pieces which were, or may have been, performed musically in their entirety between 1590 and 1608 in Florence, Rome and Mantua,[2] can be regarded as a tragedy in the Aristotelian sense because of their choice of subject, place and characters. Instead of depicting the tragic entanglements of kings and their like, situated in palaces or other appropriately courtly surroundings, early operas are generally set outdoors in country settings and are concerned with the loves of gods, semi-gods, shepherds and nymphs. In this respect they belong instead to the contemporary tradition of the pastoral play, a dramatic genre that evolved only in early modern times, even though it referred to the long-standing, but non-dramatic bucolic tradition of Greek and Roman classical authors. The most influential contemporary examples of this new type of pastoral play in Italy were Torquato Tasso's *Aminta* and Giovanni Battista Guarini's *Il pastor fido*. As in these plays, early operas do not represent the rough reality of rural life or the realistic preoccupations of peasants and farmers – these were rather the subject of a particular branch of Italian comedy in the sixteenth century – but, rather, a distant and idealised Arcadian Golden Age, where everlasting spring and the absence of hard daily labour seemed almost naturally to favour love, reciting poetry and singing as the favourite pastimes of the inhabitants.

Like all early operas, Alessandro Striggio's and Claudio Monteverdi's *Orfeo* is also deeply imbued with such a pastoral background and atmosphere: the characters are gods such as Pluto and Apollo, semi-gods like Caronte (Charon) and Orfeo (Orpheus), the allegorical figures La Speranza (Hope) and La Musica (Music), and finally nymphs and shepherds, who – with the exception of Euridice (Eurydice) – do not even bear proper names, but are introduced as character-types and designated only as Pastore, Ninfa or Messaggiera (messenger). The name of the messenger – Silvia – is mentioned only once by one of the shepherds within the dialogue.

With respect to the musical side of early opera the use of musical models from antiquity was out of question anyway, since only a few fragments were known and these were of a non-dramatic nature. It is hardly surprising, therefore, that the composers of early opera drew on a multitude of contemporary models for their forms, musical styles and compositional techniques, and used these within the new dramatic contexts. For all these closed forms in early opera – strophic 'arias' for one or more voices, aria-like strophic or half-strophic declamation models for specific poetic forms, madrigal-like compositions for chorus or soloists, instrumental sinfonias or sung and danced *balletti* – concrete models can be found in the richly diverse Italian musical culture of the sixteenth century, which already employed various forms of solo singing with instrumental accompaniment.

Since the middle of the century the polyphonic madrigal had become an unprecedented field of experiment with prosodically correct and varied recitation of poetry, with expressive treatment of melodic shapes, tempo and *ambitus* of declamation and with a sensitive use of tonality, modulation and dissonance, reflecting the semantic and affective aspects of the text. The new compositional techniques of the polyphonic madrigal also involved horizontal or vertical juxtaposition of characteristically constructed motives or *soggetti*, effective contrasts between shorter passages or sections of a piece, alternations of dynamics or sound qualities (for instance in polyphonic dialogues or echo pieces), and a subtle and refined integration of diminutions and other types of ornamentation. The general theatrical culture of the sixteenth century provided early opera with ideas and practical knowledge of scenery and scenography, the spectacular use of machinery and costumes on stage, and conventions for staging and mimic representation in acting and dancing which were themselves rooted in contemporary norms of courtly behaviour. In the lavishly staged musical *intermedi* to spoken plays, and in polyphonic madrigal-comedies, genuinely musical devices of characterisation for single roles, for persons belonging to different social strata and for various situations ranging from tragic to comic had already been established, including the conscious use of appropriate stylistic levels and of specific instrumentation. It can be shown that many of these traditions were integrated in a particularly varied and intensified manner into Monteverdi's and Striggio's *Orfeo*.

While on the one hand early opera could rely on a variety of existing compositional and scenographic devices, two genuinely new achievements of the genre must be mentioned. The first concerns the treatment of longer dramatic monologues and dialogues, for which a flexible type of musical declamation for irregular lines was needed, and one that was not as schematic as the use of a recitation tone in liturgical chant, nor based on fixed models such as the strophic variation schemes devised for the recitation of epic poems. Among the first composers who tried to find solutions to this challenge were Emilio de' Cavalieri, who fostered the idea of recitation in singing or 'recitar cantando', and Jacopo Peri, who defined this particular field as a 'cosa mezzana' halfway between sung and spoken recitation. Peri especially seems to have looked for possibilities of combining the flexibility of contemporary theatrical declamation, as a highly stylised and elevated form of speech in comparison with normal spoken language, with the genuinely musical need to use fixed pitches. Peri's 'stile recitativo' consists almost entirely of syllabic declamation and – in accordance with a realistic view of scenic dialogue – avoids repetitions of entire phrases and even single words. To the vocal part is added an instrumental accompaniment which consists mainly of chords underlining the main accents of the lines. The bass line is not conceived as an independent voice in the sense of classical polyphony, but follows the declamation of the text in the vocal part in a seemingly spontaneous manner. The improvisatory character of the accompaniment is also the reason why Peri allows for a certain 'harmonic negligence' which would have been forbidden by the rules of strict counterpoint. Monteverdi does not really follow Peri's specific concept of *stile recitativo*, but replaces the idea of a seemingly written-down, self-accompanied improvisation for a singer with a musically calculated and carefully constructed kind of musical declamation, which resembles much more the delicate and subtle ways of rendering a text in the tradition of the polyphonic madrigal than it does improvised recitation.

The second genuine achievement of early opera grew out of the necessity to develop a comprehensive musical dramaturgy and architecture for compositions that were much longer and much more complex than almost all other contemporary musical genres. Composers had to find structural means to integrate the various textual, musical and scenographic elements into an all-embracing frame so that the result was not simply a series of various alternating musical moments, but an internally related construction that allowed for a dramatically effective increase and relaxation of tension. In this respect, Monteverdi's *Orfeo* went far beyond the attempts at musical drama by Peri, Caccini or Cavalieri, which seem to be only preliminary by comparison with Monteverdi's achievement.

The first Mantuan performances of 1607 and Striggio's libretto

The Academy of the Invaghiti, before whose members *Orfeo* was first performed, was founded in 1562. Alongside speeches, disputations and literary debates it also sponsored theatrical performances in its early years; during the reign of Duke Vincenzo Gonzaga, however, only the performance of *Orfeo* can be securely documented. Members of the ducal family and high palace officials were members of the academy, among them Alessandro Striggio, librettist of *Orfeo* (who took the academic name 'Il Ritenuto'). Monteverdi's dedication in the printed score makes clear that the first performance of *Orfeo* was given under the patronage of the duke's eldest son, Prince Francesco Gonzaga. Iain Fenlon has made accessible the surviving correspondence connected with the performances of *Orfeo* in spring 1607, in particular an exchange of letters between Francesco Gonzaga and his younger brother Ferdinando in Pisa, and the Grand Duke of Tuscany.[3] From this it is clear that the first performance, on 24 February 1607, took place in the presence of Duke Vincenzo, who had already attended the rehearsals, and that it was given probably before a largely, or wholly, male audience, since the duke arranged a further performance on 1 March 1607 before all ladies of the city.[4] Little is known of the circumstances of the performances or the details of casting or the production. From the letters mentioned above, it becomes clear that the Grand Duke of Tuscany loaned a soprano castrato, Giovanni Gualberto Magli, a pupil of Giulio Caccini, who took the roles of Music in the Prologue and Proserpina in Act IV; he also took a third role, possibly that of Speranza in Act III. A further role – very probably the title part – was sung by the poet-singer Francesco Rasi, who was in Mantuan employment during this period.[5] The singers of the other parts are uncertain,[6] though it is generally assumed that the female roles were not sung by women. As far as the scenic realisation of *Orfeo* at the first Mantuan performances is concerned, John Whenham has convincingly argued that it probably used, like Peri's and Rinuccini's *Euridice*, only two sets: an Arcadian landscape for Acts I, II and V and an underworld scene for Acts III and IV; the additional instrumental items after Acts II and IV would give time for the necessary scene changes and would permit a continuous performance;[7] Silke Leopold has also ascribed to this ritornello 'a scenic function, as if it were a curtain between Arcadia and the underworld'.[8]

It is possible that the version of the opera given at the premiere was different from the one that has come down to us, for the printed librettos of 1607 transmit a different ending from that of Monteverdi's 1609 score.

After Orfeo's lament at the beginning of Act V Striggio has a chorus of Bacchantes enter on stage calling for Orfeo's death for his rejection of the female sex. In this Striggio was probably building directly on the precedent set by the *Fabula di Orpheo* by the Tuscan Humanist Angelo Poliziano, which was given at Mantua in 1480. In Monteverdi's printed score this ending is replaced by the appearance of Apollo as a *deus ex machina* who ends the earthly suffering of his son by carrying him off into the heavens in a grand final apotheosis. The precise reason for the revision is unknown, though it may have been made for a projected third performance at Mantua in 1607 for a visit there of the Duke of Savoy (the prospective father-in-law of Francesco Gonzaga).[9] The new ending gives a greater emphasis on Counter-Reformation ideas, as happens in several of the act-end choruses. Apollo teaches Orfeo that peace and true joy can only be attained in heaven: in contrast, all earthly joys are false.

The action is shaped by Striggio in a large, uncluttered span spreading across the five acts, though employing a variety of artistic, dramaturgical and architectural devices, many of which already suggest the forms in which they can be turned into music. As has already been observed, the structure of the opera is to a large extent symmetrical, with Orfeo's central aria before Caronte in Act III forming both a culmination and a central axis. Acts II and IV respectively mark the death of Euridice and her final loss, while Acts I and V, played before the same scene of Thracian fields, stand in a nearly antithetical relationship to each other: if the scene in Act I represented a place of joy, with the singing of numerous nymphs and shepherds, then in Act V it is without comfort and hope, and deserted apart from the answering echo.

The strict adherence to the action of the myth and the skilful integration of the acts into a consistent dramatic whole are to a large degree the result of focusing on the figure of Orfeo himself. All the other characters emerge only once, or at most twice in the action: Orfeo is at the centre of all five acts and is in each case involved in a turning point of the action. Each act is rounded off by a final chorus which comments on the preceding action, except for Act II, where the final chorus continues the lamenting of the shepherds and thus forms part of the action itself.

The dramatic scheme of the libretto includes a variety of metrical structures within each act, with a greater use of closed forms than is found, for example, in Rinuccini's libretto for *Euridice*. From a first act constructed almost entirely of closed forms, the libretto moves through acts in which different combinations of open and closed forms are explored, to a final act which contains very little by way of closed forms. At first sight this seems at odds with the symmetrical layout of the plot, but the progression from unity to a relative dissolution of formal order – even rhyme is largely abandoned in Act V – can be seen to mirror the contrast between the Arcadian *locus amoenus* at the beginning of the opera and the joyless desert that it becomes at the end, reflecting Orfeo's changing mental states.

Music and meaning in Monteverdi's score

The score format in which Monteverdi's *Orfeo* was published in 1609 places it among a small group of similar prints that were probably not intended for performance, but as lasting and publicly visible commemorations of otherwise ephemeral events, and, above all, as demonstrations of princely patronage. Thus the dedication (dated 22 August) of the print of *Orfeo*, issued at Venice by Ricciardo Amadino, celebrates the Mantuan hereditary prince Francesco Gonzaga, who commissioned the opera, and the publication of the score was probably financed for that purpose by his father, Duke Vincenzo.

Following the title page and dedication, a page of the print is dedicated to listing the characters of the opera, largely in order of appearance, though without, unfortunately, naming the actors who took the roles, and to providing an unusually detailed list of the instruments required in the score:

> Duoi Gravicembani.
> Duoi contrabassi de Viola.
> Dieci Viole da brazzo.
> Un Arpa doppia.
> Duoi Violini piccoli alla Francese.
> Duoi Chitaroni.
> Duoi Organi di legno.
> Tre bassi da gamba.
> Quattro Tromboni.
> Un Regale.
> Duoi Cornetti.
> Un Flautino alla Vigesimaseconda
> Un Clarino con tre trombe sordine.

Even more unusually, there are points in the score where we are given information on the use of these instruments, and even on their placement.[10] As in the sixteenth-century tradition of the musical *intermedio* the instruments are used for musical characterisation of the situation and also of certain of the characters. Muted trumpets and trombones are reserved for the ceremonial Toccata played 'before the raising of the curtain' ('avanti il levar de la tela'), with fanfare-like upper parts – essentially the same fanfare that Monteverdi used again at the beginning of his 1610 Vespers, and one that has been interpreted as a musical emblem of the Gonzagas. The *balletti* and choruses in the pastoral first act are accompanied by large instrumental groups, consisting, as in the *balletto* 'Lasciate i monti', of strings, *chitarroni*, harpsichords, harp and sopranino recorder (an instrument particularly characteristic of the shepherds' domain), or, as in the chorus 'Vieni, Imeneo, deh vieni', 'with the sound of all the instruments'. In contrast, the underworld is assigned the rasping tones of the Regal, which accompanies Caronte's singing in Act III, trombones (the score calls for five, though only four are mentioned in the initial list) and bass gamba; these instruments are, for example, used together to accompany the concluding chorus of Act III. At the scene change before Act V, as the ritornello from the Prologue is heard again, the score notes explicitly that the 'Cornetti, Tromboni & Regali' assigned to the underworld scenes are now to be silent, their place taken by 'viole da braccio, Organi, Clavicembani, contrabasso & Arpe, & Chitaroni, & Ceteroni'. In some passages in the score, particularly when Orfeo and the shepherds sing at the beginning of Act II and in 'Possente spirto', Orfeo's aria of entreaty in Act III, the changes of instrumentation and, thus, the timbres of the ritornellos are specified precisely. Something similar, though probably with a more strongly dramatic intent, applies to certain prominent passages in the recitative sections – in the messenger scene of Act II, and in Act IV when Orfeo breaks off his song in praise of his lyre and turns to look at Euridice, losing her for ever by breaking Pluto's prohibition. Here changes in the instrumental distribution of the continuo parts are indicated precisely, even for particulars of Orfeo's lines.

Apart from the beginning of 'Possente spirto', with its change from violins to cornetts, which relate to the underworld and may suggest a memory of the beloved, and finally to the harp, Orfeo himself seems above all to be associated with stringed instruments – the *viole da braccio* in the ritornello of 'Vi ricorda, o boschi ombrosi' (Act II), and in the sinfonia to whose sounds Caronte falls asleep in Act III (incidentally the only place in the score where a dynamic indication – 'pian piano' – is noted), and also in the violin ritornellos for the aria 'Qual onor di te fia degno' in Act IV. It is possible that, as in Marco da Gagliano's *Dafne* of 1608, the impression should be given that the singer actually plays his instrument, and perhaps the singer of Orfeo's part accompanied some passages or songs himself on stage; Francesco Rasi, the most likely candidate for the lead role in the Mantuan performances of *Orfeo* is known to have sung to his own accompaniment in theatrical representations on other occasions.

In some places instruments are used for deliberate spatial effects: thus, the score indicates that the ritornello to Orfeo's 'Vi ricorda o boschi ombrosi' was played 'di dentro' – possibly behind the stage or from a neighbouring space – and at the beginning of Act V there is an instruction that two *organi di legno* (organs with wooden pipes) and two *chitarroni* should be located one pair on the left and one on the right of the stage; this instruction probably relates to the accompaniment of the following passage, which employs echo effects.

The instruments do not, however, only have the function of characterising different contexts and dramatic situations; on a different level, the ritornellos and sinfonias are also components within the musical architecture. At the lowest level of internal structuring are the ritornellos, which provide, in strophic songs and choruses as well as in some of the declamation models, a clear formal division between the individual stanzas; in addition, in some acts individual sinfonias play a role in the structural organisation of the whole: among these are the ritornello following the chorus 'Lasciate i monti' in Act I, and the five-part string sinfonia in Act III, which is played before Caronte's appearance and again after Orfeo's desperate pleading, thus becoming part of the symmetrical structuring of Act III. Finally, there is the sinfonia that is played before and after the Prologue sung by Music (La Musica). This is also used in a shortened form between the stanzas of the Prologue, and then twice more, in connection with the scene changes before Acts III and V, constituting both a skilful dramaturgical device, and a semantically charged reminiscence of the figure of Music.

Musical recitation and the dramatic use of semantic layers

The shifting relationship between recitative and closed forms in *Orfeo* is, naturally, reflected in the organisation of Monteverdi's music. Orfeo's solos in Acts I and V represent in some respects the extreme poles of this process. The text of 'Rosa del ciel' in Act I, with its nineteen lines of unrhymed *versi sciolti*, forms a contrast with the otherwise largely strophic arrangement of the act. Orfeo's expanded lament, which occupies most of Act V, is, at fifty lines of text, by far the most extended solo section of the whole libretto.

In the musical setting both recitative scenes begin with an extended passage over a pedal note of G in G-Dorian, the mode in which Orfeo is first presented in the opera in 'Rosa del ciel', the mode in which he makes his plea in Act III, in which he makes his desperate lament in Act V, and, finally, the mode in which he sings a duet with Apollo as they ascend into the heavens. The parallel openings of 'Rosa del ciel' and the lament of Act V are instructive with respect to the entirely changed situation: although

Ex. 7.1

Ex. 7.2

Orfeo sings both times essentially within the octave d–d', the two situations call forth very different manners of singing. In 'Rosa del ciel' the recitation moves within the main intervals of the mode so that the song stands, as it were, in agreement with the mode (Ex. 7.1). In the lament of Act V, however, apart from the voice's almost motionless opening on d, the recitation almost completely avoids the main notes of the mode and thus conveys in a very precise musical way the estrangement that Orfeo now feels from the landscape that once seemed so familiar (Ex. 7.2).

Comparison of the two monologues is interesting in one further way. In 'Rosa del ciel' Orfeo's tonal level of G-Dorian always moves towards D major when Euridice is mentioned, as when Orfeo mentions seeing her for the first time ('pria ti vidi'), when he sighed for her ('per te sospirai') and, finally, at the end of his monologue when, instead of returning to his own modal final he turns, in an almost scenic gesture, to Euridice's final of D major in anticipation of her response. Her short first solo also circles around the final of D, even if not, as in Orfeo's perception a radiant D major; but almost immediately there is a surprising change to E major, which Monteverdi must have meant to be, at the least, disconcerting, though he may also have intended to suggest even more, since E major later becomes the tonal sphere associated with death.

At the beginning of Act V, on the other hand, Orfeo is alone on stage, and he seems to avoid any contact with living creatures; his desperate monologue is directed to the surrounding landscape and answered only by the disembodied voice of the echo. In his musical setting, Monteverdi divides it into clearly defined sections. He sets the initial section of twelve rhymed lines as a recitative over the sustained pedal notes G, A and G, characterised tonally predominantly by the ranges of G minor (Orfeo's tonal centre) and A major (related to the sphere of the underworld); the second section is a kind of echo madrigal of twenty lines, at the end of which the echo disappears as Orfeo demands that it should not give back just individual words, but the whole of his complaint. The monologue concludes with eighteen eleven-syllable lines, which are arranged syntactically into three equal groups of six lines, at the end of which Orfeo rejects the entire female sex in six lines that have the only *sdrucciolo* endings in the libretto. Through its arrangement into clearly defined contrasting sections, which Monteverdi underlines by caesuras and/or changes of key and tonality, the scene foreshadows the Lament of Arianna.

The two dramatic turning points of the action, in Acts II and IV, in which, respectively, Euridice's death is reported, and she finally returns to the realm of the shades, exhibit parallels in their multilayered and refined tonal organization. In Act II (Ex. 7.3), the appearance of the Messenger is marked by a sudden tonal break with the prevailing mood of celebration and joy which has circled round the two finals of g for Orfeo and C for the shepherds. The Messenger's recitative, which includes many disturbing dissonances, lies to a large extent within the tonal ranges of A minor/ major and E major. Jacopo Peri had used remarkable contrasts of tonality in the messenger scene of his *Euridice*, but these were no more than surprising affective moments. With Monteverdi, however, these are deployed within a refined musical dramaturgy. In what follows the tonal spheres of the shepherds and the Messenger, separated as they are by turn in mediant and/or false relations, seem at first so decidedly separate that it appears they can never meet. Only as Orfeo utters three questions in a single line – 'D'onde vieni? Ove vai? Ninfa, che porti?' (From whence do you come? Where are you going? Nymph, what [news] do you bring?) – does Monteverdi bring him from a lack of understanding to the Messenger's sphere through the chord progression F major to C major, G major to D minor, A minor to E major.[11] However, only as she announces the death of Euridice in a cadence on A major, does Orfeo fully reach her tonal sphere, uttering a desperate

Ex. 7.3

'Ohimè', and then moves a step further to Euridice's tonal level of D. The Messenger then begins her description of the death of Euridice on D minor.

The tonal types A major, A minor and E major, in which the Messenger announces the disaster, then come to represent almost throughout the score the spheres of death and/or the underworld; this can be seen not least in Act IV, where Orfeo is overcome by doubt that Euridice is actually following him: throughout the scene (Ex. 7.4) the tonal area of D major can be seen as alluding musically to Euridice, E major/A major/A minor to death/the underworld, and F major to Plutone (Pluto). Thus, when Orfeo finally turns, he sings for a moment in his own G minor, changing to D major as he sees Euridice's eyes. As the

Ex. 7.4

vision of Euridice is eclipsed, the music cadences from E to A, and a Spirit of the Underworld, speaking in Plutone's tonal sphere of F, tells Orfeo that he has broken Plutone's law and is unworthy of grace. Before her final return to the realm of the shades, Euridice speaks once more. She begins on Orfeo's G minor, but her line twists round to E major at the all-too-sweet sight ('vista troppo dolce') of Orfeo coupled with the painfulness of death, to which she is now bound. Though her speech now revolves around E major and A major, at the final cadence she touches her tonal level of D on 'mio', and at the mention of her 'consort' ('consorte') she arrives at Orfeo's G. The underworld spirit who then sings makes clear the finality of Euridice's fate on the tonal centre of E.

In his treatment of tonality in this section of recitative Monteverdi creates a complex system of reference in which musical codes are assigned to specific semantic layers. These are used not only for large-scale effects, but become constituents of a subtle and nuanced semantic system for whole scenes (and, perhaps, for the entire score) in which literally no chord seems without significance.

The dramatic significance of high, middle and low styles

The formal organisation of the libretto makes clear the considerable importance of closed forms for the musical conception of *Orfeo*. The most important types that Monteverdi uses here are strophic models, frequently with instrumental ritornellos between the stanzas, for the most part using the same musical material to which the stanzas are set. Such strophic forms cover a broad spectrum of song types, from those in which the vocal line and bass remain essentially the same from stanza to stanza, to very freely handled strophic declamation models, in which the continuo line may be varied in the length of its notes for each stanza while the melodic line may be either varied or entirely new.

Examples of the first, simple type of a strophic song lie behind the structure of the first part of Act II in an expanded passage which reaches from the beginning of the act up to Orfeo's 'Vi ricorda, o boschi ombrosi'. At the beginning of the act Orfeo sings a stanza, 'Ecco pur ch'a voi ritorno', whose rhyme scheme and eight-syllable lines match the four stanzas of 'Vi ricorda o boschi ombrosi' itself.

Monteverdi could, therefore, have begun the act by anticipating the music of 'Vi ricorda' and, as in Act I, used repetition for an architectural arrangement of the entire scene. Instead he gives this initial stanza a form of its own by allotting different music to each half of it, and repeating the first half to form an aba structure not indicated by the text. This is notated

Ex. 7.5

Ex. 7.6

in duple time, though its rhythmic structure is triple, with an upbeat (Exx. 7.5 and 7.6). The preceding five-part sinfonia exhibits the same ambiguity of notation and sounding rhythm and is developed from the same musical material. Between this beginning and 'Vi ricorda o boschi ombrosi' there are six further stanzas, all of four seven-syllable lines. This would have made a continuous strophic setting possible, moving from one to two shepherds to full chorus. Here again, though, Monteverdi makes another conscious compositional decision, treating each pair of stanzas as a separate strophic song, with the music for the final pair being given first to the two shepherds and then to the five-part chorus.[12] Each of these arias, like Orfeo's 'Vi ricorda', has a three- or five-part ritornello before the first stanza, and between the subsequent stanzas, with the same phrase structure as the stanza itself and some motivic connections with it, though usually with more rapid rhythms and an altered melodic movement in the parts. The clear phrases in all the parts, linked with stereotyped rhythmic patterns in the instrumental bass and partly also in the vocal lines, suggest a dance-like character for this type of aria. The two stanzas sung by two shepherds – 'In questo prato adorno' and 'Qui Pan, Dio de' Pastori', and also Orfeo's 'Vi ricorda' are notated in blackened notes – the so-called 'hemiola minor'. In Orfeo's aria, the preceding ritornello is actually notated in C, but since all the notes are blackened, as in older mensural practice the semiminims in fact represent blackened minims, the crotchets (fusae) should actually be read as blackened semiminims, and the continuous blackening can only be recognised from the

Ex. 7.7

Orfeo

Vi ri-cor-da o bo-schi om-bro-si, vi ri-cor-da o bo-schi om-bro-si, De' miei lun-gh'a-spri tor - men-ti

blackened *semibrevis*; the sounding result is, however, in triple time, which Monteverdi varies between 6/8 and 3/4 at each half tactus; as in Orfeo's aria at the beginning of the act it similarly represents a subtle type of notation (Ex. 7.7).[13] In the first part of Act II, then, it was clearly Monteverdi's decision to elaborate Striggio's two strophic types into five different strophic models with different times and various notational forms to produce variety (*varietas*), which is reinforced by the changing instrumentation of the ritornellos.

There is no doubt though that the entire opening of Act II, including the singing of Orpheus himself, must be considered a 'low' style level; this is clear from the choice throughout of simple strophic models whose texts and music lie in the generic tradition of the canzonetta; they are without purposeful interpretation of the text, harmonic experiment or, to a large extent melismas or other ornaments, and their low style is confirmed by frequent prosodic inelegance and even incorrect stresses of a kind otherwise hardly ever found in *Orfeo*. This may already be seen in Orfeo's first aria, 'Ecco pur a voi ritorno', with its undemanding range, and with its syncopated leap of a fifth on 'ritorno' producing a disproportionately long musical stress for the final, unstressed, syllable, and the even cruder emphasis on the final, unstressed, syllable of 'fatte'. Such occurrences are frequently found in the following songs of the shepherds as well as in Orfeo's 'Vi ricorda'; such passages suggest not carelessness or compositional inability, but rather an intentionally deployed low style. Monteverdi's concern here may have been to prove that the comprehensive abilities of Orfeo as singer included even the stylistically low level of the shepherds, or that it was possible for him to adjust to the lower level of the shepherds and to sing convincingly in an apparently artless manner. The intricacies of the notation make clear, nonetheless, that even within an apparently stylistically low level Orfeo is able to introduce musical refinement, which can only be understood by a careful reading of the score, but is completely hidden in the actual singing.

Within the symmetrical structuring of the opera, the strophic songs of Act II are balanced in Act IV by what is, strictly speaking, the only other simple strophic song with ritornellos, Orfeo's song to the power of his lyre, 'Qual onor di te fia degno?' The structure of its three stanzas – one

Ex. 7.8

eight-syllable line, followed by two of seven syllables and one of eleven – is the most modern of Orfeo's strophic songs. Within the libretto they provide the only example of that new type of strophic model with different line lengths and often varied strophic forms recently introduced into Italian poetry by Gabriello Chiabrera. The aria also introduces a new musical type, with a constantly moving bass, cadences at the half- or full tactus in the ritornellos, and continuous upward and downward scale patterns underlying the vocal stanzas. This quasi-ostinato, also known as a 'walking bass', produces a rapid harmonic rhythm which, for lack of intermediate cadences, seems like a restless *perpetuum mobile*. Over this strophic bass Monteverdi invents melodies – for two violins in the ritornellos, representing Orfeo's lyre, and for solo voice in the protagonist's stanzas – in the form of strophic variations in which details of melody and rhythmic organisation remain recognisable over long spans (Ex. 7.8).

Against such simple, often dance-like strophic songs, there is a second type of strophic model in *Orfeo* which should be considered as representing a different level of style. This is the more freely handled declamation model over a repeated bass, of a type used since the fifteenth century for the improvised performance of classical poetic types such as sonnets, sestinas, capitoli or stanzas of *ottava rima*. In *Orfeo* such models are used at particularly prominent points of the score, the first of these being Music's Prologue.

Monteverdi used for this a bass scheme of sixteen notes, of which the first five notes are used in all the stanzas for the first eleven-syllable line

Ex. 7.9

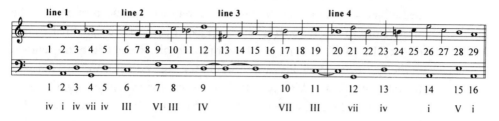

(*endecasillabo*), notes 6–9 for the second, 9–11 for the third and 12–16 for the fourth; in the first and third lines the first eight syllables are declaimed over the sustained recitation note D. The same, repeated bass, whose prime function is to define the harmonic progression, is used for all four stanzas, with line endings regularly marked by a cadence. The pitch progression of the bass changes significantly in the setting of the last stanza, where Monteverdi breaks off the cadence before reaching the *finalis* in a capricious way so that the stanza ends openly – a musical code for the halting of every breeze so that all attention may be dedicated to the story that is to follow.

In comparison with the progression of pitches, the rhythmicisation of the bass is more freely handled; elongation or shortening of individual notes of the model are determined here by the varying declamation in the vocal line, in which Monteverdi follows exactly the prosody of the different lines. An essentially similar melodic framework consisting of a sequence of twenty-nine notes (counted from the first stanza, note repetitions not included) lies behind the vocal part of all the stanzas, though minor omissions, regroupings or amendments can be found in the concrete melodic forms of the five stanzas (Ex. 7.9).

The way in which Monteverdi handles his selected recitation model in the Prologue may represent a composer's elaboration of an essentially improvised art. A feature of all five stanzas here is a severely syllabic type of text setting with correct prosody throughout, with no text repetition or melismatic writing. This restraint was probably prompted by the subject matter of the text. This speaks of high matters: in the first stanza Music addresses the Mantuan rulers as heroes of royal blood, whose sublime worth was so high that the attempt to tell their renown ('fama') was too high for mortal voice. Warlike heroism and praise of the ruler were reserved, in the system of the poetics of the time, for the noble genre of the epic.[14] In the remaining four stanzas, too, Music sings of high matters – of the extraordinary effects of music, which can evoke the most diverse passions, whose sonorous harmony not only beguiles the ears, but also awakens in the soul the desire for heavenly things; she sings, too, of the example of Orfeo, who was able to soothe wild animals and even to make hell subject and thus to acquire immortal renown ('gloria immortal'). (The subject of Orfeo's renown is taken up again explicitly in the final chorus of Act III.) To this extent the subject of the *favola*, which tells of the renown of the Thracian singer, also appropriates the high position and the 'fama' of the present rulers of Mantua. Music sings in a soberly simple style to teach ('docere') her listeners; the use of classic four-line stanzas of eleven-syllable lines requires suitable music, and for Monteverdi, the choice of a strophic recitation model seems to correspond exactly to the requirements of an elevated style with all ornamentation renounced.

Elsewhere in the score Monteverdi avails himself of comparable strophic variation models, not least in the central scene of Act III, where Orfeo encounters Charon (Caronte) after being led by Hope (Speranza) to the gates of the underworld. Caronte orders Orfeo to stop by singing three four-line stanzas of eleven-syllable lines: that is, with the same layout as the stanzas of the Prologue. Monteverdi again uses a variation model here, though this time of only eleven notes in the bass (only in the third stanza, at the word 'acerba', is a twelfth, leading note inserted). The more rapid declamation might be connected with Caronte's heightened emotion over the unseemly penetration of a mortal to the gates of the underworld. Monteverdi's treatment of Caronte's strophic variation model differs from that of the Prologue in a further way since, as in most other songs of the period for solo bass, the instrumental bass and the bass voice largely duplicate each other. Caronte makes clear that he is capable of speaking his words prosodically and musically in a well-established form, and Monteverdi provides for this, as in the Prologue, a continuous syllabic declamation without melismas or ornaments; there is no hint that the watchful ferryman should be an amusing figure, as he is in Stefano Landi's *La morte d'Orfeo* of *c.*1619, where he is assigned a merry drinking song.

After Caronte's initial stanzas there follows a five-part sinfonia, which is probably to be played by 'Viole da braccio, un Organo di legno e un contrabasso de Viola da gamba', as it is when it is repeated later after Caronte falls asleep, this time 'pian piano' in order not to wake him. After this sinfonia, which probably represents Orfeo playing his lyre,[15] Orfeo sings the central aria of the opera, 'Possente spirto', in which Monteverdi demonstrates the most elaborate kind of handling of such declamation models in the opera and at the same time portrays Orfeo's far greater musical skill as compared with Caronte's correct, but essentially unrefined strophic recitation. The textual basis of the aria is the classical form of the *capitolo*, which here embraces six stanzas of three lines (*terza rima*) and the mandatory final *commiato*. In five of the six stanzas Monteverdi

Ex. 7.10

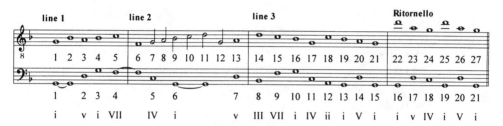

uses a recitation formula in the continuo line, consisting of fifteen notes for the vocal stanza and a further six for the following ritornello (Ex. 7.10; note repetitions are ignored). As in the Prologue, the allocation of the lines of text to the sections of the bass is fixed: thus line 1 of each stanza is sung over notes 1–4, line 2 over notes 4–7; line 3, on the other hand, spans notes 8–15, but is among other things lengthened owing to the instrumental insertions between the three lines.

The principal reason for the stretching of individual bass notes lies in the way in which Monteverdi treats the vocal line here. For the first four stanzas the printed score includes two vocal lines printed one above the other – two alternative versions, one of unornamented, syllabic declamation, the other written in a style overflowing with ornaments and requiring virtuoso ability on the part of the singer. A comparison of the two versions is instructive, because it becomes clear that we are not dealing with the addition of simple diminution patterns as taught in contemporary treatises. Instead, Monteverdi frequently uses the ornaments for purposeful harmonious enrichment of the declamation: the very first ornament on the word 'spirto', for example, rises to a tension-filled fourth above the bass and falls to a dissonant second before settling on the concluding note; and the word 'nume' rises to a major seventh above the bass. There are comparable, frequently quite free deviations from the unornamented melody in numerous other places, lending the ornamented version a colour that the unornamented version largely lacks. Monteverdi's scheme covers an extraordinarily broad spectrum of different kinds of ornament, from the simple decoration of an individual note or the filling out of intervals, as in the older diminution practice, to the new types of vocal ornament described by Caccini as 'trillo' or 'groppo', and well-planned sequences of melodic flourishes, from refined, almost heterophonic oscillating of the voice in relation to the instrumental bass, as for instance in the third line of the second stanza at 'com' esser può', to dotted Lombard rhythms and slurred quavers almost in an 'alla francese' manner, as in the fourth stanza. The reproduction of the unornamented version in the printed score may not simply serve a practical purpose regarding possible revivals of the opera with fewer virtuoso singers; rather, it serves to throw a sharper light on the breathtaking technical skill and the wealth (*varietas*) of the ornamented version. Whether this represents the version written for the singer of the first performance or was prepared by Monteverdi for the publication of the score can no longer be established.

Monteverdi does not only differentiate between the stanzas of the aria on the level of variation in the vocal line. He also uses varied instrumentation in the ritornelli: two violins (stanza 1), two cornetti (stanza 2) and double harp (stanza 3), two violins and 'basso da brazzo' (stanza 4). In stanza 5 we hear continuo alone – the organ with wooden pipes and chitarrone which have accompanied the whole aria – and finally, in stanza 6, three 'Viole da braccio, & un contrabasso de Viola'. There is, therefore, a consistently planned dramaturgy for this aria, and the abandoning of the bass model and withdrawal of ornamentation for the last stanza requires some explanation, since we might have expected the model to have been used throughout, as in the Prologue.

The first time Monteverdi moves away from the bass formula is in the fourth stanza, after Orfeo calls out his own name in an extended show of melismas. There follows an unexpected interpolation of seven notes in the bass, which do not belong to the recitation formula, for the remaining words of the first line, 'che d'Euridice i passi', before the formula reappears and leads to the end of the second line. The deviation from the formula at this point, taken together with a lack of ornaments, should probably be read as indicating that with the naming of Euridice Orfeo momentarily loses the thread of the aria, which he then forces himself to take up again in order to bring the stanza to an end; the ornaments selected now are also suddenly far more conventional.

While so far in the aria there have been no word repetitions, Orfeo now repeats the entire third line of the stanza, 'Ahi chi niega il conforto a le mie pene?' (Ah! Who will deny comfort to my pain?), to a still more emotionally laden musical line over a running, nearly chromatic bass. The last stanza, in which Orfeo addresses Caronte directly and seeks to win his sympathetic consideration, is sung to a four-part chordal string accompaniment, which returns again to the fifteen notes of the bass formula, and even the bass notes of the final *commiato* line can be interpreted as an extended variant of the section used earlier for the instrumental ritornellos. Apart from a more expanded ornament in the last line, measured recitation now prevails, and the string chords might be understood as the accompaniment of a lira da braccio. In 'Possente spirto', then, Monteverdi paints a singer certain of his abilities at the outset, who is first disturbed and finally overwhelmed by his emotions, but then controls them again in the final stanza.

Caronte now responds to Orfeo's entreaty. Striggio probably envisaged a recitative at this point, since he provided four seven-syllable and two eleven-syllable lines:

Ben mi lusinga alquanto	Much does it beguile me,
Dilettandomi il core	Delighting my heart,
Sconsolato cantore,	Disconsolate lover,
Il tuo pianto e 'l tuo canto.	Your complaint and your singing.
Ma lunge, ah lunge sia da questo petto	But far from this breast shall pity be,
Pietà, di mio valor non degno effetto.	An emotion unworthy of me.

Caronte reveals that he has remained unmoved by Orfeo's refined and artful singing, and to underline this musically Monteverdi chose, instead of writing a recitative, to make him repeat music that he had sung before hearing 'Possente spirto', even though this music had been invented for a different verse form.

It is worth looking closely at the words that Caronte sings. Orfeo's complaint and singing have beguiled him ('mi lusinga') by delighting ('dilletandomi') his heart. In the third stanza of the Prologue to the opera Music also uses the verb 'lusingare' – 'Mortal orecchia lusingar talora' – speaking of her ability to beguile mortal ears by singing to the lyre, and it is precisely this level of Orfeo's success that Caronte confirms. However, the verb 'dilettare' in the second line indicates why he is not moved. The term corresponds to 'delectare' in the rhetorical tradition, which in the ancient three-style system was assigned to the middle style, which is appropriate for matters of love and to ornamenting speech ('ornatus') in a particular way. In contrast, 'movere' (to move), which causes emotion and, as a consequence, compassion, is not a feature of the middle style, but of the high style alone, which, as a grand, elevated or passionately intense style, is able to stir the listener.[16] Caronte thus implies in his response that Orfeo, in his singing, has made a fundamental error in his choice of means: a love song, full of artistry in its ornamentation, is not suitable to excite Caronte's compassion – quite the opposite.

Orfeo understands Caronte's unmistakable message and reacts accordingly: his response to Caronte's speech is no longer measured strophic song and is entirely without ornamentation. Monteverdi places Orfeo's speech in an agitated high register of the voice, follows the exclamation 'Ahi!' with semiquavers in a manner that he was to use a year later for the most excited parts of the *Lamento d'Arianna*, and uses rapid, restless declamation soaked with dissonance to give Orfeo's despair free rein, culminating in a refrain section at the end in which he calls upon the gods of the underworld to return Euridice to him. In this passage Orfeo achieves exactly that affective style, seemingly artless and spontaneous despite its refined compositional technique, which Caronte had indirectly indicated was required even for the possibility of stirring emotion. Orfeo proves with this speech that his art could also be suited to a high-style situation. During the following, quiet sinfonia (first heard at Caronte's first appearance) the boatman falls asleep in a magical way; Orfeo attributes this to the power of his lyre and decides in the following recitative to cross to the other bank, concluding with a repetition of the refrain section of his preceding speech.

The use of strophic forms in *Orfeo* is effected throughout in a varied, but in every case carefully calculated way, with exact consideration for the respective implications of situation, persons and height of style. The examples discussed above make clear that Monteverdi left nothing to chance, handling the musical declamation and the use of ornaments in differentiated and subtle ways; he also occasionally takes liberties with the text in order to produce a more telling characterisation. Orfeo's role in the opera appears in a symmetrically disposed arrangement of solos: the recitatives of Acts I and V, the strophic songs and the disasters that follow in Acts II and IV, and the large-scale strophic variation for the 'prayer' of Act III, which forms the central point of the opera. The opera thus becomes a sort of manual of early seventeenth-century art-song. In addition, the incorporation of high, middle and low style levels, placed side by side in connection with a highly differentiated musical dramaturgy in the recitative passages, creates a fascinating musical cosmos.

In this work of genius, Monteverdi took the still young genre of completely sung drama to its first, lonely high point in comparison with the other surviving operas of those years, especially since only an individual scene of *Arianna* survives and that not even in the complete dramatic context in which it appeared in the opera. After a centuries-long slumber *Orfeo* has, particularly during recent decades, taken its rightful place on the stages of our time.

8 The Mantuan sacred music

JEFFREY KURTZMAN

When Monteverdi was hired by Duke Vincenzo Gonzaga to join the court musicians at Mantua, he described himself as a player of the *vivuola*. Yet it is obvious that he was also expected to compose, for he had already published several collections of music for three and four voices, two of which were of sacred music. Indeed, Monteverdi's very first publication, at the age of fifteen (1582), was a set of twenty-three three-voice motets, many based on antiphon texts for various of the Offices, which he entitled *Sacrae cantiunculae tribus vocibus*. In the very next year the young Claudio displayed his growing compositional skill by expanding his texture to four voices for a set of eleven *Madrigali spirituali*, only the bass voice of which survives today. It was only after these initial forays in religious music that the young composer turned his hand to three-voice secular *Canzonette* (1584) and his first two books of five-voice madrigals (1587 and 1590). So by the time he entered Gonzaga service, Monteverdi had already established himself as a significant composer of both sacred and secular music in northern Italy.

Only one more book of madrigals appeared during Monteverdi's first decade in Mantua (in 1592), but during that time he had already composed those madrigals on texts of Giambattista Guarini's *Il pastor fido* that would make him both famous and notorious because of the polemics with the conservative theorist Giovanni Maria Artusi that lasted from 1600 to 1608. Several of these madrigals were contrafacted and published with Latin spiritual texts by a Milanese rhetorician, Aquilino Coppini, in 1607. Before 1610, Monteverdi published no more sacred music, a gap of twenty-seven years from his *Madrigali spirituali*, yet that does not mean he was completely silent in the religious sphere during this period. Unfortunately, so much of Monteverdi's music, especially his sacred music, was never published, and far more was lost than ever appeared in print. We only have hints of what he must have produced from various remarks and citations in letters and other documents. The first such reference is from late 1595 when Monteverdi and four or five other singers accompanied Duke Vincenzo on a military expedition against the Turks in Hungary.[1] Monteverdi may well have provided the Mass sung in S. Andrea prior to the departure of the troops. According to the report of the expedition's chronicler, four or five masses were said in the duke's quarters every day, and on solemn feasts Vespers were sung by the singers accompanied by an organ. Most of the masses were likely sung in chant, but polyphony, presumably composed by Monteverdi, who was listed as *maestro di cappella* of the expedition, was probably performed at solemn Vespers.

In summer 1599 Monteverdi again accompanied Duke Vincenzo on a journey, this time to Spa in Flanders. Although we have no accounts of music on this excursion, it is again probable that Monteverdi provided not only secular music, but also the music for sacred services during this trip.[2] Monteverdi's own first mention of sacred music comes from two years later in his first surviving letter. Written while the duke was again in Hungary on a military expedition (though this time Monteverdi was left behind with his wife, who was shortly expecting their first child), the letter seeks appointment as *maestro di cappella* of both the chamber and the church ('e della camera e della chiesa'), a position most recently occupied by Benedetto Pallavicino, who had just died. In this letter Monteverdi expresses his desire for 'greater opportunity' to demonstrate his capacities to the duke's 'most refined musical taste as of some worth in motets and masses too' (letter of 28 November 1601). He seems here to be speaking of his eagerness to write motets and masses rather than referring to music he had already written.

What did Monteverdi mean by 'the chamber and the church'? The ducal church of S. Barbara already had its own *maestro di cappella*, Giacomo Gastoldi, who served in that role from 1588–1609. In Chapter 4 of this book, Roger Bowers cites the church of S. Croce at the edge of the ducal palace and Vincenzo Gonzaga's chapel in the Corte Vecchia as locations where Monteverdi and his predecessors as *maestro di cappella* were active as composers of sacred music. In addition, there was a chapel in the Castello S. Giorgio, another edifice in the palace complex. Yet these facilities were small and unlikely venues for the five- and six-voice masses and eight-, twelve- and sixteen-voice motets published by Pallavicino, and if Monteverdi had provided sacred music for any of these locations, it would have had to be for few-voiced ensembles. Moreover, if he had done so, why would he have expressed his desire to demonstrate his capacities to the duke in motets and masses, since the duke would already have been well acquainted with his sacred music? In my view, it is more likely that the service music in these private venues normally comprised plainchant and *falsobordone*, with possibly music of a more elaborate nature on rare occasions composed by the succession of *maestri di cappella* at the court. Had any of them produced substantial quantities of elaborate polyphony for these chapels, it is likely that some documentary trace would by now have come to light.

By 1603, Monteverdi had indeed been appointed *maestro di cappella* for Vincenzo Gonzaga (Bowers argues plausibly for December 1601), but the most likely venues for any sacred music Monteverdi wrote in this capacity were the cathedral church of Mantua, San Pietro, which lies directly across the piazza from the ducal palace and had no permanent *maestro di cappella* of its own, and the church of S. Andrea, constructed by the famous architect Leon Battista Alberti, just around the corner. The duke's *cappella* performed with some frequency in S. Pietro, and the Gonzagas celebrated numerous major events in S. Andrea, such as the Feast of the Ascension, which included the annual 'Sensa' festival celebrating Gonzaga rule in Mantua. On this feast in 1608 Duke Vincenzo established in S. Andrea a new order of knighthood in honour of Christ the Redeemer.[3] Special events at other churches in the city were also organised by the Gonzagas, and it is highly likely that the duke's *cappella* provided the music. The installation in the Jesuit Church of the Holy Trinity of an altarpiece by Peter Paul Rubens figuring Vincenzo Gonzaga and his family adoring the Holy Trinity could have featured a performance of the trinitarian motet 'Duo seraphim', or an early version of it, eventually published with the 1610 Vespers (Bowers suggests the consecration of Luigi Gonzaga in the same church at the end of the same year, which is also a possibility). Mantuan reaffirmation of the cult of the Virgin Mary in 1611 included the consecration of the Immacolata in the Capuchin Church and the renewal of the confraternity of the Immacolata in the Church of San Francesco.[4] Such events at other churches in Mantua suggest that by 'della chiesa' in his 1601 letter, Monteverdi may well have been using the term generically rather than specifically, i.e., he was asking to be responsible for all church music sponsored by the duke outside S. Barbara, rather than to be the *maestro di cappella* of any particular church.

That Monteverdi provided sacred music for liturgical celebrations is clear from a passage in the famous *Dichiaratione* of 1607, published in the *Scherzi musicali* of that year, in which Giulio Cesare Monteverdi, speaking for his brother, answered the charges of Artusi with his famous doctrine of the *prima pratica* and *seconda pratica*. Giulio Cesare justified responding in place of Claudio because his brother did not have the time, 'not only because of his responsibility for both church and chamber music, but also because of other extraordinary services'.[5]

Monteverdi's interest in sacred music was reasserted a year later when, exhausted and sick from preparations for the Gonzaga wedding festivities of May and June 1608, he retired to his father's house in Cremona. From there his father, a physician, wrote to the duke on 9 November requesting his son's dismissal from service, fearing that Claudio would perish from the bad Mantuan air should he return. But in the event that he could not obtain dismissal, his father pleaded, 'If Your Most Serene Highness commands only that he serves in the church, that he will do.'[6] In this instance the word 'church' probably referred specifically to S. Barbara, for Giovanni Gastoldi, its *maestro di cappella*, was very ill at the time and not expected to live long. Subsequent letters from Monteverdi's father and the composer himself, however, were in vain, for when Gastoldi died in January 1609, an interim *maestro* was appointed to S. Barbara and Monteverdi was ordered to return to court, though the duke did confirm a previously promised annual pension of a hundred *scudi* for the composer in recognition of his service and merit.

During 1608 and 1609, Coppini issued two more books of Latin sacred *contrafacta* of Monteverdi's madrigals in Milan. Italian spiritual *contrafacta* of three of his *Scherzi musicali* from 1607 and two otherwise unknown pieces appear in a Brescian manuscript entitled *Canzonette e madrigaletti spirituali* dated 1610.[7]

Monteverdi's hectic, difficult and penurious life at Mantua certainly prompted him to think about seeking another position, as hinted in another passage of his father's letter of 9 November 1608:

> I . . . beseech you that . . . you permit him the requested discharge, assuring Your Most Serene Highness that all his well-being he will always recognise as coming from your generosity, for if from the favour of your generous dismissal it happens that he serves a prince, I know that in this respect he will be viewed favourably.[8]

However, Monteverdi could not be hired by another court without the duke's permission or without being honourably dismissed from his service. Moreover, since court life had proved unpredictable and unbearable to him in so many ways, the only alternative was to seek a position as *maestro di cappella* of a major church, where the duties followed the liturgical calendar and were not subject to unanticipated pressures and sudden whims. However, Monteverdi had published no sacred music for twenty-seven years and no music for any liturgy at all. This lacuna in his public profile appears to have been the impetus for embarking on the publication of what would come to be known as the Mass and Vespers of 1610.[9] This print is a very large collection of fifteen compositions, and Monteverdi must have assembled it from music he had already written as well as a number of new works. By the summer of 1610 the collection was well under way and the vice *maestro di cappella*, Bassano Cassola, reported in a letter to Cardinal Ferdinando Gonzaga:

> Monteverdi is having printed an *a cappella* Mass for six voices of great
> studiousness and labour, having obliged himself to handle for every note and in
> every way, always reinforcing the eight [*recte* ten] points of imitation that are in
> the motet 'In illo tempore' by Gombert, and together [with it] he is also having
> printed psalms for Vespers of the Madonna, with various and diverse manners
> of invention and of harmony – and all are on the *cantus firmus* – with the idea
> of coming to Rome this autumn to dedicate them to His Holiness.[10]

The Mass Cassola describes was apparently Monteverdi's musical answer
to Artusi's public attacks on his compositional technique (the last of which
had been published only two years previously). In this Mass, as will be
discussed further below, Monteverdi wove a dense, imitative polyphonic
texture not only based on a motet dating from at least seventy-three
years earlier, but in several respects also reflecting the style of polyphony
from that period. Cassola's letter emphasises the strenuous effort it took
Monteverdi to produce this work, suggesting that perhaps Monteverdi
was not as practised and skilled in the *prima pratica* as his brother had
declared. Cassola also mentions the variegated psalms (Magnificats were
often listed under the rubric *salmi*) and their foundation in the *cantus firmus*
of the psalm tone, a procedure in composing psalms that was largely out of
date by 1610. What Cassola does not mention are the introductory Response,
four virtuosic few-voiced motets, the 'Sonata sopra "Sancta Maria"', and the
hymn 'Ave maris stella', which are also included in the collection.

The print is entitled *Sanctissimae Virgini missa senis vocibus, ac ves-*
perae pluribus decantandae, cum nonnullis sacris concentibus, ad sacella
sive principum cubicula accommodata. Opera a Claudio Monteverde nuper
effecta ac Beatiss. Paulo V. Pont. Max. consecrata.[11] It thereby has a double
dedication in honouring the Virgin, but with Monteverdi's personal
dedication addressed to Pope Paul V. The Vespers psalms and hymn
Monteverdi chose are those of the eight major feasts of the Virgin in
Monteverdi's day, prompting that entire section of the print to carry the
heading *Vespro della Beata Vergine*. Even though the publication was
evidently designed to assist Monteverdi in obtaining another position,
it had close ties to the Gonzagas, who honoured Mary as the patroness
and protectress of the city of Mantua, and who claimed a special relationship with Pope Paul V as well. Indeed, a general papal indulgence was
declared for the city in the church of S. Andrea in 1607 and the city
celebrated a reaffirmation of the cult of Mary in 1611.

The introductory Response of the Vespers service is even based on the
toccata fanfare that opened Monteverdi's *Orfeo*, a work commissioned
by Prince Francesco Gonzaga, whose fanfare has been understood by
several scholars as a kind of Gonzaga family entrance piece. Moreover,

the chant used in the hymn 'Ave maris stella' reflects a variant found in the rite of the ducal church of S. Barbara at Mantua.[12] In fact, there is no incompatibility between Monteverdi's having written some, possibly even most, of the compositions in the Mass and Vespers of 1610 for specific occasions in Mantua, and their subsequent function in print as an advertisement of his skill and invention for a possible appointment elsewhere.

The dedication of the print is dated 1 September 1610, and later that autumn Monteverdi did indeed go to Rome to present the collection to the Pope as Cassola had said he would. He also had hopes of obtaining a position in the Roman seminary for his son Francesco. Monteverdi seems to have travelled to Rome somewhat surreptitiously, for a letter from the Mantuan official, Rainero Bissolati, of 7 October speaks of bumping into the composer accidentally on the street and learning that he was staying at an inn.[13] As a representative of the Duke of Mantua, Monteverdi would normally have lodged in the palace of Vincenzo's brother, Cardinal Ferdinando, and the official insisted Monteverdi move to the palace for the remainder of his visit. Perhaps the composer was secretive at this stage of his journey because he was feeling out the possibility of employment at one or another major Roman church or with a cardinal or Roman nobleman. In any event, Monteverdi returned to Mantua by Christmas, and despite high praise from Cardinals Montalto and Borghese, two of the most important cardinals in the Roman curia, he came home empty-handed – without a post for his son in the seminary, and without a new job for himself. Remnants of his visit to Rome are a copy of the Missa 'In illo tempore' in a Sistine Chapel manuscript and an alto part-book of the 1610 print leather-bound and embossed with the coat of arms of Pope Paul V in the Biblioteca Doria Pamphilij.[14]

A few months after his return to Mantua, Monteverdi sent to Prince Francesco Gonzaga a setting of the Vespers psalm 'Dixit Dominus' for eight voices 'which Your Highness ordered me to send, together with which I am also sending you a little motet for two voices to be sung at the Elevation, and another for five voices for the Blessed Virgin' (letter of 26 March 1611). Attempts to identify these compositions with Monteverdi's published church music are probably in vain, since, as indicated above, he composed far more, especially in the field of sacred music, than he ever published. No sign of either the Elevation motet or the motet for the Virgin survives. Even though Monteverdi and his publisher eventually issued four settings of 'Dixit Dominus' for eight voices, he must have composed many more over the course of his long career, and it is far more likely that the 'Dixit' sent to Prince Francesco perished with so many other Monteverdi manuscripts in the sack of Mantua by Imperial troops in 1630.

On 11 May 1611, the vigil of the Feast of Christ the Redeemer (Ascension Day) was celebrated in S. Andrea with Vespers by Monteverdi.[15] One is tempted to think this was the first performance of the recently minted *Vespro della Beata Vergine*, but the feast of the Redeemer would normally have required the psalm cycle for most male feasts and a hymn proper to that feast instead of the cycle for the Virgin. The eight-voice 'Dixit Dominus' Monteverdi sent to Prince Francesco in late March could have been performed as the first psalm on this occasion, and he could well have written additional music between his return from Rome and the middle of May. Nevertheless, four of the compositions in the 1610 print – the Response, the psalms 'Dixit Dominus' and 'Laudate pueri', and the Magnificat – are also suitable for Ascension Day, so it is indeed possible that at least some of Monteverdi's Vespers music published in 1610 was heard on this occasion, together with other new music that fulfilled the liturgical requirements of that particular service.

There exists a report from Christmas 1611 of another performance of Vespers music by Monteverdi in the cathedral of Modena. A local chronicler declared that the *maestro di cappella* there 'had certain psalms sung, by Monteverdo [sic], *maestro di cappella* of the Duke of Mantua, which were to everyone's disgust'.[16] Speculation that these were the psalms from the 1610 Vespers are again somewhat misguided, since the psalm cycle for Christmas Vespers is not the same as for the Virgin, except for the overlap of 'Dixit Dominus' and 'Laudate pueri' (the latter for First Vespers only).

At some time in the period between summer 1610 and 1612, Monteverdi composed a sacred solo madrigal on a text by Angelo Grillo, which was sung by the famous court singer Adriana Basile, 'a sublime singer and an angelic voice … who, marrying the voice with the instrument, and with gesture giving soul and speech to the strings, brings forth the sweet tyranny of our souls, while leaving them in our bodies on earth, takes them with the hearing to heaven'.[17]

In July 1612, both Claudio and Giulio Cesare Monteverdi were dismissed from their posts at the Mantuan court by the new duke, Francesco Gonzaga, who had succeeded his recently deceased father. We hear no more of sacred music by Monteverdi from his Mantuan years with the exception of his audition for the position of *maestro di cappella* at S. Marco in Venice, where the 1610 print is mentioned in the document announcing his election.

The music of the Mass and Vespers of 1610

Monteverdi's first sacred collection is grandiose in style and scope. Its fifteen compositions are as follows:

Missa 'In illo tempore' for six voices
'Domine ad adiuvandum': Response to versicle 'Deus in adiutorium' for six voices
   and twelve instruments
'Dixit Dominus': psalm for six voices with optional six-part instrumental ritornellos
'Nigra sum': motet for solo tenor
'Laudate pueri': psalm for eight solo voices
'Pulchra es': motet for two solo sopranos
'Laetatus sum': psalm for six voices
'Duo seraphim': motet for three solo tenors
'Nisi Dominus': psalm for ten voices in *cori spezzati*
'Audi coelum': motet for solo tenor and tenor echo, concluded by six-voice chorus
'Lauda Jerusalem': psalm for seven voices
'Sonata sopra "Sancta Maria"': instrumental sonata with prayer 'Sancta Maria ora
   pro nobis' intoned as an eleven-fold litany in the soprano voice
'Ave maris stella': hymn for eight voices with five-part instrumental ritornellos
Magnificat: canticle for seven voices and six instruments
Magnificat: canticle for six voices

Monteverdi's print opens with the contrapuntal *tour de force* described in Bassano Cassola's letter, the Missa 'In illo tempore' for six voices. This work is almost archaic in its rigid adherence to a highly imitative six-voice texture, though with organ continuo added. The organ part, however, almost exclusively follows the lowest sounding note of the vocal parts, and any organist of the time would have played much of the rest of the vocal texture as well. In fact, a manuscript organ *partitura* of this piece survives in the Cathedral of Brescia in which all the vocal parts are reproduced.[18]

Monteverdi advertises his contrapuntal technique, in a manner unique among contemporary sacred music publications, by listing at the beginning of the piece the ten motifs drawn from Nicolas Gombert's motet of the same name (Ex. 8.1). It is apparent from this ploy and from Cassola's letter that Monteverdi conceived the Mass as displaying his contrapuntal expertise, demonstrating to Artusi that he was not only the foremost practitioner of the *seconda pratica*, but also a master of the *prima pratica*.

Gombert's motet was first published in 1538. It is noteworthy that Monteverdi reached this far back into the sixteenth century for his first large-scale effort in the imitative polyphonic style rather than drawing on a more recent work. His choice of the Gombert motet was probably influenced by two factors: its motives have a strong harmonic profile, and it is in the C-Ionian mode with no trace of the traditional eight Church modes. Monteverdi's almost reactionary contrapuntal style yields a composition that is nearly unremitting in its six-voice texture based on time-honoured contrapuntal complexities: pervasive imitation at varying time intervals, canon, inversion, retrogression, augmentation, diminution, paraphrase, sequences, countersubjects and invertible counterpoint. The first of

Ex. 8.1

the borrowed motifs is the most important, appearing in both the opening Kyrie and the closing Agnus Dei II (expanded to seven voices), as well as functioning as the head motif and closing motif in several other sections. At times Monteverdi uses more than one of Gombert's motifs simultaneously, while all ten make prominent appearances at various points throughout the Mass–all of them, for example, in the Gloria.

Monteverdi's unrelenting six-voice polyphony contrasts with more recent contrapuntists, such as Lassus, Palestrina, and Victoria, who were much more flexible in their handling of textures, motifs, and imitation. Only two sections of the Mass, the 'Et incarnatus est' in the Credo and the Benedictus, are principally homophonic. Both begin on an E major triad, expressively contrasting in their texture and tonality with the prevailing, almost monotonous Ionian mode of the rest of the Mass in order to highlight the mystery and uniqueness of their common textual reference to the incarnated Son of God. Despite the emphasis on Gombert's motifs and conservative style, many sections of the Mass conclude with descending

Ex. 8.2a Kyrie II

Ex. 8.2b Kyrie II

sequences based on scales or broken thirds, generating a more modern, forceful, harmonic impetus toward final cadences. These sequences also occur with some frequency within individual sections, providing relief to the ubiquity of Gombert's motifs (see Exx. 8.2a, 8.2b). Such sequences constitute the entirety of the Sanctus, with the exception of the homophonic Benedictus. Following the Mass, the fourteen pieces listed above fulfil in succession almost all the musical needs for a Vespers service on any feast of the Virgin in the Roman Rite. The psalms and Magnificat (with two alternative choices of the latter) are also those required for the Common of virgin saints. The four motets and the 'Sonata sopra "Sancta Maria"' have generally been recognised as substitutes for the plainchant psalm antiphons from the Proper in the Roman Rite, though a few scholars have disputed

Ex. 8.3 Second Psalm Tone

Ex. 8.4 Sancta Maria ora pro nobis

San - cta Ma - ri - a   o - ra   pro   no - bis

this on the grounds of liturgical impropriety (see below). Monteverdi provided no motet or instrumental piece to substitute for the Proper Magnificat antiphon. Thus, Monteverdi's Vespers are designed for a single category of feast, though as indicated above, the Response, the Magnificat, and the first two psalms can also serve for most other feasts, and there is no reason to exclude the possibility that a choirmaster might have chosen only certain elements from this and any other publication for a particular Vespers service.

As Monteverdi's own rubrics indicate, all the psalms and the Magnificat are based on Gregorian chant psalm (and Magnificat) tones (see the second psalm tone, Ex. 8.3). In addition, the Response is built upon its Gregorian recitation tone, the 'Sonata sopra "Sancta Maria"' employs a simple litany chant addressed to the Virgin (see Ex. 8.4), and the hymn employs its traditional melody as the upper voice (see Ex. 8.5, close to the version in the rite of S. Barbara). These chants are utilised in a number of different ways in these compositions. In the two Magnificats and the 'Sonata', and sometimes in the psalms as well, it appears as a long-note cantus firmus in one or another voice. In the Response and the psalms the chant is thoroughly integrated into the texture, often moving at the same speed as the other voices. Only in the hymn, where the chant is far more melodious than the psalm tones, does it occupy a prominent melodic role as the upper part of four- and eight-part textures, and as the solo line in the three monodic verses.

In all these pieces the chant is ubiquitous rather than simply making an occasional appearance, as in most other uses of a Gregorian cantus firmus in the early seventeenth century. Since the psalm tones are melodically limited and repetitive, Monteverdi builds around them the most varied textures, ranging from virtuoso solo and duet textures, to six-, seven- and eight-part polyphony and homophony. These varied textures generate what came to be known as the *concertato* style: the division of a

Ex. 8.5 Ave maris stella: Monteverdi's apparent unknown source

A - ve_____ ma - ris stel- la, De - i ma-ter al - ma, At-que sem-per Vir - go, Fe-lix coe-li por-ta.

composition into several different contrasting segments through changes of texture, metre and rhythm, performing forces, tempo and style. This differentiation between modern, *concertato* techniques and the conservative, traditional cantus firmus is one of the chief characteristics and highlights of Monteverdi's chant-based compositions in the 1610 Vespers. He opposes modern, opulent variety against the conservative rigidity of the cantus firmus, creating a palpable tension that is a major factor in the aesthetic effect of these settings.

Among the elements in this opulence is the employment of instruments, whether optional or obbligato, in several of the cantus firmus pieces. As already mentioned, the Response is contrafacted from the instrumental toccata that opened the opera *Orfeo*. The harmonic stasis of this toccata is ideally suited to function as a counterpoint to the chant, which consists almost entirely of the static reiteration of a single tone. Monteverdi introduces greater variety into the Response by interpolating an instrumental ritornello in triple metre, which, in its third statement, is accompanied by the voices. Nevertheless, Monteverdi denotes the instruments as optional.

Obbligato instruments are a main feature of the seven-voice Magnificat, which restructures the six-voice Magnificat by assigning many of its vocal roles to instruments. Here the instruments, like the voices, sometimes engage in virtuoso ornamentation, but also play ritornellos, provide counterpoint to the vocal cantus firmus, or, as in the first and last verses, double the voices. The instruments also play ritornellos in 'Dixit Dominus', where they are optional, and in the hymn, where they are not indicated as optional, but might well be considered so. The inclusion of a version of the Magnificat without instruments and the possibility of omitting instruments in other pieces allows for a performance of the main elements of the service by a choirmaster who did not have such instruments at his disposal.

The single composition primarily instrumental in its conception is the 'Sonata sopra "Sancta Maria"' for eight string and wind instruments with organ in addition to the solo soprano voice. This piece is also *concertato* in style, changing metre frequently, and shifting textures from eight-voice polyphony to virtuoso duets of violins or cornettos and quick antiphonal responses between strings and wind instruments. Modern dotted rhythms abound, engaging even the bass instruments. The short vocal cantus firmus appears in the soprano voice only intermittently – eleven times – above the instrumental ensemble.

Apart from the instrumental parts notated by Monteverdi, contemporary performance practice allowed for generous instrumental doubling of vocal parts, especially in thicker textures. Many early music performers today make ample and appropriate use of instruments for doubling in the psalms, the six-voice section of the motet 'Audi coelum' and the four- and eight-voice verses of the hymn. While Monteverdi's own instrumental ensemble provides sufficient instrumental colour, it is not inappropriate to employ other contemporary instruments, such as recorders or flutes, as well.

The remaining four pieces comprise motets for solo voices and continuo, which could just as well be a theorbo, or theorbo with organ, as organ alone (the harpsichord is generally not a suitable continuo instrument for sacred music). These pieces have no connection to a cantus firmus and represent the most modern style of solo singing, requiring a wide vocal range, excellent intonation and well-developed oratorical skills on the part of performers. 'Nigra sum', for solo tenor, is one of Monteverdi's greatest achievements in its consistent melodic and harmonic construction around the principal concept expressed in the text, 'surge' (arise).[19] 'Pulchra es', for two sopranos, illustrates the modern, virtuosic duet style in which one voice takes the lead and the other follows in imitation, often running in parallel thirds with the first. 'Duo seraphim', for three tenors, exhibits extraordinary virtuosity, comparable to Orfeo's aria, 'Possente spirto' in Monteverdi's opera. The motet divides into two segments, the first for two voices, representing the two seraphim, and the second for three voices in response to the Trinitarian text 'et hi tres unum sunt' (and these three are one). All three tenors sing the most extreme virtuoso embellishments, a tour de force of vocal exhibition, which is also characterised by a strong sense of melodic and harmonic direction. The final motet, 'Audi coelum', a prayer to the Virgin for solo tenor with an echo voice responding to the final syllables of several of its words, eventually expands its texture to an imitative six-voice choir when the text reads, 'omnes hanc ergo sequamur' (let all of us, therefore, follow her). The solo first part is largely in recitative style with virtuoso melismas interpolated on several occasions. The echoes sometimes form puns on the words they imitate, since the final letters or syllables echoed constitute words in their own right (e.g., 'gaudio'/'audio', 'benedicam'/'dicam', 'orientalis'/'talis'). A service without instruments other than organ could even include these motets if singers of sufficient capacity were available.

As with most collections of music in the seventeenth century, there are many unknowns regarding the origins and functions of the print itself as well as suitable ways of performing its music. Early commentary debated whether the collection was intended for a single service or constituted a random assemblage of pieces.[20] Graham Dixon has proposed that the music was originally designed for a Vespers of S. Barbara and only later redirected toward the Virgin Mary.[21] The fiercest controversies have raged over the role of the four motets and the 'Sonata sopra "Sancta Maria"', interspersed in the original print between the psalms. In earlier writings on the Vespers, scholars tended to consider them separate from the Vespers liturgical service, since they do not match (though two of their texts overlap) any of the liturgical antiphons for a Marian Vespers. Nevertheless, four of the five texts are Marian in their orientation, and ever since a seminal article by Stephen Bonta in 1967, the growing weight of evidence has pointed to a widespread contemporary practice of substituting texts and even instrumental music for the liturgical antiphons in Vespers services, and most scholars have come to believe that the print was intended to provide music for a single liturgical service, though choirmasters could easily have extracted individual items from the collection.[22]

In recent years, controversy has also arisen regarding the proportional relationships in performance of sections in duple metre versus those in triple metre. Roger Bowers has argued in favour of a strictly mathematical proportional relationship, while I have proposed a more flexible approach based not strictly on numerical proportions, but rather on the unit of beat, the *tactus*.[23] Four of the pieces in Monteverdi's 1610 print employ high clefs, so-called 'chiavette', in the notation of the voices (G_2, C_2, C_3, and C_4 or F_3 clefs; the 'standard' clefs are C_1, C_3, C_4, F_4). Many scholars, myself included, have presented substantive evidence arguing that the high clefs entailed transposition downward, typically by a fourth, in performance. Bowers has recently disputed this point as well, though other scholars have found his arguments deficient.[24] Although there will always be some questions remaining open regarding Monteverdi's Mass and Vespers of 1610, many of the issues confronting earlier scholars are gradually becoming better understood and resolved through the accumulation of evidence from a wide variety of contemporary sources.

INTERMEDIO III

'Laetatus sum' (1610)

JEFFREY KURTZMAN[1]

Seven of the fourteen compositions comprising Monteverdi's *Vespro della Beata Vergine* are based on psalm or Magnificat tones, so it is appropriate that this analysis be devoted to one of those pieces. However, with the exception of the two settings of the Magnificat, which are parallel in many respects, the role of the psalm tone in the construction of each psalm differs significantly, and the psalms differ radically from the Magnificats. Therefore, the analysis of no single composition can serve as a model for the others, and each must be addressed separately, with quite different observations to be drawn from each. Of these seven compositions, the six-voice Psalm 121 (*Book of Common Prayer* 122), 'Laetatus sum', is the most complexly organised and the one whose compositional techniques most adumbrate methods of organising *concertato* psalms in subsequent decades. Rather than the chant serving as an organising force, as in the other psalms and the two Magnificats, the structure of the text is the principal organising element. The cantus firmus is mixed together with repetitive bass patterns, imitative polyphony, chordal homophony, virtuoso solo melismas, duets, trios and *falsibordoni*. The chant appears only intermittently, either as a solo vocal line or as a single voice in a four- or six-part texture. When it does appear, the chant is usually accorded some prominence either by its position in the texture or by long note values.

Psalm texts normally consist of two-verse couplets, with each verse divided into two hemistiches. Even if a psalm text does not strictly follow this pattern (such as a grouping of three verses, or a single verse with three separate segments), the structure of the psalm tones – which are rigidly divided into two hemistiches (see Ex. 8.3 in the preceding chapter) – force this two-part organisation upon the text.

The text of 'Laetatus sum', as found in the Latin Vulgate, is as follows (the first word in each couplet is in bold type):[2]

[155]

1. **Laetatus** sum in his quae dicta sunt mihi:
   In domum Domini ibimus.

I rejoiced in what was said to me:
   We will go to the house of the Lord.

2. Stantes erant pedes nostri
   In atriis tuis, Jerusalem.

Our feet were standing
   In your halls, Jerusalem.

3. **Jerusalem**, quae aedificatur ut civitas,
   Cuius participatio eius in idipsum.

Jerusalem, which is built as a city,
   Is one with itself.

4. Illuc enim ascenderunt tribus, tribus

   Domini, Testimonium Israel,
   Ad confitendum nomini Domini.

For there the tribes ascended, the tribes of the Lord,
   The witness of Israel,
   For acknowledging the name of the Lord.

5. **Quia** illic sederunt sedes in judicio,
   Sedes super domum David.

For there the thrones sit in judgment,
   The thrones over the house of David.

6. Rogate quae ad pacem sunt Jerusalem,
   Et abundantia diligentibus te.

Pray for the peace of Jerusalem,
   And prosperity for those who love you.

7. **Fiat** pax in virtute tua,
   Et abundantia in turribus tuis.

Let there be peace in your strength,
   And abundance in your ramparts.

8. Propter fratres meos et proximos meos,
   Loquebar pacem de te.

For the sake of my brothers and my neighbours,
   I was saying, 'Peace be with you.'

9. Propter domum Domini Dei nostri,

   Quaesivi bona tibi.

For the sake of the house of the Lord our God,
   I sought good things for you.

10. **Gloria** Patri et Filio et Spiritui Sancto,

Glory to the Father and the Son and the Holy Spirit,

11. Sicut erat in principio et nunc et semper,
    Et in saecula saeculorum. Amen.

As it was in the beginning and now and forever,
   For all ages. Amen.

The psalm proper consists of four couplets and one additional verse, while the last two verses comprise the lesser doxology, which is appended to the end of all psalms when serving in the liturgy. Monteverdi, as he typically does, sets the beginning of the doxology off from the rest of the psalm to emphasise its role as a distinct textual unit. His approach to the structure of the text is highly original: he sets each couplet's first verse, as well as the isolated final verse of the psalm proper (i.e., every odd-numbered verse), to an identical walking bass in steady crotchets

Ex. III.1

Ex. III.2

Ex. III.3

(Ex. III.1). This is the first known appearance of a repetitious bass in an Italian psalm setting; later, in the 1630s and 1640s, ostinato basses became common in Italian psalmody. The walking bass as well as the remainder of the psalm is in the second mode, transposed a fourth upward to G by means of a one-flat signature (*cantus mollis*), as was normal for this mode. The note E is also quite often flattened by means of an accidental, making the mode analogous in many respects to the modern G minor. The second mode serves to harmonise the second psalm tone chant (see Ex. 8.3 in the preceding chapter), likewise transposed up a fourth.

What prompted Monteverdi to devise such a rhythmically steady, repeated bass is likely the concept of stasis and durability conveyed in the text through the perennial prosperity and peace of Jerusalem. The walking bass, with its octave leaps and reversals of direction, also has a lively character suitable to the ethos of rejoicing with which the psalm begins and continues. Another bass pattern, slower in its movement and with some variation in its repetition, supports verses 2 and 6 (Ex. III.2). This pattern is not entirely new, but rather a variant of the walking bass which begins in the major (*cantus durus*) rather than the minor (*cantus mollis*) (see Ex. III.3, in which the two basses are compared). Moreover, as John Whenham has pointed out, its second phrase bears a notable resemblance to the typical *Romanesca* bass.[3] Yet another two bass patterns are employed for verses 4, 8, and the doxology (Exx. III.4a and III.4b).

Ex. III.4a

Ex. III.4b

Ex. III.5

The first of these, a sustained G minor triad interrupted briefly by its dominant, underlies lengthy virtuoso melismas at the beginning of verses 4 and 8 (see Ex. III.5, verse 4). At the beginning of the doxology the sustained triad turns to G major, yielding at first not to its dominant, but rather to another sustained chord on C, finally turning back to D as dominant after the second G major triad. The fourth bass, which each time follows immediately after the third, is varied through truncation and diminution in verse 8, and the varied version returns once more for the final verse of the doxology. Following Gioseffo Zarlino's classification and description of the twelve modes, the regular cadences of the second mode, transposed to G, are on D, B-flat and G.[4] According to Monteverdi's contemporary, the theorist and composer Adriano Banchieri, the most common cadence notes for the second psalm tone transposed up a fourth are also D, B-flat and G.[5] In fact, Monteverdi's most prominent cadences are on the major triads of G and D (both half- and full-cadences on D), with only three cadences on B-flat in the entire psalm, embedded in the fourth bass pattern.

As indicated above, the psalm tone appears irregularly in 'Laetatus sum'. The psalm text begins with the tenor voice alone singing the second tone in comparatively slow note values, though with its leading note sharpened in order to create a strong cadence on G. The psalm tone is not heard again until verse 4, after the lengthy melismas on 'Illuc', where the cantus part sings the first hemistich to the recitation tone, harmonised in measured *falsobordone* by the other voices. For the second hemistich ('ad confitendum nomini Dei nostri'), the recitation tone shifts to the altus voice at its original *cantus durus* pitch level of F, then is repeated in the cantus back in *cantus mollis* on B-flat, both times in long note values, distinguishing the psalm tone from the rest of the texture. The psalm tone is next heard after the lower voices have presented the first hemistich of verse 6 ('Rogate quae ad pacem sunt Jerusalem'). At that point the cantus alone sings the entire first hemistich of the tone, including its *initium*, joined by the lower voices as the tone continues for the second hemistich. The other soprano voice, the sextus, takes up the tone in verse 7 ('Fiat pax in virtute tua') for another full statement, accompanied throughout by the three lowest voices. The chant is more hidden in the texture of verse 8 ('Propter fratres'), appearing after the opening melismas in the sextus voice as a recitation tone for the first hemistich, then in the altus a fourth lower (*cantus durus*) for the second hemistich ('Loquebar pacem de te'), only to be repeated in the sextus, once again in *cantus mollis*. Parallel to verse 4, the second hemistich is sung in longer note values by both the altus and sextus. The chant then disappears until the final verse of the doxology ('Sicut erat in principio'), where the first hemistich of the recitation tone is again heard in the cantus part, commencing with an unmeasured *falsobordone*.

Whether in this psalm, where the repetitive bass patterns enforce not only a certain continuity, but also a degree of uniformity, or in the other psalms and the two Magnificats, where the psalm or Magnificat tone is a principal unifying factor in its repetitions, Monteverdi's imagination and skill are revealed in the variety of textures and modes of expression he opposes to these elements of conformity. Indeed, the aesthetic effect of these compositions based on the psalm and Magnificat chants is due in substantial measure to the tension Monteverdi achieves between repetitious consistency on the one hand and substantial variety on the other. This compositional principle can readily be seen by comparing the beginnings of verses 1, 3 and 9 of 'Laetatus sum', all built over the walking bass pattern, which supports gradually increasing textures in each of its reiterations (see Exx. III.6a, III.6b, III.6c). The second bass pattern also supports a variety of textures and styles, ranging from a solo intonation of the psalm tone to paired duets to imitative textures. The fourth bass pattern normally underlies a full six-voice sonority. This type of structural process, whereby the bass remains the same or largely the same, while the upper parts are varied, is known as strophic variation. Monteverdi is sparing in his madrigalesque interpretations of words of the text in his 1610 psalm settings, and 'Laetatus sum' offers limited scope for the analyst seeking word-tone relationships. The suitability of the

Ex. III.6a

Ex. III.6b

Ex. III.6c

lively walking bass to the general emotional orientation of the text has already been mentioned. John Whenham has called attention to the first verse's first-person singular, set for a single voice part, while the first-person plural of the second verse results in a six-voice texture.[6] The words 'civitas' (city, in reference to Jerusalem) in verse 3, and 'pax' (peace) and 'abundantia' (prosperity or abundance) in verse 7 also receive modest melismatic emphasis. Otherwise one can only point to such vague relationships as the solid, steady imitative descending scales in the first hemistich of verse 2 figuring 'Stantes erant pedes nostri' (our feet were standing) or the energetic reiterations of 'ad confitendum' (for acknowledging) in the second hemistich of the fourth verse. Whenham has also taken the *Romanesca* bass as a possible reference to Rome as the centre of the Christian world, analogous to the text's 'Jerusalem' as the centre of the Hebrew world of King David's time.[7] Even though Monteverdi is often praised for his attention to the rhetorical setting of his texts and to careful word declamation, that is not always true, for there are many instances in his works where purely musical factors clearly take precedence over the text.[8] Such is the case at the beginning of verses 4 and 8, where the first word of the fourth verse is the adverb 'Illuc' (there), while the first word of the eighth verse is the preposition 'Propter' (because of or for the sake of). Although both words fulfil important grammatical functions in their respective verses, neither is the type of word that justifies either by itself nor by its significance in the verse such extraordinary melismatic treatment, and Monteverdi's only reason for setting them in this manner is his obvious desire to interrupt the regularity of the musical verse patterns he has already established in order to begin these two verses with virtuosic display. At the beginning of the doxology, however, when the sustained bass that supported these virtuoso melismas returns in its major version, the melisma abandons its virtuosic character in favour of a six-voice, imitative texture. Here the melisma is fully appropriate to the first word of the verse, 'Gloria', which Monteverdi sets melismatically several times in the course of the 1610 Vespers. The shift to a six-voice imitative texture, supported now by G major and C major harmonies, underscores the separateness of the doxology as a textual unit.

In 'Laetatus sum', it was not so much words, but rather the musical structure that was foremost in Monteverdi's mind. Although that structure is organised around the verse structure of the psalm text, individual words and phrases count for little in his compositional workshop in this piece.

9 Music in Monteverdi's Venice

IAIN FENLON

In November 1619 Francesco Dognazzi, *maestro di cappella* to the Duke of Mantua whose forebears had been Monteverdi's employers, arrived in Venice (see Monteverdi's letter of 8 March 1620). When Santi Orlandi, who had been in charge of music at the Gonzaga court, had died in the previous July, Monteverdi had been invited to return to the Duke's service. In Venice, where rumours of Monteverdi's departure from his post at S. Marco were already rife, Dognazzi's mission was to advance the cause of a return to Mantua. In this he failed. Writing to Alessandro Striggio, a Mantuan court secretary who had been Monteverdi's librettist for *Orfeo*, Monteverdi enumerated some of his reasons for staying in Venice:

> Nor is there any gentleman who does not esteem and honour me, and when I am about to perform either chamber or church music, I swear to Your Lordship that the entire city comes running.
>
> Next, the duties are very light since the whole choir is liable to discipline except the director of music – in fact, it is in his hands, having a singer censured or excused and giving leave or not; and if he does not go into chapel nobody says anything. Moreover, his allowance is assured until his death: neither the death of a procurator nor that of a doge interferes with it, and by always serving faithfully and with reverence he has greater expectations, not the opposite; and as regards his salary, if he does not go at the appointed time to pick it up, it is brought round to his house. And this is the first particular, as regards basic income; then there is occasional income, which consists of whatever extra I can easily earn outside S. Marco, of about two hundred ducats a year (invited as I am again and again by the wardens of the guilds [*signori guardiani di scole*]. Because whoever can engage the director to look after their music – not to mention the payment of thirty ducats, and even forty, and up to fifty for two Vespers and a Mass – does not fail to take him on, and they also thank him afterwards with well-chosen words.
>
> Now let Your Lordship weigh in the balance of your very refined judgement that amount which you have offered me in His Highness's name, and see whether – on good and solid grounds – I could make the change or not.
>
> (Letter of 13 March 1620)

Here, and in a number of other letters, Monteverdi underlines the range of employment that was available in the palaces, churches, convents

Fig. 9.1 Upper hall of the Scuola di S. Rocco, Venice

and confraternities of the city. In Mantua, where the composer had lived and worked for over twenty years, musical life was substantially centred on the court and, though to a much lesser extent, the cathedral.[1] Venice, with its much larger population, republican political structure and cosmopolitan character, was different. Monteverdi's specific mention, in his letter to Striggio, of the opportunities provided by the confraternities, is amplified by the remarks of the English traveller and eccentric Thomas Coryate, who visited Venice in 1608, an experience which he described in some detail in his *Crudities* published in London three years later. Among the wonders of the city, 'hastily gobled up' (as the title page puts it), were a number of musical events, principally the celebration of the feast day of S. Rocco, which Coryate had attended in the main hall of the Scuola di S. Rocco (Fig. 9.1). There, surrounded by Tintoretto's vast glowing canvases, he had

> heard the best musicke that I ever did in all my life both in the morning
> and the afternoone, so good that I would willingly goe an hundred miles
> a foote at any time to heare the like . . . This feast consisted principally of
> musicke, which was both vocall and instrumental, so good, so delectable, so
> rare, so admirable, so super excellent, that it did even ravish and stupifie all
> those strangers that never heard the like . . . For mine own part I can say this,
> that I was for the time even rapt up with Saint Paul into the third heaven.[2]

Coryate's lyrical description then continues by praising the choir of twenty voices and the large instrumental ensemble (he noted ten trombones, four cornetts, two violas da gamba, three violins, two theorbos and seven organs), precisely the kind of forces that we normally associate with Venetian polyphony of the High Renaissance. By the early seventeenth century, when Coryate visited Venice, reports of the sumptuous public musical life of the city on such occasions had become reasonably common. The great occasions of church and state were celebrated with increasingly elaborate music and ceremony, while at the larger confraternities (*scuole grandi*), where patronal feast days were elaborately marked, professional musicians and instrumentalists were employed.[3] A fundamental element in these arrangements was the choir of the basilica of S. Marco. As the principal church of Venice (though not its cathedral) and the private chapel of the doge (though in practice controlled by the *Procuratori di San Marco de supra*, three of the most distinguished and powerful members of the Venetian patriciate), S. Marco was the focal point of official civic and devotional life, and many of the musicians employed there also worked on an occasional basis elsewhere in the city. Competition between the singers and instrumentalists of the basilica to find additional work was intense, and on more than one occasion the authorities were obliged to intervene in order to regulate the practice. This was partly in an attempt to eliminate the negative effects that the pursuit of lucrative outside employment was having on the performance of duties at S. Marco itself.[4] On his arrival in Venice as *maestro di cappella*, Monteverdi inherited not only this formidable body of singers and instrumentalists which performed a central role in the musical life of the city, but also a post with a distinguished history.

During the sixteenth century, the position of choirmaster had been held by an impressive succession of musicians, beginning with Adrian Willaert who occupied the post from 1527 until his death in 1562.[5] The extent of Willaert's achievement can be gauged by the increasingly elaborate music that was performed at S. Marco during his time there, including the double-choir Vespers psalms which he elaborated on the basis of existing practice, as well as by the variety of his own numerous publications. As a teacher he was one of the most influential figures of the century, and after his death the succession at S. Marco passed to his pupils, first to Cipriano de Rore (who remained in the post for only one year) and then to the composer and theorist Gioseffo Zarlino. During Zarlino's time as *maestro di cappella* the organists of S. Marco began to assume an important role as composers. This was partly due to Zarlino's preferences. His chief interest lay in his work as a theorist, which brought him considerable status in intellectual circles and membership of the prestigious if short-lived Accademia della Fama,[6] and his own compositions are neither as numerous nor as varied in style as those of Willaert. At the same time, the increasingly heavy burdens of state and religious ceremonial brought with them extra duties. New music was required for such occasions, and the day-to-day organisation of the chapel was now more complex; in response to the taste for large-scale pieces, the chapel had expanded, and extra musicians were added on special occasions.

The first notable organist-composer at S. Marco was Claudio Merulo, appointed in 1557, but it was with the employment of Andrea Gabrieli that the musical activities of S. Marco entered a new phase. During his youth Andrea had been organist at one of the Venetian parish churches, but in his thirties he spent time at the Bavarian court at Munich. There he came under the influence of Orlande de Lassus, arguably the most famous composer of the time, who directed a large choir of singers and instrumentalists. When he returned to Venice, Gabrieli brought with him ideas that had been refined by his experience of music written for *cori spezzati*, with the choir separated into two or more groups and the singers supported by instruments. Although Andrea also wrote more modest church music suitable for smaller establishments, it was the large-scale works for two or more choirs that earned him his reputation, and it was this style that was widely imitated, particularly by his own pupils. Of these the most important was Giovanni Gabrieli, Andrea's nephew, who followed in his uncle's footsteps by working under Lassus at Munich for a time and then returning to become organist at S. Marco in 1585, in succession to Merulo.[7]

The major musical monument to the polychoral style in the period immediately after Willaert is the *Concerti* of 1587, in which most of the motets are by Andrea Gabrieli; published within two years of his death, the collection, which was assembled for the press by Giovanni, has the character of a commemorative volume. With some of their texts taken from the liturgy for the major feast days in the Venetian calendar, and others in the vernacular, the *Concerti* preserves the musical elements of annual ceremonial occasions, of both civic and religious importance, when the ducal *trionfi* were carried in procession and all the ritual apparatus of the state was on display.

By the beginning of the seventeenth century, the choir of S. Marco was arguably the finest music establishment of any church in Italy outside Papal Rome. This was due not to historical accident, but rather to an evolving policy which valued music as an essential component of the official rhetoric of Venetian self-presentation. The music and ceremonial of the Venetian church and state were regarded by its ruling patricians as intimately related and vital components of the elaboration, through artistic means, of the 'myth of Venice', a political concept that stressed the unique qualities of Venice and deployed them as a powerful weapon of propaganda.[8] At the centre of the myth was the idea of the singularity and perfection of the Republic. On one level the city was admired for its extraordinary topography and sheer physical beauty, and throughout the Renaissance period foreigners expressed their astonishment at the richness of the city's churches, the elegance of its palaces, the mosaics of S. Marco, and the public ceremonies surrounding the doge. Along the Rialto, with its mixture of traders and merchants from every part of Europe and the Orient, sights were to be seen that could not be found anywhere else in Europe. Praise of Venice invariably began with applause for its unparalleled sights and urban charm as a city quite literally (and, as legend emphasised, miraculously) founded upon the seas.

The notion of Venetian political stability and freedom from internal discord had been developed in the fifteenth century by humanists who identified Venice with models of republicanism drawn from classical antiquity. In this way the Venetian constitution came to be seen as the receptacle of ancient political wisdom and the reason why Venice, almost alone among the Italian states, had remained unconquered for more than a millennium. For Venetians, the myth was a precious political asset which the patrician classes used to foster a civic spirit in this densely populated, overcrowded, and cosmopolitan city. In the decades after the Council of Trent, consolidation of its social fabric was attempted by the increased use of the city and its main spaces for an annual cycle of ceremonies and rituals, strengthened by the enhanced conception of Venice not only as the Perfect Republic but also as the City of God. Throughout Europe, public ceremonies and processions frequently functioned as expressions of the political order, but in Venice the practice was of considerable complexity and, in its most elaborate form, the ducal procession (*andata*) involved close interweavings of history and myth, music and liturgy.[9]

In its most developed version, as enacted on some forty occasions in the course of the year, the *andata* included all the principal officeholders together with some minor officials, the ambassadors of foreign states, the canons of S. Marco, the patriarch, and, at the physical core of the procession, the doge himself. As the most elaborate Venetian processional form, the *andata* effectively became an image of the city itself, accessible to those who had never seen it through Matteo Pagan's monumental series of eight woodcuts (Fig. 9.2), as well as in maps and engravings of scenes from Venetian life, presumably produced for pilgrims, tourists, and bibliophiles rather than for Venetians themselves. While the hierarchical ordering of the procession was fixed, the

Fig. 9.2 Matteo Pagan, Procession in the Piazza San Marco (detail)

personnel who walked in the *andata* were constantly changing; those who participated did so as the temporary holders of official positions. In addition to the principal actors, the *andata* also displayed the ducal *trionfi*, symbolic objects including eight banners, six silver trumpets, a candle, a cushion, a faldstool, and a sword, presented to Doge Sebastiano Ziani by Pope Alexander III in 1177. These gifts, which as Francesco Sansovino, the author of the first guidebook to the city recognised, empowered the doge as a princely equal of popes and emperors, were carried in the ducal procession on all the major occasions in the ceremonial year.[10] They were both historical relics and emblems of status and authority.

In addition to the silver trumpets, which were sounded, the doge's trumpets and shawm players also took part in the *andata*; they are clearly depicted in a number of images of the event, including Franco's engraving showing the arrival of the ducal procession at S. Giorgio Maggiore to hear Vespers on Christmas Day (Fig. 9.3). The canons of S. Marco also walked in the ducal procession, and it was through their participation that the *patriarchino*, the rite peculiar to S. Marco, could be transposed from one place to another. When this took place, an act of appropriation was secured through musical and liturgical means. In consequence, when Mass was celebrated as part of the ducal procession to a particular church or convent, it was done so according to a liturgy that since 1456 had been

Fig. 9.3 Giacomo Franco, The doge arrives at S. Giorgio Maggiore to hear Vespers on Christmas Day

exclusively associated with the basilica. In this symbolic practice the use of the *patriarchino*, polyphonically decorated by the choir of S. Marco, served to emphasise the doge's authority. In effect the *patriarchino* was a liturgy of state.

Although the *andata* was both exclusive and hierarchical, its basic arrangement was supplemented on occasion by the addition of other social groupings such as the confraternities, the trade guilds or even a particular parish. This broadened participation and was presumably intended to underline the allegedly harmonious corporate organisation of the city, another basic underpinning of the myth of Venice. While the *scuole* represented the notion of communal devotion and charity, the guilds symbolised the complementary idea of commerce as the foundation of civic concord. On many of the more important feasts in the

Venetian calendar, the choir of S. Marco walked in the *andata*; so too did the singers employed by some of the wealthier *scuole*. In expanded form, these processions amplified the liturgy outside the basilica by making use not only of the central civic space of the city but also of other areas far from the Piazza S. Marco. In this way, civic and liturgical acts that were usually associated with ducal authority were able to broaden their audience, which could participate not only passively (by observing) but also actively by walking in the procession, chanting litanies and singing *laude*. At the same time, the wide geographical dispersal of the *andata* knitted together *sestieri* (the districts into which the city was divided for administrative purposes), parishes, confraternities and guilds in a closely woven fabric of religious and civic observance.

It is likely that Monteverdi's litany settings were originally composed for some such occasion, perhaps involving a processional element. Certainly such events required considerable preparation, as the composer himself remarked in his letters. One of the most elaborate of all that took place during Monteverdi's lifetime was the sequence of ceremonies celebrating the foundation of the votive church of S. Maria della Salute on the Grand Canal to give thanks for the end of the plague of 1630–1 (Fig. 9.4), a major epidemic in which one third of the population perished. On a number of separate occasions stretching from October 1630 until November of the following year, which together constituted the seventeenth century's most substantial addition to the tradition of Venetian civic and religious ritual, Marian litanies were sung and the basilica's prized Byzantine icon of the Madonna Nicopeia carried in procession. It has been suggested that a number of Monteverdi's extant works, including two of the settings of the 'Salve Regina' and the *concertato* Gloria published in the *Selva morale e spirituale* (1641) were composed for these ceremonies.[11]

As Coryate's experiences suggest, Venetian ceremonies were also able to incorporate a wider audience that included foreigners, such as the visitors for whom the city itself was a place of pilgrimage in its own right – the home of an impressive assortment of relics, chief among them the body of St Mark, which had been brought from Asia Minor in the Middle Ages – as well as an important staging post on the great spiritual journey to the Holy Land. The feast of Corpus Christi is perhaps the most spectacular example of state appropriation of an event of universal spiritual significance for a mixture of economic, political and devotional reasons.[12] On this occasion, foreign pilgrims joined in the traditional procession in the Piazza, one of many that took place annually (Fig. 9.5); each one, accompanied by a member of the Venetian nobility, carried a candle that was subsequently placed in front of the Holy Sepulchre in

Fig. 9.4 S. Maria della Salute

Jerusalem. In this process, the city became a psychological and symbolic extension of the sacred space of Jerusalem itself, and the ceremonies in the piazza and the basilica, carried out in the presence of the doge, an official benediction of a great Catholic enterprise. The Corpus Christi procession is a reminder that although the motivations for Venetian civic and religious rituals were complex and interlocking, the audience for them was certainly not uniform but expanded and contracted for different occasions.

The major annual feast days in the Venetian calendrical cycle corresponded to those in the Roman calendar, but to these were added others that commemorated important events in Venetian history. In this way the characteristically Venetian was associated with the universally Christian;

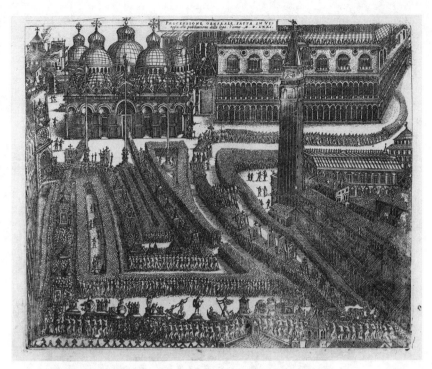

Fig. 9.5 Giacomo Franco, Procession in the Piazza S. Marco

patriotism and faith were thus conveniently and inextricably fused. The most obvious example of such paired and complementary meanings arises in the case of St Mark himself, whose cult lay at the centre of Venetian mythology. As the possessors of the Evangelist's body, supposedly transferred to the city in 827, the Venetians modelled their relationship to Mark on that of the popes to St Peter. In Venetian eyes Venice was as autonomous as Rome, and the doge's authority, inherited from Mark, as absolute and independent as that of the occupant of the Chair of St Peter. In the course of the Middle Ages, Mark had come to personify not merely the privileges of the doge, but the Republic itself. As a fifteenth-century canon of S. Marco, Gabriele Fiamma, put it: 'I was born a Venetian and live in this happy homeland protected by the prayers and guardianship of St Mark, from whom that Most Serene Republic acknowledges its greatness, its victories and all its good fortune.' The churches of the city bristled with paintings showing events from the life of the Evangelist; no fewer than four major feast days were dedicated to St Mark and his symbol was extensively used as an image of Venetian authority throughout the empire. In the city itself, the ducal palace, the basilica and piazza of S. Marco constitute a distinctive civic and ceremonial space symbolic of the unity of the religious and political features of the Venetian

constitution. In view of the strong identification of the Venetian
Republic with St Mark, it is not surprising that liturgical or paraliturgical
texts in praise of Venice's principal patron saint are so common in the
repertories of music written by musicians working in the city, especially
those associated with the basilica itself. Through such means the constitution and government of Venice were both celebrated and sanctified on
major ceremonial occasions.

In addition to its symbolic value as the emblem of a harmonious state,
music was essential to the propagation of the Venetian myth through
performance. As with every other aspect of the organisation of S. Marco,
the choir was ultimately under the direct control of the Procurators, and
their records reveal the importance of music to them and a concern to
attract musicians of quality to the basilica. Although the Procurators
often attended auditions and made recommendations about new
appointments, in practice the daily decisions about disciplinary matters,
the choice of repertory and the routines of rehearsal were made by the
maestro di cappella. Asides in Monteverdi's letters reveal that the major
Christian festivals at Christmas ('this solemn feast is the greatest that the
director of music has in the entire year' (Letter of 30 October 1627)) and
Easter were the most demanding. On one occasion the composer apol-
ogised to Striggio for not sending his opinion about the libretto for
Le Nozze di Tetide:

> This delay on my part came about because of the hard work that had to be
> done on the Mass for Christmas Eve, for what with composing it and
> copying it out I had to give up the entire month of December, almost
> without a break . . . now finished with the labours of Christmas Eve and
> Christmas Day, I shall have nothing to do in S. Marco for some little time.
>
> (Letter of 29 December 1616)

Elsewhere Monteverdi refers to the 'many duties I shall have at S. Marco
during Holy Week' (letter of 7 March 1619) and letters from July 1620
suggest that preparations for the feasts of the Most Precious Blood and
the Visitation of the Blessed Virgin Mary, which occurred on the first two
days of the month, brought additional burdens (see Letter of 11 July
1620). So too did the annual celebration of the victory against the Turks at
Lepanto in 1571, which coincided with the feast day of S. Giustina, whose
relics are in Padua. On that day (7 October), the traditional *andata*
processed from S. Marco to the church and convent of S. Giustina in
the north of the city. The occasion is reflected in musical compositions
such as Giovanni Bassano's five-voice motet 'Beata virgo et martyr
Iustina', published in his *Motetti per concerti ecclesiastici* (1598) and
presumably written for the annual celebration. Although none of

Monteverdi's works is definitely known to have been written for the feast day, he refers more than once in letters to the amount of musical preparation that was required. In late 1627 Alessandro Striggio invited the composer to visit Mantua, and in his reply Monteverdi wrote that he would not be able to come during the month of October 'since I have to attend to certain feasts ordered by our Most Serene Doge'.[13] Two weeks later the composer explained to another correspondent that he was unable to leave Venice

> until the seventh of the next month, for on that day the Most Serene Doge goes in procession to S. Giustina to give thanks to God our saviour for the joyous naval victory. He is accompanied by the entire senate, and solemn music is sung. As soon as this function is over, I shall get on the boat with the courier and come to obey Your Excellency's commands.
>
> (Letter of 25 September 1627)

Such special occasions apart, the daily round centred on music for Mass and Vespers; this latter service was particularly elaborate on major feast days, when the *Pala d'oro*, the large gold altarpiece which is the major treasure of the basilica, was opened to public gaze. Built in Constantinople in 976, the *Pala* was enlarged with gold panels in the twelfth century, decorated with jewels after the sack of Constantinople in the thirteenth, and placed in its present frame in the fourteenth. On weekdays and minor feasts it was hidden behind a special wooden altarpiece, painted by Paolo Veneziano and his sons in 1345. But on the major feasts of the church year an elaborate mechanism was used to remove Paolo's altarpiece and to unfold the *Pala d'oro* for the population to see. On these occasions, the singers of S. Marco used to perform the psalms in plainchant, but from some time about the middle of the sixteenth century it became established that psalms should be sung in eight parts arranged in two choirs. By Monteverdi's time there were more than fifty days in the church year when this happened.

Identification with the Republic through participation in civic and religious ceremonial was only one kind of allegiance, which structured the lives of seventeenth-century Venetians; at a local level there was the parish and the *scuola*. Most citizens would have belonged to one of the two hundred *scuole piccole*, whose memberships were often restricted according to criteria of occupation or national origin and which were sometimes patronised by wealthy patrician families who acted as benefactors.[14] Many were attached to parish churches; others were tied to a specific function such as assisting prisoners condemned to death. Such pious confraternities were to be found in all Italian cities during this period, but nowhere else was there anything quite like the principal Venetian institutions of this sort, the *scuole grandi*. Their main function, like that of the *scuole piccole*, was to promote virtuous living and to distribute benefits, both material and spiritual, among both their members and impoverished outsiders; in addition they provided manpower for the Venetian galleys. Membership was open to both rich and poor, but priests and nobles were excluded from positions of responsibility in the *scuole* (though not from membership itself). By the sixteenth century their financial resources had become very great, and much was spent on the construction and decoration of their meeting houses. At the time there were some who believed that such ostentatious behaviour was not becoming conduct for bodies that were essentially charitable foundations, but the results were much admired, and by the second half of the century, the *scuole* had established themselves as one of the sights of Venice.

Although the *scuole grandi* were independent foundations, they were regulated by the state and were expected to participate in processions on public occasions. As the ceremonial life of Venice became more elaborate in the course of the sixteenth century, so the demands upon this public and civic aspect of the activities of the *scuole* increased. By Monteverdi's time it seems to have become common practice for musicians from the basilica to be imported by the *scuole* on important occasions (most commonly the patronal feast) to perform pieces from their repertory. An account book which gives details of the music performed on the feast day of S. Rocco in 1595 reveals that a large body of singers and instrumentalists was involved, including the *cappella* from S. Marco and Giovanni Gabrieli, all under the direction of Giovanni Croce.[15] It was precisely an occasion of this sort that sent Thomas Coryate into raptures a few years later, and which Monteverdi had in mind when he wrote of his work for them. Another witness, Jean- Baptiste Duval, secretary to the French ambassador to Venice, was present at Vespers celebrated for the members of the Scuola di S. Teodoro in the church of S. Salvatore on the feast day of their patron saint in 1607. Of the musical arrangements, he wrote:

> There was given in that place a concert by the finest musicians, both vocal and instrumental, principally by six small organs besides that of the church (which is very fine), and by trombones (or sackbuts), oboes, viols, violins, lutes, cornets, recorders and flageolets.[16]

Yet though it is difficult to know how important the *scuole grandi* were to the development of Venetian musical repertories, it is clear that each of them contributed a good deal to the musical life of its immediate area, acting as a focal point for local enactments of civic and religious ritual. Singers and instrumentalists were involved in the High Mass that was celebrated in each of the *scuole* on the first Sunday of every month. Following this, the musicians formed a vital part of the procession that wound its way from the *scuola* to the church with which the foundation was particularly associated; after a further Mass was celebrated there the procession returned to the meeting house. On the remaining Sundays of the month the musicians of each *scuola grande* participated in a Mass in one of the religious houses in the local vicinity. Such events formed an important part of Monteverdi's professional life.

Outside the *scuole grandi* there was a considerable amount of music in the other churches of the city. This was particularly true of the two large mendicant churches of SS Giovanni e Paolo and the Frari. The former maintained a permanent choir, an organist and a music master to teach the novices. A number of *scuole piccole* were also attached to the church; among them was that of S. Pietro Martire, a reasonably wealthy institution that was able to support musicians for a polyphonic Mass twice a month as well as on the feast day of its patron saint. At the Frari, Duval was present at the celebration of Mass in 1608, when music was provided by 'trombones, spinets, bass viols, violins, lutes and oboes', and the following year, during Compline, he recorded the participation of 'two portative organs ... trombones, lutes, theorbos, cornetts and bass violins.[17] Many medium-sized parish churches also paid for music on important occasions. This is not surprising: many members of the choir of S. Marco held ecclesiastical status (sometimes in defiance of propriety), and this enabled the Procurators to provide them with additional income from benefices, so that many Venetian churches had a formalised connection with at least one musician from S. Marco. The Procurators were well placed to distribute such sinecures, for in addition to administering the church treasury they were also executors for a large number of estates that had been entrusted to their care. Through this system of additional payments and benefits, they attempted to maintain a high quality of musical life at S. Marco; at the same time the practice may occasionally have benefited musical activity at a parish level. Even in the smaller parish churches singers and instrumentalists would be employed, if only once a year.

Although little is known of domestic music making beyond the fact that Venice was one of the most important centres in Europe for both the manufacture of instruments and the printing of music, which must in itself have made a considerable impact upon the musical and social life of the city. Middle-class post-mortem inventories often list music books and instruments, suggesting both a degree of musical literacy and the widespread ownership of lutes and clavichords in particular. Both were portable, and in the summer months were often played in gondolas. This

Fig. 9.6 Giacomo Franco, Gondolas in Summer

kind of social *divertissement* can be seen in an early seventeenth-century engraving by Giacomo Franco (Fig. 9.6), which shows precisely the sort of activity that the English visitor Richard Lassells described some decades later: 'They steere for two miles upon the laguna, while the musick plays, and sings epithalamiums all the way along, and makes Neptune jealous to heare Hymen called upon his Dominions.'[18] Musical performances were clearly a popular activity in the houses and palaces of the patriciate, and in the embassies of the various foreign nations that contributed to the cosmopolitan atmosphere of the city. Similarly, the Palladian villas which the aristocracy built in the countryside of the *terraferma* must have resounded to madrigals and other kinds of music-making, or so we must infer from the scenes shown in Paolo Veronese's fresco cycle in the Villa Barbaro at Maser, or Giovanni Antonio Fasolo's on the walls of the Villa Caldogno, near Vicenza.

A number of Monteverdi's private Venetian patrons can be identified. The *Lamento d'Apollo* (part of the ballet *Apollo*) was performed in the palace of Giovanni Matteo Bembo in January 1620 (see Monteverdi's letter of 1 February 1620), and the *Combattimento di Tancredi e Clorinda*, an avant-garde theatre piece setting stanzas from Tasso's *Gerusalemme liberata*, was given its first performance in Girolamo Mocenigo's palace during Carnival 1624. The short opera, *Proserpina rapita*, was commissioned by the same family to celebrate the wedding of Lorenzo Giustiniani and Giustiniana Mocenigo in April 1630. Elsewhere in the city Monteverdi worked for a number of patrons including the English ambassador Sir Isaac Wake, the Florentine community at SS Giovanni e Paolo, and the Milanese 'nation' attached to the Frari. Monteverdi also provided music for the private oratory of Marc'Antonio Cornaro, *primicerius* (the senior ecclesiastic) of S. Marco (letters of 8 and 17 March 1620); some of the small-scale motets published in the 1620s may reflect this connection.

From the descriptions of visitors, archival documents, and sometimes from the printed music itself, a good deal can be reconstructed about the music performed outside the basilica of S. Marco – in parish churches, confraternities, during official public ceremonies and processions, and even in the squares and streets of the city. For many visitors it was not only the physical beauty of Venice that was compelling but also the endless spectacle and ceremony in this city of processions. These features of Venetian musical life continued past the watershed of the late 1630s, when the first public operas were presented in a number of existing theatres built and owned by patrician families. In addition to this phenomenon, to which Monteverdi himself contributed in the last years of his life, musical activity also began to shift to the four main Venetian *ospedali*, charitable institutions which maintained musical chapels. Yet despite the superficial brilliance of the city and its institutions, the economic, political and social realities were different. By the time of Monteverdi's death, every intelligent Venetian knew that the game was up. Behind the myth, decorated and supported by music and the other arts, the structure was already rotten. Despite the brilliance of Venice in the remaining decades, the Republic was in the process of irreversible decline; when Napoleon arrived to dismantle what remained, no resistance was offered.

10 The Venetian secular music

TIM CARTER

Monteverdi's move to Venice as *maestro di cappella* of the basilica of S. Marco in 1613 ostensibly forced a shift in his professional commitments away from court music in favour of the church. However, the impact was not necessarily as marked as one might expect. In fact, notwithstanding the size and complexity of Monteverdi's two 'Venetian' collections of sacred music – the *Selva morale e spirituale* (1641) and the posthumous *Messa ... et salmi* (1650), plus a few pieces in anthologies – the composer published surprisingly few of the sacred and spiritual works that he must have written during his thirty years at S. Marco. Conversely, and despite appearances (five madrigal books published by 1605, only three from 1614 to 1638, plus a further posthumous volume in 1651), Monteverdi's secular output remained significant in terms both of surviving works and of what we know (from his letters and other sources) of his musical commitments.[1]

However, there are a number of difficulties in assessing this output. One, also shared with the sacred music, concerns chronology. Monteverdi published his Sixth Book of Madrigals in 1614, his Seventh in 1619 and his Eighth in 1638. Between the Seventh and Eighth Books came reissues of Monteverdi's first six books of madrigals (1620–22), of the Seventh (1622, 1623, 1628) and of the 1607 *Scherzi musicali* (1628); the 1623 edition of the *Lamento d'Arianna* (also including the *lettera amorosa* and *partenza amorosa* from the Seventh Book); an edition corrected by Monteverdi of Arcadelt's four-voice madrigals (Rome, 1627); the second book of *Scherzi musicali* of 1632; and a few settings included in anthologies edited by Venetian associates such as Giovanni Battista Camarella (?1623)[2] and Carlo Milanuzzi (reissue of 1624), or by the printers Bartolomeo Magni (1624[11]) and Alessandro Vincenti (1634[7]). One might expect him to have issued more new music, but this was a period that saw a severe downturn in the music-printing trade, and perhaps Monteverdi also felt that – having gained a prestigious appointment – there was little further benefit in publication in terms of reputation and potential mobility. However, the nineteen-year gap between the Seventh and Eighth Books, plus the fact that the latter, at least, contains music going back several decades in some shape or form – most notably the *Ballo delle ingrate* (the first version of which was performed on 4 June 1608) – makes it difficult to locate individual settings in a specific time and place such as to be able to discern straightforward lines of development.

The Mantuan secular music appears more cohesive not just because of its chronology but also because it was composed within a consistent, if evolving, environment in terms of courtly tastes, poetic choices, performing forces and a relatively stable genre. One prime agenda, at least for modern scholars, has of course been Monteverdi's realisation of the ideals of the *seconda pratica*, with the poetry the mistress, rather than servant, of the music. Monteverdi remained concerned with the issues, if we are to believe his correspondence with the theorist Giovanni Battista Doni in 1632–3 – his letter of 22 October 1632 notes that that he was still writing the treatise, now titled *Melodia, overo Seconda pratica musicale*, that he had promised in the postface to the Fifth Book of Madrigals as the outcome of his controversy with Giovanni Maria Artusi. The preface to the Eighth Book also takes matters one step further. But the Venetian secular music seems more disparate and fragmented, swimming both with and against contemporary tides that seem to have muddied the waters of the composer's pristine ideals.

Doni was less than convinced of Monteverdi's theoretical acumen. He also felt that the composer had taken some wrong turns. Although the theorist acknowledged the mastery of the monodic *Lamento d'Arianna* (due in large part, he said, to Ottavio Rinuccini's poetry), he felt that the polyphonic version included in the Sixth Book of Madrigals was a mistake made 'at the request of a Venetian gentleman':[3] the tone is dismissive, as if no one of good taste (viz. Florentines, of which Doni was one) would have countenanced so perverse a treatment of an expressive recitative. While it is now clear that much of the Sixth Book is Mantuan in origin (and even, perhaps, orientation), we know that Monteverdi did indeed provide secular music for Venetian gentlemen during his time in the city. His letters reveal that his official duties included writing music for four state banquets per year (as on 15 June (St Vitus's Day) 1623 and 1626) and for public and private ceremonies in honour of visiting dignitaries (Władisław Sigismund, Crown Prince of Poland, in March 1625; at the residence of the English ambassador on 17 July 1627; Grand Duke Ferdinando II and Prince Giovanni Carlo de' Medici for a banquet in the Arsenale on 8 April 1628, involving setting for two voices and continuo of five sonnets by Giulio Strozzi, *I cinque fratelli*).[4] He also cultivated close relationships with prominent Venetian noblemen such as Giovanni Matteo Bembo (in whose palace the lament from the Mantuan ballet *Apollo* was performed in January 1620), Marc'Antonio Cornaro, the Giustiniani, Girolamo Mocenigo, the poet Giulio Strozzi, and later, members of the Accademia degli Incogniti.

For the Giustiniani, in 1622 Monteverdi negotiated on their behalf to have Giovanni Battista Andreini and his *commedia dell'arte* troupe come to Venice, and in April 1630 the composer provided an entertainment, *Proserpina rapita*, for the wedding of Lorenzo Giustiniani to Giustiniana Mocenigo.[5] Giustiniana's father, Girolamo, had also provided the occasion in Carnival 1624 for which Monteverdi wrote the *Combattimento di Tancredi e Clorinda*, performed in the Mocenigo palace as part of an evening's entertainment that also included 'madrigali senza gesto'.[6] In addition to these Venetian connections, Monteverdi also retained contacts with prominent individuals elsewhere in Italy. In 1614 he sent a copy of his Sixth Book and other music to the poet Angelo Grillo (Livio Celiano); he was invited by Ottavio Rinuccini to visit Florence in 1617; in 1619–20 he acted as agent for Paolo Giordano Orsini, Duke of Bracciano, to print Francesco Petratti's *Il primo libro d'arie*; on 13 June 1620 he attended a meeting of Adriano Banchieri's Accademia dei Floridi in Bologna (he became an honorary member of its successor, the Filomusi, in 1625 or 1626); in 1623–4 he sent music to Cesare d'Este, duke of Modena; and on 9 March 1630, he sent a canzonetta probably to Marchese Enzo Bentivoglio.[7]

Although these external relations appear fairly casual, Monteverdi also had other, more formal obligations outside Venice that made their impact on his secular output. The Gonzagas appear soon to have regretted their hasty dismissal of the composer in 1612, especially after the melomane Ferdinando Gonzaga became duke (following the death of Duke Francesco in December 1612, although Ferdinando, a cardinal, was crowned officially only in 1616). Alessandro Striggio and other Mantuan agents repeatedly attempted to persuade Monteverdi back to Mantua – which the composer equally repeatedly resisted on the grounds, he said, of his superior working conditions in Venice. Duke Ferdinando also used the fact that Monteverdi remained a Mantuan citizen (and therefore a feudal subject) to pressure him to write music for Mantuan entertainments. He was not always enthusiastic: although the *ballo Tirsi e Clori* (later included in the Seventh Book of Madrigals) was performed in Mantua in January 1616, the proposed *intermedi*, *Le nozze di Tetide*, for the wedding of Duke Ferdinando and Caterina de' Medici (February 1617) remained unfinished, even if Monteverdi did set the prologue to Giovan Battista Andreini's *La Maddalena*, a *sacra rappresentazione* performed as part of the celebrations. A libretto received from Mantua in spring 1618, Ercole Marigliani's (Marliani) *Andromeda*, was eventually staged in Carnival 1619–20 (with another *ballo*, *Apollo*). Plans to celebrate Caterina's birthday on 2 May 1620 with a performance of *Arianna* came to naught, but Monteverdi wrote music for Carnival 1620–1 and set at least two of the *intermedi* for Marigliani's *Le tre costanti* performed in early 1622 celebrating the marriage of Eleonora Gonzaga and Emperor Ferdinand II. Later (1627), he also worked on the commission for an opera *La finta pazza Licori* for the festivities associated with the coronation of Duke Vincenzo II Gonzaga.

Although Monteverdi was still highly ambivalent over his relationship with Mantua, he was not averse in principle to some kind of court appointment. He was reportedly tempted by an offer made in 1623 to move to the Polish court; he also worked hard to secure, in the face of stiff competition, the commission for theatrical music for the wedding (December 1628) of Odoardo Farnese, Duke of Parma, and Margherita de' Medici, comprising six *intermedi* for Tasso's *Aminta* and a tournament (he also produced a *mascherata* for Carnival 1627–8).[8] Further, Eleonora Gonzaga's marriage to Emperor Ferdinand II led to Monteverdi's increasingly close relations with the Habsburg court, where he seems to have been sending music regularly in the early 1630s, if not before, and which, we shall see, had a clear impact on the Eighth Book of Madrigals.

This puts in a somewhat different light Monteverdi's repeated claims to Alessandro Striggio and others of his delight in Venice – other evidence suggests that Monteverdi's tenure at S. Marco was not always untroubled – and it seems that had the right offer been made, the composer would have seriously considered moving. Although the Sixth Book of Madrigals appeared without a dedication – and therefore made a statement of new-found independence – the Seventh had one in fulsome, even grovelling terms to Caterina de' Medici (the composer received a necklace in return that he eventually pawned to bail his son, Massimiliano, from the Inquisition), while the Eighth was originally dedicated to Emperor Ferdinand II, hastily revised on the emperor's death to address his successor, Ferdinand III. In both cases, Monteverdi clearly had an ulterior motive: securing the pension of one hundred *scudi* per year granted him by Duke Vincenzo Gonzaga in early 1609 became an obsession, forcing the composer into tortuous twists and turns to keep the Gonzagas on his side. Similarly, in the late 1620s and early 1630s, Monteverdi tried a different tack, petitioning the Habsburgs (feudal lords of the Gonzagas) to help secure an ecclesiastical benefice in Cremona to meet the pension.[9] Monteverdi noted to Alessandro Striggio in 1627 that he was proposing to present Empress Eleonora with some of his compositions to this end: this also seems to be why he took holy orders (he is styled 'Molto Illustre & Molto Reverendo Signor Claudio Monteverde' on the title page of the 1632 *Scherzi musicali*). Eleonora Gonzaga had a penchant for Italian *balli* (such as those included in the Seventh and Eighth Books), and also welcomed Mantuan musicians to Vienna: for example, in January 1631 the brothers Giovanni Battista and Orazio Rubini, the violinists (and chitarrone players) who had performed in *Orfeo*, their sister

Lucia Rubini and Margherita Basile (the latter the sister of the famous Adriana Basile) as virtuoso sopranos, and the tenor Francesco Dognazzi plus an organist from Verona.[10] But as a result, it is difficult to locate Monteverdi's Venetian secular music in a single environment. Some of it is clearly for Venice, some for Mantua, some for Vienna, and some for elsewhere in Italy. The resulting stylistic and other inconsistencies make this music hard to reduce to a single, straightforward model.

'Bella gerant alii ...'

The publication of the Seventh and Eighth Books may have been opportunistic in terms of taking advantage of specific events (the wedding of Duke Ferdinando Gonzaga and Caterina de' Medici in 1617; the coronation of Ferdinand III as King of the Romans in 1636). The 1623 edition of the *Lamento d'Arianna* may have been in response to (the threat of?) the setting being published in a Roman anthology that same year, *Il maggio fiorito: arie, sonetti, e madrigali, à 1.2.3. de diuersi autori* (Orvieto, Michel'Angelo Fei and Rinaldo Ruuli, 1623[8]); it would seem that Virginia Andreini, the original singer, had somehow released a piece that had hitherto been kept in her own performance repertory.[11] The 1632 *Scherzi musicali* is an odd collection that may have been somehow pirated by the Venetian printer Bartolomeo Magni (who signed the dedication), unless the composer felt that his new ecclesiastical status warranted staying in the wings. None gives the impression of being part of a consistent publishing strategy, and even though the preface to the Eighth Book makes great, if sometimes confused, theoretical claims for its contents, the collection as a whole still smacks of being a rather random miscellany (although it does have strongly directed themes, as we shall see below). Indeed, the mere fact that Monteverdi (or his publisher) sought to give some external order to these volumes – the Seventh Book a 'concerto' with madrigals sequenced by ascending number of voices (broadly speaking) followed by the 'altri generi di canti' mentioned in the title page, and the Eighth by the two-part division of *canti guerrieri* and *amorosi* – is perhaps symptomatic of their heterogeneity.

The poetry, too, is a rather eclectic mix of the good and the bad, and the famous and (to us, at least) anonymous. Monteverdi retained his interest in Battista Guarini from the Fourth and Fifth Books (but in the madrigals rather than *Il pastor fido*), and jumped on the Marino bandwagon, at least in the Sixth and Seventh. Giambattista Marino had taken Italy by storm with the publication of his *Rime* in 1602, and although in the Sixth Book Monteverdi tended to stick with the more conservative sonnets, in the Seventh, he embraced Marino's madrigalian kisses and love-bites with at least some of the enthusiasm typical of the period. Monteverdi appears to have had some fondness for Rinuccini (the librettist of *Arianna* and the *Ballo delle ingrate*), and not just because of his collaborations for Mantuan 1608 wedding festivities. Petrarch, on the other hand, adds gravitas both to the Sixth Book and to the Eighth, and perhaps also (in the latter, at least, as in the first two of four spiritual madrigals opening the *Selva morale e spirituale*) is a sign of an ageing composer resisting the moderns and hankering after the past. The relative absence from the Seventh and Eighth Books of the poetry of Gabriello Chiabrera is more surprising – at least in terms of his contemporary popularity – but a number of the 'anonymous' poems are in a strongly Chiabrera-like vein, such as the canzonettas 'Chiome d'oro' and 'Amor, che deggio far' in the Seventh Book, both in a later version of the poetic and musical styles of the 1607 *Scherzi musicali* (which is full of Chiabrera). On the whole, however, these poetic choices are fairly middle of the road in a deliberate or, more likely, accidental search for *varietas*.

Monteverdi's turn to Marino has been a source of some opprobrium on the part of those who think the composer should have had better poetic taste, just as Marino himself has often been charged with single-handedly causing the decline of Italian poetry into the decadent manner-ism of *secentismo*.[12] It is true that one soon tires of considering where kisses should best be planted: on the eyes (the source of tears) or on the mouth (to cause a smile) is the debate in 'Vorrei baciarti, o Filli' (Seventh Book), though Marino has in his repertory plenty of other options from the neck downwards. Yet he is not a bad poet, and indeed he seems to have opened up themes that became emblematic for Monteverdi's late secular works. The prologue-like 'Tempro la cetra, e per cantar gli onori' opening the Seventh Book sets the tone: 'I tune my lyre, and to sing the honours of Mars I raise my style', begins the poet in grandiloquent vein, 'but I try in vain', for the lyre 'always sounds of nothing but love'. Marino used a similar gambit in 'Altri canti di Marte e di sua schiera', which begins the *canti amorosi* in the Eighth Book: 'Let others sing of Mars and of his troops, I sing of love.' But according to the common conceit from the Classical period on, love and war are but two sides of the same coin. Ovid's 'Militat omnis amans, et habet sua castra Cupido' (*Amores* I.9) translated in Rinuccini's 'Ogni amante è guerrier, nel suo gran regno' (Eighth Book) sets the pattern, and of course it had become a commonplace of the Petrarchan lyric during the Renaissance. Just as warriors lay siege to a castle, so do lovers to the hearts of their beloveds; just as soldiers are wounded or even die, so are lovers, at least in various metaphorical senses; Cupid's arrows, like those of any enemy, pose mortal threats to life and soul; the soldier-lover can retire in defeat, or can fight the impossible fight, gaining heroic glory even in death. But while the conceit is conventional enough, it infiltrates the Eighth Book so pervasively that there must be something else at stake.

In the preface to the Eighth Book, Monteverdi explicitly linked the 'war' imagery with his reinvention of the *concitato genere*, the 'aroused' style associated with 'that *harmonia* that would fittingly imitate the utterance and the accents of a brave man who is engaged in warfare' (Plato, *Republic*, 399a) to complement the 'soft' and 'temperate' styles (*molle*, *temperato*) that, the composer said, were already in common use.[13] He linked it explicitly (following Plato) to poetic metre – the pyrrhic – which could be recreated in music by taking a long note (a semibreve; as it were, [part of] a spondee) and dividing it into sixteen repeated semiquavers. However, the *concitato genere* is also generally taken to include other 'martial' musical devices evoking the sounds of battle such as fanfares and running scales, often in G major. Monteverdi had used such patterns in earlier works to represent anger (as in parts of the *Lamento d'Arianna*), but in pieces such as the *Combattimento di Tancredi e Clorinda* or the *concitato* moments of 'Or che 'l ciel e la terra e 'l vento tace' it becomes elevated to a theoretical principle. Monteverdi uses it to claim originality and precedence (given that, he says, others have now adopted the style),[14] to bolster his search for musical means to imitate the gamut of human passions, and to provide works suited for 'the music of great princes [which] is used in their royal chambers in three ways to suit their delicate tastes: in the theatre, in the chamber, and for dancing'.

The 'great princes' for whom much of the Eighth Book appears designed are, of course, the Habsburgs. The textual references are obvious enough in 'Altri canti d'Amor, tenero arciero' ('o gran Fernando'), 'Ogni amante è guerrier: nel suo gran regno' ('l'Istro real' and 'o gran Fernando Ernesto', i.e., the Danube and Ferdinand III), the *ballo* 'Volgendo il ciel per l'immortal sentiero – Movete al mio bel suon le piante snelle' (the Danube, the Spanish Ebro, and 'l'opre di Ferdinando eccelse e belle'), and the *Ballo delle ingrate*. These references involved changes to the original texts (Rinuccini designed both 'Ogni amante è guerrier' and 'Volgendo il ciel' in honour of Henry IV of France) and their musical settings. For the latter, a case in point is the *Ballo delle ingrate*, originally written for Mantua, which in addition to the textual changes appears to contain revised music (for example, the central episode for Plutone seems more modern than would have been possible in 1608).

The reference in the revised *Ballo delle ingrate* to 'il Re *novo* del romano impero' would seem to associate the piece with Ferdinand II's son, Ferdinand III, newly elected and crowned as King of the Romans in December 1636, therefore ensuring his succession to the title of Holy Roman Emperor (which occurred on Ferdinand II's death on 15 February 1637). The other *ballo*, 'Volgendo il ciel', might also relate to the same occasion, although its references are more generic and so could date from any time when one or other Ferdinand was achieving 'noble and fair deeds'. Attempts to identify precise performances of these two *balli* have failed, although 1636 seems to have been a further key date in Monteverdi's Habsburg relations given that he appears to have sent a good deal of music to Vienna in that year, either on request or just in the hope of taking advantage of the coronation.[15]

However, Monteverdi's presentation volume for the Habsburgs did not just contain music adapted for their use: its very design now appears quite carefully crafted to suit an Austrian court with a Gonzaga empress. The martial imagery clearly refers to the Habsburgs' own activity on the battlefield: the Thirty Years' War (1618–48), one of the bloodiest in European history, seemed (wrongly) to have reached its end with the Peace of Prague (ratified on 15 June 1635) and then Ferdinand III's election and succession.[16] This presumably explains the evident triumphalism through the book, plus the notion that glorious military victories have now yielded to leisure and more amorous pursuits. But there is another play here as well. The pendant sonnets that open the *canti guerrieri* and *canti amorosi*, the anonymous 'Altri canti d'Amor, tenero arciero' and Marino's 'Altri canti di Marte e di sua schiera', juggle with a motto that had started life in Ovid's *Heroides*, 13.84, as Laodamia begs Protesilaus 'Bella gerant alii, Protesilaus amet' (Let others wage war, may Protesilaus fall in love). The hemistich *Bella gerant alii* was adopted from the 1560s as the motto of Cardinal Francesco Gonzaga (1538–66, appointed cardinal in 1561), cousin of Duke Guglielmo, and appears gradually to have moved into Habsburg circles in the first half of the seventeenth century as Gonzaga–Habsburg ties became strengthened, particularly after the arrival in Vienna of Eleanora Gonzaga. By 1654, the Savoyard academician Emanuele Tesauro (in his *Il cannocchiale aristotelico*) could associate Cardinal Francesco's device with a specifically Habsburg, and 'famous', extension: *Bella gerant alii, tu felix Austria nube* (Let others wage wars, you, happy Austria, marry). Better known from the eighteenth century as a motto regularly associated with Habsburg epithalamia and panegyrics, by the second half of the nineteenth century it was widely adopted by historians as somehow emblematic of Habsburg policies of expanding territories and spheres of influence through dynastic marriages rather than on the battlefield.[17] Monteverdi quite literally composes it into his collection.

Stylistic problems

The Eighth Book is so *sui generis* that it is not surprising that it was never reprinted; it was also expensive to buy, and hard to manage in terms of its layout and performance resources (left-over copies were still on sale in 1662).[18] Scholars have also had difficulties getting to grips with it in stylistic terms, a problem that applies as well to the much more neglected (though more often reprinted) Seventh Book. We can appreciate the Petrarchan grandeur of 'Or che 'l ciel e la terra e 'l vento tace', or the Gabrieli-like play of sonorities pitting vocal group against group, and instruments against voices, in 'A quest'olmo, a quest'ombre et a quest'onde' (Seventh Book); we can be thrilled by the erotic rub of dissonance in duets such as 'Interrotte speranze, eterna fede' (Seventh) and 'Ardo e scoprir, ahi lasso, io non ardisco' (Eighth); we can even weep at the fate of a lovelorn lamenting nymph, although it is not clear that we should. Yet the *concitato genere* in the Eighth Book, while impressive (in the *Combattimento*), quickly turns into a mannerism (in 'Ardo, avvampo, mi struggo, ardo: accorrete') unless it can be taken with a pinch of comic salt (as in 'Gira il nemico insidioso Amore'). Here and elsewhere, Monteverdi seems just to be playing with empty madrigalisms: conventional word-painting devices extending back into the sixteenth century albeit with a few modern twists. This is not quite the serious literary purpose that we have come to expect of the founder of the text-expressive *seconda pratica*.

Of course, we should not blame Monteverdi for failing to meet our own anachronistic expectations. Yet he, too, seems to have been caught in a bind by stylistic developments in contemporary vocal music. Giulio Caccini's epochal collection of songs for solo voice and basso continuo issued as *Le nuove musiche* (1602) created a set of problems for more serious composers wedded to older styles and genres. Monteverdi achieved his own compromise between the five-voice madrigal and the new continuo styles in the last six madrigals of the Fifth Book; he took a step backwards in the more conservative (for the most part) Sixth Book; and then surrendered in the Seventh which, as many have noted, contains pieces for one to four and six voices, but not the canonic five save for the final *ballo* (*Tirsi e Clori*). He also avoids five-part writing in the Eighth Book save for the two 'alla francese' pieces in the *canti amorosi*, 'Dolcissimo uscignolo' and 'Chi vol aver felice e lieto il core' (and again in the *ballo* 'Movete al mio bel suon le piante snelle'). But while six or more parts become Monteverdi's texture of choice for grandiloquence, he seems unwilling to write just for solo voice and continuo save when in operatic vein. He can, of course, do it well enough: 'Ohimé ch'io cado, ohimé' (Milanuzzi, 1624) and 'Quel sguardo sdegnosetto' (1632 *Scherzi musicali*), strophic-bass cantatas in the manner of his Venetian colleagues such as Alessandro Grandi, are real gems. But when it comes to texts requiring a bit more expressive punch, Monteverdi, like some other of his contemporaries, seems to have decided that the duet for equal voices and continuo (two sopranos or, more often, two tenors) permitted the declamatory flexibility of the solo song while also allowing for expressive dissonance and, should the text call for it, a measure of contrapuntal display.[19]

The chief advantages of the continuo madrigal were that individual voices could emerge from the texture for the sake of musical or dramatic characterisation, and that the voices did not have to sing continuously to maintain the musical momentum. The chief disadvantage was a tendency for the musical argument to fragment into short-breathed phrases that, failing long-range harmonic planning, would appear merely successive rather than processive. The specific technique of the sixteenth-century madrigalist to maintain continuity across phrases, by setting up but then 'avoiding' musical cadences (*fuggire la cadenza*), was directly related to the textural need to keep in motion at least one voice, and often more, so as to elide between sections. However, with that constraint removed by virtue of the instrumental accompaniment, cadences were more often emphasised than avoided. The resulting stop–start tendencies could be lessened by virtue of harmonic variety and by carefully building melodic climaxes over stretches longer than the two-bar phrase. Monteverdi gets to the point where he can do it very well indeed – especially when he builds progressions on scale degrees (tonic, subdominant, supertonic, dominant) in ways that tend toward functional tonality – although he seems to be struggling in some of the Seventh Book duets that perhaps are earlier in composition than their counterparts ('O viva fiamma, o miei sospiri ardenti' and 'Ah che non si conviene' are potential examples).

This tendency to fragmentation could also be countered by a more formalist approach to text-setting, or by the choice of texts that were themselves formal in construction. Of the twenty-nine settings in the Seventh Book, no fewer than seven are sonnets, one is an *ottava rima* stanza ('Ohimè, dov'è il mio ben, dov'è il mio core?', with eight hendecasyllabic lines rhyming ABABABCC), and three have strophic texts (two canzonettas and the *ballo*). Of the seventeen poetic madrigals, two ('Vaga su spina ascosa' and 'Soave libertate', both by Chiabrera) are entirely in seven-syllable rhyming couplets and could almost be canzonettas, and a third ('Non è di gentil core') is manipulated by Monteverdi so that the first two lines return at the end to round off the setting.[20] Seven-syllable rhyming couplets also appear, somewhat unusually, in the *partenza amorosa*, 'Se pur destina e vole' (however, the *lettera amorosa*, 'Se i languidi miei sguardi', is more typically in *versi sciolti*). Formal texts do not necessarily create formal music – indeed, some of the sonnets are set in ways that seem emphatically to make them not-sonnets (something similar occurs in the setting of Petrarch's 'Vago augelletto, che cantando vai' in the Eighth Book, with its refrains) – although Monteverdi makes full use where appropriate of the standard techniques of strophic-bass variation, partitioning the poetry into sections each of which have the same instrumental bass line but vary the melody on top: this is clear in 'Tempro la cetra, e per cantar gli honori' (two quatrains and two tercets) and also in 'Ohimè, dov'è il mio ben, dov'è il mio core?', where the eight lines of the *ottava rima* stanza are presented (as is conventional) two by two, with each two-line section set to the standard bass pattern known as the *romanesca* above which the voices weave fantastic variations.

In these cases, the use of repeating bass lines is determined by an association between earlier improvisatory practices linked to specific poetic forms (*arie da cantar sonetti, arie da cantar ottave rime*, etc.): the technique also had its influence on operatic prologues (as to *Orfeo*; and 'Tempro la cetra' is of the type, if not the form). Other poetic forms that would generally involve some manner of repetition are strophic canzonettas, where the music for each stanza of the text would be the same ('Non partir ritrosetta' and 'Su, su, su, pastorelli vezzosi' in the Eighth Book), or similar ('Chiome d'oro' and 'Amor, che deggio far?' in the Seventh). In early seventeenth-century technical terms, such a piece would be called an 'aria', which denotes a form (strophic repetition, with or without variation) rather than a style (arias may be in a recitative-like idiom or a more tuneful one). The tuneful type of aria, which may be in duple or triple time, will tend to have more strongly shaped melodies and goal-directed harmonic motion, the latter often created by other types of repetitive bass patterns. Triple-time arias will often be dance-like in style and even function (as in *Tirsi e Clori*). Given that most duple-time dances were slow, the tuneful type of aria in duple time had to rely on other means of generating melodic/harmonic momentum by way of phrases with a strong rhythmic drive and symmetrical and/or repetitive structures (this is what Monteverdi may have meant by the 'canto alla francese').

Already in *Orfeo*, Monteverdi had used the 'walking' bass line moving in regular rhythms to create musical propulsion through each stanza of a strophic aria, as in Orfeo's 'Qual onor di te fia degno', sung as he leads Euridice from Hades in Act IV. The technique appears again in the duple-time *scherzi musicali*, and then in 'Chiome d'oro' and 'Amor che deggio far?' Such walking basses will tend to articulate cadential patterns on one or more degrees of the scale and therefore will be, or at least seem, repetitive within themselves. In 'Chiome d'oro', a bass line moving relentlessly in crotchets and similar to the one of 'Qual onor di te fia degno' (and also heard elsewhere in the opera, at 'Dunque fa degno Orfeo' in Act II), underpins both the instrumental ritornellos (three variations over the same four-bar cadential bass pattern) and the vocal stanzas. Such 'walking' and similar basses could also be used outside formal arias as a means of musical propulsion on the one hand, and unity on the other. Monteverdi had already demonstrated the technique in 'Laetatus sum' in the 1610 Vespers, where the setting of a long text is held together by the recurrences of such a bass line, and the bass patterns of 'Chiome d'oro', and also its ritornello, appear in the six-voice setting of 'Beatus vir' (plus two violins and optional trombones) in the *Selva morale e spirituale*. Other pieces in the Seventh Book such as 'Io son pur vezzosetta', 'Soave libertate', and 'Vaga su spina ascosa', although madrigals, are not so different in feel.

It is a moot point whether 'Chiome d'oro' and other pieces of its type are set to a 'ground bass', strictly speaking: its repeated units are too short and irregularly sequenced. Other cases are more straightforward, how-ever. In the duet 'Zefiro torna, e di soavi accenti' (in the 1632 *Scherzi musicali* and in the Ninth Book), Monteverdi takes a syncopated triple-time harmonic sequence from contemporary dance music, the *ciaccona*, and strictly repeats it fifty-six times, while the voices sing of the delights of spring that will, toward the end of the setting (shifting into dolorous recitative) be contrasted with the grieving state of the lover, who then alternates weeping with singing. The virtuosity here lies in just how many different melodic patterns – and word-painting devices – Monteverdi can weave over a simple two-bar cadence formula.[21] Another example is the *Lamento della ninfa*, with its central section set over thirty-four repeti-tions of a bass line descending from tonic to dominant through the melodic minor scale. This descending tetrachord appears elsewhere in Monteverdi (and in the music of his contemporaries) and has been called an 'emblem of lament', although we shall see (in the 'Intermedio', below) that there are other possible readings.

Here, structural musical devices (a ground bass) would seem to assume an expressive, or at least semiotic, purpose. This, in turn, would suggest that recent appraisals of the formalism of Monteverdi's Venetian secular music need to move beyond a simple triumphalist rhetoric (music becomes music rather than some spurious form of speech) or a pejorative one (the composer is forced into formalist games by the aridity of Marinist poetry). But it is also a result of the fundamental stylistic problem facing Monteverdi's version of the 'new music'. While the duet texture is significantly richer than a monody, it is still fairly limited in terms of what one can do with the voices: the basic choice is between homophony on the one hand, and counterpoint on the other. In the setting of Guarini's sonnet 'Interrotte speranze, eterna fede' (Seventh Book), the two tenors start on a unison then move a third apart and move predominantly in thirds to the cadence at the end of the first quatrain. The music for the second quatrain repeats that of the first. The homophony continues through the first tercet (which ends with the same cadence as the first and second quatrains), and breaks only at the start of the second (at 'Questi ch'a voi quasi gran fascio invio'), which marks the beginning of the main clause of Guarini's text: the interrupted hopes, eternal faith, the flames of a tormented heart – the lover bundles all these together and sends them to his beloved as a bouquet of 'harsh, fierce torments' that 'will be your trophies, and my pyre'. The change of texture at 'Questi' (the first tenor alone) makes a rhetorical point and serves to clarify the overall syntax,[22] but it also marks the release of pent-up frustration: the second tenor bursts in far too soon with 'donna crudel' from the next line of the poem. The voices then move to imitation for the final line, both to mark the point of the text and to emphasise its unending pain.

This is all well and good with the right text, but it can easily become formulaic, and at times one can sense Monteverdi chafing at the bit. In the duet 'Non vedrò mai le stelle' (Seventh Book), Monteverdi sets an anonymous poem where the lover says that he will never see the stars without recalling the eyes of his unyielding beloved, and without asking them (the stars) why they should reflect such beauty of one who betrays his faith ('O luci belle / deh siate sì rubelle / di lume a chi ribella è sì di fede ...'). The trope is familiar from 'Sfogava con le stelle' in the Fourth Book and appears elsewhere in the Seventh (for example, 'Al lume delle stelle'): an opening factual statement (by the lover or a narrator) leads to an 'I say' (or 'he said'), an exclaimed vocative ('O') and some kind of imperative (stars, make her pity me) or question (stars, why does she not pity me?).[23] In 'Sfogava con le stelle', the 'O'-moment prompted a shift from the predominantly homophonic opening to glorious double counterpoint with the five voices extending across their full range. Monteverdi achieves a similar effect in 'Non vedrò mai le stelle' within the more limited means of the duet: the opening moves largely in homophony (shifting to counterpoint for the 'harsh cause of my torments'), but after 'I say', the 'O' is set for a solo tenor in a luxuriously expansive line over four bars before resuming the text ('o luci belle, / deh siate sì rubelle'). The first tenor then comes back to those 'luci belle' – the focus of his obsession – now echoed by the second tenor leading to a cadence that makes no syntactic sense whatsoever. What follows, however, is even more extraordinary, as the music shifts to triple time ('o luci belle, / deh siate sì rubelle ...') for thirty-eight bars where the text is mangled beyond recognition as the singers, and Monteverdi, revel in glorious lyric expression until they rein themselves in, returning to duple time for the last two lines of the poem.

We can argue over whether Monteverdi does this because the poetry is clumsy ('belle ... rubelle ... ribella') and syntactically obscure, or whether he has just been inspired by the heat of the rhetorical moment. The latter seems more than just wishful thinking, given that he repeats the trick in later settings both secular and sacred. The result is even more effective in the duet 'O sia tranquillo il mare, o pien d'orgoglio' (Eighth Book, and seemingly popular enough to be repeated in the Ninth), where in a much better sonnet the lover sits on the cliff top awaiting his beloved until he realises that she will not return ('Ma, tu non torni'), that the air scatters his lament, and that he is foolish to entrust his heart to a women and his prayers to the winds. The lyrical triple-time at 'Ma, tu non torni' (fifty-eight glorious bars for the two tenors) again far exceeds its textual bounds but gives the moment a remarkable rhetorical intensity as the 'lament' of the lover takes song.

Songs and singers

One lover, two lovers, or all lovers? The advantage of monody was that it fostered an identity of singer and character, be that character specific (Arianna, say) or generic. Any more than one voice threatened this illusion of verisimilitude. The sixteenth-century polyphonic madrigal had long taken this 'problem' in its stride (witness all those Dido laments set for five voices), but with the advent of opera and of the *stile rappresentativo*, it could no longer be ignored. Monteverdi certainly writes 'representative' pieces where singers present characters: the term is used for the central section of the *Lamento della ninfa* and the *Ballo delle ingrate*, and it applies to all the (semi-)theatrical pieces in Monteverdi's Venetian publications (*Tirsi e Clori* in the Seventh Book, the *Combattimento di Tancredi e Clorinda* in the Eighth). It also applies to those pieces that present literally a single 'speaking' voice: in the Seventh Book, 'Tempro la cetra', and the *lettera amorosa* and *partenza amorosa*, all three in the male poetic voice (although the *lettera amorosa* is written for soprano);[24] and in the Eighth, the 'Poeta' who delivers the prologue to the *ballo* 'Movete al mio bel suon le piante snelle'. Yet when two, three, or more voices 'speak' for one, the rules of the game must shift significantly, and even more when issues of gender come into play. In *Tirsi e Clori*, Monteverdi adheres to gendered norms: the shepherd Tirsi sings in a rambunctious triple time, while Clori has seductive recitative. The case of 'Eccomi pronta ai baci' (Seventh Book), however, is less straightforward.

The text has a woman addressing her lover, Ergasto ('Here am I ready to be kissed . . . but don't bite me'), and Monteverdi's male-voice setting (TTB) can only be read as bar-room bragging, voyeuristic fantasy, or comic parody, unless we just accept that voices and voice-types matter not one whit, at least in certain types of settings.[25]

Much hinges on the nature of poetic, in particular lyric, expression and the subjectivities involved therein. Texts that are diegetic (in Plato's sense of the term) – i.e., predominantly narrative – locate as subject either the author, or in more convenient post-structuralist terms, the text (which narrates itself). While the text might be given an individualised voice (say, as Testo in the *Combattimento*), its rendering by a plurality does not threaten verisimilitude to the same degree as in mimetic texts, which imitate one or more subjects seemingly independent of the author, or of the text (as Plato has Socrates say, when Homer 'tries as far as may be to make us feel that not Homer is the speaker'). Poems referring predominantly to third-person pronouns (he, she, it) will more easily be assimilated to the diegetic than those using the first-person, at least if 'I' is to be distinguished from 'we'. 'You'-poems (e.g., addressing a beloved) occupy a middle ground depending on whether the actual or implied 'I' (voicing the vocative) is strong or weak. Monteverdi plays with these modalities in quite intriguing ways.[26]

In the four-voice 'Tu dormi, ahi crudo core' (Seventh Book), the upper three voices (SAT) present the accusation against the beloved ('Do you sleep, o cruel heart?'). When the first-person pronoun first appears ('Io piango . . .', 'I weep'), the fourth voice (B) enters with a chromatic point of imitation then followed by the other parts. Individuating the bass voice in some way to articulate the poetic 'I' is not unusual, even in sixteenth-century polyphonic madrigals, and Monteverdi does it again in the Seventh Book in 'Parlo miser o taccio' ('S'*io* taccio . . .'), and 'Augellin che la voce al canto spieghi' ('Per pietà del *mio* duolo'), and in the Eighth, including 'Or che 'l ciel e la terra e 'l vento tace' ('Guerra è il *mio* stato') and 'Ogni amante è guerrier, nel suo gran regno' (the long central solo episode at '*Io* che nell'otio nacqui e d'otio vissi'). In the case of the duets, on the other hand, 'I'-moments can be marked out by a shift just to one voice, or indeed by having the voices move so closely together that they sound almost as one.

However, of all the potential 'I's being presented here – the poet, the composer, the fictive lover, the text – one tends to be forgotten: the performer. The changes prompted by the new music in early seventeenth-century Italy were not just stylistic but also to do with the performance practices of virtuoso singers and instrumentalists. It is surely no coincidence that so much of the Seventh and Eighth Books seems quite literally to be about voice. In one of the strangest pieces of the Seventh Book (indeed, perhaps of Monteverdi's entire secular output), 'Con che soavità labbra odorate' for solo soprano and nine instruments,[27] the poet enjoys both kissing his beloved's lips and listening to what emerges from them, but he cannot do both at the same time: what sweet harmony it would be if words could kiss and kisses speak. Monteverdi's point is, of course, that this impossibility can be achieved through the singing voice and its instrumental accompaniment, and the harmony he produces is sweet indeed. This preoccupation with (vocal) sound and its expressive capabilities extends through those settings that play on the singing of birds reflecting, or contrasting with, the condition of the lover's heart: 'O come sei gentile / caro augellino . . .' and 'Augellin che la voce al canto spieghi' in the Seventh Book, and 'Vago augelletto che cantando vai' and 'Dolcissimo uscignolo' in the Eighth. Guarini's poem 'O come sei gentile', for example, is riddled with references to song – both the bird's and the lover's – that prompt Monteverdi to write florid embellishments in the manner of the more elaborate duets in *Orfeo* (compare Apollo and Orfeo at the end of Act V) or the 1610 Vespers. Other, newer signs for 'singing' are tuneful triple times, as in 'Zefiro torna, e di soavi accenti' (Now I weep, now I sing). Indeed, one setting in the Eighth Book is quite literally about the performing voice: in 'Mentre vaga Angioletta' (again by Guarini), the poet describes the effect of hearing a virtuoso soprano, such that his heart matches her flourishes, roulades, accents and turns, and then, oh miracle of love, soars like a nightingale. Monteverdi begins his narrative with an unaccompanied solo tenor, but as the heart takes on the spirit of music ('Musico spirto prende'), the continuo enters, and then as Angioletta awakes the heart to a garrulous, masterful harmony ('garula e maestrevol armonia'), so does a second tenor. This leads to a compendium of all the tricks of the singer's trade – redoubled, as it were, by the two tenors – piling on the vocal fireworks until the poet's heart takes ecstatic flight on wings of song in an extended triple-time peroration.

'Mentre vaga angioletta' is usually read as an account of contemporary vocal technique, but it is, rather, one of the effect of singing and of song: the subject is not Angioletta's voice, but the heart and soul's response to it.[28] The result may seem self-conscious, but it is also extraordinarily powerful. Monteverdi's Venetian secular music is difficult to locate in terms of chronology, environment and function. It is also stylistically inconsistent and even at times troublesome in its mixtures of old and new, and of the conventional and the inspired. But what rings, and sings, throughout is the excitement of discovery at just what the human voice can do. Here, at least, Monteverdi constantly surprises us at every turn. He may even have surprised himself.

INTERMEDIO IV

Lamento della ninfa (1638)

TIM CARTER

The *Lamento della ninfa*, included by Monteverdi in his Eighth Book of Madrigals, the *Madrigali guerrieri, et amorosi* (1638), has been a focus of hot debate over aesthetic and expressive issues in the composer's Venetian secular music. It was identified by Ellen Rosand in 1979 as a prototypical example of a ground-bass pattern moving from tonic to dominant through a descending minor tetrachord – the so-called 'emblem of lament' that then, in diatonic or chromatic form, and with or without a cadential extension, permeated Baroque music, via Purcell's *Dido and Aeneas* (Dido's concluding 'When I am laid in earth') to the Crucifixus of Bach's B minor Mass, even extending into the Classical period and beyond (the opening of Mozart's D minor string quartet, K. 421). In 1987, Gary Tomlinson sought to reconcile his disparaging view of Monteverdi's apparent decline from Renaissance subtlety into Baroque sterility with his undoubted sense of the power of this 'through-composed dramatic *scena*': the *Lamento della ninfa* is 'a brilliant anomaly' – 'In it, from the foundation of Marinism, with materials touched by memories of lighter styles, Monteverdi erected an enduring monument to the Petrarchism of his youth.' In 1991, Susan McClary picked up on Tomlinson's notion of it being a 'dramatic *scena*' and explored the piece as a prototypical (again) mad-scene, worthy of comparison with Donizetti's *Lucia di Lammermoor*, Richard Strauss's *Salome*, and Schoenberg's *Erwartung*. More recently, the debate has hinged on how Monteverdi's use here of a triple-time aria style (if it is) signifies a shift of emphasis from recitative to aria as the prime form of musical expression – clearly significant for what would emerge in later Baroque opera and cantata – and even from a 'second practice' to a 'third'.[1]

Certainly, the *Lamento della ninfa* is a very odd piece. The text is a relatively straightforward canzonetta by Ottavio Rinuccini that must have been written before its first musical setting appeared in print, a solo song by Antonio Brunelli published in 1614. Brunelli's monody, plus a duet by Johann Hieronymus Kapsberger (1619) and an anonymous solo voice setting in a Florentine manuscript, treat the text fairly straightforwardly. Rinuccini's poem is in ten stanzas, each ending with the same two-line refrain:

Non havea Febo ancora	Phoebus had not yet
recato al mondo il dì,	brought the day to the earth,
ch'una donzella fuora	when a maiden out of
del proprio albergo uscì.	her own house appeared.
Miserella, ahi più, no, no,	*Wretched girl, ah, no, no more*
tanto giel soffrir non può.	*can she suffer such coldness.*

These three settings treat the poem strophically, with the same music for each subsequent stanza. A fourth setting, for solo voice by Giovanni Battista Piazza (1631), takes an altered version of just the first stanza and turns it into a tripartite structure: a regular duple time for 'Phoebus had not yet / brought the day to the earth / when a maiden out of / her own house appeared', then a brief recitative-like 'She said, grieving and sad', and a concluding section in triple time: 'Wretched girl, what shall I do? / I will not suffer such grief' ('Misera, che farò / tanto duol non soffrirò').[2]

Piazza is the first to articulate different voices in the text, however briefly, in keeping with trends in the 1630s: to do so, he needed to change the words. Brunelli's setting is for tenor, as is the anonymous one, whereas Kapsberger's is for two sopranos, and Piazza's for solo soprano. The apparent choice of gender may or may not be significant (soprano parts may, of course, be for castratos) given that Rinuccini's canzonetta is in a single poetic voice, a narrator whose gender appears fairly irrelevant. After the opening narration to set the scene (three stanzas), the poetic 'I' reports the words of the nymph but remains resolutely detached from them:

'Amor,' diceva e 'l piè	'Love,' she said and stopped
mirando il ciel fermò,	her foot, gazing at the sky,
'dove, dove la fe	'where, where is the faith
che 'l traditor giurò?'	that the traitor swore?'
Miserella, ahi più, no, no,	*Wretched girl, ah, no, no more*
tanto giel soffrir non può.	*can she suffer such coldness.*

Piazza, however, separates the narrator from the nymph by altering the refrain: 'She said . . . "Wretched girl, what shall I do?"' Monteverdi followed the hint by giving the opening narrative to two tenors and a bass (stanzas 1–3, each minus the refrain), and the central lament (stanzas 4–9) to a solo soprano with the lower voices using the refrain to 'comment' on the scene and even to offer the nymph their sympathy, and then the final stanza again just for the trio to present the lesson: 'Thus in lovers' hearts, / Love mixes fire and ice.' His delaying of the refrain to the central lament makes a certain sense, allowing the trio to respond realistically to a particular situation rather

than setting the wretched 'donzella' up for a fall right from the start. This
lament is over the descending tetrachord ground bass; the first and final
sections are further marked for separation by being in C major rather than
the central section's A minor.

Giving a separate voice to the nymph locates this piece within the *stile
rappresentativo* – in which the singer takes on a separate, identified persona –
and Monteverdi uses the label 'Rapresentativo' for the central section,
although not, significantly, for the framing stanzas for the two tenors and
bass who remain characterless (albeit now more strongly gendered male, one
assumes). He also directs this central section to be sung 'in time to the
emotion of the soul and not to that of the beat' (*a tempo dell'affetto
dell'animo e non a quello della mano*), whereas the narrative frame is to be
performed in a more regular manner. The notion of a flexible tempo is
somewhat at odds with the triple metre of the lament and also, of course,
with the relentless repetition of the ground bass (thirty-four statements). But
some generic confusion ensues. Canzonetta texts were normally set as arias
in the early seventeenth-century sense of repetitively strophic settings of
strophic poetry (hence Brunelli's and Kapsberger's). Such arias might be
set in a declamatory recitative-like style, or more often in a more tuneful one
(in a regular triple or duple metre). Yet Monteverdi's *Lamento della ninfa* is
in effect through-composed (although there is repetition in the ground
bass), and its central triple time, while seemingly regular in metrical terms,
is meant to be sung freely.

There is no doubt that the central section is a *lamento* or a *pianto* (so
Monteverdi variously calls it). It is not in the grand manner of laments for
noblewomen, which conventionally remained in impassioned recitative
(Arianna, Penelope, Ottavia), but then, a nymph is a lowlier character for
whom singing – rather than musical 'speaking' – was a more feasible
mode of self-representation, at least in early Baroque opera. But like
Arianna, at least (and also Monteverdi's *Orfeo*, if we treat his opera as
adhering to the Aristotelian unity of time), our nymph laments at the
right time of day (just before dawn), and also in the right place (outdoors).[3] The music itself is less clearly marked, despite the apparent
emblematic significance of the descending tetrachord ground bass. Such
bass lines (whether or not as a ground) are also found in this period in
what are, strictly speaking, non-lamenting contexts: Monteverdi uses
them (with the diatonic tetrachord in D minor) to represent love's
'sweet delights and sighed-for kisses' ('i dolci vezzi, e sospirati baci') in
the madrigal 'Altri canti d'Amor, tenero arciero' at the beginning of his
Eighth Book; the major descending tetrachord appears in the bass lines
of love duets in *L'incoronazione di Poppea*; and the minor descending
tetrachord underpins the final love duet in Cavalli's *La Calisto* (1651).

Similarly, Purcell's G minor version of the trope is anticipated by Hecuba's despairing invocation of the Underworld spirits in Act I, scene 6 of Cavalli's *La Didone* (1641). It may be but a short step from love, or invocation, to lament, but the comparisons suggest that, like most conventional signs, this one can be somewhat slippery, with its meaning needing to be fixed by way of contextual determinants.

So what contextual determinants exist for the *Lamento della ninfa*? The prior settings of the text do not help very much, given their consistency of narrating voice (even in the Piazza, for all the change of rhetorical register). In Monteverdi's Eighth Book, this is one of the *madrigali amorosi*, situated between the five-voice setting of Guarini's 'Chi vol aver felice e lieto il core' (Whoever wishes to have a happy, joyful heart should not follow cruel Love, that flatterer who kills the more he jokes and laughs) and the trio (ATB) 'Perché te 'n fuggi, o Fillide' (Why, o Fillide, do you flee? Alas, ah, Filli, listen to me, turn your beautiful eyes toward me . . . I am Aminta). Does our nymph exemplify the moral of Guarini's cynical warning against the flames of love, or is she the Fillide whose heart colder than ice cannot be moved by a newly (perhaps always) faithful Aminta? Looking not so further afield, is she the 'Ninfa che scalza il piede e sciolta il crine' extolled by two tenors and a bass – the nymph who, barefoot and with hair loosened, has set grief aside to go singing and dancing in the meadow but is pursued by Lillo who would accompany her with his lyre if only she would pause – or is she the pretty girl whom another, evidently humorous if not bawdy, male trio (ATB), in 'Non partir ritrosetta', urges not to flee so that she might herself hear a lament that is, to judge by its music, clearly parodic.[4] Will our nymph eventually find her Aminta, Lillo, or three dirty old men expending their sighs in erotic wishful thinking, or will she become an ingrate condemned to eternal punishment for her refusal any more to yield to love? Is hers the only serious piece in the somewhat tongue-in-cheek *madrigali amorosi* or is she herself a parody of the abandoned woman, a humorous counterpart to Arianna or Penelope who attracts male sympathy only with a knowing nudge here and a wink there?

Monteverdi forces these questions precisely because he has given the nymph a voice rather than hiding her behind a narrative screen. Performers must select from multiple options: she can be deranged, angry, bitter, piteous, jealous, cynical, regretful, wistful, proud, or even self-deprecating – there is more than one 'affetto dell'animo' here, any or all of which are probably better than her just being bound by convention to sing and then, so Rinuccini's text has it, fall silent. Listeners, too, cannot avoid decisions: are we moved, amused, or simply detached observers presented with an object lesson in love? Perhaps we should just be glad that we have the choice.

11 The Venetian sacred music

JOHN WHENHAM

Monteverdi's appointment in 1613 as *maestro di cappella* of S. Marco, Venice, brought him financial security in a post that also allowed him a good deal of freedom to accept commissions elsewhere, both in and outside the city. His initial salary of three hundred ducats was raised by the Procurators of S. Marco to four hundred in August 1616,[1] making him, in his own words

> certainly not rich, but neither am I poor; moreover, I lead a life with a certain security of income until my death, and furthermore I am absolutely sure of always having it on the appointed pay-days, which come every two months without fail. Indeed, if it is the least bit late, they send it to my house [in the chancellery of S. Marco]. Then as regards the *cappella* I do as I wish, since there is the assistant choirmaster ... and there is no obligation to teach.   (Letter of 10 September 1627 to Alessandro Striggio)

Monteverdi's reference here to his assistant choirmaster is a reminder that he was not alone in shouldering the responsibilities of providing music for S. Marco. He inherited, and was later able to appoint, assistants who were not only performers, but also able composers of sacred music – Marc'Antonio Negri (singer and assistant choirmaster from 1612), Alessandro Grandi (singer from 1617, assistant choirmaster from 1620) and Giovanni Rovetta (singer from 1623, assistant choirmaster from 1627). Moreover, S. Marco employed two organists, among whom, again, were able composers – Giovanni Battista Grillo (first organist from 1619), Carlo Fillago (first organist from 1623 to his death in 1644), Francesco Cavalli (singer from 1616, second organist from 1639). Like Monteverdi, their work was not confined to S. Marco. Cavalli had been organist of the great Dominican church of SS Giovanni e Paolo (Fig. 11.2) from 1620 to 1630 and Fillago was organist there from 1631 to 1644, concurrently with his work at S. Marco; Grillo was also organist of the Scuola Grande of San Rocco from 1612 until his death in 1622.[2] During the last decade of Monteverdi's life Rovetta seems to have shouldered some of the responsibilities that might otherwise have fallen to the older composer: he was in charge of the musicians who sang at the installation of Cardinal Cornaro as Patriarch of Venice in 1632, and of the music performed at S. Giorgio Maggiore in 1638 to celebrate the birth of the future Louis XIV of France; his *Messa e salmi*, Op. 4 (1639) includes the Mass sung for this occasion, an early example of a Mass published without Sanctus or Agnus Dei. It had earlier been the custom in Venice to sing Masses with shortened settings of the last two movements.[3]

Motets, Salve Regina settings, the Litany

Before Monteverdi himself saw any of his Venetian church music into print some twenty works by him were published in anthologies issued in Austria and Italy, and more were issued after his death. These works, published between 1615 and 1651, form a rich and substantial body of music too little explored by modern performers, and include almost equal numbers of settings for one, two, and four to six voices respectively. They are mainly motets – settings of texts that were not part of the fixed liturgy of the Church – which were generally sung at Venice during the Offertory and the Elevation of the Host at Mass, and between psalms at Vespers.[4] Motets were specifically called for on the doge's *andata* to the Church of the Redentore on the Giudecca (third Sunday in July), when Low Mass was said by the Prior of the Church's Capuchin community with motets sung at the Offertory and Elevation by singers of S. Marco,[5] and it was motets, as well as 'a certain cantata in praise of the doge' (words and music now lost) that were sung for the annual wedding of Venice to the sea on Ascension Day, when the choir of the Patriarch of Venice, on board the patriarch's *peota*, and the choir of S. Marco, on board the state barge, the Bucintoro, sang music in turn.[6]

Some of Monteverdi's motet texts draw freely on psalms, the Song of Songs and other parts of the Bible; other sources include Books of Hours, and even the liturgy itself – 'O beatae viae' (1621[4]) is proper to the Feast of S. Rocco (16 August) and 'Exulta filia Sion' (1629[5]) arranged from the Communion for the Mass at Dawn on Christmas Day. The solo motet 'Ecce sacrum paratum convivium' (1625[2]) is very unusual: it mixes images of the celebration of Mass with the Last Supper, conceived as a Roman feast with guests reclining on couches at table. The exquisite duet 'Sancta Maria, succurre miseris' (1618), which employs the same plainsong as the 1610 'Sonata sopra "Sancta Maria"', draws its text from the Magnificat antiphon at first Vespers on the Commemoration of the Blessed Virgin of Mount Carmel (16 July) in the Roman rite, and it may indeed have been one of the works that Monteverdi performed when he celebrated this feast at the Carmelite Church in Venice in 1627 (see letter of 24 July 1627). (I have not traced the text in the rite of S. Marco.) The

Ex. 11.1 'Cantate Domino' (1615[13])

Ex. 11.2 'Currite populi' (1625[2])

appearance in the text of the petition 'intercede for the devout female sex', however, might also have prompted its use as a more general devotional motet to be sung in convents.

Sometimes we need to take care to recognise the occasion for which a motet is intended. 'Exultent coeli' (1629[5]) has two verses sandwiched between a five-part chorus of rejoicing and a suave triple-time trio of praise to the Virgin Mary, which begins over the so-called 'Passacaglia' bass (Ex. 11.3). The two verses are, however, proper to two completely different Marian feasts – the Conception (8 December) and the Annunciation (25 March); clearly, then, both verses should not be sung on the same occasion. Other texts can be used for a number of occasions – 'Venite videte martirem' (1645[3]), for the feast of any martyr, and 'Currite populi' (1625[2]) and 'En gratulemur hodie' (1651[2]) in both of which the saint's name is left to be filled in by the performer.

The styles of the motets range from a strophic aria with violins – 'En gratulemur hodie' (1651[2]) – to works like 'Ego flos campi' (1624[2]) and 'Ego dormio' (1625[1]), written throughout in a declamatory style. Some follow Alessandro Grandi's motets by including a final alleluia: for example, 'O beatae vie' (1621[4]) and 'Currite populi' (1625[2]). Many include at least an element of triple-time writing, to suggest singing (Ex. 11.1), or urgency (Ex. 11.2), or just as a beautiful melody in the manner of Venetian arias of the 1620s and 1630s (Ex. 11.3). Occasionally, passages in triple time

Ex. 11.3 'Exultent coeli' (1629[5])

are used as refrains: in even the earliest published of Monteverdi's motets –
the duet 'Cantate Domino' (1615[13]) – the opening triple-time music
(Ex. 11.1) recurs as a refrain, contrasted with highly ornamented writing
in the duple-time sections.

Among the works included in anthologies are three settings of the
Marian antiphon 'Salve [o] Regina' (1624[2], 1625[2] and 1629[5]/R1641),
which was sung at S. Marco, with its associated devotions, after Vespers
or Compline between the Octave of Pentecost and the first day of
Lent (i.e. for most of the Church year); the first of the settings is an
extended and powerful setting for solo tenor employing a triple-time
refrain, the second a simple declamatory setting, also for solo tenor,
and the third a setting in which Monteverdi uses three voices in solo
declamation and in melting passages of chromaticism and triple-time
aria writing. This last was reprinted in 1641, together with two further
'Salve Regina' settings, one a languorous duet (SV284), the other
(SV283) an extraordinary setting which combines the text 'Audi caelum',
which Monteverdi had set in its own right in 1610 and which is set here in
a declamatory style, with the 'Salve Regina' text set largely in aria style
with violins.

Among five works by Monteverdi published in 1620 by his former
composition pupil and colleague at Mantua, Giulio Cesare Bianchi, is
a setting for six voices of the Litany of Loreto (1620[4] and reprinted in
1626[3] and 1650). The many polyphonic settings of this litany – a series of
invocations and petitions framed at one end by the words 'Kyrie eleison'
and at the other by a troped 'Agnus Dei' – that were written for Venice
during the seventeenth century and sung in processions seem to have been

prompted by a wave of Marian devotion following the Venetian victory at the Battle of Lepanto (1571), which was declared by Pope Pius V to have been due to the intervention of the Madonna of the Rosary.[7]

Bianchi was also responsible for publishing four technically undemanding, but very attractive, motets by Monteverdi for five and six voices in 1620[3]. Two of them, whether consciously or not, contain reminiscences of music that Monteverdi had written earlier. 'Cantate Domino' reuses for the phrase 'Cantate et exsultate' music that he had first employed at the end of the madrigal 'Ecco mormorar l'onde' (1590), and 'Domine ne in furore' the type of close imitation found in 'Nisi Dominus' (1610). The other two, very moving settings of essentially the same text – 'Adoramus te, Christe' and 'Christe, adoramus te', drawn from the Hours of the Cross – are suited to the devotions of Holy Week or for an occasion such as Holy Cross Day, when a relic of the Holy Blood was displayed in S. Marco and Monteverdi had, in his own words, 'to be ready with a concerted mass, and motets for the entire day' (letter of 21 April 1618).

The *Selva morale* (1641) and *Messa . . . et salmi* (1650)

Just as at Mantua, Monteverdi himself published only one collection of sacred music at Venice, the massive *Selva morale e spirituale* of 1641, including spiritual madrigals, music for the Mass, motets, and music for Vespers (psalms, hymns, Magnificats, 'Salve Regina' settings).[8] A further major collection of his work, including a Mass, Vespers psalms and the litany, was published posthumously in 1650 in a volume possibly edited by Francesco Cavalli, who contributed a Magnificat setting to the collection. The Mass setting in 1650 (like that of 1641 written in a deliberately conservative style) is fascinating for the way in which Monteverdi generates most of its material from only a few basic ideas – a falling scale and two rising thirds heard at the beginning of the first Kyrie, the inversion of this, and sequences of rising and falling thirds filled in and elaborated with additional melodic and rhythmic figures. Paradoxically, this exercise in tight motivic integration produced from Monteverdi one of his most attractive and engaging compositions.

The evening service of Vespers calls for the singing of five psalms and a hymn specified for each Feast, and the Magnificat. The Vespers psalms published in 1641 are mainly those for the so-called 'male cursus' ('Dixit Dominus', 'Confitebor tibi', 'Beatus vir', 'Laudate pueri', 'Laudate Dominum omnes gentes'); the 1650 book balances this by including psalms for the 'female cursus' ('Dixit Dominus', 'Laudate pueri', 'Laetatus sum', 'Nisi Dominus', 'Lauda Jerusalem'). For the choirmaster working in the Roman rite, to whom the 1641 and 1650 volumes were probably addressed, the first five psalms in the *Selva* alone provided music for

First Vespers of Apostles and Evangelists, Martyrs and Confessors, and also, for example, for Vespers on Christmas Eve. The idea of a service in which all, or most, of the music is by a single composer may seem an anachronistic idea, the concern of present-day concert promoters and record producers rather than the working musicians of Monteverdi's day. However, on special occasions in Venice, such as the Mass at S. Marco celebrating the end of the plague in 1631, and the celebration of Vespers for St John the Baptist's Day, 24 June 1620, described by Constantijn Huygens, Monteverdi was noted as the sole composer of the music,[9] and as he himself pointed out in a letter on 13 March 1620, he could earn up to fifty ducats for providing two Vespers services and a Mass for patrons outside S. Marco.

Monteverdi dedicated the *Selva morale* to Eleonora Gonzaga, daughter of Duke Vincenzo Gonzaga of Mantua and widow of the Emperor Ferdinand II, a dedication analogous to that of the other great collection of his old age – the *Madrigali guerrieri, et amorosi* of 1638, which was dedicated to Eleonora's son, the Emperor Ferdinand III. The dedication of the *Selva* combines tributes to both Vienna and Mantua, and Linda Maria Koldau has argued that some, if not all its contents were chosen for publication with Vienna and the empress's chapel in mind: that the opening madrigals, with their *vanitas* theme, reflect Viennese sensibilities, that the book's *stile antico* Mass would have been suitable for Eleonora's private devotions, and that the inclusion of the Lament of Arianna as a sacred *contrafactum* – the *Pianto della Madonna* – at the end of the book was another tribute to Eleonora, for whose brother Francesco's wedding in 1608 *Arianna* was originally written.[10]

The *Selva morale* opens with the group of *vanitas* settings – five settings of Italian 'moral' texts on the transitory nature of love, earthly rank and achievement, even existence itself. The first three are five-part madrigals, two on quite substantial texts by Petrarch, including 'Voi ch'ascoltate in rime sparse il suono', the sonnet with which Petrarch opened his own *Canzoniere*; the third sets a short epigrammatic madrigal by Angelo Grillo, a Benedictine friar and admirer of Monteverdi.[11] The other two settings – 'Spuntava il di' and 'Chi vol che m'innamori?' – are of strophic texts with refrains, scored for three voices.

The first of the madrigals, 'O ciechi', is drawn from Petrarch's *Trionfo della morte*. If the *Selva* is, indeed, the sacred counterpart of the *Madrigali guerrieri ed amorosi* of 1638, then this is the sacred counterpart of its opening madrigal 'Altri canti d'Amor' (Let others sing of Love . . . I sing of Mars) which celebrated Ferdinand III's military prowess and set the programme of the book. 'O ciechi, ciechi' is a reminder of the ultimate futility of power, riches and military conquest. The 'point' of the madrigal makes this clear:

U' sono or le ricchezze? u' son gli onori	Where now their riches? Where their honours now?
E le gemme e gli scetri e le corone	Where now their gems and sceptres, and their crowns,
E le mitre e i purpurei colori?	Their mitres, and the purple they had worn?

The arranger of the text has, in fact, taken these lines out of order: in Petrarch's *trionfo* they appear before the first thirteen lines set by Monteverdi. And if we look at the three lines, not set by Monteverdi, that precede them, we can see that the 'point' is directed clearly at popes and emperors:

Ivi eran quei che fur detti felici,	Here now were they who were called fortunate,
pontefici, regnanti, imperadori;	Popes, emperors, and others who had ruled;
or sono ignudi, miseri e mendici.	Now are they naked, poor, of all bereft.
U' sono or le ricchezze? u' son gli onori	Where now their riches? Where their honours now?
. . .	. . .

The style of the setting places it firmly with Monteverdi's later compositions and there seems every reason to suppose that, though the other spiritual madrigals may have had their origins in performances at Venice, perhaps in the oratory of the *Primicierius* of S. Marco (Marc'Antonio Cornaro; see Monteverdi's letter of 17 March 1620), this was written specifically as a prologue to the *Selva morale*.

The madrigals are followed by a Mass setting in *stile antico*, a magnificent *concertato* setting of the Gloria for seven voices and instruments, and three *concertato* settings of sections of the Creed – 'Crucifixus', 'Et resurrexit' and 'et iterum venturus est', which can be used, according to their rubrics, as substitutes for the corresponding sections of the complete Mass setting. It is not clear whether the Gloria is also intended as a substitute for its counterpart in the Mass, though there is no reason from a liturgical point of view why it should not be used in this way.

The seven-part Gloria has intrigued scholars as much as it has attracted performers. It lasts some twelve minutes in performance, requires virtuoso singers and instrumentalists and is conceived as a large-scale structure in five sections which anticipates the sectional Mass settings of the later Baroque.[12] The thrilling figuration with which it begins is brought back both at the end of the first section and at the end of the setting to round off the structure

(Ex. 11.4); and the musical texture encompasses slowly moving harmonies for 'et in terra pax' analogous to those of the opening of 'Or che 'l ciel e la terra' from the *Madrigali guerrieri*, as well as passages of *concitato* writing, suggesting the power of God, at 'Domine Deus ... omnipotens'. Because of the magnificence of this setting, scholars have felt that it must have been written for a special occasion, and their attention has focussed on a Mass celebrated on 21 November 1631 as part of the ceremonies marking the end of the plague that had swept through northern Italy, killing nearly fifty thousand people in Venice alone. The ceremonies culminated in the dedication of the site on which a new church was to be built – the church of Santa Maria della Salute which now dominates the entrance to the Grand Canal (Fig. 9.4). We know that a Mass setting composed by Monteverdi was performed at S. Marco on this occasion, the Gloria and Creed of which involved *trombe squarciate*. For many years it was assumed that these instruments were trombones, leaving open the possibility that the Gloria from the *Selva morale* might indeed have been part of the Mass of Thanksgiving and leading to the ingenious theory that various other items of the *Selva morale* might also have been associated with the foundation of the Salute.[13] However, recent work has shown that *trombe squarciate* were trumpets, not trombones, and suggests that the assumed link between the seven-part Gloria and the Mass of Thanksgiving was essentially wishful thinking.[14] There are, in any case, more regular occasions in the church year when a Gloria of the grandeur of that in the *Selva morale* or, indeed, the double-choir Gloria attributed to Monteverdi in a Neapolitan manuscript (SV307),[15] might be substituted for a simpler setting: the Masses of Christmas and Easter, following the abstinence of Advent and Lent, are cases in point.

The psalms of the *Selva morale* and the 1650 book are not set out, as in Monteverdi's 1610 publication, to give the impression of complete, unified services. Instead, the books present several settings of various psalms and hymns, two different Magnificats and three settings of the 'Salve Regina'. From the practical point of view, then, they provided choirmasters with resource books from which they could draw individual settings appropriate to particular feast days.

The styles, techniques and structures that Monteverdi uses in his motets can also be seen, transferred on to a larger canvas, in his psalm settings. Five of the psalms – 'Beatus vir' (SV269) and 'Laudate pueri' (SV271) from 1641, 'Laudate pueri' (SV196), 'Laetatus sum' (SV199) and 'Lauda Jerusalem' (SV203) from 1650, all of them for five voices – are simply through-composed, with generally continuous imitative textures, little solo writing and cadences 'escaped' by allowing one or more voices to initiate a new point of imitation. With their generally restrained

Ex. 11.4

dissonance usage and word-painting ('Lauda Jerusalem' (SV203) is something of an exception in this respect) they are clearly related to the sixteenth-century tradition of motets, though their basic units of notation are the crotchet and quaver, rather than the semibreves and minims that we see in the works that Monteverdi wrote in deliberately 'old' styles.

The most extravagantly madrigalian of all the psalm settings is the six-part 'Nisi Dominus' (SV201) of 1650 in which almost every verbal image is found a musical equivalent: triple time to produce a laboured texture for 'Vanum est vobis' (it is vain for you . . .) contrasted with lines that rise through a seventh for 'ante lucem surgere' (. . . to rise up before dawn); surging semiquaver passages followed by a sequence of harsh dissonances for 'surgite postquam sederitis, qui manducatis panem doloris' (you get up before you have gone to bed, you who eat the bread of misery); rapid rising scales for the 'sagittae in manu potentis' (arrows in the hand of a mighty man). There is even a passage of repeated dominant–tonic chords of a kind found in the *Combattimento di Tancredi e Clorinda* for the phrase 'non confundetur cum loquetur inimicis suis in porta' (he shall not be confounded when he speaks with his enemies at the gate).

Interestingly, the other setting of 'Nisi Dominus' in 1650 (SV200), for three voices and two violins, contains musical imagery for 'rising up' and the flight of arrows that seem to be initial versions of the ideas worked out more fully in the larger version. In SV200, however, these are preceded by melodies using paired quavers in the style that Monteverdi also used for 'Confitebor tibi' (SV267) in 1641, a setting that he labelled 'alla francese' (in the French manner) and which can be performed either by solo voice and strings or by five voices. There are other parallels between the two settings, including the use in both of an elaborate Italianate solo for the opening of the 'Gloria Patri' before the words 'sicut erat in principio' prompt a return to the (possibly) French melodic style with which the settings began.

Monteverdi's settings of 'Confitebor tibi' present an even greater variety of approaches to the use of aria styles than the motets. The two settings in 1650, for example, have essentially the same music, though in the first case (SV193) only a solo voice is used and in the second (SV194) the music is divided between the two voices, with one occasionally reinforcing the other. The text, punctuated by ritornellos for two violins, is set as variations over a bass whose figuration is itself varied from one statement to another. In the second 1641 setting (SV266) Monteverdi sets a pair of verses for each of the three voices (soprano, tenor, bass) in turn, and then the last three verses for a trio, all over essentially the same bass.

The first of the 1641 'Confitebor' settings (SV265) is the most interesting of all. Here Monteverdi uses a primary group of three solo voices, adding a further five to produce a full eight-part texture for verses 2 and 6 of the text, the first half of verse 9 and the 'Gloria Patri'. The three soloists sing, for the most part, in triple time and in imitative textures. The full eight-part texture is used as a refrain – a rich harmonic progression in block chords. The reasons for Monteverdi's choice of textures seems largely to be related to the meaning of the text. The sudden emergence of the full texture at verse 2 underlines the phrase 'Magna opera Domini' (Great are the works of the Lord), at verse 9 the phrase 'Sanctum et terribile nomen eius' (holy and fearsome is His name), and at the end of the setting the words 'Gloria Patri' (Glory be to the Father'). Only at verse 6 can the use of the refrain not be explained textually; here it seems to have been used for musical balance in the otherwise long transition between verses 2 and 9.

The use of aria styles and refrains is characteristic of a number of Monteverdi's more extended psalm settings. In the first 'Laudate pueri' setting of 1641 (SV270) Monteverdi builds most of the psalm from just two blocks of material – duple (A) and triple (B). He then alternates the two blocks, allowing B to evolve gradually, while A remains recognisably the same. In refrain structures, the refrains are often either in triple time within a predominantly duple setting or vice versa, as in the first of the 'Lauda Jerusalem' settings in 1650 (SV202). In the otherwise continuous texture of the five-part 'Beatus vir' II (SV269, 1641) the opening phrase of the setting recurs after verses 4, 6 and 9.

In fact, all three settings of 'Beatus vir' employ the initial words as a refrain, perhaps to emphasise the fact that the whole psalm is devoted to the attributes of the 'blessed man who fears the Lord'. The seven-part setting in 1650 (SV195) begins with both duple- and triple-time settings of the refrain. The duple-time version is then brought back after almost every verse (only verses 5–6 and 7–8 are run together without refrain), and both versions round off verse 9. The refrain sometimes overlaps the end of the verse to produce telling textual counterpoints – the blessed man rejoices at the same time as the wicked man perishes in verse 9 of the psalm; and he appears again in the middle of the 'Gloria Patri', producing the phrase 'Beatus vir ... semper, et in saecula' (Blessed is the man ... for ever and ever).

The most often performed of the 'Beatus vir' settings is the first of the two in the *Selva morale* (SV268), for six voices and instruments, and here again Monteverdi uses the phrase 'Beatus vir qui timet Dominum', or just 'Beatus vir', as a refrain. The setting as a whole is given an A–B–A[1] structure in which the outer sections are an elaboration of music that Monteverdi originally created for the duet 'Chiome d'oro' (Hair of gold) in the Seventh Book of Madrigals (1619). These outer sections are set over a 'walking bass', with recurring patterns of notes (though not quite a ground bass), and the central section in triple time over yet another recurring pattern (again, not quite a ground bass). Stylistically, the walking bass and suave triple-time aria writing are typical of Venetian songbooks of the 1620s and 1630s and the use of variation patterns here, in the seven-part Gloria, and in the four-note ostinato of the gloriously exuberant setting of 'Laetatus sum' (SV198) in the 1650 collection, with its variety of obbligato instruments (violins, trombone and bassoon), forms the culmination in Monteverdi's work of the process that Massimo Ossi sees as beginning in the Fifth Book of Madrigals (1605).[16]

The four settings of 'Dixit Dominus', two in 1641 (SV263 and 264) and two in 1650 (SV191 and 192) are all for eight voices, the two 1641 settings also calling for two violins and four *viole da braccio* or trombones, ad. lib. The two settings in 1650 are clearly indicated as being for two four-part choirs, and the first, possibly both, of the 1641 settings should also be set out in this way.

Only the second 1650 setting (SV192), marked 'alla breve', with semibreve and minim as its basic note-values, belongs clearly to the tradition of psalm settings for double choir begun at S. Marco by Adrian Willaert. The setting is initiated in plainsong for the first part of verse 1 and then proceeds with the choirs singing one verse each in alternation until the second part of verse 5, where the full eight-part texture is heard for the first time at 'Tu es sacerdos in aeternum' (Thou art a priest for ever). Thereafter, Monteverdi organises the exchanges between the choirs more freely, though ensuring that each is essentially self-sufficient, as prescribed for *cori spezzati* writing by another of his predecessors at S. Marco, Gioseffo Zarlino.[17] David Bryant argued that double-choir settings of this kind were performed with both choirs standing together in the *pulpitum magnum cantorum* (also known as the Bigonzo – the tub), located at the south front of the choir screen (the *iconostasis*) (Fig. 11.1), a location in which the choir certainly sang on some occasions, as reflected in Canaletto's well-known drawing of 1766;[18] more recently, Laura Moretti has suggested that Vespers psalms for double choir were performed with the two choirs standing opposite each other in the two *pergole* (also called the *nicchie*) on the north and south sides of the chancel, just inside the choir screen; there was originally only one of these: a second was constructed at about the time that Willaert introduced double-choir polyphony at S. Marco.[19] In either case, the first choir consisted of soloists while in the second choir parts were doubled.[20]

The first setting of 'Dixit Dominus' in 1641 (SV263) and the first of the two 1650 settings (SV191) are related through Monteverdi's extensive reworking of the same material. If we believe that a more complex setting is likely to have been developed from a simpler, then the 1650 setting, which is 259 bars in length in Malipiero's edition and for voices and continuo only, is likely to be the earlier of the two, and the 1641 setting,

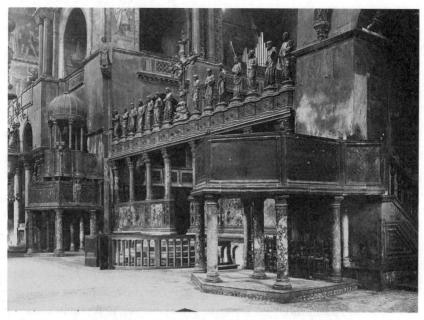

Fig. 11.1 S. Marco, the Bigonzo, Iconostasis, Pergola and North Organ Loft

303 bars long and for voices and instruments the later reworking. The entire setting of verses 3 to 7 and the 'Gloria Patri' of the 1650 setting (bars 36–146 and 202–59) are reworked in 1641 (bars 93–227 and 245–303) with most of the twenty-four extra bars in 1641 coming from the reworking of verse 3. The relationship between the two settings is disguised on first hearing by the extended new setting of verses 1 and 2 in the 1641 version (ninety-two bars) and the replacement of Psalm Tone 8G, placed prominently in the top line at the opening of 1650, with neutral chanting on one note (in the 1641 setting, we hear the psalm tone only briefly, in the borrowed material of verse 3).

The grandeur, rich scoring, and scale of the two 1641 settings of 'Dixit Dominus' (each lasts about nine minutes in performance), are analogous to the large *concertato* settings of the Gloria and Magnificat I (SV281) in the same book, and they seem eminently appropriate for the psalm which begins almost every festal Vespers in the Roman rite, and many in the liturgy of S. Marco. Like the Gloria and Magnificat, they are sectional structures. The first (SV263) is organised mainly in pairs of verses (verse 3 and 8 excepted), the second mainly verse by verse in a fluid juxtaposition of small ensemble and fuller writing. In this latter setting (SV264) the full scorings emphasise the idea of a powerful God, sometimes speaking loudly from Heaven, or exulting (verse 8), or represented as helping to crush the enemies of the psalmist (or, in this context, Venice), as we can hear in verse 2 ('until I make thine enemies thy footstool'), the second half of verse 3 ('rule thou in the midst of thine enemies'), and verses 6 and 7, in which a wrathful God smites kings and fills the places with dead bodies. In setting verse 3 Monteverdi uses double counterpoint, so that the phrase 'rule thou' (*dominare*) is placed sometimes above, sometimes in the middle of the texture, surrounded by a contrasting motif for 'in the midst of thine enemies' (*in medio inimicorum tuorum*) (Ex. 11.5).

Music at S. Marco . . .

In the seventeenth century S. Marco was not the cathedral of Venice, as it is now, but the state church of the Venetian Republic (the seat of the Patriarch of Venice was S. Pietro in Castello at the eastern extremity of the city). As the state church, S. Marco was at the centre of the intermingling of piety with Venetian history and state ceremonial that characterised and reinforced the myth of the Most Serene Republic (see above, Chapter 9). Moreover, because of its antiquity, S. Marco had been allowed to retain its own liturgy – that is, its own ordering of texts for the days of the Church year – even after a uniform Roman rite had been imposed on most other churches following the Council of Trent.[21] The provisions of this liturgy, and the customs of S. Marco which dictated the types of music to be sung at particular services, raise interesting questions when we try to identify the occasions for which Monteverdi's surviving music might have been used there.[22]

Christmas Eve, for which Monteverdi was expected to write a new Mass setting each year (see his letters of 29 December 1616 and 2 February 1634), provides us with a useful case study of the relationship between his surviving music and his work at S. Marco. The services for Christmas Eve at S. Marco were Vespers, Compline, Matins and Mass, and involved both singers and instrumentalists. The way in which these services were celebrated in the late sixteenth and early seventeenth centuries was described by Giovanni Stringa, *maestro di coro* of S. Marco, in his revision of Francesco Sansovino's *Venetia, città nobilissima*, published in 1604.[23] According to Stringa, the doge entered the church about two hours before sunset, and as soon as he arrived Vespers was celebrated 'with the sweetest sounds of voices and instruments ... by the salaried musicians of the church and by others hired specially to make a greater number, since on that evening they perform [*si canta*] in eight, ten, twelve and sixteen choirs to the wonder and amazement of everyone.'[24]

For Christmas Eve, the customs of S. Marco prescribed the opening of the great golden altarpiece, the *Pala d'oro* (Fig. 9.5), and that the psalms of Vespers should be sung in eight parts by two choirs. The five psalms appointed for Vespers on Christmas Eve were the so-called 'Cinque

Ex. 11.5

Laudate', all of which begin with a form of the word 'laudare' – 'Laudate pueri' (Psalm 112 (*Book of Common Prayer* 113)); 'Laudate Dominum omnes gentes' (Psalm 116/117); 'Lauda anima mea' (Psalm 145/146); 'Laudate Dominum quoniam bonus' (Psalm 146/147: 1–11); 'Lauda Jerusalem' (Psalm 147/147: 12–20). As James Moore has shown, the *Vespero delli cinque Laudate* held a special position in the liturgy of S. Marco and was used for a very large number of major feast days in its annual cycle.[25] Settings of these special psalms survive in publications by Monteverdi's predecessors and successors – Giovanni Croce (1597), Rovetta (1644 and 1662), Cavalli (1675) and Natale Monferrato (1675) – and share several characteristics – all are for eight voices divided into two (self-sufficient) four-part choirs, and their style is simple, with no solo writing even when continuo is used; the choirs change at the ends of verses or at the half-verse; and the settings are 'short psalms', without extensive development of any paragraphs of text. They are, thus, *salmi spezzati* which look back in style and structure to the psalms of Adrian Willaert in the sixteenth century.[26] Monteverdi's surviving sacred music includes only two settings of 'Laudate' psalms – 'Laudate Dominum omnes gentes' SV273 and 274 (both 1641) for eight voices, neither of which is in the requisite style.

The singing of Vespers psalms in eight parts, for two choirs, was not limited to those days at S. Marco for which the *Cinque Laudate* psalms were set, but for all important feasts when the *Pala d'oro* was opened.[27] The implication is that these, too, were sung as *salmi spezzati* and not in the more modern styles found in Monteverdi's surviving work: only his setting of 'Credidi' (SV275, 1641) falls quite clearly into the older category of double-choir setting; 'Memento Domine David' (SV276, 1641) and the second 1650 'Dixit Dominus' (SV192) also belong to the earlier tradition, though the first includes short passages of two-part writing supported by continuo only, and in the second Monteverdi does not simply alternate the two choirs verse by verse, but combines them in a more varied, less predictable series of textures.

For many of the most important feasts of the year, then, it would seem that a restrained, conservative style of double-choir psalm settings was employed at S. Marco, and continued to be employed there well into the seventeenth century. And try as one might to explain away the discrepancy, it is not likely that the more modern *concertato* styles that characterise so many of Monteverdi's surviving psalm settings would have been appropriate for these occasions. There are, however, feast days in the S. Marco calendar for which Monteverdi's settings could have been used, and they include feasts important to Venice which were celebrated in the presence of the doge, and therefore probably involved instruments in addition to the organ.[28] These include First Vespers of S. Lorenzo

Giustiniani (8 January), S. Marco (25 April, when 'Vespers was sung . . . with the greatest possible solemnity'[29]), S. Antonio di Padova (13 June) and SS Vito and Modesto, all of which call for the first five psalms set in Monteverdi's 1641 book.[30]

If the psalms for Christmas Eve were sung in eight parts by two choirs, how do we account for the large number of voices and instruments, performing in eight, ten, twelve and sixteen 'choirs' as described by Stringa? The answer must be that they performed either large-scale motets or instrumental music, or both, between the psalms, and/or they joined together for the performance of the Magnificat, which forms the climax (though not the end) of Vespers, when the altar is ceremonially censed.[31] Monteverdi's opulent Magnificat I (SV281, 1641) may have been composed for an occasion such as Christmas Eve Vespers at S. Marco, as may some of his motets.

Immediately after Vespers, Compline was said, without music, and followed by Matins, chanted by the canons and other priests of S. Marco. At the end of Matins, at about two hours after sunset, the celebration of Mass began, and here it must have been that Monteverdi's involvement was at its greatest. Mass ended, according to Stringa, at about four hours after sunset, lasting, if he is correct, about two hours, which would certainly have allowed time for the performance of a large-scale *concertato* Mass, including a movement like the seven-part Gloria (SV258).

Mass concluded the celebrations of Christmas Eve after some six hours in church. On Christmas Day itself High Mass was celebrated, according to Stringa, 'with as much solemnity as the Mass of the previous evening', and, perhaps, with much the same music. After lunch the doge came into church to hear a sermon and then proceeded *in trionfo* to the church of S. Giorgio Maggiore, on the island opposite the ducal palace, to hear Vespers (Fig. 9.3). This service was sung in plainchant by the canons of the church.[32]

We have, in short, little of the music by Monteverdi that might have been sung at S. Marco on a great occasion such as Christmas. And if we are looking to reconstruct a Monteverdian Vespers at S. Marco using his psalm settings we have to look at those feast days that did not, seemingly, call for rather old-fashioned music. S. Marco was, however, only one arena of his activities in Venice and it may be that some of the settings in 1641 and 1650 belong to his work outside the ducal chapel.

. . . and elsewhere in Venice

We know of several occasions on which Monteverdi served in the Venetian *scuole* and in churches where the Roman rite was used, and to which the restrictive customs of S. Marco did not apply. On 4 November 1620, and again on 3 and 4 November 1635, he was employed by the Milanese community in Venice to provide music for the Feast of S. Carlo Borromeo, probably in the huge Gothic church of S. Maria Gloriosa dei Frari (letter of 21 October [1620] and Fabbri, *Monteverdi*, p. 233). In 1623 and 1627 he provided music for the Scuola Grande di S. Rocco for its patronal feast day (16 August) (for the location, see Fig. 9.1).[33] On 15 July 1627 (see letter of 24 July 1627),[34] he furnished music for First Vespers of the Blessed Virgin of Mount Carmel at the Carmelite Church (all the psalms for this can be provided from 1650 and some from 1641). And on 23 February 1630 he wrote that he had been 'taken up with certain ecclesiastical compositions for some of the nuns of San Lorenzo'.

Once certainly, and once probably, Monteverdi was employed by the Florentine community at Venice to provide music for them. The first of these occasions was for the Requiem celebrated at SS Giovanni e Paolo (Fig. 11.2) on 25 May 1621 following the death of Grand Duke Cosimo II, the cost of which was put at around three thousand ducats by the Florentine Resident.[35] The ceremony was described in a booklet written

Fig. 11.2 SS. Giovanni e Paolo, Venice

by Giulio Strozzi, which shows that Monteverdi directed music (now lost) written by himself, Giovanni Battista Grillo and Francesco Usper.[36] Strozzi commented with some admiration on Monteverdi's setting of Psalm 129/130:

> A most suave *De profundis* at the Elevation of the Host . . . sung as a dialogue as if by souls standing in the torments of Purgatory and visited by angels, produced admiration for the novelty and excellence of the art.[37]

The text of Psalm 129 is not in dialogue form, so it must have been manipulated by Monteverdi. Though this example is lost, we do have another instance of his turning a text into a dialogue in the third 1641 setting of Psalm 116/117 – 'Laudate Dominum omnes gentes' (SV274). This psalm, which consists of two verses only, plus the 'Gloria Patri', presented composers with a challenge if they were to construct more than a very brief setting. Monteverdi's 1650 setting in a sense avoids the problem: it is, unusually, for solo voice and contrasts ornamented declamation for verse 1 with triple time in verse 2 (recitative and aria, as it were), while the 'Gloria Patri' is set over two short ostinato basses. In the first setting of 1641 (SV272) Monteverdi uses line repetition and contrasts of texture to build a large-scale structure. In SV274, however, he creates a dialogue where none existed: two sopranos, perhaps representing angels, engage in dialogue with the remaining six voices, perhaps representing the people. They urge the people to praise the Lord, but are at first met only by the single word 'quoniam', which, in this context becomes a question – 'because?' (in the sense of 'why?'). Only after the sopranos have answered this, by singing 'Because his mercy is confirmed upon us', do the people respond at greater length, at first seeking further confirmation, and then singing the complete psalm text, led by the 'angels'. The 'Gloria Patri' is then sung by the 'angels', whose voices finally seem to disappear into the distance.

The other occasion on which Monteverdi may have served the Florentine community is the one for which we have an eye-witness account of his performance – the Vespers for the Feast of St John the Baptist heard by Constantijn Huygens on 24 June 1620 at the church of 'SS Giovanni e Lucia' (most probably SS Giovanni e Paolo).[38] There is no known evidence bearing directly on the Feast of S. Giovanni Battista for 1620, but a report of Ippolito Buondalmenti, the Florentine Resident at Venice, written on 23 June 1629, suggests that the Florentine community ('Nazione fiorentino') at Venice regularly celebrated the feast day of S. Giovanni Battista, who was their protector saint, with elaborate church music. Buondalmenti reported that, following the death of Filippo Mannelli, consul of the Florentine community, the whole community had met and resolved to celebrate the Feast of S. Giovanni Battista with customary solemnity since this greatly enhanced their reputation in the city. Accordingly, solemn First Vespers had been celebrated that day; only one member of the community, the representative of the Lords Guadagni, had opposed the extravagant expenditure involved.[39] The psalms set for both First and Second Vespers of S. Giovanni Battista in the Roman rite are those of the male *cursus*, settings for which are found in both Monteverdi's 1641 and 1650 books, and the hymn for Vespers of the feast – 'Ut queant laxis' – is set in 1641 (SV279a).

In the end, and despite his having served as a church musician at S. Marco for thirty years, Monteverdi's Venetian sacred music poses almost as many questions about place of performance as his 1610 publication. We are, however, left with a body of music that is as rich and inventive as anything that Monteverdi wrote in the secular sphere during his later years. The smaller-scale works cover the gamut from Florentine-style declamation to the song styles and variation structures characteristic of Venetian song-books of the 1620s and 1630s. And the large-scale sectional structures of some of the 'Dixit Dominus' settings, the seven-part Gloria, and the first Magnificat of 1641 set the ground for the development of such settings through the seventeenth and into the eighteenth century.

Magnificat SV281 (1641)

JOHN WHENHAM

The Magnificat is a 'canticle', a non-metrical, song-like passage of text drawn from books of the Bible other than the Book of Psalms. The Magnificat – the Song of the Blessed Virgin Mary – comes from the Gospel of St Luke, 1:46–53, and represents Mary's joyful response to the message given her by the Angel Gabriel that she was to bear the son of God. In the Catholic liturgy this canticle was set to be read or sung daily towards the end of the main evening Office of Vespers. It forms the climax of the service, and while it is being sung a priest censes the altar. The Magnificat is preceded by the singing of an antiphon specific to the particular day on which it was being performed, and followed by the 'Gloria Patri' and a repetition of the antiphon. This whole unit is then followed by a prayer and the dismissal of those who have celebrated Vespers.[1]

The text of the Magnificat is laid out in the *Liber Usualis* (an abbreviated compendium of texts and music for the Mass and Office) as follows. (The English version is the one given in the *Book of Common Prayer*.)

1. Magnificat * anima mea Dominum.	1. My soul doth magnify the Lord
2. Et exsultavit spiritus meus: * in Deo salutari meo.	2. And my spirit hath rejoiced in God my saviour
3. Quia respexit humilitatem ancillae suae: * ecce enim ex hoc beatam me dicent omnes generationes.	3. For he hath regarded the lowliness of his handmaiden: for behold all generations shall call me blessed.
4. Quia fecit mihi magna qui potens est: * et sanctum nomen eius.	4. For he that is mighty hath magnified me: and holy is his name.
5. Et misericordia eius a progenie in progenies: * timentibus eum.	5. And his mercy is on them that fear him throughout all generations.
6. Fecit potentiam in brachio suo: * dispersit superbos mente cordis sui.	6. He hath shewed strength with his arm: he hath scattered the proud in the imagination of their hearts.

7. Deposuit potentes de sede, * et
exaltavit humiles.

7. He hath put down the mighty from
their seat, and hath exalted the humble
and meek.

8. Esurientes implevit bonis: * et
divites dimisit inanes.

8. He hath filled the hungry with good
things: and the rich he hath sent
empty away.

9. Suscepit Israel puerum suum, *
recordatus misericordiae suae.

9. He remembering his mercy hath
holpen his servant Israel.

10. Sicut locutus est ad patres nostros, *
Abraham et semini eius in saecula.

10. As he promised to our forefathers,
Abraham and his seed, for ever.

11. Gloria Patri, et Filio, * et Spiritui
Sancto.

11. Glory be to the Father, and to the Son,
and to the Holy Ghost.

12. Sicut erat in principio, et nunc, et
semper, * et in saecula saeculorum.
Amen.

12. As it was in the beginning, is now and
ever shall be, world without end.
Amen.

Ex. V.1

In a celebration of Vespers sung entirely in plainsong, the Magnificat would
have been sung to one of eight Magnificat Tones – one for each of the Church
modes; the Tone would have been chosen to match the mode of the antiphon
that preceded and followed the Magnificat. The convention of matching the
Magnificat Tone to the mode of the antiphon, however, becomes unworkable
if a particular Tone is embedded in a polyphonic setting such as Monteverdi's,
and the antiphon must instead be transposed to end on a convenient pitch.

The Magnificat Tone is constructed in two sections, with a median and
a final cadence: Ex. V.1 shows the Magnificat Tone for Mode 1, ending on
D, with the first two verses of the Magnificat underlaid. The asterisks in
the Latin text above show the point at which the plainsong choir should
reach the median cadence.

Monteverdi's polyphonic setting is a large-scale work lasting some ten
minutes in performance. It is scored for eight voices in two four-part choirs,
with two violins and continuo, to which can be added parts for four *viole*
(probably the lower members of the violin family, rather than viols) or four
trombones if the choir director wishes; if he does this, the piece is effectively in
fourteen parts, plus continuo, promoting it to the sort of large-scale music
that Giovanni Stringa suggested was used at S. Marco on occasions such as
Christmas Eve.[2] There are several instances in the psalms of the *Selva morale*
when Monteverdi also suggests that optional extra instruments can be added;
he does not usually supply the parts for these – the choir director has to invent
them for himself. In this case, however, Monteverdi made an error when he

delivered his manuscripts to the printer: he omitted to give the printer the parts for the Alto and Bass voices of Choir II, and instead gave him two parts for the optional *viole* (scored in alto and bass clefs) which were duly printed in the published part-books; no one at the time seems to have noticed the mistake. (I say this, though, without having checked all the surviving copies of 1641 to see whether a correction was made during the printing process.) On the one hand this leaves editors and performers with the problem of adding the missing voice parts, a problem that is most difficult in the densely imitative settings of verses 5, 9 and 10: on the other hand, both the supplied *viole* parts and cues in the organ part help the editor to know when the 'optional' instruments would have been used by Monteverdi. The score published in Malipiero's edition faithfully reproduces the surviving parts, offering no solution to the problem of the missing voices. It is unusable as a performing edition, but essential as a point of reference for comparison with reconstructed versions or for making a fresh reconstruction. The Fondazione Claudio Monteverdi edition, edited by Denis Stevens, provides a reconstruction of the lost vocal parts, as does the edition published by King's Music, with reconstruction by Andrew Parrott; it also preserves the original note-values where Stevens reduces them.[3] The bar numbers are the same in both editions. Other performer-editors provide their own solution in their recordings. The subtle differences that these produce need to be borne in mind when analysing the work, though they need not inhibit a broad understanding of Monteverdi's setting.

In terms of the material that he invents, Monteverdi treats some verses of the text as separate units, but runs others together. Verses 1 and 2, which form a single syntactical unit, also form a single musical unit; verses 3 to 5 are treated separately; verses 6 to 8 are run together, as are verses 9 and 10; the two verses of the 'Gloria Patri' are set to different material.

The setting opens with two statements in triple time, probably for the whole ensemble, of the word 'Magnificat'; this is then followed by a solo tenor singing the same word to the first part of Magnificat Tone 1. Since the Tone begins on the note F, the function of the initial triple-time music is probably to establish Mode 1 clearly, through its two cadences on D. The full phrase 'Magnificat anima mea Dominum' then follows, with Choir II at first following Choir I in triple time and then joining it in a full texture in duple time. In this full texture the second half of the Magnificat Tone is sung by Tenor 2. The entire unit is then repeated for verse 2, with the bass a fifth higher; Monteverdi manages ingeniously to reuse the Cantus 1 line from bars 15 to 21 over the new harmonic range at bars 38 to 44. In this second unit only the first part of the Magnificat Tone is sung, probably by Alto 2 (bars 26 to 29); the only alternative is Bass 2.

Verse 3, expressing Mary's pleasure at being favoured by God, is conceived as a triple-time aria for two sopranos with violins. It begins with sixteen bars with vocal antecedents followed by instrumental consequents and a further nineteen bars in which the process is reversed. As the soloists repeat the phrase 'beatam me dicent' they are joined by the other voices and instruments suggesting the host of 'other generations'. The actual phrase 'omnes generationes', however, interrupts the flow of the aria with duple-time declamation encompassing the falling fifth that characterises the end of the Magnificat Tone.

Although Monteverdi does not use the Magnificat Tone in an easily identifiable form after verse 1, two characteristics of its shape – the rising fourth within which its first part is contained and the scale falling through a fifth from its second part – are reused. The imitative line that characterises verse 4 is a scale falling through a fifth from A (the reciting note of the Tone); this is heard in Tenor 1 and Cantus 2, and differs from the Psalm Tone only by virtue of its sharpened F. Similarly, the chromatic line with which Monteverdi chose to suggest God's mercy at the beginning of verse 5 rises through a fourth; its ending, for the words 'a progenie in progenies', is formed by a sequence of two falling scales each encompassing a fifth, the sequence also serving to suggest the sense of 'from one generation to another' (Ex. V.2). As the setting of the verse proceeds these two elements are counterpointed against each other in a texture that draws in all the voices and instruments.

So far, none of the musical units has extended beyond fifty bars. The setting of verses 6 to 8, however, is 126 bars long. At this point in the text we move suddenly away from the idea of a merciful God in verse 5 to that of a powerful, even vengeful one, scattering the proud, putting down the mighty, sending the rich empty away. This prompts Monteverdi to write a setting that begins in his *genere concitato*, with the words 'Fecit potentiam in brachio suo' (He hath shewed strength with his arm) set over repeated G major harmonies; it begins with a bar in duple time followed by triadic, fanfare-like motifs in triple time (Ex. V.3). This is not the *genere concitato* as defined in the preface to the Eighth Book of Madrigals (1638), but one of the styles that become associated with it through their use in madrigals in the *concitato* section of the book: see, for example, the setting of the words 'le battaglie' (the battles) in bars 136–9 of 'Altri canti d'Amor' or the opening of 'Ardo, avvampo, mi struggo'.

Monteverdi brings this fifteen-bar *concitato* passage back as a refrain at the beginning of verses 7 and 8. In all three verses the triple-time passage gives way to a repeat of the duple-time bar, this time for two voices only (two sopranos (verse 6), two basses (verse 7), two tenors (verse 8)) to launch the setting of the complete verse. Each verse is set differently: in verse 6 the word 'dispersit' (he hath scattered) gives rise to virtuoso semiquaver writing; in verse 7 the mighty are put down from their seat in a line that descends to bass D, while the humble and meek are exalted in

Ex. V.2

Ex. V.3

Ex. V.4

a rising triple-time aria-like line. Given that Monteverdi was committed to writing for two voices only for verse 8, by the pattern of scorings that he had chosen, the idea of filling the hungry could not be matched with a full texture; however, the emptiness of the rich is suggested by the two tenors arriving at an 'empty' unison D for the word 'inanes'.

Verses 9 and 10 are linked together by motifs that sound distinct, but are in fact linked by their use of falling thirds, enabling Monteverdi to combine them contrapuntally within chains of 6/5–5/3 progressions that drive the harmony forward (Ex. V.4). The sequence of falling thirds in the

Ex. V.5

bass is combined with a scale descending through a fifth (the Psalm Tone again), an affecting series of dissonances and resolutions results (Ex. V.5).

When the the 'Gloria Patri' begins with solo tenors singing an ornamented version of the descending scale, falling this time through only a fourth before the line is swept upward to its cadence; again, the harmony begins with a sequence of falling thirds. At 'Sicut erat in principio' (As it was in the beginning) Monteverdi avoids the temptation to revert to the music heard at the beginning of the piece, as he does in some psalm settings, and invents instead a melody for tenor and the 'optional' *viole/* trombones whose quaver patterns are then followed through in the other voices until the approach to the cadence. Here Soprano 1 sings the descending scale from the end of the Psalm Tone at its original pitch. Soprano 2, Soprano 1 and Tenor 1 then end the setting with the descending scale pitched a fourth higher, singing the words 'semper et in saecula saeculorum' (always, for ever and ever) in the dotted rhythms used in verse 5 for the phrase 'a progenie in progenies' (from one generation to another).

The Magnificat is scored for eight voices in two choirs. However, when Monteverdi writes for solo voice, as he frequently does in this and some of his eight-part psalm settings, the harmony is only completed by the continuo accompaniment. Was such writing received at St Mark's as an acceptable development of the tradition of writing for double choir? And if the choirs were located in the *pergole*, did each have a continuo instrument located there, or were the main organs of the church used? No definitive answers have yet been found for these questions.

12 Monteverdi's late operas

ELLEN ROSAND

From Monteverdi to Monteverdi

This conceit, famously coined by Nino Pirrotta, summarises a central problem raised by Monteverdi's operas: the stylistic gulf between the first, *Orfeo*, and the last, *Il ritorno d'Ulisse in patria* and *L'incoronazione di Poppea*.[1] Scholars have generally rationalised this gulf by invoking the different systems of patronage of ducal Mantua and republican Venice, where the respective works were performed, as well as the composer's own development over the course of the three and a half decades that separate them. Aside from the different circumstances surrounding the performance of the works – *Orfeo* was staged in a room of the ducal palace before a small group of aristocrats, while *Ulisse* and *Poppea* were produced in a public theatre before a socially mixed audience of several hundred – the composer himself had naturally matured. The sometime faithful servant of the Gonzaga household had become *maestro di cappella* at S. Marco, the dominant musical personality in Venetian society, a figure of enormous prestige. The change was not only psychological, of course: the late operas come after the composition of many madrigals (the Sixth to Eighth Books, published from 1614 onwards, after he had left Mantua for Venice, comprise some seventy madrigals) and a lengthy, sustained commitment to sacred music, as well as a number of smaller-scale dramatic or para-dramatic works written for private patrons. The monumental Eighth Book of Madrigals (1638) – with its dialogues and solo madrigals, its dramatic *balli*, the *Combattimento di Tancredi e Clorinda*, and the *Lamento della ninfa* in *stile rappresentativo* – demonstrates, in fact, the full range of Monteverdi's conception of musical drama just as he was about to embark on the final, Venetian phase of his operatic career. The contents of the Eighth Book can be said to manifest the stylistic changes from *Orfeo* to *Poppea*.

Monteverdi meets opera in Venice

This was the very moment when public opera was beginning to take hold in Venice, owing to the efforts of a travelling company of musicians, led by Benedetto Ferrari, and the patrician patrons who initially made a theatre available for them, the Tron brothers Francesco and Ettore. Having produced the first 'Venetian' opera during Carnival 1637, at the Tron's Teatro S. Cassiano, to great acclaim, Ferrari's company returned there in 1638 for a second opera; and in 1639 they moved to a new theatre at SS Giovanni e Paolo, owned by another patrician family, the Grimani, where they staged two more operas. In the meantime a second company, this one organised by a local musician, Francesco Cavalli, took over at S. Cassiano and produced an opera: five operas in three seasons, and none of them by the Venetian *maestro di cappella*, arguably the most famous opera composer in Italy. Monteverdi's absence was noticed by at least one commentator, who as early as 1638 expressed the hope that the composer would soon produce an opera for the public theatre, as everyone else seemed to be doing. Even if he never actually did so, this observer concluded, Monteverdi's voice would be heard, since he was so powerfully behind the whole operatic venture in the first place.[2]

The composer's entry into the Venetian operatic marketplace may have been delayed, but it was decisive: four works in as many years with the last in the year of his death, 1643. In 1640, two operas by Monteverdi were staged, one a revival, the other brand new. The revival, *Arianna*, originally performed in Mantua some three decades earlier, inaugurated the Giustinian Teatro S. Moisé, Venice's third opera house; the new opera was *Il ritorno d'Ulisse in patria*, at SS Giovanni e Paolo.[3] It seems that Ferrari had a hand in both productions. A sonnet by him addressing Monteverdi as the 'oracle of music' appeared in the libretto printed in connection with the *Arianna* revival,[4] and his company was responsible for staging *Ulisse*. By offering the legendary *Arianna*, Monteverdi may have been testing the waters. Or else he was pressed for time: to judge from the libretto that accompanied the revival, it was nearly identical to the original production. Although the choruses were omitted and the prologue revised to suit the new venue, it still differed markedly, in both genre and style, from the operas currently on the Venetian boards. We know nothing of its reception by Venetian audiences, but we may imagine that they preferred the melodious arias and variety of characters they had become accustomed to in the works of Manelli, Ferrari and Cavalli.

Il ritorno d'Ulisse was evidently more to their liking. After ten performances at SS Giovanni e Paolo, each of them before a packed crowd,[5] it was taken on the road by the Ferrari–Manelli troupe; following a series of performances in Bologna, it was revived in Venice the next year. The cast, likely the same in all productions, included Giulia Paolelli as Penelope, Maddalena Manelli, as Minerva, her husband Francesco, the composer, probably Nettuno, and their son Costantino as Amore.[6] The success of the opera was pre-ordained, even overdetermined, for the libretto was specifically designed to draw the composer out of operatic retirement. This is clear from a letter addressed to Monteverdi from the author, Giacomo Badoaro, who reports that he had embarked upon this, his first substantial literary effort, for the sole purpose of encouraging the composer to display his operatic mastery to the city of Venice.[7] Until now, according to Badoaro, Venetian audiences have been deceived by mere appearances. The emotions they have seen portrayed on stage have left them cold and unmoved, because they were warmed by a merely painted sun; only the great master Monteverdi, the true sun, radiates sufficient heat to truly ignite the passions. Badoaro is extremely pleased with the results, he says, though he can hardly recognise his own handi-work in its Monteverdian garb, and hopes the composer is pleased as well, since he has revealed to the world the true spirit of theatrical music, which is not well understood by modern composers.[8]

The most concrete testimony to the success of *Ulisse*, however, is provided not by any performance statistics nor by an interested party's hyperbole, but by Monteverdi's next opera, *Le nozze d'Enea e Lavinia*, also performed at the Teatro Grimani in 1641, which was closely modelled on *Ulisse*. The author of the formerly anonymous libretto, recently identified as Badoaro's friend Michelangelo Torcigliani, makes this clear in his preface to the printed *Argomento e scenario*. He reports that he conceived his text in response to the 1640 premiere of *Il ritorno d'Ulisse* and completed it for performance in the present year (1641) to follow the revival of Badoaro's much-applauded work – though he worries that his libretto will seem particularly inferior when directly juxtaposed with Badoaro's.[9]

Like Badoaro, Torcigliani aimed specifically to please the composer. Recognising that Monteverdi

> likes [rapidly] shifting affections because they offer him the opportunity of showing the marvels of his art with a full range of pathos, adapting the notes to the words and the passions in such a way that the singer laughs, cries, becomes enraged, compassionate, and does everything else they ask of him, and the listener is drawn by the same impetus into experiencing the variety and force of those same passions

he tells us that he avoided 'extraneous and irrelevant thoughts and ideas, and paid greater attention to the affections, as Signor Monteverdi wishes; in order to please him I also changed and omitted many of the things I had originally included.'[10]

After expressing the fear that his libretto might have been unworthy of such a great man as Monteverdi, and that the musical setting would only emphasise the infinite disparity between poet and composer, Torcigliani is relieved to report that Monteverdi had covered the weaknesses of the libretto with his glorious music, concluding that 'theatrical music would forever be in Monteverdi's debt for having been restored to a state more perfect than it ever was, even in ancient Greece.'[11] Although, sadly, the music for *Le nozze d'Enea* has not yet surfaced, much about it can be gleaned from the previously quoted *Argomento e scenario* and the various surviving manuscript librettos. These sources also shed light on the surrounding works, *Ulisse* and *Poppea*, and, together with them, on the aesthetics of Monteverdi's late style.

Il ritorno d'Ulisse in patria

Classicism

Although opera in mid-seventeenth-century Venice was very different from that in Florence and Mantua half a century earlier, there were academic theorists and librettists in Venice who were as intent as their Florentine predecessors on reviving classical tragedy in opera – perhaps as a means of justifying their own involvement in what was so patently a popular, commercial activity. Many of the early Venetian librettists, including Badoaro and Torcigliani, belonged to one particular academy, the Accademia degli Incogniti, where such issues were debated as part of a general interest in exploring the relevance of ancient classical models to modern Venetian culture. It is within the context of their discussions that *Ulisse* – and then *Le nozze d'Enea* – emerged. The librettist of *L'incoronazione di Poppea*, Gian Francesco Busenello, belonged to the same academy. Indeed, the three authors were friends.

Il ritorno d'Ulisse was the first Venetian opera to diverge from the mythological pastoral. In contrast to its predecessors, which were identified by title only, the libretto bears the generic description 'tragedia'. (The original Mantuan libretto of *Arianna* had also been subtitled *tragedia*, but the Venetian libretto of 1640 was not. Another libretto of 1640, *Adone*, by another Incognito author, Paolo Vendramin, was, however, also called a tragedy.) The choice of generic description was significant. It embodied the classicising impulse of the Incogniti authors. By adhering to the rules of tragedy, as derived from translations of Aristotle and Renaissance commentaries on the *Poetics*, they could legitimise their efforts. These rules were designed to enhance the expressive power of the genre by increasing its verisimilitude.

The most complete explication of the rules of tragedy as exemplified by *Ulisse* is found, not coincidentally, in the published *Argomento e scenario* to *Le nozze d'Enea*, a libretto that was also subtitled 'tragedy'. According to Torcigliani, tragedies required heroes that were well known, because, 'those things believed to be true seem to move the affections more than those believed to be imaginary, and also stay in the memory longer.' And because they were so well known, the adventures of these heroes could not be altered without causing disbelief in the audience. Therefore the drama had to remain faithful to its source. Convincing presentation of such true stories, moreover, required that the unities of time, place and action be observed. They recommended five acts for their dramas, so that the intervals between the acts could accommodate the time that could not actually transpire on stage. Like time, they argued, action should be mimetically convincing. This required that each of the characters behave with decorum, that he speak in accordance with his condition, sex, age and mood, which the librettist could facilitate by variety of metres in the poetry.[12]

Ulisse follows these prescriptions with remarkable fidelity. It is based on the last twelve books of the *Odyssey*, a text cited more than once by Aristotle for exemplifying some of the most important features of tragedy. This is the portion that concerns the last leg of resourceful Ulysses' homeward journey, from the time he is deposited by the Phaecians, asleep, on Ithacan shores, to his reunion with his ever-faithful wife, circumspect Penelope. Its hero is indeed well known, and the libretto draws all its incidents and characters from Homer, preserving decorum by having them express themselves in an appropriate and consistent manner. It observes unity of place: Ithaca; unity of action: everything revolves around Ulysses' reunion with his wife; and unity of time: it transpires during a single revolution of the sun. And it is in five acts.

Sources and authenticity

Although *Ulisse* was a great success in its own day, and was considered a worthy demonstration of Monteverdi's dramatic gifts, it soon disappeared from history, not to be rediscovered until the late nineteenth century, when an anonymous score, roughly contemporary with the original production, turned up in the Vienna State Library.[13] Because of discrepancies with the only libretto known at the time, a manuscript bearing the composer's name, the attribution of the music to Monteverdi was called into question. The discovery of ten more manuscript librettos, most of them dating from the eighteenth century and probably copied from the same exemplar, has done nothing to modify the discrepancies. These include a different number of acts (five in the librettos, three in the score); a different prologue (the librettos all have Il Fato, La Prudenza, and La Fortezza, whereas the score features Humana

Fragilità, Il Tempo, La Fortuna and Amore); and a different ending.[14] The score closes with a love duet between Ulisse and Penelope, while in the librettos this is followed by a chorus of Ithacans that draws a brief moral referring back to the prologue (suggesting that it became irrelevant once the prologue was replaced). In addition, many passages in the librettos, ranging from an entire scene (Act V, scene 2) to individual lines, are either omitted or rearranged in the music (most prominently Penelope's lament in Act I, scene 1).[15]

The discrepancies may not have disappeared, but they are no longer seen to undermine Monteverdi's authorship. On the contrary, the larger ones can be understood as exemplifying the difference between a literary text, designed to be read, and an operatic text, designed to be heard; and the smaller ones are now considered one of the strongest arguments in support of authenticity by demonstrating the kinds of tightening and recasting of text familiar from Monteverdi's other works. Close examination of the score, in fact, removes one of the biggest discrepancies: the many crossed-out and erased scene numbers indicate that it too was originally in five acts, but was changed to three during the course of copying, either while the original production was in rehearsal, or when it was being revised for the Bolognese or Venetian revival.[16]

Structure

The five-act structure of Badoaro's libretto may be just the most overt sign of its classicising impulse, but it is intrinsic to the drama. Shaped on a scale that matches that of its monumental source, the libretto moves inexorably from the poignant opening scene of Penelope's lonely grief at Ulisse's continued absence through the gradually spreading awareness of his return. Indeed, the most remarkable quality of *Ulisse* is its dramatic momentum: once launched, Ulisse's progress toward his goal is unrelenting; resolution becomes increasingly inevitable. The drive toward that resolution is carefully planned to accelerate over the five acts, for each of them culminates with an action that marks a successive step in Ulisse's journey homeward: Act I ends with his rejoicing at his arrival in Ithaca, Act II with his reunion with Telemaco, Act III with his vow to slay the Suitors, Act IV with his defeat of the Suitors, and Act V with his reunion with Penelope.

Intrinsic as five-act structure may be to Badoaro's text, it is no less so to Monteverdi's setting. Each action (and act) is sealed with expansive lyrical expression for Ulisse: the first with his strophic aria 'O fortunato'; the second with his arioso to Telemaco, 'Vanne alla madre'; the third with his joyous laughter, 'Rido, ne so perché'; the fourth with his impassioned battle cry; and the fifth with the love duet. Within the larger context of ascetic, speech-like exchanges that characterise so much of this score, these lyrical passages stand out and heighten the significance of the crucial moments they mark. It is the composer himself, not the librettist, who is responsible for underlining these particular moments with lyricism. There is nothing in the form of Badoaro's text – no metric regularity, no closed rhyme scheme, no word repetition – nothing but dramatic force and feeling, to suggest lyrical setting. With the exception of the final love duet, signalled in the libretto by a distinct change in metric structure and formal alternations between Ulisse and Penelope (from *versi sciolti* to regularly rhymed and alternating *quinari*), the act-closing lyrical emphasis was essentially Monteverdi's creation. In Act I, for example, he regularises a shapeless eleven-line speech to make the aria, and in Act II he sets a rhymed quatrain in triple-time arioso style, expanding its first line through expressive repetition and repeating it at the end for closure ('Vanne, vanne alla madre, va, vanne vanne alla madre, va'); he turns Badoaro's strongly metric but asymmetrical five-line text at the end of Act III into a little bipartite aria, dilating with particular relish upon Ulisse's laugh ('Rido, rido, ne so perché, rido, rido, rido, rido ne so perché'). The already dramatic conclusion of Act IV is intensified by Monteverdi's vivid exploitation of the *genere concitato*. Here he divides Ulisse's five lines into a pair of two-line phrases separated by a *sinfonia di guerra* and culminating in a furious accompanied statement of the concluding line, much repeated: 'Alle morti, alle straggi, alle morti, alle straggi, alle rovine, alle rovine, alle rovine.'

Highlighted by the composer, the five stages of Ulisse's progress are measured against Penelope's obdurate immovability. In opposition to Ulisse's motion, her stasis is reaffirmed at or near the beginning of each act – with her long recitative lament (I.1); her adamant counter-arguments against her lascivious servant Melanto's exhortations to love ('Amor è un idol vano'; 'Non dèe di nuovo amar', II.1); her refusal to accede to the Suitors ('Non voglio amar, non voglio', III.3); and her angry response to Telemaco's enthusiasm for the beauty of Helen, ultimate cause of the Trojan war and of Ulisse's absence ('Beltà troppo funesta, ardore iniquo', IV.1). But what is so impressive is that the distance between the two characters, at its maximum in the first act, diminishes in each successive one. Ulisse moves closer to his intractable object, while Penelope remains unyielding until the very end of the opera.

Needless to say, this powerful structure is obscured in the three-act version, in which the new, exceedingly long Act II begins in the middle of the old Act II (after scene 4, coinciding with the shift from Eumete's pastoral landscape to the heavens) and extends through the old Act IV. The final act remains the same in both versions. The reason for the conversion to three acts is unclear. Perhaps it was designed to reduce the number of required *intermedi* (from four to two) for the production in Bologna; or perhaps the scene change from landscape to heavens in the old Act II would have been more easily accomplished if it occurred between acts. It is probably no coincidence that the one manuscript libretto of *Le nozze d'Enea* that appears to have been copied from a score is also in three acts.[17] Perhaps both of these classical texts, the last of the five-act librettos of this period, were 'modernised' in performance to suit Venetian taste and the exigencies of production.

Speech and song

Badoaro's text is largely designed as recitative. Offering few overt invitations to song, its *versi sciolti* are only rarely interrupted by formal aria texts (there are only eight). But the composer capitalised on many shorter passages in the libretto that were set apart by a distinctive rhyme or metre by setting them lyrically (as in some of the act-closing passages already mentioned).[18] One recalls Badoaro's flattering remark that he hardly recognised his text in Monteverdi's setting. Perhaps this is what he meant.

In Monteverdi's hands lyricism, applied as well as withheld, is a powerful aspect of characterisation. It is effectively withheld from Penelope; her intransigence is matched and intensified by her austere and speech-like mode of expression, her reluctance, or inability, to release her voice in song.[19] Not until she has been thoroughly convinced that the old man who slew the Suitors is really her husband in disguise can she release the pent-up feelings that have prevented her from singing – we must assume – for the entire twenty years of his absence; the final recognition scene is the subject of Intermedio VI, below. Ulisse, in contrast, is hardly as restrained. Although he often expresses himself in passionate recitative, he can burst into song to express his emotions (as at the end of Acts I and II). Telemaco, too, is prompted to song by an excess of feeling: an exhilarated aria as he flies back to Ithaca in Minerva's chariot, a heady duet with the goddess, and a passionate one with his long-lost father.

Melanto and the Suitors also lapse readily into song, the language of love, or lust. Song comes even more naturally to some of the other characters: gods and goddesses, possessed of supernatural attributes, sing as easily as they fly; roulades, elaborate passage-work, and trills decorate their every word, displaying their natural superiority over mere mortal singers. Eumete, the swineherd, even speaks in song, the natural language of the pastoral world to which he belongs. He sings textual passages that other characters would deliver in recitative. Following the lyrical invocation of nature with which he introduces himself, he sings his welcome to the old beggar who is Ulisse in disguise and to Telemaco, whom Minerva has brought back to Ithaca; and he sings the news of Telemaco's return and Ulisse's proximity to Penelope. If Eumete is congenitally unable to speak except in song, Iro, the parasite, is the opposite: he cannot sing at all. A misfit in the pastoral world, he is unable to master its language: he splutters and stutters, even in his one aria. There is no melody in him.

L'incoronazione di Poppea

Modern taste

Monteverdi's third and last Venetian opera, *L'incoronazione di Poppea*, was performed in 1643, two years after the double bill of *Ulisse* and *Le nozze d'Enea*, at the same theatre, SS Giovanni e Paolo.[20] Cristoforo Ivanovich, whose *Minerva al tavolino* offers a chronology of Venetian opera from its beginnings in 1637 up to 1687, also lists a revival at the same theatre in 1646.[21] Although this revival has been called into question on the basis that Venetian theatres were closed at that time because of the war of Candia, recent evidence indicates that closure affected only the prose theatres, that opera houses were open, and that *Poppea* probably was revived, as Ivanovich claimed. One of the two surviving scores, though dating from the early 1650s, may in fact have been copied from the score used for the 1646 revival.[22] Another revival, this one securely documented by a printed libretto, occurred in Naples in 1651 under the title *Il Nerone*, but without any reference to the name of the composer. Although the identity of only one of the singers of the Venetian premiere is known for certain, Anna Renzi (Ottavia), others can be tentatively identified from the cast of *La finta savia*, the opera that shared the season at SS Giovanni e Paolo with *Poppea*: Anna di Valerio (Poppea), Stefano Costa (Nerone) and 'Rabacchio' or 'Corbacchio' (Valletto).[23]

The libretto by Gian Francesco Busenello contrasts markedly with those of its two predecessors, in ways that seem purposeful. Busenello was by far the most experienced of Monteverdi's Venetian librettists. By the time of *L'incoronazione di Poppea*, he had already produced two operatic texts for Francesco Cavalli (*Gli amori di Apollo e di Dafne* and *La Didone*). This might explain some of the differences between his libretto and those of Badoaro and Torcigliani – the greater number of closed forms, for instance, which Monteverdi would have set as arias. No less than Badoaro and Torcigliani, Busenello was a member in good standing of the Accademia degli Incogniti, but his aims, already revealed in his two previous librettos, were clearly different – he sought to justify his operatic activities by appealing to modern taste rather than classical doctrine. Accordingly, Busenello eschewed tragedy in his subtitle for *Poppea*, adopting instead the distinctly modern, anti-classical, 'opera musicale', redolent not of Aristotle but of the popular theatre. As a source for his drama, he did not choose an ancient epic praised by Aristotle, but a more modern Roman history as recorded by Tacitus (*Annals* 7–28). And whereas *Ulisse* adhered purposefully to its source, Busenello flaunts his freedom in the preface to his libretto:

> Nerone, enamoured of Poppea, wife of Ottone, sent him under the pretext of embassy, to Lusitania so that he could take his pleasure with her – this according to Cornelius Tacitus. *But here we represent things differently.*

He then goes on to outline his drama.

> Ottone is desperate at being deprived of Poppea. Ottavia, wife of Nerone, orders Ottone to kill Poppea; he promises to do so, but lacking the spirit to deprive his beloved of life, he dresses in the clothes of Drusilla who loves him. Thus disguised, he enters Poppea's garden. Love disturbs and prevents that death. Nerone repudiates Ottavia, in spite of the counsel of Seneca, and takes Poppea as his wife. Seneca dies, and Ottavia is expelled from Rome.

The drama does indeed take liberties, especially with the historical sequence of events and the portrayal of the characters. Most significant, perhaps, is the placement of Seneca's death. Although Busenello's outline links it chronologically with Ottavia's exile, in Tacitus it occurs some three years later, while in the libretto it occurs earlier, in the previous act, directly at the midpoint of the opera.

While he does at least cite Tacitus, Busenello fails to mention a number of his other sources, namely Suetonius (*The Lives of the Caesars*, 6, 8) and Dio Cassius (*Roman Histories*, 61–2), which he drew upon for his characterisation of Seneca, and the anonymous tragedy *Ottavia* (then ascribed to Seneca himself), which not only offers the prototype for the relationship of two nurses to their mistresses (as in Busenello's Arnalta and Nutrice to Poppea and Ottavia respectively), but provides a template for the stichomytheic debate between Nerone and Seneca in Busenello's Act I, scene 9, as well as for Ottavia's final lament, 'Addio Roma'.

Busenello's attitude towards his sources is intentionally contradictory. By simultaneously flaunting his departure from and minimising his dependence on them, he could maintain an anti-classical pose, as if in explicit defiance of the Aristotelian strictures regarding verisimilitude. Likewise with the unities: he found it expedient to observe these particular Aristotelian rules in *Poppea*, despite the licence for their abuse provided by modern taste. Like *Ulisse* (and *Le nozze d'Enea*), *Poppea* clearly transpires during a single revolution of the sun. Busenello was a pragmatic modernist: his choices depended on his needs. He could just as well respect one rule – the unity of time – as he could reject another – five-act structure, in favour of three.

Formal structure

Busenello's choice of three-act structure over five, however, was not merely an attempt to seem modern. For that structure is fully as intrinsic to *Poppea* as the five-act structure is to *Ulisse*. Both of the intervals between the acts allow for the passage of imagined, rather than repre-sented, time that enables a crucial event that has just transpired to accumulate its full resonance. By the end of the first act, Seneca's doom has been sealed – as Poppea, who has suggested it, knows; as Nerone, who has ordered it, knows; and as Ottone, who has overheard Nerone's order, knows as well. Most importantly, the audience knows. But the key player in this particular intrigue, Seneca himself, has not yet learned of his fate. The pause before the second act heightens anticipation of what his response might be.

The interval between the second and third acts works in a similar way. The audience has just witnessed the failure of Ottone's attempt on Poppea's life. Here, they expect the interval to provide time for the information to reach the other characters. Despite the passage of that time, however, when Drusilla opens Act III, she has not yet heard the news. Her ignorance is particularly ironic, since she will be accused of the crime. Monteverdi exacerbates the situation by providing Drusilla with an inappropriately happy song, 'Felice cor mio'.

But there is a larger dramatic structure in *Poppea*, a binary division more closely linked to the meaning of the work. That division is articu-lated by Seneca's death in the middle of Act II. In the first half of the libretto, while the stoic philosopher is alive, his position and influence act upon the other characters, most of whom show at least some signs of conscience: Ottavia's moral and religious beliefs prevent her from aven-ging Nerone's betrayal, despite her rage. Ottone, too, cannot permit himself to yield to his anger and resists the temptation to kill Poppea for vengeance. Even Arnalta's conscience bothers her; she cannot con-done Poppea's immoral ambition and feels pity for Ottone. And Nerone, who must confront Seneca most directly, cannot overcome the inevit-ability of his old tutor's logic.

After Seneca's death, however, the whole moral fabric of this world unravels: Ottavia plans a murder and becomes a blackmailer; Ottone agrees to kill Poppea and exploits Drusilla's love, making her an accessory to the crime; Arnalta accepts Poppea's ambitious expediency and thinks of her own fortune; and Nerone, justified by the failed murder attempt, repudiates Ottavia, the very action Seneca had refused to condone. Seneca's death has unleashed the tide of immorality that is so shocking in *Poppea*. His death is the necessary prerequisite for the complete decay and ethical perversion ultimately embodied in Poppea's coronation: the world has turned upside-down, become carnival.

We have no external evidence that Busenello designed *Poppea* for 'the oracle of music' – no letters addressed to the composer, no revealing prefaces. Yet he surely gave Monteverdi what he liked: those

> rapidly shifting affections that offered him the opportunity of showing the marvels of his art with a full range of pathos, adapting the notes to the words and the passions in such a way that the singer laughs, cries, becomes enraged, compassionate, and does everything else they ask of him, and the listener is drawn by the same impetus into experiencing the variety and force of those same passions.[24]

The grand monologues of Ottone, Ottavia and Seneca, the angry confrontation of Seneca and Nerone, the sensual dialogues of Nerone with Poppea and with Lucano, demonstrate the full range of the composer's ability to portray human character and human passions. In calling upon his singers to laugh, cry, become enraged or compassionate, Monteverdi, like the great dramatists of classical antiquity, ensured that his audience would experience those same emotions, and thereby be purged of them.

Sources and authenticity

It is one of the ironies of musicology that Monteverdi's authorship of *L'incoronazione di Poppea*, which was celebrated as the composer's crowning achievement from the time a score was uncovered late in the nineteenth century (only a few years after *Ulisse*), and even adduced as the standard by which *Ulisse* was deemed lacking, is now considered uncertain by some scholars. *Ulisse*, in contrast, is now generally accepted as Monteverdi's.[25] The traditional attribution of *Poppea* relied on the standard Venetian chronologies (Ivanovich above all), but the surprising absence of contemporary evidence linking the work to Monteverdi, combined with growing suspicions about the accuracy of the chronologies, has led scholars to question his authorship. Doubts were fuelled by the advanced age of the composer, the identification in the two extant scores (in Naples and Venice) of music by other composers, and the practice of *pasticcio* current at the time (notably in the companion of *Poppea* at SS Giovanni e Paolo in the same season, *La finta savia*, which boasted the collaboration of six different composers).[26]

The uncertainty has been exacerbated by the nature of the surviving source material, which though more substantial than for any other opera of the time – some twelve different items, comprising, in addition to the two scores, manuscript and printed librettos, and a printed scenario – is frustratingly inconclusive. Only one of these sources links the work to Monteverdi (a manuscript libretto in Udine),[27] and only two of them can be plausibly associated with the Venetian premiere of 1643 (the same Udine manuscript and the scenario). Virtually all the other sources that can be dated, including the scores, are posthumous.[28]

While the authorship question cannot be definitively resolved with the material at hand, it is now generally agreed that both scores contain music by younger composers, most notably the much-beloved duet 'Pur ti miro', that concludes both scores (but is missing in the Naples libretto), which was likely composed by either Francesco Sacrati, Filiberto Laurenzi, Benedetto Ferrari or Francesco Cavalli.[29]

Music and text

Despite the ambiguity of the sources, and the probable presence of music by other composers in the scores, Monteverdi's hand is strongly in evidence throughout the opera. Eric Chafe has demonstrated this with respect to tonal design, especially as it embodies conventions of tonal allegory developed in the composer's earlier works.[30] It is perhaps most obvious, however, in Monteverdi's treatment of the libretto, the distinctive ways in which he altered Busenello's text. The composer's insistence on making texts his own, from the sonnets of Petrarch to the Roman Catholic Mass, is well attested. No other composer of the time (or of any time) is known to have taken the same kind of liberties.

Monteverdi's impact on Busenello's libretto is manifested in many ways, but his interventions in the text itself can be reduced to two general types, which often reinforce one another: intercalation or rearrangement of lines, and word repetition. Although the second of these techniques is used sporadically in *Ulisse*, both of them are much more appropriate in *Poppea*. Intercalation, which increases the interaction between characters, can transform stilted dialogues into more natural ones that imitate the dynamic familiarity of real life; Busenello's already naturalistic confrontations lend themselves particularly well to such treatment. Likewise, the psychological potential of repetition, particularly when exaggerated, finds an ideal testing ground in characters like Busenello's, whose motivations are not always on the surface. Excessive repetition of key words can sometimes go beyond the content of the text itself to reveal the speaker's deeper feelings.

One of the most effective instances of intercalation, coupled with exaggerated verbal repetition, occurs in the grand confrontation between

Ex. 12.1 L'incoronazione di Poppea, Act 1, scene 9 (Nerone and Seneca)

Seneca and Nerone in Act I, scene 9, a confrontation that lies at the very heart of the drama:

N.	La forza è legge in pace, e spada in guerra,	Force is the law in peace, and sword in war
	E bisogno non ha della ragione.	and has no need for reason.
S.	La forza accende gli odi, e turba il sangue.	Force kindles hate and excites the blood.
	La ragione regge gli uomini e gli Dei.	Reason governs men and gods.
N.	Tu mi sforzi allo sdegno; al tuo dispetto,	You are rousing my anger; despite you,
	E del popol in onta, e del Senato,	the people, the senate, despite
	E d'Ottavia, e del cielo, e dell'abisso,	Octavia and heaven and hell,
	Siansi giuste od ingiuste le mie voglie,	whether my wishes are just or unjust,
	Oggi, oggi Poppea sarà mia moglie.	Today, today Poppea will be my wife.

The musical setting (Ex. 12.1) is crucial to the passionate effect of this argument, particularly the intercalation of Nerone's and Seneca's lines and the *concitato* setting of the repeated words. Text and music portray more than an adversarial relationship here. They reveal the basic differences between the two men. Hysterical repetition of text bespeaks Nero's excitability, and his loss of control – perhaps even his guilty conscience: he doth protest too much. Seneca's moral self-confidence, on the other hand, his self-righteousness, is embodied in his straightforward, conclusive responses to Nerone. He has little need to repeat text to justify his position. This single example can stand for many. Poppea's manipulation of Nerone into agreeing to repudiate Ottavia and sentence Seneca to death is carried out by means of a series of judiciously placed intercalations, hesitations and word repetitions. Similar techniques intensify the irony of Drusilla's happiness in the face of Ottone's ambivalence toward her.

The nature of these revisions is very different from those in *Ulisse*. The composer intervened on a larger scale in the earlier work. His restructuring of entire speeches and scenes has an impact on the overall shape of the drama. The much more numerous interventions in *Poppea* are concerned with details; but although their individual impact is much more limited and subtle – an emphasis here, a motivation there – their cumulative effect is profound, contributing to the portrayal of psychologically complex characters, who reveal different aspects of themselves in their various confrontations with others.

An Incognito debate: questions of meaning

Considering that they were composed within two years of one another, *Il ritorno d'Ulisse* and *L'incoronazione di Poppea* seem remarkably different in almost every respect. One is a classicising drama, a 'tragedia' based closely on a single, well-known source, from which all of its characters and incidents are drawn. In five acts, its trajectory is steady and explicit: it moves inexorably, in a straightforward narrative progression, to its happy ending. Its themes seem clear – the rewards of patience, the power of Love over Time and Fortune – and they are clearly prepared in the prologue. The other work, a modern 'dramma musicale', is apparently more problematic. Based on a patchwork of sources (some unacknowledged), telescoped and rearranged and mixed with characters and situations invented by the librettist, its meaning seems far from clear – or if clear, far from acceptable. Nominally it celebrates the victory of Love, the love of Poppea and Nerone that triumphs over all obstacles – over objections of state, over legality and morality. But Love, fuelled by lust and by Poppea's ambition, is only victorious at the expense of Virtue. The philosopher Seneca dies, the legitimate empress, Ottavia, is exiled and the faithful lovers Ottone and Drusilla, emblems of constancy, are banished from Rome. The love rewarded in *Ulisse*, then, would seem to be the very opposite of that celebrated in *Poppea*.

Monteverdi's first and last Venetian operas are in dialogue with one another. They set up a debate that would have been familiar in the libertine salons of the Accademia degli Incogniti: between the classics and modern taste, between what we might call sacred and profane love; and the composer's second Venetian opera, the missing *Le nozze d'Enea*, would have added a further voice to that debate. Together, the three works form a kind of historical trilogy, deriving from the consequences of the fall of Troy: the return of Ulysses to Greek Ithaca, the foundation of Rome, and the dissolution of the Roman Empire. Running through as a thread is the theme of love, its mythical power and its implications for a larger social order. In *Ulisse* and in *Le nozze d'Enea*, the licit love of marriage confirms that order. In *Poppea* it is undermined and destroyed by the triumph of passion. Such moral alternatives would have had political resonance for Venetian audiences, relating to the celebrated virtue of their own republic. But whatever lessons Monteverdi's contemporaries may have taken from his last operas would have depended, then as now, on the passionate conviction of the composer's art.

Il ritorno d'Ulisse (1640), Act V, scene 10

ELLEN ROSAND

Ulisse has repeatedly turned to song to express his growing optimism – with Minerva, with Eumete, with Telemaco, and in his defeat of the Suitors. His confrontation with Penelope, so long awaited by him and by us, will be different. Resourceful Ulisse will not attempt to reach her with music, but with speech, the mode of expression she herself had adopted, we imagine, ever since his departure. Monteverdi takes special pains with Ulisse's speech, mustering his most carefully controlled eloquence. Here, notably, Badoaro's libretto is adequate to the task; the composer adds very little, content to exploit rhetorical emphases – parallelisms, repetitions, enjambements, images – already built into the text.

In a series of brief speeches, each countered by Penelope's stolid denial of her feelings and refusal to trust her senses, Ulisse enlists all his powers of persuasion, an effort marked, among other things, by repeated attempts to dislodge Penelope from her fixation on D, symbol of her faith – he moves several times to A, finally to G. He presses his suit with wide-ranging, strongly shaped melodic lines, extended phrases and expressive harmony. Her resistance, in contrast, is expressed in speech-like music of narrow compass placed low in her range, short phrases, strongly cadential harmony, and uniformly slow harmonic rhythm.

Ulisse's eloquence is in full flight when he first appears on stage, resplendent in his own clothes. As he has been announced by Telemaco with a strong cadence on G – 'Eccolo affé' – his entrance on high E introduces an abrupt shift, with E harmonised as a first-inversion dominant of A (the key of Love): 'O delle mie fatiche / Meta dolce e soave, / Porto caro, amoroso / Dove corro al riposo' (Oh sweet and gentle goal of my labours, dear, loving port, where I seek rest). These words are beautifully performed by Ulisse's gradually unfolding melodic line, a six-bar phrase extended through a series of suspensions and secondary dominants that delay harmonic resolution until the end. The descending suspension-filled melody of his 'fatiche' finally, after repeated postponement, curls briefly upwards before descending once more to reach its 'sweet goal' and come to rest.

Ever resourceful, in each of his subsequent attempts to move her he tries a different tack – he questions her response ('is *this* how you welcome your husband?'), he works to evoke her pity and guilt ('for you I risked death?'), and finally he asserts his identity ('I am that very Ulysses'), reminding her that he killed the Suitors – but she rejects each of his statements in turn as lies, deception, magic. Only when Ericlea, anguished witness to the scene, finally intervenes to testify on Ulisse's behalf does Penelope begin the painful process of yielding. Voicing her doubts for the first time, she struggles with the conflicting claims of love and honour. Love inspires a new key, F, but thoughts of honour lead back to D. Seizing upon the opening provided by her conflict, and especially by her poignant, provocative reference to her chaste bed, the ever wily Ulisse makes his final plea in his longest speech of the scene. Badoaro could hardly have served him better here, presenting him with ten sinewy lines almost completely devoid of rhyme and featuring a series of four consecutive enjambements (in this, and subsequent examples, italics indicate text repetitions added by Monteverdi):

Del tuo casto pensier io so, *io so* 'l costume,	Of your chaste thoughts I know the habit,
So che 'l letto pudico,	I know that your unsullied bed,
Che tranne Ulisse solo, altri non vide,	which none but Ulysses has ever seen,
Ogni notte da te s'adorna e copre	is adorned and covered every night by you
Con un serico drappo	with a silken cloth
Di tua man[o] contesto, in cui si vede	woven by your own hand, in which is depicted
Col verginal suo coro	with her virgin companions,
Diana effigiata	Diana's image.
M'accompagnò mai sempre	I was always accompanied
Memoria così grata.	by this sweet memory

Taking up the image of her chaste bed, Ulisse begins his argument in understated prose; his simple repeated notes form tonic triads over an unmoving bass in G. But the enjambed lines in the middle of his speech (lines 4–9) inspire one last melodic ascent of an octave, extended over nine bars and reaching a climax on the same high E, and resolution on the same low A, as his very first speech in the scene. The tension here created dissipates in the final four-bar phrase, in which Ulisse returns calmly – and self-confidently – to G for a cadence. Recalling the passionate opening of the scene, this final burst of eloquence finds its mark: 'Yes,' she responds, 'yes, yes, yes.'

Penelope's capitulation, as designed by the librettist, unfolds in three stages: recitative, aria and duet, but the text is little more than a sketch. Its overwhelming effect, all the more powerful for being so long withheld, belongs to the composer. Badoaro makes no formal distinction between her previous responses to Ulisse and this one, continuing with *versi sciolti*:

Or sì ti riconosco, or sì ti credo,	Now yes, I recognise you, now yes I believe you,
Antico possessore	ancient master
Del combattuto core.	of my beleaguered heart.
Onestà mi perdoni,	Forgive my rudeness,
Dono tutte ad Amor le sue ragioni.	I lay all the blame on Love.

But text repetition, melodic patterning and triple metre burst out in full force as Monteverdi and Penelope come alive again. The composer's setting of the first three lines grants them the weight they have earned.

Or sì, *or sì* ti riconosco,	Now yes, I recognise you,
sì sì sì sì, or sì ti credo, *sì sì*,	now, yes, I believe you,
Antico possessore	ancient master
Del combattuto core.	of my beleagured heart.

Unlike all her previous responses to Ulisse though, in this one Penelope accepts C and G (his keys) although she still reverts to her D for the cadence.

Then, to Ulisse's passionate encouragement to unfetter her tongue and unleash her voice, she responds with an aria, her only aria in the opera (and one in which the orchestra plays an unusually important role, in substantial ritornellos that repeat each vocal phrase). It is firmly planted from beginning to end in C major. The remarkable effect of this aria, too, is largely the composer's doing. To be sure, Badoaro has suggested lyrical setting by providing Penelope with three pairs of *versi sciolti* – alternating *settenari* and *endecasillabi* – in which she calls upon nature to rejoice with her. However, though the content of Badoaro's text certainly invites lyrical setting, it is highly irregular and resistant to formal structure. To begin with, the three couplets are not strictly parallel: the first one is an invocation, urging the heavens, fields and breezes to rejoice, while the second and third are descriptive of the singing birds, the murmuring streams, the greening grass and whispering waves, which now rejoice and are consoled. Nor do all three share rhyme or metre: only the second and third have an internal rhyme and end with a *sdrucciolo*. But Monteverdi regularises (as well as expands) the text. He constructs an aria of three strophes, dividing each of them into two very unequal parts, a pair of *settenarii* and a *quinario*, as follows:

Illustratevi o cieli,	Shine out, oh heavens,
Rinfioratevi o prati,	bloom again, oh fields,
Aure gioite.	Breezes, rejoice.
Gl'augelletti cantando,	The birds singing,
I rivi mormorando	the murmuring brooks
Or si rallegrino.	are now rejoicing.
Quell'erbe verdeggianti,	The verdant grass,
Quell'onde sussuranti,	the whispering waves
Or sì consolino.	now console themselves.

Though based on unequal textual segments, the two sections form a beautifully balanced bipartite structure (A and B), the composer compensating for the textual disparity through repetition and melismatic expansion of the B section, introducing effective text-interpretative gestures for 'gioite', 'rallegrino', and 'consolino'. The orchestral ritornello, which echoes each section, wonderfully enacts the text: Penelope's call for nature to join in her rejoicing is answered by the string band.

The aria remains in C, a significant departure from the key in which Penelope has found herself for most of the opera. Penelope's sense of freedom or abandon is displayed in the elaborate melismatic decorations, especially in the B sections of the stanzas (but also in A, particularly on 'onde sussuranti'). The regular succession of vocal and instrumental phrases conveys the sense that the entire world is infected with Penelope's joy. Penelope shifts to A minor and to expressive recitative in duple metre to declaim Badoaro's final summarising couplet: 'Già che'è sorta felice / Dal cenere Troian la mia Fenice', (now that my phoenix has happily arisen from the Trojan ashes), a conclusion that paves the way for the final duet in the same key, A minor, the key of love.

Her rediscovery of song, the language of love, inspires equal lyricism in him. Long abstemious in word repetition, they both indulge now. As he urges her to unfetter her tongue, his own tongue becomes unfettered: triple metre, expansive text repetition, and repeated emphasis on his high E warm his response: 'Sciogli *sciogli, sciogli* la lingua, *deh* sciogli / Per allegrezza i nodi, / sciogli un sospir, *un sospir,* un'ohimè, la voce snodi'.

Following her aria, their voices finally join in a duet, the first time they have sung together, sharing the language of love they have not spoken in twenty years. Rarely has an operatic duet earned its meaning so completely, so credibly. In one final editorial intervention, a thorough recasting of libretto material, Monteverdi renders this duet a fitting conclusion to all the preceding action. Badoaro's text is rather shapeless, though one can discern an overall telescoping of line lengths from seven syllables to five, three, and four ('Sospirato mio sole', 'Non si rammenti', 'Del goder', 'sì, sì vita'), and finally to three-syllable lines again at the end ('sì sì sì').

U: Sospirato mio sole	My longed-for sun.
P: Rinovata [ritrovata] mia luce!	My refound light.
U: Porto, quiete e riposo.	Quiet and peaceful harbour.
U and P: Bramato, sì, ma caro,	Desired and dear.
bramato sì, ma caro, caro, caro.	
bramato sì, ma caro, caro,	
P: Per te gli andati affanni	For you I learn
A benedir imparo.	to bless my past torments.
U: Non si rammenti	No longer remember
Più de' tormenti;	the torments;
P: sì, sì vita, sì sì	*yes, yes, my life, yes, yes.*
U: Tutto è piacer.	All is pleasure.
P: sì, sì vita, sì, sì.	
P: Fuggan dai petti	Let flee from our breasts
Dogliosi affetti;	all painful feelings,
U: sì sì sì core sì sì.	
P: Tutto è goder.	All is joy.
U: sì sì sì core sì sì.	
[a2 Venuto è il dì]	

score	*libretto*
U and P *(a due)*	
Del piacer	P: Del goder
Del goder	U: Del piacer
Venuto è il dì.	P: Sì, sì vita
Sì, sì, *si* vita,	U: Sì, sì core
sì, sì *sì* core	**Both:** Sì, sì, sì.
sì sì sì *sì.*	

The duet begins with a succession of six *settenari*, the first four for the lovers in alternation, the last two for Penelope alone. These are followed by a pair of three-line stanzas of *quinari*, one for each of the lovers, ending in a shared line; and finally four alternating *quaternari*, again ending in a shared line. Monteverdi transforms the first part of this exchange (lines 1–3) into a well-shaped lyrical statement in which the reunited lovers first alternate (as in Badoaro), with Ulisse's ascending line mirrored by Penelope's descending one. But then, after a shift from triple to duple metre, they overlap (Penelope's line 4, repeated many times by both), creating suspensions with one another; finally joining together to sing in parallel thirds (line 4 again) – a progression that re-enacts in miniature their *rapprochement*. As the metre shifts from triple to duple and back again, the harmony vacillates between A and D, interspersed with a few secondary dominants. Penelope then sings lines 5 and 6 alone, as in Badoaro; her music is a sequential augmentation of their previous shared material.

The final, longest section of the duet is constructed over an ostinato bass – an attenuated version of a *ciaccona*, extended from four to six triple-metre bars by means of a deceptive cadence. Here the composer intercalates two of Badoaro's textual units – the *quinari* and *quaternari* – so that once again the music of the lovers overlaps. First Ulisse sings his stanza ('Non si rammenti'), Penelope joining him with text taken from their later exchange ('Sì, sì vita, sì, sì'). Then their positions are reversed: Penelope sings her stanza ('Fuggan dai petti') with Ulisse supplying counterpoint to text taken from their later exchange ('sì, sì, sì core, sì, sì'). That later exchange never takes place: instead the lovers sing those lines together in sixths to bring the duet to a close on A. This final simultaneous passage is by far their longest in the opera. The unstable harmony, avoidance of cadences, unpredictable repetition of various textual units and irregular overlaps between voices, sometimes with different, sometimes the same text, the repetitive vocal lines and rhythmic disjunctions – repeated shifts between duple and triple metre, syncopations – create an almost dizzying effect, which does not resolve until the concluding passage of parallel sixths. Here the reunited lovers sing the same text simultaneously for the first and only time in the opera, first in C, then in A. Even the ostinato pattern dissipates here, losing itself in the bliss of their union, so long postponed, so deeply desired.

13 Monteverdi studies and 'new' musicologies

Monteverdi studies have been associated with the so-called 'new musicology' since the first time the latter was mentioned in print, in a column reviewing the 1991 meeting of the American Musicological Society for the *New York Times*.[1] Papers on Bob Dylan, desire in Skryabin, reflections of Nazi ideology in German musicology during the Second World War, and the gendered rhetoric of the Monteverdi/Artusi controversy served the author as signs of

> of a gradual transformation of ... musicology ... The new musicology ... turns ... to the movements that dominate literary studies, ... not primarily interest in aesthetic issues ... they might focus on the social implications of a work, or ... how a work reveals the artists' position in society or argues for a particular view of sexuality and power.

Using the phrase 'new musicology' three more times as he cautiously welcomed a 'classic paradigm shift', the writer conferred the status of a movement on an eclectic group of papers whose authors had never met. Yet the label, and the sense that it referred to some kind of movement, stuck. It was in part because the Monteverdi paper sparked criticism when it was published, leading the author to compare 'new musicology' to the 'second practice', that the label 'new musicology' has had a special resonance in Monteverdi studies.[2] This essay will survey the intersections of Monteverdi studies with the new approaches to music scholarship that emerged, mainly in the United States, over the last twenty years. Characterised by successive efforts to assimilate the newest insights and methods of other disciplines, the phenomenon might be better described as an 'interdisciplinary' or 'critical turn' in musicology, rather than as any single 'new' musicology.

Critical turns: new criticism, new historicism, feminism

Three of the most important Monteverdi scholars of the last quarter century, Gary Tomlinson, Ellen Rosand and Susan McClary, were among the first musicologists of any sort to make these turns. In the early 1980s, Tomlinson published a pair of path-breaking articles that hovered between 'new criticism' (close reading of a text without considering any contexts) and 'new historicism' (seeking to understand the 'cultural work' of a text – its ways of addressing cultural anxieties – in its original historical context).[3] Tomlinson began where Nino Pirrotta's interest in Monteverdi's poetic choices left off.[4] Taking account of the literary fashions and critical perspectives that would have been part of Monteverdi's intellectual world ('new historicism'), Tomlinson used close reading ('new criticism') to decipher how Monteverdi might have read the poems he set.[5] Tomlinson thus produced a new way of thinking about the 'via naturale all'imitatione' that was to make Monteverdi's recitative soliloquies so compelling to posterity. Developing his ideas in a subsequent book, Tomlinson argued that Monteverdi was at his best when he read poetry as a humanist – and at his worst when, later in life, he read with the surface-obsessed sensibility associated with the poet Giambattista Marino.[6] Tomlinson's critical work articulated in new terms the long-standing perception that Monteverdi had straddled a paradigm shift in Western music, reinvigorating scholarly interest in the word/music question and in the ways its answers might illuminate Monteverdi's importance. The ongoing interest in applying literary and linguistic theory to Monteverdi's musical texts – notably of Jeffrey Kurtzman and Mauro Calcagno – can be traced to Tomlinson's literary turn.[7]

Ellen Rosand's 1985 article 'Seneca and the interpretation of *L'incoronazione di Poppea*'[8] combined close reading and a fuller engagement with new historicism into a model for interpreting early opera critically that young scholars continue to emulate. Rosand meticulously historicised Gian Francesco Busenello's libretto for *Poppea*, linking it to specific concerns of Venice's Accademia degli Incogniti, to which he belonged. She showed how Busenello made the character of Seneca figure those concerns, so that despite his obvious human flaws Seneca became the moral centre on which the opera's morally problematic plot turns. Turning to close reading of Monteverdi's music, Rosand wrote from the assumption that Monteverdi's focus was more on the representation of credible human characters than on the representation of language that had been Tomlinson's concern: in her view, Monteverdi had shaped characters from the details of musical speech he created for them. The result was an interpretation that read *Poppea* as a whole, much as a literary critic might read *Hamlet*, and that showed how *Poppea* addressed important issues of its time. Rosand thus opened the field for alternative readings of *Poppea* and other early operas that treat them both as aesthetic objects and as historical evidence about the concerns of a particular cultural and historical moment.[9] Moreover, her work sparked ongoing interest in how Monteverdi engaged problems of representation.

Two essays in Susan McClary's *Feminine Endings* marked the most dramatic emergence of a 'new musicology' in Monteverdi studies, piquing traditional scholars' fascination and ire in ways that Tomlinson's and Rosand's dalliance with new historicism did not. What was so new about McClary's approach? First, the notes to her essays suggest breathtakingly wide interdisciplinary reach, encompassing references to Bakhtin, Barthes and Bourdieu on the one hand to feminist critics like Catherine Clément, Sandra Gilbert, Ann Rosalind Jones, Kaja Silverman and Gaytari Spivak on the other. McClary's sweeping eclecticism burst musicology's disciplinary boundaries and redefined what might count as historicist study of music. Although she cited not a single archival document or 'primary' musicological source, the material McClary did cite enabled her to historicise early modern gender norms, as a background against which to read Monteverdi's creation of various musical rhetorics to represent a range of early modern gender positions – the sexually innocent and musically unfocused Euridice; the sexually active and musically goal-directed Proserpina; the seductive and musically masterful Poppea; the powerful yet, in his emotional extravagance, faintly effeminate Orfeo. By her ability to link immediately audible details to late twentieth-century intellectuals' ideas about early modernity, McClary made Monteverdi's music intelligible, as art and as history, to a wider public than early-music scholars usually reach.

Second, McClary's essays introduced musicologists to the notion that both gender and sexuality are historically and culturally specific constructs. On the face of it, this notion seems unproblematic: gender and sexuality are historically specific ways of interpreting certain physically observable 'facts' about animals' bodies, just as modality and tonality are historically specific ways of interpreting physically observable 'facts' about the properties of sound. Yet the very phrase 'constructions of gender' destabilised a fundamental premise of twentieth-century musicology. If Monteverdi's representations of gendered human beings could be understood as deliberately crafted in response to cultural norms about gender we no longer share (so that his characters would be intelligible to his contemporaries), then it followed that some aspects of his music were neither 'universal' nor 'transcendent'. Thus McClary challenged one of the foundations of traditional music history: the belief that some musical works, by some composers, merit performance and study because they communicate human truths that transcend their conditions of origin. After McClary, it would be harder to sustain the belief that a scholar's or a critic's work was to explore and explicate Monteverdi's unquestioned, trans-historical genius.

Third, it follows from the idea that gender and sexuality are constructed, that whatever we might have thought to understand directly about Orfeo or Arianna, Seneca or Poppea, might be a misunderstanding based in late-modern or post-modern assumptions. No matter how carefully we had reconstructed Monteverdi's reading habits, his poetic choices or the political agendas of his librettists, unless we also understood the social structures of his time we could not grasp the meanings his characters projected to his first listeners. McClary's work thus exponentially raised the standards for new historicist scholarship on Monteverdi. After her, to write credibly about Monteverdian matters touching on gender or sex would require that musicologists come to terms with the large body of historical and critical scholarship on early modern ideas of gender, sex and embodiment, as well as with literary, theatrical and musical histories. Further, it would become increasingly difficult to ignore the fact that real bodies – both early modern ones and late twentieth- or twenty-first-century ones – were involved in the performance and representation of some highly sexualised texts ('Si, ch'io vorrei morire' (SV89), for example), and consequently increasingly difficult to ignore the implications for real, embodied persons of musical texts that represent sexual violence or betrayal ('Eccomi pront'ai baci' (SV135), or the laments of Arianna and the nymph of 'Non avea Febo ancora recato il dì' (SV163)).

These three points amounted to a revolution in musicology, not just in Monteverdi studies. But McClary's was not a total revolution. The Monteverdian essays in *Feminine Endings* develop their argument from three assumptions that had long pervaded Monteverdi studies. First, for McClary, as for Tomlinson and Rosand, Monteverdi's musical constructions seem to respond to forces that are easily described in language; thus music remains the *serva* of culture, notwithstanding its dominion over listeners' feelings. Second, like Tomlinson, McClary sees Monteverdi's musical *oeuvre* as straddling two 'orders of things': she explores the relatively early *Orfeo* as a document of late Renaissance ideas about gender in relation to rhetoric and sees in the late *Poppea* an example of different gender/rhetorical norms. Third, McClary's argument is wholly grounded in the assumption that musical meaning is discerned by listening to music, rather than by making it. Still, her work raised important questions. How did the rhetorical prowess represented as a male privilege in early opera come to be reassigned mainly to female characters by the 1640s? How did representations of rhetorically extravagant women come to envoice complaints against inappropriate power? Could representations of women, or instances of real women's vocality, have functioned as resistance to patriarchal authority? These were questions others would take up in the 1990s, often with arguments made partly through interpretations of Monteverdi's music.

After 1993: analysis, performance, historiography and criticism

Monteverdi studies flourished in the 1990s and the first years of this century, sparked in part by commemorations of the 350th anniversary of his death.[10] Much new work emerged from premises quite independent of the United States' fashion for critical readings, but new ideas about analysis, performance, historiography and the relationship of music to gender, sexuality and embodiment increasingly informed each other, speeding the progress of Monteverdi studies' critical turn. 'Close', 'new historicist' and 'feminist' critical readings of Monteverdi's music were both enabled and enriched by new musical analytical models introduced in the 1990s. An ongoing problem for scholars of early seventeenth-century music is the lack of a single unifying theory: much of the repertoire seems to hover between modal and tonal organisation.[11] In 1992, Eric Chafe's *Monteverdi's Tonal Language* proposed a way of describing the pitch organisation of Monteverdi's music in terms of hexachord, system and mode that has come to be generally accepted in the United States.[12] Chafe used his own descriptions as the basis for provocative close readings of many madrigals from the Fourth and Fifth Books, and of the 'tonal allegories' of such larger works as *Orfeo*, the *Ballo delle ingrate*, *Il ritorno d'Ulisse*, and *L'incoronazione di Poppea*. In 1993, Tim Carter and Geoffrey Chew each used a kind of layer analysis derived from Schenkerian techniques to support, respectively, points about the possible meanings of 'aria' in early seventeenth-century music and the Neoplatonic implications of Monteverdi's rhythmic and modal procedures in the Eighth Book of Madrigals.[13] Echoing the much earlier analytical work of Susan McClary's dissertation, their methods enabled close readings of Monteverdi's music that were entirely independent of the *oratione* (the rhetorical standpoint, or the words) that, the composer had claimed, commanded his musical choices as a *padrona* would her *serva*.[14] The same year Jeffrey Kurtzman produced a close reading of the Eighth Book's 'Or che'l ciel e la terra' that took seriously the taxonomic impulse of Monteverdi's preface and showed how Monteverdi might have used an equally taxonomic reading of Petrarch's poem to produce the madrigal's surprisingly varied, but coherent large-scale form.[15] More recently, Anthony Pryer has used an inspired combination of historical and analytical study to show how Monteverdi reworked excerpts from *Orfeo* in the Sixth Book madrigal 'Zefiro torna e'l bel tempo rimena' (SV108). While none of this work sutures Monteverdi's music to a social context, as critical musicologists try to do, it does shed remarkable light on Monteverdi's compositional process.[16]

The last fifteen years have seen a steady expansion of knowledge about such things as tunings, cleffing, transposition, string technique, options for continuo practice and the physical spaces and ritual functions of some canonic Monteverdi works.[17] Immensely helpful to both performers and scholars by allowing us richer, more carefully historicised notions of how this music sounded, little of this work explicitly engaged the intellectual revolutions of critical musicology. An important exception is the work of Richard Wistreich. His 1994 article, 'La voce e grata assai, ma...: Monteverdi on singing' brought both vocal expertise and post-modern scepticism to bear on a wide range of early seventeenth-century descriptions of singers, yielding a nuanced survey of vocal tastes and of the cultural meanings that might have been ascribed to different kinds of voices.[18] Although not specifically about Monteverdi, Wistreich's more recent work must be counted as among the first examples of music scholarship to assimilate successfully Judith Butler's theory that identity is performative (brought into being by repeated actions understood to constitute a social category), McClary's notion that music can construct social identities, and a rigorous reconstruction of historical conditions from primary sources.[19]

More than any other scholar, Gary Tomlinson was responsible for introducing new historiographical methods into Monteverdi studies. His *Monteverdi and the End of the Renaissance* advocated adapting anthropologist Clifford Geertz's method of 'thick description' to the study of early music, although Tomlinson's own range of cultural reference, while rich, did not extend very far outside the traditional literary sources.[20] In his next book, however, Tomlinson's thought took the anthropological turn more sharply. *Music and Renaissance Magic* focuses on music as a cultural practice, rather than as a set of autonomous works created by exceptional individuals. Almost all the music Tomlinson mentions was improvised with the intention of effecting real – if 'magical'– change in the world; ephemeral, this music was locked forever in a realm of ineffable, time-bound performances that seem impervious to historical knowledge.[21] Not at all concerned with this music's aesthetic qualities, Tomlinson sought instead to understand an aspect of Renaissance musical culture profoundly foreign to the modern sensibility, and thus to de-familiarise the parts of that culture that twentieth-century scholars believed we understood. Monteverdi's music figured only toward the end of the book, when Tomlinson revisited his own critical readings of 'Sfogava con le stelle' (Fourth Book of Madrigals) and the Lamento della Ninfa (Eighth Book) in terms of his argument that magical thinking had been an unspoken assumption of 'Renaissance' culture that was rapidly disappearing by the 1630s. These examples ensured that Tomlinson's ideas about both magic and music historiography became touchstone concerns of Monteverdi scholarship – if often contested ones.

Theoretically dense, *Music and Renaissance Magic* introduced Monteverdians to three ideas from the work of the French historian Michel Foucault, each of which diminishes the centrality of individual composers and individual works. 'Archaeology' reads the traces that survive from the past to detect levels of meaning unavailable to the people who produced those traces.[22] Directly opposed to hermeneutics, which seeks to decipher (not only detect) the meanings in specific texts, archaeology opposes both close and historicist readings. 'Geneaology' is the history of the position of the subject; it accounts for the constitution of knowledges and discourses without positing the existence of a 'transcendental' subject who could be imagined as outside discourse: the knowing (or reading, composing, performing) subject is understood to have been formed by the knowledges and discourses in which she or he might, as an artist or a scholar, intervene.[23] Because both knower (say, a performer-scholar) and known (say, a Monteverdi madrigal) have been formed differently by discourse, knowledge itself is a relationship suffused with power and difference – not a set of discoverable facts. An 'episteme' is the historically specific set of *a priori* assumptions on which knowledge is based in a given time or place. These assumptions, detectable by archaeology, will most often not be part of any knower's (or artist's) conscious thought: they are taken for granted, as 'the order of things'.[24] Tomlinson's *Music in Renaissance Magic* capitalised on Foucault's notion that some time near the start of the seventeenth century a modern 'episteme of representation' (in which the relationship between, say, signs and signifiers was, by definition, the product of arbitrary, temporary artifice) and a pre-modern 'episteme of resemblance' (in which everything in the 'world' was conceived as related to everything else in a seamless web of existence and in which play with the intrinsic resemblances between, say, a musical mode, a planet and a word or thought could produce effects of power). Although it was not Tomlinson's point, his book can leave a reader interested in Monteverdi with the impression that the composer was not a transcendental subject, but a historically contingent one, formed by one Foucauldian episteme, who lived through – and contributed to – the transition to another.

Although Tomlinson's third book, *Metaphysical Song*, has little to say about Monteverdi, Monteverdi scholars must nonetheless reckon with its arguments.[25] Following up on Tomlinson's anthropological and Foucauldian turns, the book traces the history of 'the hearing of the operatic voice as a medium putting its listeners in touch with invisible, supersensory realms'.[26] Tomlinson puts some familiar narratives of opera history in touch with equally familiar narratives of intellectual history, choosing the points of contact strategically so as to show the relationship between profound shifts in metaphysics and concepts of subjectivity on the one hand, and shifts in the way singers, composers and listeners have understood the theatricalised voice of opera on the other. *Metaphysical Song* is controversial. In his focus on metaphysics, and on 'song' as a noun rather than 'singing' as a verb form, Tomlinson can seem to have transported music into the realm of pure thought. The book can seem to dismiss the meanings that might attach, consciously or not, to the act of singing – one of the most complex and culturally variable actions a human body can perform. Moreover, although Foucauldian method shows ways to evade entrapment in the myths of 'great composer', 'great works' and transcendental mastery, in practice Tomlinson's essay falls back on works, composers and indeed, philosophers that his readers already know, re-inscribing a set of gendered and classed structures of knowledge and power that many post-modern intellectuals strive to dismantle. Nonetheless, Tomlinson's essay points to the interpretative possibilities that arise from a Foucauldian approach to two preoccupations of Monteverdi studies – the relationship between language (culture) and music and the almost magical properties attributed to the act of singing by those who listen.

Among the strongest threads of 'new musicology' in Monteverdi studies are those that explored the relationships linking the composer's music to issues of gender, sexuality and embodiment. This strand of scholarship might casually be called 'feminist', as its correlate is in literary studies, but many of its musical exponents eschew the self-consciously political stance the word implies. Inspired by Susan McClary's work, their authors often drew methodologically on traditional history, Rosand's new historicism or Tomlinson's anthropological turn to explore representations or performances of femininity, and to recover the contributions performers had made to the musical traces associated with Monteverdi's name. For example, Beth Glixon used archival documents to develop a vivid picture of the material conditions of singers' lives from Anna Renzi (Octavia in the first production of *Poppea*) to Giulia Masoti, active in the late 1660s. Reading singers' contracts straightforwardly but shrewdly, Glixon showed that by Masoti's generation, women singers could dictate terms to composers and librettists.[27] Thus, Glixon shows a material side of the seventeenth-century trend to represent some women's voices as powerful and resistant, to which McClary had already drawn attention. A rich conversation developed around McClary's notion that the lament was a feminine genre. I combined new historicism with close reading to interpret Monteverdi's lament for Arianna in relation to early modern prescriptive culture on womanhood, and to argue that the lament's repeated performance by female amateurs transformed the lament itself into prescriptive culture – an occasion for women to practice such patterns of behaviour as ferocious but futile rage and self-silencing.[28] Tim Carter used traditional historical method to consider the possibility that the lament might have been as much improvised by Virginia Ramponi Andreini as composed by Monteverdi.[29] Using historical anthropology (rather than Foucauldian archaeology) Anne MacNeil rediscovered the ritual function of laments to mark the liminality in rites of passage, especially marriages, as well as the use of laments in training young boys for rhetorical power. Both uses have implications for the utility of the constructed 'feminine' in early modern Italian culture.[30] Working from performativity theory, Bonnie Gordon argued that the very sound of a woman's voice in the lament-like recitative that ends the *Ballo delle ingrate* resisted the ritual intention to silence women.[31] More recently, Rachel Lewis has broken through the implicit notion that gender-sensitive readings are mainly of interest to women, showing the usefulness of such reading to address the attribution problems of *Poppea* from a critical rather than a source-studies perspective.[32]

Four recent monographs exemplify the range and sophistication that both critical and traditional musicology can reach. Tim Carter's *Monteverdi's Musical Theatre* profits from the author's ubiquity in the field of Monteverdi studies over the last generation: there has been no novelty of analysis, historiography or critical perspective to which Carter has not responded, and few that he has not actively fostered.[33] His book synthesises traditionally gathered historical material about theatrical production norms, genres, libretti, sources and so forth, with critical readings of Monteverdi's principal theatrical works that are perspicacious, provocative, and, most importantly, pertinent to both performers and audiences. Massimo Ossi's methodologically traditional *Divining the Oracle* addresses two long-standing nodes of Monteverdi scholarship – the composer's straddling of traditional and modern musical worlds, and the relationship, in his compositions and verbal thought, between *oratione* and music.[34] Reading letters and music against each other, Ossi shows Monteverdi to have actively embraced (if not created) his position as music's leading modernist; to have consciously engaged questions of genre and large-scale musical design throughout his life; to have been more interested in music's ability to communicate affect than its ability to serve language *per se*; and, through skilled use of *ostinati* and *ritornelli*, to have arrived at a conception of musical communication that held the claims of music and text in equilibrium. Wendy Heller's erudite *Emblems of Eloquence* uses Rosand's methods to answer McClary's questions about representations of women in seventeenth-century opera.[35] Heller reconstructs from primary sources the discourse on womanhood that circulated in early modern Venice, and the ways that discourse interacted with the Republic's political self-fashioning. Her chapter on the character of Octavia in *Poppea* is a fine example of her historicist achievement: she painstakingly recovers the conceptions of Nero's queen that circulated in the classical Roman literature and history that mid-century Venetians knew and deftly shows how Monteverdi's compositional decisions can be seen as choices among them, further analysing the diva Anna Renzi's contribution to the character's first reception. Finally, Bonnie Gordon's *Monteverdi's Unruly Women* brings ideas from McClary, Tomlinson and others to bear on the issue named in her book's subtitle – 'the power of song in early modern Italy'.[36] Gordon's book is not ultimately about Monteverdi. For her, the composer is a rhetorical convenience – the creator of relatively well-known works through which to explore the relationships that link musical behaviours to the rest of the world. Gordon's focus is on women's bodies as understood in the medical literature, common sense, erotic imaginings and fantasies of difference that circulated in Monteverdi's time and on the ways that singing of and/ or about embodied women would have been understood by both singers and listeners in early modern culture. Subtly contesting Tomlinson's emphasis on the metaphysical, Gordon produces historicised readings of Monteverdi works that privilege the physical force of the sounds that came from women's throats, showing how and when those sounds might have been perceived to contest patriarchal authority, how and when they may have helped to articulate the shift of episteme through which she, like so many others, believes Monteverdi lived.

Unanswered questions

Like McClary and Tomlinson, Heller and Gordon move away from the idea that a critical musicologist's work would be to explore and explicate instances of Monteverdi's genius, although they leave intact the curious disembodiment (and apparent independence from material, quotidian realities) that music historians have long conferred on 'great composers'. If the explication of a transcendental subject's genius is not our work and if, for better or worse, helping to solve source and performance-practice quandaries never was – what is the use of critical musicology's work on Monteverdi? 'Monteverdi' provides these authors and many others with a well-known repertoire through which to propose new critical or historiographical methods; to probe music's relationship to modern subjectivity; to explore ways that the music of another time and place might illuminate our understanding of historical others' experience. Finally, these authors invite us to contemplate the reasons that this music, produced by a set of unspoken beliefs about knowledge, power and sound very different from our own, should continue to move us. That might be agenda enough to ensure an ongoing stream of scholarship, some of it interesting to performers and audiences.

The four papers chosen by the *New York Times* fifteen years ago to exemplify a 'new musicology' represented four themes it was poised to develop further – musical desire, popular culture, scholarly ideology and music's imbrication with gender; only two of those, desire and gender, have been much explored by Monteverdi scholars. But the recent essays of Andrew dell'Antonio and Iain Fenlon tracing the uses of Monteverdiana to Italian fascism invite curiosity about the liveliness – indeed, the dominance – of Anglo-American scholarship on Monteverdi in recent years.[37] How has that liveliness interacted with the social, economic and political transformations engendered by Anglo-American 'neo-liberalism' since the Thatcher–Reagan alliance of the 1980s or with the delicate relationship between Anglo-American Monteverdi enthusiasts and Italy's early-music communities, both performing and scholarly, and the equally delicate relationships linking both to the artistic self-fashionings of the new Europe? To what extent might such political questions be implicated in the rise of distinctive, seemingly national, styles of performing Monteverdi's music, each appealing directly to potential listeners' identifications or disidentifications with contemporary pop? Might they be implicated in the startling critical inattention to Monteverdi's sacred music? Might these or similarly self-reflexive questions illuminate critical musicology's odd inattention to representations of sexual violence, class antagonism, ethnic tension and empire and perhaps prompt a new burst of scholarship, both historicist and critical, in just these areas, along with newly conceived performances?

How might thinking about Monteverdi's constructions of sexual and ethnic violence illuminate the ways both 'difference' and 'violence' itself were understood in early modern Mantua and Venice? Based on what we know about where, when and how these representations were performed, what can we say about this music's role in either resisting or inscribing particular patterns of violence in the modern sensibility? How might these representations satisfy our own expectations about the place of violence, and narratives of violence, in musical pleasure or aesthetic experiences? Could we imagine producing *Il combattimento di Tancredi e Clorinda* now as Luciano Berio meant to in the 1960s, as an anti-war gesture? Or does the *Combattimento* instead outline exactly the volatile mingling of sexual, ethnic and religious arrogance (the fear, loathing and love of a particular other) from which Anglo-American culture's current imbroglios in the Middle East have sprung? Might the *Combattimento* have become the most important of Monteverdi's works to study from critical and widely historicising perspectives, and the most inflammatory?

But there may be still deeper questions to be asked. Almost all the new work on Monteverdi to have emerged in the last fifteen years, critical or not, has remained tethered to three premises: 1) that Monteverdi lived through the transition from one episteme (or paradigm, or poetic sensibility) to another; 2) that the relationship between words (or culture) and music was most easily figured as a binary, whether hierarchical or, in Ossi's conception of it, complementary; and 3) that the primary means of experiencing music – as aesthetic pleasure, knowledge/power, or meaning – is through listening. The latter two, and perhaps all three, can easily seem to manifest the presence of the 'episteme of representation' in modern thought about music. This is an episteme in which music is ... only music and not a force that can make things happen in the world, nor a means by which to know what the other, language-bound disciplines of cultural inquiry cannot decipher. Yet the episteme of representation has been disintegrating since Foucault named it in 1966, shortly before the four-hundredth anniversary of Monteverdi's birth. Evidence that the process extends to musical culture includes the rapidly successive interdisciplinary turns of musicology in recent years. The focus on performance and performativity (exemplified by Wistreich and Gordon), on the continuum linking music to a soundscape (exemplified in early modern studies by the work of Bruce Smith), on the opacity of musical events to either hermeneutic or archaeological scrutiny (argued by Carolyn Abbate) seem to be leading us right out of the episteme of representation, toward an episteme in which music *is* a force.[38] It is hard even to imagine what the emerging episteme might be; but it seems likely that by the time we come to celebrate the four-hundredth anniversary of Monteverdi's death, some of its principles will be taken for granted, disappearing from hermeneutic view. There is no telling what questions, if any, about Monteverdi and his epoch might seem pertinent in that world.

14 Monteverdi in performance

RICHARD WISTREICH

On 24 June, the feast of St John the Baptist, I was taken to Vespers in the church of SS Giovanni and Lucia where I heard the most perfect music I had ever heard in my life. It was directed by the most famous Claudio Monteverdi, *maestro di cappella* of S. Marco, who was also the composer and was on this occasion accompanied by four theorbos, two cornettos, two bassoons, one *basso di viola* of huge size, organs and other instruments all equally well handled, not to speak of ten or twelve voices. I was delighted with it. (CONSTANTIJN HUYGENS, 1620)[1]

A competent and credible performance, good enough that the audience could experience the work. The instrumental forces approximated an authentic ensemble. True, the bowed strings were all modern, except for a viol da gamba [sic] played beautifully by a woman unnamed in the program. But there were theorbos, a portatif organ, harpsichord and, most interestingly, three cornettos. The cornetto was on the verge of obsolescence even in Monteverdi's time. It looks like a warped oboe without any keys, but it is played with puckered lips, like a trumpet. In fact, it sounds a lot like a thin-voiced trumpet. When used in ensemble with the trombones Wednesday, it produced a beautiful, archaic sound ... there were seven solo singers, some of whom specialize in early music, and all of whom had the technique and stylistic knowledge to sing Monteverdi convincingly ... All in all, a fitting season opening for the National Arts Centre Orchestra. (RICHARD TODD, 1998)[2]

In these two reports of performances of Vespers music by Monteverdi, separated by more than 350 years, there are striking resemblances between the things that each writer chose to mention and those they did not. Both are fascinated by the performing forces, singling out certain instruments for particular comment – names, numbers and unusual, even exotic, features. Each mentions the singers as well, but generically, not as individuals. There are hints at the skills of the musicians but neither writer chooses to focus on the music he heard in terms either of its content, structure, meaning or genre (sacred music), nor its relationship to the event at which it was heard – in the first case as part of a service in a church and in the second, a performance in a concert hall. Instead, they both engage with Monteverdi's music as something that *happens*, a visual as well as an aural experience for an audience focused on the performers, rather than with the music as 'composition' or sound object.

The second account, however, is also imbued with the writer's sense of the self-consciously historicist dimension of the event he witnessed, not to mention the apparent need, even as recently as 1998, to explain its novelties. His reference to the 'technique and stylistic knowledge' necessary to validate the performance as 'convincing', draws attention to the wide range of technical considerations and interpretative challenges involved in bringing Monteverdi's music to life in circumstances far removed from those in which it was first created. These challenges persist at the beginning of the twenty-first century, despite, or perhaps even because of, the enormous developments in 'historically informed performance' in the past forty years or so.

In turning any score into a performance, there is a huge amount of information which is not written down, either because it is simply not possible to explain on paper or because the composer or publisher takes it for granted that the musicians will 'know' what to do, based on their training, experience and shared sense of prevailing conventions. Trying to reconstruct this kind of knowledge and then apply it over such a distance of time resembles the most ambitious archaeological or detective work. It involves piecing together sometimes tiny fragments of information of different kinds from pictures, letters, payment records, music treatises, surviving instruments and buildings, and a host of other sources. Much of the information available now about the performance practice of Monteverdi's music, covering questions of organology, playing technique, notation, performing spaces, instrumentation, liturgical contexts, dance forms and much else besides, has been painstakingly accumulated and disseminated during the recent past by scholars and practising musicians – these days quite likely one and the same – often researching and testing out ideas 'on the job'. This chapter focuses on Monteverdi the practical musician and the singers and instrumentalists for whom he wrote his music – their skills and their mutual understanding of the conventions that informed the relationship between composer and performer.

Music director

Monteverdi became *maestro* of Duke Vincenzo Gonzaga's household music establishment in Mantua probably in December 1601 after more than a decade's service as one of its rank-and-file members. The duties, although involving supplying the demand for new compositions in a wide variety of genres, were also relentlessly 'hands-on'. In the words of Pietro Maria Marsolo, *maestro di cappella* at Ferrara Cathedral, writing in 1612 to express his interest in Monteverdi's recently vacated post, 'it is not sufficient for a *maestro di cappella* just to be a good composer: he must also know how to utilize singers as well as instrumentalists, prepare and direct them well, have a good ear and be quick to remedy any deficiency'.[3] These combined responsibilities imposed a heavy burden – indeed, Monteverdi suffered what amounted to a breakdown through overwork and stress in 1608. But throughout his career, both at Mantua and Venice, he was fortunate enough to work with fine and able musicians, both 'stars' and the members of the rank-and-file who, by the very nature of the job, would have been not only technically highly assured in every aspect of singing or playing, but also deeply enculturated to the collective responsibilities and conventions governing their work.

Monteverdi's full-time team in Mantua included about a dozen male and five female singers, eight or nine players of members of the violin family, two keyboard players (of organ, harpsichord and spinet), a harpist, guitarists and a small ensemble of about five assorted wind players, as well as his respected assistant director, Don Bassano Cassola.[4] Although individual freelance musicians from the locality as well as occasional guest stars from other courts might be brought in to augment their forces when necessary, the core ensemble of household musicians had to cover most of the music of the court in all relevant genres, from church music to opera. Their duties were very varied, from the regular provision of liturgical music in the ducal chapel to intimate concerts in the Gonzaga family's private rooms, music for court social dancing, and the weekly Friday-evening performances of concerted madrigals and other chamber music in the Hall of Mirrors. They also served as the main body of musicians for a variety of larger-scale and more public occasions, including multi-media theatrical events staged for special entertainments – banquets, receptions, ballets and, of course, occasional major undertakings such as the productions of plays, operas and *intermedi* commissioned for important celebrations such as dynastic marriages.[5]

When he moved to Venice in 1613, Monteverdi inherited an even larger group of salaried musicians. There was a full-time *cappella* of about twenty singers (which he soon expanded to twenty-four by 1616) in addition to the thirty or so *giovani di coro* who sang the plainchant each day and may also have performed polyphonic Masses in traditional polyphony when the main *cappella* was absent. There was also an ensemble of sixteen instrumentalists – wind, bowed string and theorbo players – regularly supplemented by up to fifteen extras brought in for feast days.[6] Monteverdi had to 'utilize . . . prepare and direct' all of these performers. His schedule in Venice was probably no less demanding than in Mantua, especially as he had to supervise and often compose music for up to forty different festivals each year, both in the basilica and in various public places including the doge's barge and for processions in Piazza S. Marco.[7] He also took on numerous other engagements in the city's palaces, churches and *scuole* (such as the service attended by Constantijn Huygens in 1620), as well as his additional activities in the opera theatre in the final years of his long life. But the major difference was that he had a bevy of assistants to help him at S. Marco. These included a highly competent *vice-maestro* and two organists, a *maestro di canto* (who supervised and taught the boys at their seminary) and a *maestro de' concerti* ('Director of Instrumentalists'), all of whom tended to be good composers as well, and between them they shared much of the day-to-day work;[8] as Monteverdi rather smugly (and perhaps creatively) reported when the Gonzaga were trying to woo him back to Mantua: 'the duties are very light ... and if [the Director of Music] does not go into chapel, nobody says anything' (letter of 13 March 1620).

Working with professional musicians

Rehearsal time in both Mantua and Venice was probably always very limited. Although Monteverdi clearly challenged his performers with demanding and innovative music, it is clear that whatever he wrote was based closely on a culture of shared conventional musical knowledge and, specifically, on what his musicians could already do. Music historians naturally tend to focus on the qualities which make the work of any one composer unique, but it is important to bear in mind that even complex music – for example, the Vespers (1610) – is made up of a relatively limited set of generic technical elements which would have been familiar to top-level musicians.

Professionals were expected not only to read music fluently but also to alter it appropriately during the act of performance by adding occasional passages of short-value scales and figures (*passaggi*) and, especially in vocal music, expressive dissonances, delays, rhythmic changes, trills, tremolos and other articulation gestures (*grazie*) in response to the words, the harmonic movement and the style and mood of the music. Conventionally in sixteenth-century music, none of these improvisatory elements was notated by the composer, as they were regarded as the preserve of the individual performer, belonging to the performance and not to the compositional act. Nevertheless, it is a feature of Monteverdi's published music (and that of many of his contemporaries) that it often includes numerous fully written-out *passaggi* and other kinds of 'performance act alterations' which he clearly expected musicians to perform as they read the notes. Whether this is a sign of a deliberate move somehow to rein in performers' over-zealous virtuosity or, rather, a function of the process of publication itself, in which the notation to some extent represents the performances of virtuoso musicians whose gestures have been appropriated into the compositional process, is open to debate.

Accompanists, on the other hand, including players of the organ, harpsichord, lute, theorbo, guitar and harp, had to know how to construct harmonies with appropriate voice-leading or arpeggiated articulations more or less unaided by the composer, reading either from a simple bass line or 'short score'. Accompanying and improvising from basic notation was, as it is now, so intrinsic to the skill of 'continuo players' that it is almost meaningless to separate it from technical mastery of each respective instrument. The most adept were even able to create transcriptions of contrapuntal pieces such as madrigals and motets on the spot, reading from a short score or even simultaneously from several part-books at once. As the veteran court musician Luigi Zenobi observed (writing around 1600), 'Among all the things that demonstrate the competence or ignorance of those who play the harpsichord, the lute and the harp ... is the rendering with masterly artifice and particularly at sight, of a work in score by an excellent composer.'[9]

Zenobi also emphasised the need for professional court singers to be able to sing securely from written music. This included reading passages in quavers and semiquavers (suggesting the written-out *passaggi* found in the most modern music of the time, as mentioned above), handling accurately big leaps such as sixths, sevenths, ninths and even elevenths (think, for example, of sight-reading the opening phrases of 'Vattene pur, crudel' from the Third Book of Madrigals (1592)) as well as singing music that is syncopated, dissonant and chromatic and perhaps all three at once. He (for Zenobi mentions only male singers) must be able to recognise the different tempo signs and their correct interpretation as well as proportional tempo relationships, 'in both old and modern works' (including, presumably, sacred polyphony in the *stile antico*). Furthermore, Zenobi expects singers to be able to spot and make instant corrections to errors in the score while performing, without 'falling off' and without help from others. These conditions surely applied to instrumentalists as well and this strongly implies that in normal circumstances, professional rank-and-file musicians were expected to sing or play directly from part-books, at sight.[10] Singers thus did not normally expect to perform composed music from memory, except in theatrical works.

Monteverdi was clearly inured to the minimal rehearsal time available in Mantua, but was aware of the potential disservice this could do to his music. On one occasion in 1607, he deputised his assistant to hold a rehearsal of a new and particularly difficult piece with 'the other gentlemen singers' before performing it, remarking that 'it is very difficult for a singer to represent the *aria* that he has not first practised and greatly damaging to the composition itself, as it does not become completely understood on being sung for the first time.'[11] Much later, when he sent the music of his sung *ballo*, *Tirsi e Clori*, from Venice, he asked the court secretary in Mantua whether he might 'let the singers and players see [the music] for an hour before His Highness hears it' (letter of 21 November 1615).

Theatre productions, however, did require longer rehearsal periods, especially when, as so often in court situations, productions had very elaborate machinery, sets and costumes and occasionally had to be mounted in specially constructed or adapted spaces. Although this might give the singers the chance to learn their music sufficiently to perform convincingly (even though late substitutions could sometimes make this a close-run thing, as with the first performance of *Orfeo*) there were plenty of other challenges to be overcome. A variety of the practical problems facing musicians preparing the performance of theatrical works was addressed in an anonymous treatise, *Il Corago* ('the Producer' or 'the Theatre Intendant') written around 1630 and covering all aspects of musical theatre, from choosing and setting a libretto to music through details of singing and acting styles and on to really basic practicalities.[12]

A typical practical problem was the question of where the instrumentalists should sit. In the earliest opera productions, such as Rinuccini and Peri's *Euridice*, staged in Florence in 1600, the continuo players who accompanied the singers sat behind the scene, so as to maintain the illusion that the actors were essentially 'speaking in song' unaided.[13] The impracticalities of this for the musicians are clear, but, just as in the modern theatre, such considerations are not always of the highest priority in the creation of a convincing spectacle. After discussion of the alternatives, the *Corago* opts for dividing the players into two groups and placing them on each side of the stage (as was done, for example, for *Orfeo* in Mantua).[14] Placed like this they would not get in the way of all the ropes and pulleys behind the scenes, neither would they obscure the view of the audience nor drown out the singers, which was the problem when they sat in front of the stage. Also, this had the advantage that the accompanying players would have close contact with the singers.

Visual and aural contact was especially important, because the musical director did not stand in front of the musicians 'conducting', in the modern sense of the word, whether in the theatre, in church or in chamber music. Certainly, in complex ensemble music, especially where sightlines or acoustics made communication tricky, someone might discreetly beat time in order to keep everyone together, but the beat was essentially a mechanical aid to accurate performances and not a means for dictating 'interpretations'. This was a particular issue when theatre singers were declaiming in *recitar cantando* style, where freedom to vary the pulse and rhythm in line with the words was a paramount consideration. On one hand, the *Corago* argues, having a beat helps ensure that things do not fall apart; but on the other, 'it is accepted wisdom and practice among singers not to have a beat ... because the perfection of the recitative style on stage consists in showing and imitating the natural way of speaking' and this sometimes involves making dramatic pauses which are not written in the music. Additionally, the audience would be seriously irritated if they had to watch someone 'waving up and down constantly for two or three hours'. The *Corago* proposes that at least the principal musician (*sonatore principale*) should be able to see and hear the stage in order to lead and coordinate the singers and instrumentalists, particularly during the rehearsals. He adds that particularly difficult passages should be 'practised several times', and if there are still a few occasions where a beat proves to be absolutely necessary then it will have to be given in the performance; otherwise, beating time should only be done during the choruses.[15]

Singers and singing

Although Monteverdi wrote exquisite music for his instrumentalists to play, it is as a singer's composer that he is most admired; vocal music makes up by far the largest part of his output and thus much of this chapter focuses on singers and singing. The composer's music constantly demonstrates his extraordinary regard and understanding for the expressive capabilities of the voice and his letters show how important a role this precise and intimate sense of singers' individual qualities played in his process of composition. But despite this, his music remains very challenging to modern singers, making what appears to be a variety of extraordinary technical demands, suggesting that even allowing for the fact that Monteverdi often had exceptional practitioners to work with, there are nevertheless important differences between today's 'art singing' and its equivalent in his time.

It is likely that Monteverdi himself had been, to all intents and purposes, a professional singer from an early age. He probably began in his native Cremona as a boy treble at the cathedral and continued after his voice broke, under the tutelage of its *maestro di cappella*, Marc'Antonio Ingegneri.[16] It is usually accepted that Monteverdi's talent as a bowed string player played an important part in his appointment at Mantua[17] and he was undoubtedly an accomplished instrumentalist (although never actually listed as such in the household accounts), but it was as a 'singer of His Highness' that he was referred to in 1594.[18] He must surely have been more than just a decent church chorister to have found a place among the small, but highly respected vocal group that Duke Vincenzo Gonzaga maintained in the 1590s.

Vocal technique and style

Monteverdi's duties as music director both in Mantua and in Venice included recruiting and auditioning rank-and-file musicians and the handful of his reports that survive in letters constitute some of the most useful evidence we have about the nature of professional singing (and playing) at this time. In 1610, Pandolfo del Grande, one of the Mantuan court tenors, was deputed to ask Monteverdi to audition a contralto from Pandolfo's own home town of Modena who was hoping to find a place in the duke's ensemble. The punctilious Monteverdi reported to his employer:

> I took him straightaway into S. Pietro [the cathedral in Mantua] and had him sing a motet to the organ. I heard a fine voice, powerful and sustained, and when he sings on the stage he will make himself heard in every corner very well without strain . . . He has a very good *trillo* and respectable throat articulation and he sings his part securely in motets . . . I have not heard him in madrigals because he was all ready to set out and place himself at Your Highness's disposal.   (Letter of 9 June 1610)[19]

By listening to the performance of just one piece, Monteverdi had been able to assess the applicant against three key benchmarks: his sight-reading (secure) and two fundamental technical elements – flexibility of throat articulation and the suitability of his voice for the different singing styles associated with church and theatre; had the singer not departed prematurely, Monteverdi would also have tested his abilities in the third kind of court singing – chamber music.

The *trillo* to which Monteverdi referred is normally understood as a specific grace applied to a single note in which the same pitch is rapidly repeated (mostly famously described by the great singer and teacher Giulio Caccini in his *Le nuove musiche* in 1602). A successful *trillo*, however, presupposes fast and accurate throat articulation of all fast notes, both even and dotted. In fact, the Italian word Monteverdi used – *gorgia* (literally 'throat') – also implies that our singer was capable of applying this rapid articulation in all kinds of short ornamental graces, often referred to collectively by the plural word *gorgie*. This ability to sing fast with throat articulation (in the sixteenth and seventeenth centuries often called simply *disposizione* – 'skill') is perhaps one of the fundamental differences between pre-Romantic and modern technique and this has implications beyond just its local application in performing ornamentation. Throat-articulation presupposes a vocal production that is in many ways counter-intuitive to the prevailing aesthetic goals of modern art-singing. It requires the larynx to 'float' and rise, rather than consciously to be kept low, which in turn affects the voice's timbre and carrying power. It also means that there will be regular changes of vocal intensity, because clear and accurate *gorgie* require a very soft vocal attack and far less projection than sustained notes.[20] Monteverdi, incidentally, added to his report that the contralto was not flawless in this respect as 'he does not really strike the *gorgia* as would be necessary, nor does he soften it at certain other places'. Singing with *disposizione* results in a simple, light timbre, based on very little diaphragm support, unlike the complex resonance and intensity which comes from constant engagement of the 'singer's formant' to produce a ringing and powerful sound that is the usual goal of present-day classical voice training.

Church, chamber and theatre

Monteverdi also noted the contralto's strong and carrying voice ('gagliarda e longa') and the implications of this for his potential as a theatre singer. Among the many requirements which Luigi Zenobi pre-scribed for a good singer was that 'he must sing in one style in church, in another one in the chamber, and in a third one in the open air, whether it be daytime or night',[21] which echoes standard references going back at least to the early sixteenth century that distinguish between church singing – essentially loud and full-voiced – and chamber singing, where a conversational level was most prized.[22] But the difference that the same singers made between sacred and secular singing may well extend beyond a simple question of loudness.

Monteverdi's writing for singers in sacred and in secular music is, in fact, technically and stylistically sometimes unexpectedly similar. A com-parison between the written-out *gorgie* in, say, Orfeo's aria 'Possente spirto' in Act III or his duet with Apollo in Act V of *Orfeo* (1607) and the setting of the words 'Sanctus Dominus Deus Sabaoth' for two and then three tenors in the *Vespers* (1610) suggests that the sacred concerto would not have sounded out of place alongside a madrigal performed in a private room of the palace; indeed, the title page of the *Vespers* declares the concertos to be 'suited to the chapels or chambers of princes'.[23] This kind of writing persists in Monteverdi's later solo, duet and consort music for the most outstanding singers of the *cappella* in Venice, much of which calls for virtuoso displays of *disposizione* and was almost certainly sung only one voice to a part. All this suggests that Monteverdi's virtuoso soloists in fact sang at the same dynamic level in both chamber and church. They would have contrasted dramatically both with the sound of a choir with perhaps several singers on each line, doubled by wind and string instruments in the occasional *tutti* sections, and also with performances by a full choir of the masses of Palestrina and Lassus, which Monteverdi kept in the repertoire of the basilica.[24] These different textures, alongside instrumental canzonas and sonatas, organ music and long stretches of plainchant sung by a choir of cantors, presented the listener in S. Marco with an extraordinarily varied feast of contrasting sounds, possibly unmatched anywhere else in Europe at the time.

In theatrical singing, audible and precise enunciation of text is crucial, especially in the prevalent *recitar cantando* style of seventeenth-century opera. It is interesting in this respect that Monteverdi mentioned that he had also found fault with the clarity of the Modenese contralto's words, although he adds that this could easily be remedied with some direct advice about voice placement. Likewise, the transitions between the 'measured speech' of recitative and song-like aria and back again, which characterises early Venetian opera singing, needed to be fluent and coherent. And, of course, theatre singers also had to act and move convincingly on stage, although we know very little indeed about how they learned this part of their craft. Interestingly, the *Corago* bemoans the fact that there are still (*c.*1630) so few singers who know how to perform theatrical recitative properly, wondering aloud why, if singers can learn to sing '*trilli*, *passaggi* and other similar gallantries', they cannot also learn to act with the necessary 'changes of voice and feeling'?[25]

The *Corago* has a very practical chapter on basic acting technique for singers, which includes such things as moving slowly to match the pace of the music, not walking around while singing and advice for those who find themselves having to sing while suspended over the stage in a cloud machine. He expresses the perennial mantra of most opera directors: 'to be a good singing actor one should above all be a good speaking actor,' and he adds that although connoisseurs may appreciate a wonderful singer who acts badly, by and large, if there has to be a choice, the public would rather have the opposite. He advises directors to put weak actors at the back or in a machine where they do not have to 'strike histrionic poses'.[26] Acting style in the Venetian theatres may in fact have been livelier than this (the *Corago* is more concerned with court theatre productions), as the early commercial operas were closely linked to the traditions of the straight theatre and especially the companies of *commedia* actors, some of whom may have taken smaller parts in operas. Most of Monteverdi's leading male roles (including those for castratos) would, however, normally have been cast from the ranks of S. Marco and other institutions in the city. The generally limited acting abilities of singers may be reflected in the hyperbolic praise meted out to performers who were good at it, such as the 'first operatic prima donna', Anna Renzi (Monteverdi's first Ottavia in *L'incoronazione di Poppea*), praised by Giulio Strozzi not only for her consummate singing technique but also for her ability to 'transform herself completely into the person she represents'.[27]

Voice types

The Modenese contralto was a man, but, unlike modern counter-tenors who are often heard singing alto parts today, he probably sang in full chest voice most of the time. Monteverdi's alto parts consistently have a range of about g to g', with very occasional extensions in each direction (but usually at the lower end), which fits the voice of a tenor, moving into falsetto only for the highest notes.[28] Here it is important to note that music of this period is sometimes notated in high clef combinations (so-called *chiavette*) for various pragmatic reasons; it is normally easily identifiable when the lowest line of an ensemble has an F3 or even C4 clef, rather than the usual F4 bass clef. Musicians knew that this was a sign for them to transpose the music lower in performance, normally by a fourth.[29] The effect of this rule is that alto parts, which before transposition might be mistaken for 'low soprano range', are revealed as no different from non-transposing alto lines. Likewise, the range of tenor parts is the same as the most common 'un-produced' male chest voice, from about c to f', with occasional extensions of a tone at the top and up to a third at the bottom; and when sung with a free larynx position, close to typical male speech register.

The transposition of high clef parts does highlight the fact that basses today sometimes find themselves singing an unusual number of very low notes in Monteverdi's music – well-known *chiavette* passages include the section 'Et misericordia' in the Magnificat à 7 of the 1610 *Vespers* and the choruses of Spirits that close Act III and open Act IV in *Orfeo*. However, it is clear that the most prized bass singers in Italy in the sixteenth and seventeenth centuries could not only sing very low but also had large ranges overall. Zenobi stipulates that a 'court' bass should have a range of twenty-two notes (three octaves), and although probably not many were quite so well-endowed, there is plenty of other contemporary evidence to support him. Monteverdi's solo parts for bass, including the roles of Plutone in the *Ballo delle ingrate*, Nettuno in *Il ritorno d'Ulisse* and Seneca in *L'incoronazione di Poppea* as well as his solo motet 'Ab aeterno ordinata sum' (1641) and a number of pieces in the Eighth Book of Madrigals testify to the availability of singers of impressive range (down to bottom D and C) and with prodigious *disposizione*.[30]

There were indeed professional falsetto singers in Monteverdi's time, but they nearly always sang soprano parts, which is the vocal range in which they have most carrying power and can best articulate text. The only church choirs in which women were permitted to sing were those in convents; otherwise ecclesiastical music foundations were exclusively male, and the soprano parts were usually sung by boys or falsettists, or both. But, if at all possible, the preference was for castratos, whose voices were much more powerful than either falsettists or boys and who were therefore in great demand by those establishments that could afford them, including the papal chapel in Rome, the court of Mantua and at S. Marco in Venice. In the late sixteenth century good castrato singers were still notoriously hard to find: Duke Vincenzo's father, Gugliemo Gonzaga, had spent years trying to recruit them from as far away as Naples, Rome and even Spain and France, with little success.[31] The supply increased slowly, so that by the time that *Orfeo* was performed in 1607, there were apparently three full-timers in the Mantuan ensemble. One of them, however, was clearly not adequate to the task and so Duke Vincenzo famously had to 'borrow' Giovanni Gualberto Magli from Grand Duke Ferdinando I de' Medici in Florence to sing the parts of the Prologue (La Musica), probably also Messaggiera and perhaps, Proserpina.[32] The Mantuan castratos presumably sang the soprano parts in much of Monteverdi's music for both church and public secular occasions, which normally excluded the appearance of women and men singing together. At S. Marco, Monteverdi strengthened the soprano section of the choir by bringing in six new castratos between 1613 and 1620, and it is for them that he and his younger contemporaries must have written their often elaborate soprano solos and duets.[33]

Women singers

Some of Monteverdi's most celebrated music, however, was written for female sopranos, although even more of it is lost, never having reached the press. Duke Vincenzo Gonzaga had established his own *concerto* of women singers in the 1590s in imitation of the famous group in Ferrara and when Monteverdi started to work in Mantua he presumably composed music for them; his wife, Claudia Cattaneo, became a member of the group some time before 1603.[34] The soprano lines of most of his Mantuan madrigals may well have been written with women's voices in mind, although it is important to remember that women normally only appeared in relatively private events in court because of prevailing notions of propriety. Monteverdi's madrigals were widely performed elsewhere in Italy and further afield (especially once they appeared in print) including in academies which did not admit women, so they must have been sung by all-male ensembles as well.[35]

The theatre, however, was an exception in this respect and it was actresses who were first able to establish wider public prominence for female singers. Monteverdi's landmark *Lamento d'Arianna* (first performed 28 May 1608) was especially composed for the actress Virginia Ramponi Andreini when she took over the role at short notice after the death of his pupil, the rising star Caterina Martinelli.[36] Monteverdi effectively harnessed Andreini's extraordinary abilities as both actress and singer in the new lament and again in the heart-rending aria for her at the end of the *Mascherata dell'ingrate* (first performed 4 June 1608), which she sang 'plaintively, abhorring [the ungrateful women's] suffering', thus initiating Monteverdi's series of great theatrical roles for leading women singers that continued until the end of his life.

In 1610, Duke Vincenzo achieved the coup of enticing the famous Neapolitan virtuosa, Adriana Basile, to his court. Among her attractions was the fact that she could apparently perform by heart over three hundred songs in Italian and Spanish, accompanying herself on guitar or harp;[37] Monteverdi thought her a finer musician than the two other most famous female singers in Italy at the time, Francesca Caccini and Ippolita Recupito.[38] The only music that we know for sure that he presented with Adriana while he was still in Mantua is a pair of now-lost madrigals by Cardinal Ferdinando Gonzaga which were performed as duets with the castrato Don Giovanni Battista Sacchi, accompanied by two theorbos and an organ.[39] It is particularly unfortunate not to have this music, as it might well have shed light on how the voices of these two types of soprano were combined, something that Monteverdi himself was to do with the two lovers, Nerone and Poppea, in his last opera. He later started to write the role of Venus for Adriana to play in *Le nozze di Tetide*, but this was abandoned, never performed, and is also now lost.[40]

Monteverdi worked, too, with Settimia Caccini (Francesca Caccini's younger sister) at the Parma festivities in 1628. Like his first Orfeo, Francesco Rasi, Settimia was a pupil of Giulio Caccini (her famous father) and thus almost certainly a specialist in highly embellished arias. Monteverdi wrote the role of Aurora in *Mercurio e Marte* for her, which she sang 'with superhuman grace and angelic voice' so that 'there was no one, however feeble of judgement who did not grow tender at the trills, sigh at the sighs, become ecstatic at the ornaments'.[41] Music conceived for specific singers whom Monteverdi could first have seen performing in the new opera theatres of Venice include the magnificent role of Penelope in *Il ritorno d'Ulisse* for a now unknown low-voiced soprano and, as we have seen, Ottavia in *L'incoronazione di Poppea*, for the celebrated Anna Renzi, whom he may have seen in her triumph as Deidamia in Francesco Sacrati and Giulio Strozzi's *La finta pazza* at the Teatro Novissimo in 1641.[42]

The title role in another lost work, *La finta pazza Licori* (The feigned madness of Lycoris), was created for Adriana Basile's singer-actress sister, Margherita, in order to exploit her particular acting talents, and from his letters we get a fascinating insight into the way that Monteverdi composed for a particular individual.[43] As he began to conceive his setting of Giulio Strozzi's comic libretto, he was anxious to get a commitment from Duke Vincenzo II about the casting of the title role, because the part 'must not fall into the hands of a woman who cannot play first a man and then a woman, with lively gestures and different emotions ... I believe that Signora Margherita will be best of all.' Two weeks on and he is hoping to send her some of the music, but before actually writing anything, he wants to know 'the actual range of her voice, as regards her highest and lowest notes'. One senses the mounting excitement as the sixty-year-old composer conjured up in his head the performance of the role on stage, which was by now inextricable from the actress who would sing the part: 'my aim is that whenever she is about to come on stage, she has to introduce fresh delights and new inventions'; two days later he writes to say that he is thinking about the various instrumental effects to accompany her different moods and emotional states. Two months on, he promises Alessandro Striggio to send the music as soon as he can copy it out, so that 'you will see that Signora Margherita will have a great deal to do on her own'.[44]

Instrumentalists and ensembles

Although Monteverdi calls for instrumental ensembles in plenty of his music, the concept of an 'orchestra' in its modern sense is anachronistic. Instrumental players were, however, often based in family or guild groups, which, to a certain extent operated as self-contained bands: this was especially so in the case of violin family and wind players. At Mantua in the first decade of the century, the ensemble of bowed string players and theorbos apparently sometimes functioned in two distinct formations, the *concerto delle vivole da ballo*, whose primary function was to accompany dance music and the *sinfonie di Salamone*, a grouping led by the composer and string player, Salamone Rossi.[45] Music for string ensembles, including those which Monteverdi wrote in his Mantuan music, was generally in five parts and intended for *viole da braccio* – the collective term for the various members of the violin family: the usual formation was one violin, three violas and a bass violin (precursor of the violoncello). The combination of two violins as part of an otherwise vocal ensemble is another familiar texture in, for example, *Orfeo*, which later became ubiquitous in Monteverdi's Venetian music.

Larger bowed instruments which could double the bass line at the octave were also often added to reinforce ensembles and these are collectively (and sometimes confusingly) named violone; they were very large viols rather than the contrabass violins (double basses) which nowadays are the lowest members of a modern string section. Monteverdi calls for a *contrabasso di viola da gamba* in *Orfeo* and again to accompany the narrator's recitative together with a harpsichord in *Il combattimento di Tancredi e Clorinda*, a work which also includes numerous instructions to the string players, including playing two-fingered *pizzicato*, a form of *sforzato* in the shape of a sudden change from *forte* to *piano* in a single bow stroke, and an instruction to die away on the final note – effects never hitherto described in printed music.[46] The mixing of violins and viols in a consort was a common practice in German-speaking lands but probably unknown in Italy and Monteverdi's specification of such a group in some of the pieces in the Eighth Book of Madrigals perhaps reflects the fact that they were written for the Imperial court in Vienna.[47] Otherwise, Monteverdi rarely asked for other sizes of viola da gamba and certainly not organised into 'viol consorts'.

At the Mantuan court, there was a 'wind band' made up of about five musicians, including a cornetto player and a trombonist who doubled on *clarino* trumpet. As was often the case, all these players were masters of a number of different instruments, but extra players might be brought in as necessary. For example, for a concert at Lake Garda in 1609, there was an ensemble of two recorders, two flutes, bagpipes, horn, cornetto and trombone, led by the principal cornetto player in the household chamber music ensemble, Giulio Cesare Bianchi.[48] On another occasion, Monteverdi was instructed to audition and sound out a new wind player to see if he would like to go to work for Prince Francesco Gonzaga at Casale Monferrato, who liked to have 'madrigals, French songs, airs and dance songs' played by a wind ensemble 'in private, in church, in procession and atop the city walls'. The unnamed candidate under consideration apparently fulfilled the requirements of the job, which included being able to play 'recorder, cornetto, trombone, flute and bassoon'.[49] The Dukes of Mantua also kept a separate ensemble of trumpeters who played fanfares at all kinds of formal state occasions, and it is almost certainly a transcription of their kind of music which is heard at the start of both *Orfeo* and the 1610 *Vespers*.

Foundation instruments

Luigi Zenobi indicated that the most important job of players of 'the foundation instruments' (harpsichord, lute, harp, theorbo, cittern, Spanish guitar and vihuela), was 'above all' that 'they must show taste and skill in playing in ensemble with a solo player or a singer'.[50] Highly prized instrumentalists such as Lucrezia Urbana, the virtuoso singer and harpist in the Mantuan ensemble who was paid not much less than Monteverdi himself, would also have performed solo in the private rooms of the ducal family, and the more modestly paid rank-and-file lutenists, guitarists and keyboard players in the Gonzaga establishment may also have fulfilled similar functions from time to time.[51] Nevertheless, it was in mixed ensembles of voices and other instruments that they needed to exercise the specialised skills of accompanying, often as part of a group of foundation instruments playing from the same bass line.

Agostino Agazzari's packed booklet, *Del sonare sopra 'l basso* (On playing above the bass) of 1607, though only twelve pages long, is one of our principal sources of information about the deployment of chordal instruments and the techniques appropriate to the ensemble accompaniment of singing, particularly in theatrical music, at the turn of the sixteenth century. New music-theatre vocal styles – above all the pre-eminence of *recitar cantando* – made new demands on accompanists just as it did on singers and these included making effective use of different timbres and textures to underpin the changing expressive demands of the drama. Nowhere is this more clearly illustrated than in the other principal critical document about continuo deployment from this time, the score of Monteverdi's *Orfeo* itself, first published in 1609.[52] The long list of instruments at the beginning of the book and the many indications in the score about which instruments should play at any time provides such a wealth of information (some of it occasionally contradictory) that there is a danger of assuming that this represents a norm of both numbers of players and diversity of instruments that should be imitated as often as possible in the production of early operas.[53]

In fact, conditions at the court of Mantua, which this score celebrates, were exceptional. The published score of *Orfeo* lists a large variety of continuo instruments, including at least two organs with wooden pipes, a regal (a reed organ, used only in the scenes set in the Underworld), two harpsichords, a double harp, three chitarrones or theorbos (to which is also later added a reference to one or more 'cetaroni' – wire-strung theorbos), three violas da gamba and two contrabass string instruments, all probably divided into two groups on opposite sides of the acting area.[54] There were also two violin consorts of five players in each (two players also doubled on 'violini piccoli'),[55] likewise deployed on opposite sides, and a wind ensemble of two cornettos and four trombones (which, like the regal, only appear in the Underworld scenes), as well as two recorders which play only in the pastoral scenes. Finally, there is an ensemble of five trumpets, including a virtuoso top line for 'clarino', who perform the opening Toccata (this group may have included drums as well).

The precise way in which Monteverdi deployed these resources in order to support the changing emotional and dramatic movement of the sung text is today a source of wonder and admiration, an early example of sophisticated 'orchestration', which seems to invite extrapolation to other theatre music less generously provided with written performance instructions. This is certainly potentially relevant to other court spectacles (including works by Monteverdi himself, such as the *Ballo delle ingrate*) but – despite what is often heard in apparently 'historical' performances in the opera house today – not really to his late operas. Continuo support for the singers in the Venetian opera houses of the 1640s was almost certainly restricted to a pair each of harpsichords and theorbos, together with a small – probably four- or five-part – consort of violin family instruments which played short ritornellos in arias and act-division sinfonias.[56] Additions of other instruments such as double basses, viols, lirones, recorders, organs, trombones, trumpets, cornettos or percussion to this textural palette and the 're-orchestration' or 'realisation' of apparently incomplete sections of the surviving scores is without solid historical foundation.

On the other hand, the role of a rich variety of instruments, both wind and stringed, in the performance of liturgical music in Venice had a venerable tradition going back fifty or more years by the time Monteverdi took over as *maestro di cappella*; indeed, the practice of combining instruments with singers in church music was already widespread in northern Italy by the 1580s.[57] The normal ensemble of instrumentalists employed, for example, in Giovanni Gabrieli's sacred concertos is about eight – two violins or violas, two cornettos and four trombones – although he also on occasion called on a far larger number of players.[58] Monteverdi's larger-scale Venetian church music calls for a very similar size and disposition of ensemble, although there was a marked move away from a predominance of cornetts in favour of violins, reflected in the changing composition of the permanent ensemble at S. Marco during the period of his tenure.[59] In his Venetian church music, Monteverdi normally only gives independent lines to a pair of violins and a bass instrument, but he often alludes to other instruments, especially trombones or *viole da braccio*, which can be employed to double the vocal lines if desired when the instruments are available; indeed, Huygens's report, quoted at the head of this chapter, is witness to Monteverdi's use of instruments in festive music, probably for this particular purpose.

The bass lines in Monteverdi's church music were reinforced by string bass instruments and by theorbos, but the principal accompaniment was the organ. In modern performances of his sacred music, especially in concert halls, we are used to seeing and hearing small portable organs accompanying the ensembles, and certainly many churches, including S. Marco, possessed such instruments; but in fact, in most north Italian churches, the large fixed organs were used for accompanying singers and instruments as well as for playing solo music. Once again, Monteverdi's unusually copious published performance advice includes some of the most detailed surviving contemporary information we have, this time about organ registration, in the *Bassus generalis* part-book of the 1610 *Vespers*.[60]

Monteverdi performance in recent times

Before the start of the full spate of the early-music revival in the 1970s, the rediscovery and production of Monteverdi's theatre works entailed compromising with existing operatic performance traditions. Musical decisions were mainly ordered to fit prevailing establishments of singers and orchestral forces and their associated singing, acting, stage production and music-directorial styles.[61] The limitations imposed by this accommodation have been remarkably tenacious, largely because of the continuing dominance of certain organisational models of professional music-making in opera houses, classical concert series and, to a certain extent, the recording industry. Nevertheless, many pioneering performers and directors have enabled historically informed performance of Monteverdi's music to take its place in the institutional mainstream through sometimes creative and sophisticated fellow-travelling in the system. As a result, music that was originally highly contingent upon utterly different performance conditions from those in which it is now situated is nevertheless continually programmed and heard in convincing performances today. But this also entails some occasionally bizarre contortions and compromises that, in turn, set up more layers of tradition and orthodoxy for future generations to reassess and perhaps subvert in their turn.

In recent decades the establishment of a relatively large pool of rank-and-file professional players equipped with appropriate instruments and technical skills has created the conditions whereby institutions such as opera houses or choral societies are able to install more or less 'historical' instrumental forces into otherwise uncompromisingly modernist theatre productions and concerts. The question of vocal style, on the other hand, remains less clear. As I have hinted, the full implications of an historically informed approach to singing remain to be confronted to the same extent as has already happened within instrumental performance; but this probably has as much to do with genre demarcations and even ideology, as with the current state of knowledge. Growing familiarity of audiences with a recognisable 'sound of early music' has contributed to a gradual move away from the integrationist aesthetics of earlier distortions of Monteverdi's notation in performances, which at its extreme included, for example, the dense reorchestrations and *verismo* singing in the productions of the Venetian operas directed by the 'historicist' Nikolaus Harnoncourt in the late 1970s.[62] This can also be said for the gradual (but by no means complete) disentanglement of Monteverdi's madrigals and his sacred music from the performance preconceptions of an essentially nineteenth-century model of choral music – large choruses, orchestras and 'interpreter conductors'.

Monteverdi's works, each carefully conceived for the musicians and for the cultural establishments for which he worked four centuries ago, are expected to serve the same order of functions today, albeit in profoundly different contexts: in opera houses, concert halls and even in the private sphere, where the intimacy of the salon has perhaps been supplanted by the CD player and iPod. Nevertheless, the assimilation of historically informed performance skills into contemporary cultural frameworks creates challenging juxtapositions that require the creativity and adaptability of musicians now, no less than other kinds of musical demands must have done in Monteverdi's time. Interestingly, the nub of the challenge to performers comes back, finally, to the negotiations that are made at the interface between the musicians and the notation from which they read. The continuing exploration of these processes in performance offers our best chance of appreciating the complexity of the relationship between composer, performer and listener, and places Monteverdi's music where it was always expected to be – at the centre of active performative interactions between all the participants.

Notes

1 Approaching Monteverdi: his cultures and ours

1. P. Fabbri, *Monteverdi*, Cambridge, 1994, p. 258.
2. M. Stattkuss, *Claudio Monteverdi: Verzeichnis der erhaltenen Werke; kleine Ausgabe*, Bergkamen, 1985, lists 337 'authentic' items; see the Catalogue and Index in this volume.
3. The standard Italian text of the letters is É. Lax (ed.), *Claudio Monteverdi: lettere*, Florence, 1994, and the standard English translation is C. Monteverdi, ed. and trans. D. Stevens, *The Letters of Claudio Monteverdi*, rev. edn, Oxford, 1995.
4. *La carte postale: de Socrate à Freud et au-delà*, Paris, 1980, trans. A. Bass, as *The Post Card: From Socrates to Freud and Beyond*, Chicago, 1987.
5. See, for example, E. Gellner, *Culture, Identity and Politics*, Cambridge, 1987.
6. Fabbri, *Monteverdi*, p. 144.
7. For a discussion of some surviving paintings of Monteverdi, see Fabbri, *Monteverdi*, pp. 267–9.
8. Vienna, Österreichische Nationalbibliothek, MS 18763, f. 115^r.
9. Fabbri, *Monteverdi*, p. 182.
10. Fabbri, *Monteverdi*, p. 6.
11. J. Glixon, 'Was Monteverdi a traitor?', *Music and Letters*, 72 (1991), 404–6.
12. Fabbri, *Monteverdi*, p. 147.
13. J. Hutchinson and A. Smith (eds.), *Nationalism*, Oxford and New York, 1997.
14. *Le rivoluzioni del teatro musicale italiano*, Bologna, 1783, vol. I, Chapter 5, p. 255.
15. *Johannes Gabrieli und sein Zeitalter*, vol. II, p. 226.
16. 'Claudio Monteverdi: Leben, Wirken im Lichte der zeitgenössischen Kritik und Verzeichnis seine im Druck erschienenen Werke', *Vierteljahrsschrift für Musikwissenschaft*, 3 (1887), 315–450, at 443–50.
17. *Gli albori del melodrama*, Milan, 1904, vol. I, between pp. 96 and 97.
18. See also A. Dell'Antonio, 'Il divino Claudio: Monteverdi and lyric nostalgia in fascist Italy', *Cambridge Opera Journal*, 8 (1996), 271–84.
19. *Early Italian Songs and Airs*, Boston, 1923.
20. See the remarks of Vincenzo Giustiniani (*c*.1628) in I. Fenlon, *Music and Patronage in Sixteenth-century Mantua*, 2 vols., Cambridge, 1980; 1982, vol. I, pp. 126–7; also the 1608 account of *Arianna* and remarks on the nature of performance in a letter from 1609, both in Fabbri, *Monteverdi*, pp. 85–7, 105.
21. Fabbri, *Monteverdi*, pp. 264–5.
22. Z. Szweykowski and T. Carter (eds.), *Composing Opera: from 'Dafne' to 'Ulisse Errante'*, Practica musica 2, Kraków, 1994, pp. 196–7.

23. Fabbri, *Monteverdi*, p. 124.
24. His contracts with the Gonzagas and Venice seem not to have survived, if they ever quite existed in the modern sense. A receipt signed by Monteverdi on 26 March 1623 was sold by private treaty at Sotheby's in London in 2004. The work, or works, to which it relates are not known, though plausibly it might refer to the *Combattimento di Tancredi e Clorinda*. See the Sotheby's Music Sale Catalogue for 7 December 2004, p. 146.
25. Letter of 6 November 1615; see also Monteverdi's letter of 28 December 1610.
26. S. Parisi, 'Licenza alla Mantova': Frescobaldi and the recruitment of musicians for Mantua, 1612–15', in A. Silbiger, ed., *Frescobaldi Studies*, Durham, 1987, pp. 55–91, at pp. 60–61.
27. One instance, in a letter to Monteverdi in 1607, is cited in D. Arnold, rev. T. Carter, *Monteverdi*, Oxford, 2000, p. 17. However, the term is not confirmed by the Italian source given in the footnote.
28. On the dating 1590 for Monteverdi's arrival at Mantua, see below, Chapter 4.
29. See, for example A. Curtis, 'La Poppea impasticciata or, who wrote the music to *L'incoronazione* (1643)?', *Journal of the American Musicological Society*, 42 (1989), 117–51; and A. Pryer, 'Authentic performance, authentic experience and "Pur ti miro" from *Poppea*', in R. Monterosso (ed.), *Performing Practice in Monteverdi's Music*, Cremona, 1995, pp. 191–213.
30. See the analysis in A. Pryer, 'Monteverdi, two sonnets and a letter', *Early Music*, 25 (1997), 357–71, especially Ex. 7, p. 365. See also the discussion of Monteverdi's modelling in Chapter 3, below.
31. This particular connection seems first to have been discussed in detail in F. Sternfeld, *The Birth of Opera*, Oxford, 1993, pp. 168–71.
32. See: J. Florio, *Queen Anna's New World of Words*, London, 1611 and L. Salviati *et al.* (eds), *Vocabolario degli Accademici della Crusca*, Venice, 1612.
33. See, for example, the study by P. Burke, *Popular Culture in Early Modern Europe*, London, 1978.
34. B. Storace, *Selva di varie compositioni d'intavolatura per cimbalo ed organo*, ed. B. Hudson, Corpus of Early Keyboard Music, vol. VII, Neuhausen, 1965, pp. 117–21.
35. Fabbri, *Monteverdi*, p. 98.
36. R. Agee, *The Gardano Music Printing Firms, 1569–1611*, Rochester, NY, 1998, p. 41.
37. See, for example, the listings on the Amazon websites.

38. Agee, *The Gardano Music Printing Firms*, p. 423, n. 27.
39. My thanks to Louise Ringrose of Universal Music for this information.
40. N. Lebrecht, *When the Music Stops*, London, 1996, pp. 351–60.
41. See N. Elias, trans. E. Jephcott, *The Civilizing Process*, Oxford, 1978, and N. Elias, trans. E. Jephcott, *The Court Society*, Oxford, 1983.
42. The *Fiori poetici* appears in facsimile in D. Stevens, *Monteverdi in Venice*, London, 2001; the Piazza poem is on p. 180.
43. See further: G. Tomlinson, *Music in Renaissance Magic: Towards a Historiography of Others*, Chicago, 1993.
44. T. Adorno, trans. R. Livingstone, *Quasi una Fantasia: Essays on Modern Music*, London, 1992, pp. 249–68, at p. 252.
45. See R. Holzer, '"Sono d'altro garbo . . . le canzonette che si cantano oggi": Pietro della Valle on music and modernity in the seventeenth century', *Studi musicali*, 21 (1992), 253–306.
46. S. Parisi, 'New documents concerning Monteverdi's relations with the Gonzagas', in P. Besutti, T. Gialdroni, R. Baroncini (eds.), *Claudio Monteverdi: studi e prospettive: atti del convegno Mantova, 21–24 ottobre 1993*, Florence, 1998, pp. 477–511, at p. 506.

2 Musical sources
1. T. Carter, 'Artusi, Monteverdi, and the poetics of modern music', in N. Kovaleff Baker and B. Russano Hanning (eds.), *Musical Humanism and its Legacy: Essays in Honor of Claude V. Palisca*, Stuyvesant, NY, 1992, pp. 171–94.
2. For a counter-argument that this music was often printed in such detail so as to make it more difficult to perform, thereby tempting the consumer while retaining the exclusivity of the composer, see T. Carter, 'Printing the "New Music"', in K. van Orden (ed.), *Music and the Cultures of Print*, New York and London, 2000, pp. 3–37.
3. See the Introduction to K. Jacobsen and J. P. Jacobsen (eds.), *Claudio Monteverdi: Il quinto libro de madrigali*, Egtved, 1985.
4. Compare J. Milsom, 'Tallis, Byrd and the "incorrected" copy: some cautionary notes for editors of early music printed from movable type', *Music and Letters*, 77 (1996), 348–67.
5. W. Osthoff (ed.), *Claudio Monteverdi: L'Orfeo, favola in musica*, Kassel, 1998. A facsimile of the Florence copy, which stems from earlier in the print-run, has been edited by E. Schmierer, Laaber, 1998.
6. T. Carter, 'Singing *Orfeo*: on the performers of Monteverdi's first opera', *Recercare*, 11 (1999), 75–118; T. Carter, *Monteverdi's Musical Theatre*, New Haven and London, 2002, pp. 97–9.
7. P. Holman, '"Col nobilissimo esercitio della viuuola": Monteverdi's string writing', *Early Music*, 21 (1993), 577–90, at 584–5, uses the same information to argue that the Vespers was put together from separate sets of parts (with, he implies, diverse origins), i.e., that it was not

conceived as a 'work'. Our two arguments are not mutually exclusive.
8. A. Rosenthal, 'Monteverdi's *Andromeda*: a lost libretto found', *Music and Letters*, 66 (1985), 1–8; Carter, *Monteverdi's Musical Theatre*, New Haven and London, 2002, pp. 226–36 (*Proserpina rapita*); E. Rosand, *Monteverdi's Last Operas: A Venetian Trilogy*, Berkeley and Los Angeles, 2007.
9. For example, letter of 26 March 1611: 'I beseech you to be so kind as to accept the *Dixit* [*Dominus*] for eight voices which Your Highness ordered me to send, together with which I am also sending you a little motet for two voices to be sung at the Elevation, and another for five voices for the Blessed Virgin. Once Holy Week is over I shall send a couple of madrigals, and anything else that I understand may be to Your Highness's taste.'
10. See his letter of 17 March 1620 (sending the score to the copyist). Monteverdi sent the copyist's quires in stages on 21 and 28 March, and 4 April.
11. S. G. Cusick, '"There was not one lady who failed to shed a tear": Arianna's lament and the construction of modern womanhood', *Early Music*, 22 (1994), 21–41; A. MacNeil, 'Weeping at the water's edge', *Early Music*, 27 (1999), 407–17.
12. For a somewhat different view, see G. Tomlinson, 'Madrigal, monody, and Monteverdi's "via naturale alla immitatione"', *Journal of the American Musicological Society*, 34 (1981), 60–108.
13. I. Godt, 'I casi di Arianna', *Rivista italiana di musicologia*, 29 (1994), 315–59.
14. T. Carter, 'Lamenting Ariadne?', *Early Music*, 27 (1999), 395–405.
15. The Venice edition does not have a dedication and so cannot be dated within the year (save perhaps by a close examination of degrading fonts in all Magni's editions of 1623); the Orvieto edition has a dedication, though with no date. Therefore we cannot tell which came first.
16. There is also another *contrafactum* as a *Lamento della Maddalena* in Bologna, Civico Museo Bibliografico Musicale, MS Q43.
17. Letter of 21 March 1620: 'I am also sending the first part of the "Lament", which I had already copied at home on a different sheet of paper, so you will also gain time with this item, being as it is the most essential part of the work.'
18. A. Chiarelli, '*L'incoronazione di Poppea* o *Il Nerone*: problemi di filologia testuale', *Rivista italiana di musicologia*, 9 (1974), 117–51; A. Curtis, '*La Poppea impasticciata* or, Who wrote the music to *L'incoronazione* (1643)?', *Journal of the American Musicological Society*, 42 (1989), 23–54.

3 A model musical education: Monteverdi's early works
1. Quintilian, [Marcus Fabius Quintilianus, *c*.35–*c*.95 AD], ed. and trans. H. E. Butler, *Institutio oratoria*, Cambridge, MA, 1920, 4.10.1.
2. The term 'parody' was first questioned by L. Lockwood, 'On parody as term and concept in

sixteenth-century music', in J. LaRue (ed.),
*Aspects of Medieval and Renaissance Music: A
Birthday Offering to Gustave Reese*, New York,
1966, pp. 560–75 ; and H. M. Brown recommended the terms 'imitation' and 'emulation',
both attested in Renaissance usage as *imitatio*
and *(a)emulatio*, for music, in 'Emulation, competition, and homage: imitation and theories of
imitation in the Renaissance', *Journal of the
American Musicological Society*, 35 (1982), 1–48.
Of subsequent articles, see in particular
R. Wegman, 'Another "imitation" of Busnoys's
Missa L'Homme armé – and some observations
on *Imitatio* in Renaissance music', *Journal of the
Royal Musical Association*, 114 (1989), 189–202;
and H. Meconi, 'Does *imitatio* exist?', *Journal of
Musicology*, 12 (1994), 152–78.
3. G. W. Pigman III, 'Versions of imitation in
the Renaissance', *Renaissance Quarterly*, 33
(1980), 1–32.
4. Pigman, 'Versions of imitation', 32.
5. H. Bloom, *The Anxiety of Influence: A Theory
of Poetry*, New York, 1973, p. 5.
6. K. Korsyn, 'Towards a new poetics of musical
influence', *Music Analysis*, 10 (1991), 3–72;
J. N. Straus, *Remaking the Past: Musical
Modernism and the Influence of the Tonal
Tradition*, Cambridge, MA, 1990.
7. T. M. Greene, *The Light in Troy: Imitation and
Discovery in Renaissance Poetry*, New Haven,
1982, p. 31.
8. L. Zacconi, *Prattica di musica*, Venice, 1592;
see J. Haar, 'A sixteenth-century attempt at
music criticism', *Journal of the American
Musicological Society*, 36 (1983), 191–209.
9. D. Arnold, rev. T. Carter, *Monteverdi*,
London, 1990, p. 124.
10. Festa's motet is No. 46 in A. Seay (ed.),
Costanzo Festa opera omnia, vol. V, Corpus
mensurabilis musicae, 25, American Institute of
Musicology, 1979, pp. 54–6. The four-voice version, printed in the 1520s, is probably the closest
to any that Festa would have recognised.
11. Details of the different versions are given in
Seay, *Costanzo Festa opera omnia*, pp. xvi–xvii.
12. *Motetta trium vocum ab pluribus authoribus
composita quorum nomina sunt Iachetus Gallicus,
Morales Hispanus, Constantius Festa, Adrianus
VVilgliardus*, Venice, 1543, No. 14.
13. A. Seay (ed.), *Costanzo Festa opera omnia*.
14. C. Burney, *A General History of Music From
the Earliest Ages to the Present Period*, London,
1789, vol. III, p. 246; F. Mercer (ed.), New York,
1935, vol. II, p. 200.
15. L. Schrade, *Monteverdi: Creator of Modern
Music*, New York, 1950, pp. 94–6.
16. Despite the title, no further volumes
appeared and none may have been envisaged by
the composer. The later canzonettas were published under different titles, and the genre had
changed appreciably by the time they appeared.
These canzonettas were ignored by earlier writers
such as H. Leichtentritt, 'Claudio Monteverdi als
Madrigalkomponist', *Sammelbände der
Internationalen Musikgesellschaft*, 11 (1909–10),

255–91, since no complete surviving source was
known. They were preceded by a collection of
four-voiced *Madrigali spirituali* (1583), still only
known through one part-book.
17. O. Vecchi, ed. R. I. DeFord, *The Four-voice
Canzonettas with Original Texts and Contrafacts
by Valentin Haussmann and Others*, 2 vols.,
Recent Researches in the Music of the
Renaissance, vols. 92–3, Madison, 1993.
18. N. Pirrotta, 'Monteverdi's poetic choices', in
*Music and Culture in Italy from the Middle Ages to
the Baroque: A Collection of Essays*, Cambridge,
MA, 1984, pp. 271–316; P. Fabbri, *Monteverdi*,
Cambridge, 1994, p. 15. For Vecchi's authorship
of his own texts, see DeFord, *The Four-voice
Canzonettas*, part 1, p. 3.
19. In the present context and in the analysis
below of 'Ecco mormorar l'onde', I use the term
'fugal' rather than the normal 'imitative', in
order to avoid confusion with the imitation of
models.
20. See N. Pirrotta, 'Early opera and aria', in
W. Austin (ed.), *New Looks at Italian Opera:
Essays in Honor of Donald Jay Grout*, Ithaca, 1968,
pp. 39–107; T. Carter, '"An air new and grateful
to the ear": the concept of *aria* in late
Renaissance and early Baroque Italy', *Music
Analysis*, 12 (1993), 127–45.
21. G. E. Watkins and T. LaMay, '"Imitatio" and
"emulatio": changing concepts of originality in
the madrigals of Gesualdo and Monteverdi in the
1590s', in L. Finscher (ed.), *Claudio Monteverdi:
Festschrift Reinhold Hammerstein zum 70.
Geburtstag*, Laaber, 1986, pp. 453–87, at p. 482.
22. For discussions of the relationships, see
G. Tomlinson, *Monteverdi and the End of the
Renaissance*, Berkeley and Los Angeles, 1987,
pp. 37–40 (Marenzio, Luzzaschi); D. Arnold,
'Monteverdi and his teachers', in D. Arnold and
N. Fortune (eds.), *The New Monteverdi
Companion*, London, 1985, pp. 95ff. (Ingegneri).
23. Watkins and LaMay, 'Changing concepts of
originality', p. 479.
24. Tomlinson, *Monteverdi*, pp. 55–6, following
A. Einstein, trans. A. H. Krappe, *et al.*, *The Italian
Madrigal*, Princeton, 1949, repr. 1971, p. 722,
suggests that this piece is modelled on the
opening madrigal of Rore's First Book of
Madrigals for five voices, 'Cantai, mentre
ch'i arsi'.
25. N. S. Struever, *The Language of History in the
Renaissance*, Princeton, 1970, p. 193.
26. A. M. Monterosso Vacchelli (ed.), *Claudio
Monteverdi: madrigali a 5 voci libro secondo*,
Opera omnia, vol. III, Cremona, 1979, pp. 21ff.
27. Marenzio's madrigal is edited by D. Arnold,
in *Luca Marenzio: Ten Madrigals for Mixed
Voices*, London, 1966. For its Petrarch text, see
P. Cudini (ed.), *Francesco Petrarca, Canzoniere*,
Milan, 1974, p. 180. Tomlinson, *Monteverdi*,
pp. 41–4, identified the Marenzio model cited
here, though it has also been suggested that
Monteverdi's madrigal was modelled on 'Sorgi e
rischiara' from Wert's Seventh Book of
Madrigals for five voices (Pirrotta, 'Monteverdi's

poetic choices', pp. 277–8), or 'I' vo' cantar', from Ingegneri's First Book for four voices (Vacchelli, (ed.), *Libro secondo*, p. 18).
28. Leichtentritt, 'Claudio Monteverdi als Madrigalkomponist', 261. The same point concerning the form was made seventy-five years later as if a new discovery by R. Hammerstein, 'Versuch über die Form im Madrigal Monteverdis', in L. Finscher (ed.), *Claudio Monteverdi: Festschrift Reinhold Hammerstein zum 70. Geburtstag*, Laaber, 1986, pp. 9–34, especially p. 16. For Ingegneri's use of the ABA form, see Vacchelli (ed.), *Libro secondo*, p. 18.

Intermedio I: 'Ecco mormorar l'onde' (1590)
1. See the Catalogue of Monteverdi's works, below. The first edition was unknown to Malipiero, whose ordering is still observed on the Consort of Musicke recording, Virgin Veritas, 5622682. On the textual problems, see A. M. Monterosso Vacchelli (ed.), *Claudio Monteverdi: madrigali a 5 voci libro secondo*, Opera omnia, vol. III, Cremona, 1979, pp. 14–15. The three madrigals all have texts by Tasso, and correspond in various technical respects: see ibid., pp. 22–4.
2. The poets are all identified in the Catalogue and Index of Works in this book.
3. 'Io non son però morto' and 'Vezzosi augelli' in C. MacClintock and M. Bernstein (eds.), *Giaches de Wert: Collected Works*, Corpus mensurabilis musicae, 24, vol. VIII (American Institute of Musicology, 1968), nos. 1 and 4, pp. 1–3 and 11–14, respectively. Another edition of 'Io non son però morto' appears in A. Einstein, *The Italian Madrigal*, Princeton, 1949, repr. 1971 vol. III, pp. 301ff. The edition of 'Vezzosi augelli' in D. Arnold (ed.), *Giaches de Wert, Madrigal 'Vezzosi augelli'*, London, 1961, is barred differently from that in the Collected Works, and transposes the written pitch up a tone.
4. C. Dahlhaus, '*Ecco mormorar l'onde*: Versuch ein Monteverdi-Madrigal zu interpretieren', in H. Poos (ed.), *Chormusik und Analyse*, Mainz, 1983, pp. 139–54.
5. Alfred Einstein thought this technique showed Monteverdi's 'impatience' and was symptomatic of the disintegration of the madrigal: Einstein, *The Italian Madrigal*, vol. II, pp. 722ff.
6. For other resemblances between 'Ecco mormorar' and 'Dolcemente dormiva', not assuming a specific link, see G. Tomlinson, *Monteverdi and the End of the Renaissance*, Berkeley and Los Angeles, 1987, p. 53.
7. It was suggested as the model by Denis Arnold, in *Monteverdi*, London, 1990, p. 56, and in 'Monteverdi and his teachers', in D. Arnold and N. Fortune (eds), *The New Monteverdi Companion*, London, 1995, p. 108.
8. *Monteverdi and the End of the Renaissance*, pp. 49–52, at p. 50.
9. Dahlhaus, '*Ecco mormorar l'onde*', pp. 151–2.
10. For some of the theoretical implications, see G. Chew, 'The perfections of modern music: consecutive fifths and tonal coherence in Monteverdi', *Music Analysis*, 8 (1989), 247–74.

11. H. Leichtentritt, 'Claudio Monteverdi als Madrigalkomponist', *Sammelbände der Internationalen Musikgesellschaft*, 11 (1909–10), 263–7.
12. Dahlhaus, '*Ecco mormorar l'onde*', p. 147.
13. In this study I have distinguished only between cadential and non-cadential material, but Dahlhaus makes further distinctions related to the style of the Baroque and Classical periods as described by W. Fischer, 'Zur Entwicklungsgeschichte des Wiener klassischen Stils', *Studien zur Musikwissenschaft*, 3 (1915), 24–84.
14. Dahlhaus, '*Ecco mormorar l'onde*', p. 154.

4 Monteverdi at Mantua, 1590–1612
1. P. Fabbri, trans. T. Carter, *Monteverdi*, Cambridge, 1994, pp. 20–2. Of the five items of available evidence, the dedication of the Second Book, indicating that on 1 January 1590 Monteverdi had not yet entered Gonzaga service, appears incontestable. The dedication of the *Selva morale* (1641) places his engagement between 30 July 1589 and 29 July 1590, and his and his father's letters of November 1608, between November 1588 and November 1589. Allowing for a very slight 'rounding up' by their writers, these latter two items join the first two in consistency with a deduction that Monteverdi was engaged at Mantua very early in 1590. Thus it was by error that in November 1615 he remarked that his service had lasted twenty-one years, rather than the correct twenty-two.
2. Mantua, Archivio di Stato (henceforth I-MAa), Archivio Gonzaga, busta 395, f. 156r (*Religiosi*), f.156v (*Cantori*); S. Parisi, 'Musicians at the court of Mantua during Monteverdi's time: evidence from the payrolls', in S. Gmeinwieser *et al.* (eds.), *Musicologia humana: Studies in Honor of Warren and Ursula Kirkendale*, Florence, 1994, 183–208, at pp. 187–9.
3. I. Donesmondi, *Dell'istoria ecclesiastica di Mantova*, 2 vols, Mantua, 1612–16, vol. II, p. 201.
4. R. Morselli, *Le Collezioni Gonzaga. L'elenco dei beni del 1626–1627*, Milan, 2000, p. 28; Stefano L'Occaso, 'Santa Croce in Corte e la devozione dei Gonzaga alla Vera Croce', *Rubens. Eleonora de' Medici Gonzaga e l'Oratorio sopra Santa Croce: pittura devote a corte*, ed. F. Trevisani and S. L'Occaso, Milan, 2005, pp. 24–32, at p. 31; D. Ferrari, 'Fonti archivistiche viennesi de interesse mantovano. Alcuni disegni di palazzo ducale presso l'Hofkammerarchiv', *Verona Illustrata*, 3 (1990), pp. 77–91, ill. 87.
5. Mantua, Archivio Storico Diocesano, Curia Vescovile, Visite pastorali 1575, II, ff. 651r–652v; S. L'Occaso, 'Santa Croce in Corte', *Quaderni di San Lorenzo*, 3 (2005), 7–35, at pp. 27–8.
6. N. Giannantoni, *Il palazzo ducale di Mantova*, Rome, 1929, pp. 73–4; G. Rodella, 'Le strutture architettoniche', in G. Algeri (ed.), *Il palazzo ducale di Mantova*, Mantua, 2003, pp. 17–52, 81–4, at pp. 38–42, 83; S. L'Occaso, 'Santa Croce in Corte'.

7. Mantua, Archivio Storico Diocesano, Curia Vescovile, Visite pastorali 1575, II, ff. 651r-2v; L'Occaso, 'Santa Croce in Corte', pp. 27–8.

8. G. Paccagnini, *Il palazzo ducale di Mantova*, Turin, 1969, pp. 14–18.

9. Mantua, MS Visite pastorali 1575, ii, ff. 652v–3r.

10. E.g. 'e della camera e della chiesa': K. B. Monteath, 'Pallavicino, Benedetto', *New Grove Dictionary of Music and Musicians*, ed. S. Sadie and J. Tyrrell, 29 vols., London and New York, 2001, vol. XIX, pp. 6–10, at p. 8.

11. E.g. I. Fenlon, *Giaches de Wert: Letters and Documents*, Paris, 1999, p. 142, and Chapter 14, below.

12. Statutes: Mantua, Archivio Diocesano, Basilica di Santa Barbara, MS 'Constitutiones Sanctae Barbarae, 1568' [hereinafter 'MS Constitutiones']. P. Tagmann, 'The palace church of Santa Barbara in Mantua, and Monteverdi's relationship to its liturgy', in B. L. Karson (ed.), *Festival Essays for Pauline Alderman: A Musicological Tribute*, Provo, UT, 1976, pp. 53–60.

13. 'MS Constitutiones', chapters 45, 46; I. Fenlon, *Music and Patronage in Sixteenth-century Mantua*, 2 vols, Cambridge, 1980, vol. I, pp. 186–7.

14. P. Tagmann, 'La cappella dei maestri cantori della Basilica Palatina di Santa Barbara a Mantova, 1565–1630', *Civiltà mantovana*, 4 (1970–1), 376–400, at 380–92.

15. Fabbri, *Monteverdi*, pp. 20–21, 22, 27, 28, 30.

16. I-MAa, Archivio Gonzaga, busta 3146, f. 64r (probably of 1591).

17. I-MAa, Archivio Gonzaga, busta 395, ff. 159v, 160r; Fenlon, *Music and Patronage*, vol. I, pp. 124–35.

18. Fabbri, *Monteverdi*, pp. 27–8; see also Chapter 14, below.

19. S. Parisi, 'Ducal patronage of music in Mantua, 1587–1627: an archival study', Ph.D. dissertation, University of Illinois (1989), pp. 141–3, 480.

20. See Fenlon, *Music and Patronage*, vol. I, pp. 146–52.

21. *A briefe discourse of the voyage and entrance of the Queene of Spaine into Italy . . . translated . . . by H. W.*, London, n.d. [?1599], pp. 3, 10, 13.

22. I-MAa, Archivio Gonzaga, busta 403, unfoliated (sub-bundle XII, folder N° 7, months August, September).

23. Fabbri, *Monteverdi*, pp. 33–4, 70–71.

24. O. Strunk, *Source readings in music history*, vol. IV, rev. M. Murata, *The Baroque Era*, New York and London, 1998, pp. 18–26; C. V. Palisca, 'The Artusi–Monteverdi controversy', in D. Arnold and N. Fortune (eds.), *The New Monteverdi Companion*, London, 1985, pp. 127–58; Palisca, 'Artusi, Giovanni Maria', in *New Grove*, vol. II, pp. 94–6; Fabbri, *Monteverdi*, pp. 34–52; T. Carter, 'Artusi, Monteverdi, and the poetics of modern music', in N. Kovaleff Baker and B. Russano Hanning (eds.), *Musical Humanism and its Legacy: Essays*

in Honor of Claude V. Palisca, Stuyvesant, NY, 1992, pp. 171–94; S. G. Cusick, 'Gendering modern music: thoughts on the Monteverdi–Artusi controversy', *Journal of the American Musicological Society*, 45 (1993), 1–25.

25. Monteath, 'Pallavicino'.

26. Tagmann, 'La cappella dei maestri cantori', pp. 379–80.

27. Fenlon, *Music and Patronage*, vol. I, pp. 107–8, 114–16.

28. I. Fenlon, *Giaches de Wert, Letters and Documents*, Paris, 1999, pp. 94–7.

29. Fabbri, *Monteverdi*, p. 285.

30. Parisi, 'Ducal patronage', p. 122.

31. E. Strainchamps, 'The life and death of Caterina Martinelli: new light on Monteverdi's "Arianna"', *Early Music History*, 5 (1985), 155–86.

32. For all these, see Parisi, 'Ducal patronage', pp. 125–7, and subject paragraphs in Part II.

33. Fabbri, *Monteverdi*, p. 55.

34. D. de' Paoli (ed.), *Claudio Monteverdi: lettere, dediche e prefazioni*, Rome, 1973, p. 391.

35. Translations in Fabbri, *Monteverdi*, p. 48; Palisca, 'The Artusi–Monteverdi controversy', pp. 151–2.

36. Fabbri, *Monteverdi*, p. 37.

37. Giulio Cesare expanded substantially on this position in his gloss on Claudio's letter printed in 1607[21]: Strunk, *Source Readings*, p. 34.

38. In his letter of 27 October 1604 Monteverdi observed that five months had elapsed since his last receipt of stipend.

39. I-MAa, Archivio Gonzaga, busta 395, ff. 3–23.

40. S. Parisi, 'New documents concerning Monteverdi's relations with the Gonzagas', in P. Besutti, T. M. Gialdroni and R. Baroncini (eds.), *Claudio Monteverdi: studi e prospettive; atti del convegno, Mantova, 21–24 ottobre 1993*, Florence, 1998, pp. 477–511, at p. 485, n.18.

41. I. Fenlon, 'The Mantuan *Orfeo*', in J. Whenham (ed.), *Claudio Monteverdi: 'Orfeo'*, Cambridge, 1986, pp. 1–19.

42. T. Carter, 'Giovanni Gualberto Magli', *Early Music*, 11 (1983), p. 577; Fabbri, *Monteverdi*, p. 79; Fenlon, 'The Mantuan *Orfeo*', pp. 17–18. See also T. Carter, 'Singing *Orfeo*: on the performers of Monteverdi's first opera', *Recercare*, 11 (1999), 75–118.

43. Translation in Strunk, *Source Readings*, pp. 19–27.

44. Letter of 28 July 1607; A. Pryer, 'Monteverdi, two sonnets, and a letter', *Early Music*, 25 (1997), 357–71.

45. C. Sartori, 'Monteverdiana', *Musical Quarterly*, 38 (1952), 399–413, at 403–6.

46. Corrected date in E. Strainchamps, 'The life and death of Caterina Martinelli', p. 167 and n. 23.

47. T. Carter, 'Lamenting Ariadne?', *Early Music*, 27 (1999), 395–405.

48. Fabbri, *Monteverdi*, p. 92.

49. Translations in Fabbri, *Monteverdi*, pp. 100–102.
50. Parisi, 'New documents', p. 491 n. 33.
51. Partial translation in Fabbri, *Monteverdi*, p. 104; Monteverdi, *Letters*, p. 50, nn.15, 16.
52. Letter of 9 June 1610; Parisi, 'New documents', p. 491, n. 33.
53. D. de' Paoli, *Monteverdi*, Milan, 1979, p. 160; J. Kurtzman, *The Monteverdi Vespers of 1610: Music, Context, Performance*, Oxford, 1999, pp. 41 n. 139, 42 n. 142.; Parisi, 'New documents', p. 496, nn. 42, 47.
54. Kurtzman, *The Monteverdi Vespers*, pp. 41 n. 138, 42–3 n. 147.
55. Parisi, 'Ducal patronage', pp. 82–5.
56. Parisi, 'New documents', p. 479 n. 4; Parisi, '"Licenza alla Mantovana"', pp. 60, 62–3, 78 (and nn. 25, 26), 80–82.
57. Parisi, 'Ducal patronage', p. 583.
58. Parisi, '*Licenza alla Mantova*: Frescobaldi and the recruitment of musicians for Mantua, 1612–15', in A. Silbiger (ed.), *Frescobaldi studies*, Durham, 1987, pp. 55–91, at pp. 60–61, 78–9.
59. Parisi, 'New documents', p. 481 and n. 12.
60. Tagmann, 'La cappella dei maestri cantori', p. 382.

5 Spaces for music in late Renaissance Mantua

1. P. Besutti, 'The "Sala degli Specchi" uncovered: Monteverdi, the Gonzagas, and the palazzo ducale, Mantua', *Early Music*, 27 (1999), 451–65, to which reference should be made for details of the rediscovery.
2. S. Lapenta and R. Morselli, *Le collezioni Gonzaga: La quadreria nell'elenco dei beni del 1626–1627*, Cinisello Balsamo, 2006, p. 28.
3. Besutti, 'The "Sala degli Specchi"', p. 453, Plate 1.
4. C. Gallico, 'Guglielmo Gonzaga signore della musica', in *Sopra li fondamenti della verità: musica italiana fra XV e XVII secolo*, Rome, 2001 (first edn 1977), 277–350; P. Besutti and R. Tamalio, 'Guglielmo Gonzaga', *Dizionario biografico degli Italiani*, Rome, 2003, lxi, 1–11.
5. P. Carpeggiani, *Bernardino Facciotto: progetti cinquecenteschi per Mantova e il palazzo ducale*, Milan, 1994.
6. Besutti, 'The "Sala degli Specchi"', 456, Plate. 6.
7. R. Morselli, *Le collezioni Gonzaga*, p. 42.
8. For a detailed analysis of the picture, see P. Besutti, 'La galleria musicale dei Gonzaga: intermediari, luoghi, musiche e strumenti in corte a Mantova', in R. Morselli (ed.), *Gonzaga: La celeste galeria: le raccolte, catalogo della mostra (Mantova, Palazzo Te, 1 settembre – 8 dicembre 2002)*, ed. R. Morselli, Milan, 2002, 407–75, at 419–20; the angels frieze is shown on p. 419.
9. For example, Mantegna's *Parnassus* in the rooms of Isabella d'Este.
10. N. Guidobaldi, *La musica di Federico: immagini e suoni alla corte di Urbino*, Florence, 1995, p. 32.
11. Mantua, Archivio di Stato (henceforth I-MAa]), Archivio Gonzaga, busta (henceforth b.) 2712, fascicolo IV, n. 7, Mantua, 15 March 1608, Antonio Costantini to Vincenzo Gonzaga at

Turin; transcribed in Besutti, 'The "Sala degli Specchi"', 459–61.
12. I-MAa, Archivio Gonzaga, b. 1516, fos. 300–302, 310–11, Venice 18 and 25 October 1586, Gabriele Calzoni to Federico Cattaneo; transcribed in Besutti, 'La galleria musicale', p. 441, n. 163.
13. For the documentary and bibliographical references synthesised here, see Besutti, 'La galleria musicale', pp. 424–5, and 432–7 ('Repertorio degli strumenti musicali in corte a Mantova, 1486–1628').
14. I-MAa, Archivio Gonzaga, b. 388, f. 266v.
15. Morselli, *Le collezioni Gonzaga. L'elenco*, pp. 134–5, 146.
16. I-MAa, Archivio Gonzaga, b. 2709, Mantua, 23 February 1607, Carlo Magni to his brother Giovanni in Rome. Reproduced and translated in J. Whenham (ed.), *Claudio Monteverdi: 'Orfeo'*, Cambridge, 1986, p. 170.
17. Besutti, 'The "Sala degli Specchi"', p. 463.
18. G. Bertazzolo, *Breve relatione dello sposalizio fatto dalla Serenissima Principessa Eleonora Gonzaga con la Sacra Cesarea Maestà di Ferdinando II imperatore*, Mantua, 1622, p. 9.
19. Lapenta and Morselli, *Le collezioni Gonzaga*, p. 167.
20. The placing in the Sala di Manto of various performances of *Orfeo* (among them those of 30 April 1933, using the edition of Giacomo Orefice, and 25 August–8 September 1990, directed by Claudio Gallico) were motivated solely by the ample size of the room, not scholarly considerations. The reconstruction as a scale model of a hypothetical 'Sala di Orfeo' in the Musée de la Musique in Paris was inspired by the Sala Imperiale although no performance took place there. On the use of the Hall of Mirrors for music, see P. Besutti, 'L'oratorio in corte tra Bologna, Modena e Venezia', in P. Besutti (ed.), *L'oratorio musicale italiano e i suoi contesti*, Florence, 2002, 365–421.
21. P. Besutti, 'La figura professionale del cantante d'opera: le virtuose di Ferdinando Carlo Gonzaga', *Quaderni storici*, 22 (1997), 409–33.
22. I-MAa, Archivio Gonzaga, b. 2162, fos. 601–602, Mantua, 23 February 1607, Francesco Gonzaga to his brother Ferdinando at Pisa. Transcribed and translated in Whenham (ed.), *Claudio Monteverdi: 'Orfeo'*, pp. 170–1.
23. F. Follino, *Compendio delle sontuose feste fatte l'anno MDCVIII nella città di Mantova per le reali nozze del serenissimo principe D. Francesco Gonzaga con la serenissima Infante Margherita di Savoia*, Mantua 1608, facs. edn., C. Gallico, Florence, 2004, p. 74.
24. I-MAa, Archivio Gonzaga, b. 2162, fos. 603–604, Mantua, 1 March 1607, Francesco Gonzaga to his brother Ferdinando at Pisa. Transcribed and translated in Whenham (ed.), *Claudio Monteverdi: 'Orfeo'*, p. 171.
25. I-MAa, Archivio Gonzaga, b. 2162, fos. 605–606, Mantua, 30 March 1607, Francesco Gonzaga to his brother Ferdinando at Pisa.
26. Monteverdi, *L'Orfeo favola in musica*, Venice, 1609, dedication to Francesco Gonzaga; for the question of 'angusta' and 'augusta' see

T. Carter, *Monteverdi's Musical Theatre*, New Haven and London, 2002, p. 78, n. 4, and T. Carter, 'The first edition of Monteverdi's *Orfeo*', *Orpheus Orfeo. Studi dedicati a Claudio Gallico*, Florence, forthcoming.

27. R. Toscano, *L'edificazione di Mantova*, Padua, 1586, p. 22.

28. E. Tamburini, 'A partire dall'"Arianna" monteverdiana pensando ai comici. Luoghi teatrali alla corte di Mantova', in P. Besutti, T. M. Gialdroni and R. Baroncini (eds.), *Claudio Monteverdi. Studi e prospettive*, Florence, 1998, pp. 415–29.

29. For the sources of this description, see ibid., pp. 420–21.

30. Follino, *Compendio*, pp. 74 and 124. The title *Mascherata dell'ingrate*, which was employed in the description of the 1608 festivities, is used here rather than the more usual title *Ballo delle ingrate* to distinguish the Mantuan version from the version of the ballet published in the Eighth Book of Madrigals (1638), the text, and probably some of the music, of which was adapted for performance at Vienna.

31. Bertazzolo, *Breve relatione*, p. 20.

32. Parisi, 'Ducal patronage', p. 161.

33. Follino, *Compendio*, p. 124.

34. Ibid., p. 29.

35. A. Solerti, *Gli albori del melodramma*, 3 vols., Turin, 1903, repr. Bologna 1976, I, p. 100: report to the Este court on the festivities (four thousand people); Follino, *Compendio*, p. 29 (six thousand people).

36. Follino, *Compendio*, pp. 99–100.

37. Ibid, p. 30.

38. C. Burattelli, *Spettacoli di corte a Mantova tra Cinque e Seicento*, Florence, 1999, pp. 103–104.

39. A chronological repertory of such forms of entertainment is given in P. Besutti, 'Giostre, fuochi e naumachie a Mantova fra Cinque e Seicento', in P. Fabbri (ed.), *Musica in torneo nell'Italia del Seicento*, Lucca, 1999, 3–32.

40. See Chapter 8, below.

41. P. Besutti, 'Un modello alternativo di controriforma: il caso mantovano', in O. Mischiati and P. Russo (eds.), *La cappella musicale nell'Italia della Controriforma*, Florence, 1993, 111–21; P. Besutti, 'Fonti e pratica del canto piano a Mantova tra Quattro e Cinquecento: i codici della messa dell'Archivio Storico Diocesano', in A. Albarosa, and S. Vitale (eds.), *Gregoriano in Lombardia*, Lucca, 2000, 73–115.

42. The collection of polyphonic music is preserved in the Biblioteca del Conservatorio in Milan; catalogue: G. Barblan (ed.), *Musiche della cappella di S. Barbara in Mantova*, Florence, 1972; it contains no music by Monteverdi.

43. Tagmann, 'La cappella dei maestri cantori della basilica palatina di S. Barbara a Mantova, 1565–1630', *Civiltà Mantovana*, 4 (1970/1), pp. 376–400.

44. On the construction of S. Barbara see T. Gozzi, 'La basilica palatina di S. Barbara in Mantova', *Atti e memorie dell'Accademia Virgiliana di Mantova*, 42 (1974), 3–91.

45. F. Dassenno (ed.), *L'Antegnati di S. Barbara (1565): l'organo della basilica palatina dei Gonzaga: riscoperta, recupero e restauro*, Mantua, 1999; R. Berzaghi 'Le ante di S. Barbara: Fermo Ghisoni e la pittura a Mantova nella seconda metà del Cinquecento', *Civiltà mantovana*, 20 (1988), 1–20.

46. Its curious history is summarised in Besutti, 'La galleria musicale', p. 424.

47. A fascinating hypothesis of a musical journey unwinding between chapels, images of saints and relics, is offered in S. Patuzzi, *Madrigali in basilica: le 'Sacre lodi a diversi santi' (1587) di G. G. Gastoldi: un emblema controriformistico*, Florence, 1999.

48. See P. Besutti, '"Ave Maris Stella": la tradizione mantovana nuovamente posta in musica da Monteverdi', in Besutti, Gialdroni and Baroncini (eds.), *Claudio Monteverdi*, Florence, 1993, pp. 57–77.

49. G. B. Grillo, *Breve trattato di quanto successe alla maestà della Regina Margarita d'Austria*, Naples, 1604, pp. 40–1.

50. L'Occaso, 'S. Croce in Corte'.

51. For Roger Bowers's hypothesis on Monteverdi's engagement in S. Croce in the sphere of his service as *maestro di cappella*, see Chapter 4, above.

52. P. Tagmann, *Archivalische Studien zur Musikpflege am Dom von Mantua (1500–1627)*, Bern and Stuttgart, 1967.

53. Besutti, 'Fonti e pratica del canto piano a Mantova tra Quattro e Cinquecento: i codici della messa dell' Archivio Storico Diocesano', in A. Albarosa and S. Vitale (eds.), *Gregoriano in Lombardia*, Lucca, 2000, pp. 73–115, at pp. 77–84.

54. C. Gallico and L.Volpi Ghirardini, 'Tre pittori per un *concerto* mantovano', in *Orpheus Orfeo. Studi dedicati a Claudio Gallico*, Florence, forthcoming.

55. See Chapter 8, below.

56. C. Gallico, 'Vita musicale in Sant'Andrea di Mantova', in *Sopra li fondamenti della verità*, 195–203.

57. G. Cadioli, *Descrizione delle pitture, sculture, ed architetture*, Mantua, 1763, repr. Bologna, 1974. I should like to thank Rodolfo Signorini for information about this church.

58. W. F. Prizer, 'La cappella di Francesco II Gonzaga e la musica sacra a Mantova nel primo ventennio del Cinquecento', in *Mantova e i Gonzaga nella civiltà del Rinascimento*, Mantua, 1977, 267–76, at 268.

6 The Mantuan madrigals and the *Scherzi musicali*

1. On musical patronage in Mantua, see I. Fenlon, *Music and Patronage in Sixteenth-Century Mantua*, 2 vols., Cambridge, 1980; 1982.

2. On Poliziano's *Favola di Orfeo*, see N. Pirrotta and E. Povoledo, *Music and theatre from Poliziano to Monteverdi*, trans. Karen Eales, Cambridge, 1982.

3. A. MacNeil, *Music and Women of the Commedia Dell'Arte in the Late Sixteenth Century*, Oxford, 2003, pp. 127–33.

4. On the theatre at Sabbioneta, see F. Sisinni (ed.), *Il teatro all'antica di Sabbioneta*, Modena, 1991.
5. On the question of the dating of the *Scherzi*, see my 'Claudio Monteverdi's *ordine novo, bello et gustevole*: the canzonetta as dramatic module and formal archetype', *Journal of the American Musicological Society*, 45 (1992), 270–6.
6. J. Kurtzman, 'An early 17th-century manuscript of *Canzonette e Madrigaletti Spirituali*', *Studi musicali* 8 (1979), 149–71.
7. C. Palisca, 'The Artusi–Monteverdi controversy' in D. Arnold and N. Fortune (eds.), *The New Monteverdi Companion*, London, 1985, pp. 127–58, at p. 127.
8. The standard source on Monteverdi's changing poetic tastes remains N. Pirrotta, 'Monteverdi's poetic choices', in *Music and Culture in Italy from the Middle Ages to the Baroque: A Collection of Essays*, Cambridge, 1984, pp. 271–316; G. Tomlinson, *Monteverdi and the End of the Renaissance*, Berkeley and Los Angeles, 1987, pp. 58–72.
9. Tomlinson, *Monteverdi*, pp. 118–31.
10. Tomlinson, *Monteverdi*, pp. 73–98.
11. On the relationship between *Il pastor fido* and Monteverdi's Fifth Book of Madrigals, see M. Ossi, *Divining the Oracle: Claudio Monteverdi's Seconda Prattica*, Chicago, 2003, pp. 83–95.
12. Regarding the Florentine festivities of 1589, and the *intermedi* in particular, see J. M. Saslow, *Florentine Festival as Theatrum Mundi: the Medici Wedding of 1589*, New Haven and London, 1996.
13. On the presence of the Pellizzari family, Antonio and his sisters, Lucia and Isabella, in Mantua, see A. Newcomb, *The Madrigal at Ferrara, 1579–97*, 2 vols., Princeton, 1980, vol. I, p. 100, and Chapter 4, above.
14. P. Misurarca, *Carlo Gesualdo principe di Venosa*, Palermo, 2000, pp. 49–57.
15. On the relationship between Giulio Cesare Monteverdi's 'Dichiaratione' and the music of the *Scherzi*, see Ossi, *Divining the Oracle*, pp. 11–119.
16. Palisca, in 'The Artusi–Monteverdi controversy', analyses the criticisms levelled by Artusi in terms of contrapuntal improprieties; for the larger intellectual and aesthetic issues underlying the dispute, see Ossi, *Divining the Oracle*, Chapter 1.
17. On the importance of the canzonetta in Monteverdi's output, see Ossi, *Divining the Oracle*, Chapter 3.
18. L. Fabri, preface to Chiabrera's *Le maniere de' versi toscani* (1599), in M. Turchi (ed.), *Opere*, Turin, 1973, p. 215; on French influences in his poetry, see G. Chiabrera, 'Il Geri. Dialogo della tessitura delle canzoni', in *Opere*, p. 574. The admiration between Chiabrera and Caccini was mutual: see Caccini's comments in the preface to *Le nuove musiche*, Florence, 1602, p. [v].
19. On Monteverdi's interest in allying himself with Chiabrera, see Ossi, *Divining the Oracle*, pp. 111–16.
20. C. Gallico, 'Emblemi strumentali negli 'Scherzi' di Monteverdi', *Rivista italiana di musicologia*, 2 (1967), 54–73.

21. Newcomb, *The Madrigal at Ferrara*, vol. I, pp. 35–45.
22. The choreography is mentioned in his letter of December 1604. On the significance of [*Endimione*] (perf. prob. Carnival 1604–5), the work discussed in this letter, see Ossi, *Divining the Oracle*, pp. 132–4.
23. On the differences between the Fourth and Fifth Books, and on the organisation of the Fourth in particular, see Ossi, *Divining the Oracle*, pp. 96–110.
24. Tomlinson, *Monteverdi*, pp. 98–113.
25. On the relationship between Monteverdi's and Caccini's settings of 'Sfogava con le stelle', see I. Horsley, 'Monteverdi's use of borrowed material in "Sfogava con le stelle"', *Music and Letters*, 49 (1978), 316–28, and, more recently, T. Carter, '"Sfogava con le stelle" reconsidered: some thoughts on the analysis of Monteverdi's Mantuan madrigals', in P. Besutti, T. M. Gialdroni and R. Baroncini (eds.), *Claudio Monteverdi: studi e prospettive. Atti del convegno Mantova 21–24 ottobre 1993*, Florence, 1998, pp. 147–70.
26. Ossi, *Divining the Oracle*, pp. 96–110.
27. Ossi, *Divining the Oracle*, pp. 58–83.
28. For a sample of different analytical approaches to Monteverdi's 'Cruda Amarilli' and 'O Mirtillo', see C. Dahlhaus, trans. R. O. Gjerdingen, *Studies on the Origin of Harmonic Tonality*, Princeton, 1990, pp. 289–98, E. Chafe, *Monteverdi's Tonal Language*, pp. 67–75, and S. La Via, 'Monteverdi esegeta: rilettura di Cruda Amarilli / O Mirtillo' in M. C. Vela and R. Tibaldi (eds.), *Intorno a Monteverdi*, Lucca, 1999, pp. 77–99.
29. Tomlinson, *Monteverdi and the End of the Renaissance*, pp. 121–31.
30. For such an assessment of the continuo madrigals, see L. Schrade, *Monteverdi: Creator of Modern Music*, New York, 1950, pp. 215–19 and, on the *Scherzi musicali*, 219–223.
31. G. B. Doni, *Trattato della musica scenica*, Florence, 1763, p. 61.
32. E. Strainchamps, 'The life and death of Caterina Martinelli: new light on Monteverdi's "Arianna"', *Early Music History*, 5 (1985), 155–86.
33. Doni, *Trattato*, p. 61, maintains that it would have been better had the Venetian patron asked for an arrangement with a 'concerto a quattro voci strumentali'.
34. On Monteverdi's use of instruments in 'Con che soavità', see Ossi, *Divining the Oracle*, pp. 153–73.
35. Pirrotta, 'Monteverdi's poetic choices', pp. 300–1.
36. On Salomone Rossi's career in Mantua, see D. Harrán, *Salomone Rossi: Jewish Musician in Late Renaissance Mantua*, Oxford, 1999, pp. 14–35; on the violin in *Orfeo*, see D. Boyden, 'Monteverdi's "violini piccoli alla francese" and "viole da brazzo"', *Annales musicologiques*, 6 (1958–63), 387–401. See also Chapter 14, below.

37. On Monteverdi's approach to instruments in his vocal music, see M. Ossi, 'Claudio Monteverdi's concertato technique and its role in the development of his musical thought', Ph.D. diss. Harvard University, 1989.

Intermedio II: 'Ahi come a un vago sol cortese giro' (1605)
1. For the resemblance between this and the complex of solos, ensemble and choral refrain that concludes the messenger scene of Peri's *Euridice*, see J. Whenham, *Duet and Dialogue in the Age of Monteverdi*, 2 vols., Ann Arbor, 1982, vol. I, p. 97.

7 Orfeo (1607)
1. See, for example, N. Pirrotta and E. Povoledo, *Music and Theatre from Poliziano to Monteverdi*, trans. K. Eales, Cambridge, 1982 and S. Leopold, *Die Oper im 17. Jahrhundert*, Laaber, 2004, especially pp. 46–61.
2. The relevant works are several shorter pastorals by Laura Guidiccioni with music by Emilio de' Cavalieri (texts and music lost), the *Dafne* (1598) of Ottavio Rinuccini of which there is a partially preserved first musical rendering by Jacopo Corsi and Jacopo Peri and a second composition (1608) by Marco da Gagliano, the two competing musical settings of Rinuccini's libretto for *Euridice* by Peri and by Giulio Caccini, *Eumelio* by Agostino Agazzari (1606) and finally Monteverdi's and Striggio's *Orfeo* (1607) and Monteverdi's and Rinuccini's *Arianna* (1608).
3. I. Fenlon, 'Correspondence relating to the early Mantuan performances', in Whenham (ed.), *Claudio Monteverdi: 'Orfeo'*, Cambridge, 1986, pp. 167–72; see also the further discussion of these materials in Carter, 'Singing *Orfeo*: on the performers of Monteverdi's first opera', *Recercare*, 11 (1999), 75–118, at 105–11.
4. Fenlon, 'Correspondence', p. 171.
5. The participation of Rasi, though without precise information on his role, was mentioned in 1612 in a poem published by Eugenio Cagnani; see Carter, 'Singing *Orfeo*', 78.
6. Tim Carter has, however, associated the role of Apollo, and possibly one of the shepherds, with the palace tenor Francesco Campagnolo; see Carter, 'Singing *Orfeo*', 112.
7. J. Whenham, 'Five acts: one action', in Whenham (ed.), *Claudio Monteverdi: 'Orfeo'*, pp. 42–7; see also Whenham, 'Producing Monteverdi's *Orfeo*: some fundamental considerations', in P. Gargiulo (ed.), *'Lo stupor dell'invenzione': Firenze e la nascita dell'opera*, Florence, 2001, pp. 73–86.
8. See S. Leopold, 'Lyra Orphei', in *Claudio Monteverdi: Festschrift Reinhold Hammerstein zum 70. Geburtstag*, ed. Ludwig Finscher, Laaber 1986, pp. 337–45, at p. 337.
9. See I. Fenlon, 'The Mantuan *Orfeo*', in Whenham (ed.), *Claudio Monteverdi: Orfeo*, pp. 1–19, at p. 18, and Carter, 'Singing *Orfeo*'.
10. See also below, Chapter 14.

11. The significance of this tonal scheme was first noted in Whenham, 'Five acts: one action', 56–62.
12. See S. Leopold, *Monteverdi: Music in Transition*, Oxford, 1991, p. 92.
13. See H. Hell, 'Zu Rhythmus und Notierung des "Vi ricorda" in Claudio Monteverdis *Orfeo*', *Analecta musicologica*, 15 (1975), 87–157.
14. Monteverdi returned to the compositional problem of a musical 'heroic' more than once, and finally tried to supplement what from his point of view was an insufficient range of musico-poetic types with the heroic *genere concitato*; on the preface to the Eighth Book of Madrigals and numerous discussions of this in the Monteverdi literature, see J. Steinheuer, 'Herzensfestungen und Luftschlösser – Zur Ikonographie militärischer Architekturen im Liebeskrieg bei Cipriano de Rore, Nicolò Fontei, Claudio Monteverdi und Barbara Strozzi', *Musiktheorie*, 21 (2006), 101–29.
15. Leopold, 'Lyra Orphei', 337–45.
16. For a brief treatment of the three styles in Classical rhetoric, see B. Vickers, *In Defence of Rhetoric*, Oxford, 1998, pp. 80–2; for further information see the following entries in G. Ueding (ed.), *Historisches Wörterbuch der Rhetorik*, Tübingen, 1992–: K. Spang, 'Dreistillehre', II, cols. 922–3, J. Wisse, 'Affektenlehre', I, col. 223 and also C. Mouchel, 'Ethos', II, col. 1523. For a detailed discussion of these associations, see J. Steinheuer, *Chamäleon und Salamander, Neue Wege der Textvertonung bei Tarquinio Merula*, Kassel, 1999, especially pp. 286–303.

8 The Mantuan sacred music
1. The expedition is described in V. Errante, '"Forse che sì, forse che no": la terza spedizione del duca Vincenzo Gonzaga in Ungheria alla guerra contro il Turco (1601) studiata su documenti inediti', *Archivio storico lombardo*, 42 (1915), 29–34.
2. Documents relating details of this trip are found in S. Parisi, 'The Brussels–Mantua connection: Vincenzo Gonzaga's state voyages to the Low Countries in 1599 and 1608', forthcoming in *Alamire Yearbook*, vol. 6/7.
3. I. Fenlon, 'The Monteverdi Vespers: suggested answers to some fundamental questions', *Early Music*, 5 (1977), 383. Fenlon is mistaken in applying a Marian liturgy to a feast of Christ. The papal indulgence proclaimed in S. Andrea in 1607 at the request of the duke would have been in the context of a solemn, probably musically ostentatious, service.
4. I am grateful to Licia Mari for information on the 1611 events as well as evidence of the duke's chapel of musicians performing in both S. Pietro and S. Andrea.
5. O. Strunk, *Source Readings in Music History*, vol. IV, rev. M. Murata, *The Baroque Era*, New York and London, 1998, p. 29.
6. P. Fabbri, trans. T. Carter, *Monteverdi*, Cambridge, 1994, p. 102.

7. J. Kurtzman, 'An early seventeenth-century manuscript of *Canzonette e madrigaletti spiri-tuali*', *Studi musicali*, 8 (1979), 149–71.
8. Fabbri, *Monteverdi*, p. 102.
9. The principal studies of this publication are J. Kurtzman, 'The Monteverdi Vespers of 1610 and their relationship with Italian sacred music of the early seventeenth century', Ph.D. dissertation, University of Illinois at Champaign-Urbana, 1972; J. Kurtzman, 'Some historical perspectives on the Monteverdi Vespers', *Analecta musicologica*, 15 (1974), 29–86; J. Kurtzman, *Monteverdi: Essays on the Monteverdi Mass and Vespers of 1610*, Houston, 1978; J. Kurtzman, *The Monteverdi Vespers of 1610: Music, Context, Performance*, Oxford, 1999; and J. Whenham, *Monteverdi: Vespers (1610)*, Cambridge, 1997.
10. Fabbri, *Monteverdi*, p. 109.
11. The title of the Bassus generalis part-book differs somewhat, beginning *Sanctissimae Virgini missa senis vocibus, ad ecclesiarum choros ac vesperae pluribus decantandae.*
12. See P. Besutti, '"Ave Maris Stella": La tradizione mantovane nuovamente posta in musica da Monteverdi', in P. Besutti, T. M. Gialdroni and R. Baroncini (eds.), *Claudio Monteverdi: studi e prospettive, atti del convegno (Mantova, 21–24 ottobre 1993)*, Florence, 1993, pp. 57–77.
13. S. Parisi, 'New documents concerning Monteverdi's relations with the Gonzagas', in Besutti, Gialdroni and Baroncini (eds.), *Claudio Monteverdi*, p. 495.
14. The Mass is in the manuscript Cappella Sistina 107.
15. This information is contained in a letter recently discovered by Licia Mari in Mantova, Archivio di Stato, Archivio Gonzaga, busta 2721, fasc. III, cc. 55–56.
16. Quoted in Fabbri, *Monteverdi*, p. 120.
17. Quoted from an undated letter by Grillo to Monteverdi in Fabbri, *Monteverdi*, p. 118.
18. The manuscript, possibly from the late seventeenth or early eighteenth century, is found together with one of the cathedral's copies of Monteverdi's print. It was penned by one Lorenzo Tonelli, about whom we currently have no other information. The six vocal parts of the Mass are transposed down a fourth in this *partitura*, in keeping with the standard practice of performing compositions notated in high clefs a fourth or a fifth lower than notated.
19. For a detailed analysis of 'Nigra sum', see Kurtzman, *The Monteverdi Vespers of 1610*, pp. 308–24.
20. See the account and bibliography of the vitriolic debate between Hans Redlich and Leo Schrade in Kurtzman, *The Monteverdi Vespers of 1610*, pp. 16–19.
21. G. Dixon, 'Monteverdi's Vespers of 1610: "della Beata Vergine"?', *Early Music*, 15 (1987), 386–9.
22. S. Bonta, 'Liturgical problems in Monteverdi's Marian Vespers', *Journal of the American Musicological Society*, 20 (1967), 87–106. On the practice of antiphon

substitutions, see also J. Armstrong, 'The Antiphonae, seu sacrae cantiones (1613) of Giovanni Francesco Anerio: a liturgical study' *Analecta musicologica*, 14 (1974), 89–150; A. M. Cummings, 'Toward an interpretation of the sixteenth-century motet', *Journal of the American Musicological Society*, 34 (1981), 43–59; and J. Kurtzman, '*Per fare il Vespro meno tedioso*: Don Pietro Maria Marsolo and the "antiphon problem"', in B. H. Haggh (ed.), *Essays on Music and Culture in Honor of Herbert Kellman*, Paris, 2001, pp. 411–22. See also the discussion of the substitution issue in Kurtzman, *The Monteverdi Vespers of 1610*, pp. 56–78.
23. R. Bowers, 'Some reflection upon notation and proportions in Monteverdi's Mass and Vespers of 1610', *Music and Letters*, 73 (1992), 347–98; Kurtzman, *The Monteverdi Vespers of 1610*, pp. 433–66.
24. See the recent discussion in R. Bowers, 'An "aberration" reviewed: the reconciliation of inconsistent clef-systems in Monteverdi's Mass and Vespers of 1610', *Early Music*, 31 (2003), 527–38; A. Parrott, 'Monteverdi: onwards and downwards', *Early Music*, 32 (2004), 303–18; and A. Johnstone, '"High" clefs in composition and performance', *Early Music*, 34 (2006), 29–54; see also Chapter 14, 'Monteverdi in Performance', below. As indicated in note 20 above, the manuscript organ partitura of the *Missa in illo tempore* in Brescia transposes all voices of the mass, which were originally notated in the high clefs, downward by a fourth.

Intermedio III: 'Laetatus sum' (1610)
1. For other analytical comments on this psalm, see John Whenham, *Monteverdi: Vespers (1610)*, Cambridge, 1997, pp. 67–72; and J. Kurtzman, *The Monteverdi Vespers of 1610: Music, Context, Performance*, Oxford, 1999, pp. 223–30.
2. I am grateful to Judith Evans-Grubb for assistance with details of the English translation.
3. Whenham, *Monteverdi: Vespers (1610)*, p. 71. The beginning of the walking bass itself follows the typical *Romanesca* outline.
4. See G. Zarlino, trans. V. Cohen, *On the modes: part four of 'Le istitutioni harmoniche'*, 1558, New Haven and London, 1983, pp. 58–61.
5. A. Banchieri, *Conclusioni nel suono dell'organo*, Bologna, 1609; reprinted New York, 1975, p. 39; and Banchieri, *Cartella musicale nel canto figurato fermo, & contrapunto*, Venice, 1614; reprinted Bologna, 1968, p. 71.
6. Whenham, *Monteverdi: Vespers (1610)*, p. 71.
7. Ibid., pp. 71–2.
8. On this subject, see T. Carter, 'Two Monteverdi problems, and why they matter', *Journal of Musicology*, 19 (2002), 417–33.

9 Music in Monteverdi's Venice
1. I. Fenlon, *Music and Patronage in Sixteenth-Century Mantua*, 2 vols., Cambridge, 1980; 1982, vol. I, pp. 22–44.

2. T. Coryate, *Coryat's Crudities Hastily Gobled up in Five Moneths Travells in France, Savoy, Italy, Rhetia*, London, 1611, pp. 251–3.

3. J. Glixon, *Honoring God and the City. Music at the Venetian Confraternities, 1260–1807*, Oxford, 2003: a summation of the author's previous writings on the subject.

4. J. Glixon, 'A musicians' union in sixteenth-century Venice', *Journal of the American Musicological Society*, 36 (1983), 392–421.

5. G. Ongaro, 'Sixteenth-century patronage at St. Mark's, Venice', *Early Music History*, 8 (1988), 81–115.

6. I. Fenlon, 'Gioseffo and the Accademia della Fama', in Fenlon, *Music and Culture in Late Renaissance Italy*, Oxford, 2002, pp. 118–38.

7. D. Arnold, *Giovanni Gabrieli*, Oxford, 1979.

8. E. Rosand, 'Music in the myth of Venice', *Renaissance Quarterly*, 30 (1977), 511–37.

9. E. Muir, *Civic Ritual in Renaissance Venice*, Princeton, 1981, pp. 189–211; I. Fenlon, 'Magnificence and civic image: music and ceremonial in early modern Venice', in Fenlon, *Music and Culture*, pp. 1–23.

10. F. Sansovino, *Venetia citta nobilissima, et singolare, descritta in XIII. Libri ... con aggiunta di tutte le cose notabili della stessa citta, fatte, & occorse dall' anno 1580, fino al presente 1663 da D. Giustiniano Martinioni*, Venice, 1663, pp. 479–80.

11. J. H. Moore, '*Venezia favorita da Maria*: music for the Madonna Nicopeia and Santa Maria della Salute', *Journal of the American Musicological Society*, 37 (1984), 299–355. Doubts on the identification of the *concertato* Gloria (published in 1641) with the 1631 celebrations have recently been expressed in J. Kurtzman and L. M. Koldau, '*Trombe, trombe d'argento, trombe squarciate, and pifferi* in Venetian processions and ceremonies of the sixteenth and seventeenth centuries', *Journal of Seventeenth-Century Music*, 8/1 (2002) and in J. Kurtzman, 'Monteverdi's Mass of thanksgiving: da capo', in *Fiori musicali: liber amicorum Alexander Silbiger*, Warren, MI: Harmonie Park Press, forthcoming.

12. Muir, *Civic Ritual*, pp. 223–30; Fenlon, 'Magnificence as civic image'.

13. Letter of 18 September 1627. See also the previous letter (10 September 1627), which says that 'The Feast of the Rosary [which coincided with the feast day of S. Giustina] being over, and His Highness back from Maderno, it will be easy for me to get to Mantua.'

14. R. MacKenney, 'The scuole piccole of Venice: formations and transformations', in N. Terpstra (ed.), *The Politics of Ritual Kinship: Confraternities and Social Order in Early Modern Italy*, Cambridge, 1999, pp. 172–89.

15. D. Arnold, 'Music at the Scuola di San Rocco', *Music and Letters*, 40 (1959), 229–41.

16. J.-B. Duval, *Les Remarques triennales*, in Paris, Bibliotheque nationale Fonds. Fr. 13977, f.45v; see A. Pirro, 'La Musique des italiens d'après les remarques triennales de Jean-Baptiste Duval (1607–1609)', in *Mélanges offerts a M. Henri Lemmonier*, Paris, 1913, pp. 175–85.

17. Ibid.

18. R. Lassells, *The voyage of Italy: or, a Compleat Journey through Italy*, Paris, 1670, p. 413.

10 The Venetian secular music

1. For the biographical information cited here, see Fabbri, *Monteverdi*, Cambridge, 1994, *passim*. New documentation is also becoming available by way of the *Herla* Project, http://www.capitalespettacolo.it.

2. The date of Giovanni Battista Camarella's *Madrigali et arie* (Venice, Alessandro Vincenti) is unclear: the title-page reads 'MDCXX' although there is a blot, and the dedication is dated 15 November with 'MDCXXXIIII' added in ink. It is dated 1623 in an Utrecht bookseller's catalogue of 1639; H. Vanhulst (ed.), *The 'Catalogus librorum musicorum' of Jan Evertsen van Doorn (Utrecht 1639)*, 'Catalogus redivivi', 9, Utrecht, 1996, fol. B4^v, no. 3.

3. In his *Trattato della musica scenica* (1633–5); Fabbri, *Monteverdi*, p. 140.

4. For an example of such ceremonial duties, see J. Whenham, 'The Gonzagas visit Venice', *Early Music*, 21 (1993), 525–42. As for *I cinque fratelli*, only the text survives. According to Margherita Costa's account of the Medici's northern tour (to pay homage to the emperor) in *Istoria del viaggio d'Alemagna del Serenissimo Gran Duca di Toscana Ferdinando Secondo*, Venice, 1628, pp. 91–120 (*Herla*, L-544), the sonnets were 'cantati da due musici di Claudio Monteverdi', i.e., were set as duets.

5. One portion survives – 'Come dolce oggi l'auretta' in the Ninth Book; T. Carter, *Monteverdi's Musical Theatre*, New Haven and London, 2002, pp. 226–36. For the identification of the text, see T. Walker, 'Gli errori di *Minerva al tavolino*: osservazioni sulla cronologia delle prime opere veneziane', in M. T. Muraro (ed.), *Venezia e il melodramma nel Seicento*, Florence, 1976, pp. 7–20, at p. 13.

6. For the *Combattimento*, see Carter, *Monteverdi's Musical Theatre*, pp. 170–95. Monteverdi also appears to have planned (1627) a companion piece on the subject of Armida; ibid., pp. 195–6.

7. The music was then given to a young female singer, Antonia Monti; *Herla*, C-3891.

8. For Poland, see S. Parisi, 'New documents concerning Monteverdi's relations with the Gonzagas', in P. Besutti, T. M. Gialdroni and R. Baroncini (eds.), *Claudio Monteverdi: studi e prospettive; atti del convegno, Mantova, 21–24 ottobre 1993*, Florence, 1998, pp. 477–511, at 503–7. For Parma, see T. Carter, 'Intriguing laments: Sigismondo d'India, Claudio Monteverdi, and Dido *alla parmigiana* (1628)', *Journal of the American Musicological Society*, 49 (1996), 32–69.

9. S. Saunders, 'New light on the genesis of Monteverdi's eighth book of madrigals', *Music and Letters*, 77 (1996), 183–93.

10. For these and other Mantuan performers in Vienna (including comedians), see the various essays in U. Aioli and C. Grazioli (eds.), *I Gonzaga e l'Impero: itinerari dello spettacolo*, 'Storia dello Spettacolo: Fonti', 4, Florence, 2005.

11. Whenham ('The Gonzagas visit Venice', 527) suggests that Monteverdi could have issued the lament in 1623 in connection with the visit of the Duke and Duchess of Mantua to Venice in that year, who had in their retinue the famed singer Adriana Basile. Virginia Andreini may also have been in Venice in 1623 as part of her husband's *commedia* company, I Fedeli.

12. This view is most strongly articulated in G. Tomlinson, *Monteverdi and the End of the Renaissance*, Oxford, 1987.

13. Monteverdi attributes the quotation to the third book of Plato's 'De rhetorica', confusing him with Aristotle; for the broader issues, see M. Ossi, *Divining the Oracle: Monteverdi's 'Seconda Prattica'*, Chicago and London, 2003, pp. 189–210.

14. For parallel examples by the Viennese composer Giovanni Giacomo Arrigoni published in Venice in 1635, see Saunders, 'New light', pp. 186–8.

15. The pieces in the Eighth Book containing separate instructions concerning their performance – the *Combattimento*, the *Lamento della ninfa*, and the *Ballo delle ingrate* – presumably do so because Monteverdi was sending them to Vienna and therefore would not direct the performances himself; these instructions then remained unedited in the materials sent for printing This probably explains the 'mistake' in the instructions for the *Combattimento*, referring to the piece having been performed 'twelve years ago' (1624 plus twelve is 1636) rather than the correct (for 1638), fourteen.

16. Similarly, the opening of the Seventh Book with a sonnet that at least promises to sing of war (but succumbs instead to love) may be a reference to the start of the war, particularly given that the Medici had sent troops to support the emperor in 1618.

17. E. Klecker, '*Bella gerant alii: tu, felix Austria, nube!* Eine Spurensuche', *Österreich in Geschichte und Literatur*, 41 (1997), 30–44. Despite the legend attributing the catchphrase to Matthias Corvinus, King of Hungary (1458–90) and of Bohemia (1469–90), or Emperor Maximilian I (King of the Romans in 1486 and Holy Roman Emperor from 1493 until his death in 1519), there is no evidence for its use prior to the early seventeenth century.

18. It is listed in the Alessandro Vincenti catalogues of 1649, 1658 and 1662; O. Mischiati, *Indici, cataloghi e avvisi degli editori e librai musicali italiani dal 1591 al 1798*, 'Studi e testi per la storia della musica', 2, Florence, 1984, nos. IX.78. IXbis.76, X.78. Due to its size, the book was also unusually expensive (16 *lire* in 1649 and 1658; 16 *lire* 10 *soldi* in 1662), some four times the average cost of a standard book of madrigals.

19. For the medium, see J. Whenham, *Duet and Dialogue in the Age of Monteverdi*, 2 vols., Ann Arbor, 1982.

20. The attribution of the text of 'Non è di gentil core' to Francesco (sometimes Francesca) degli Atti is incorrect; see Whenham, *Duet and Dialogue*, vol. II, p. 77. Degli Atti, a singer in Graz, published a setting of this text in Bartolomeo Mutis's *Musiche a una, doi a tre voci* (Venice, 1613; edited in *Denkmäler der Tonkunst in Österreich*, 125 [1973]), but he was not the poet. Other settings (e.g., by Alfonso Fontanelli and Sigismondo d'India) do not repeat the first lines at the end in the manner of Monteverdi.

21. Though not all the word-painting is appropriate; see T. Carter, 'Two Monteverdi problems, and why they matter', *Journal of Musicology*, 19 (2002), 417–33.

22. Compare Mauro Calcagno's discussion of deictics in '"Imitar col canto chi parla": Monteverdi and the creation of a language for musical theater', *Journal of the American Musicological Society*, 55 (2002), 383–431.

23. T. Carter, '"Sfogava con le stelle" reconsidered', in P. Besutti, T. M. Gialdroni and R. Baroncini (eds.), *Claudio Monteverdi Studi e prospettive*, Florence, 1998, pp. 147–70.

24. The claim that 'Se i languidi miei sguardi' (the *lettera amorosa*) is in the male voice might seem surprising, given that it has become something of a (female) soprano showpiece; also the genre of the love letter would seem normally to be gendered female (following Ovid's *Heroides*). However, the speaker 'rimarrò prigioniero', will remain a prisoner of his beloved's blonde tresses that are praised inordinately in Claudio Achillini's text.

25. Compare M. Ossi, '"Pardon me, but your teeth are in my neck": Giambattista Marino, Claudio Monteverdi, and the *bacio mordace*', *Journal of Musicology*, 21 (2004), 175–200.

26. Here I draw upon K. Berger, *A Theory of Art*, New York and Oxford, 2000, pp. 165–212; M. Murata, 'Image and eloquence: secular song', in T. Carter and J. Butt (eds.), *The Cambridge History of Seventeenth-Century Music*, Cambridge, 2005, pp. 378–425. I also owe a debt to Mauro Calcagno's ongoing work on subjectivities in the Renaissance madrigal.

27. The reading 'labbra adorate' that appears in some work lists (and translations of this text) seems to be a corruption.

28. Compare B. Gordon, *Monteverdi's Unruly Women: The Power of Song in Early Modern Italy*, Cambridge, 2004, pp. 131–60.

Intermedio IV: *Lamento della Ninta* (1638)

1. E. Rosand, 'The descending tetrachord: an emblem of lament', *Musical Quarterly*, 55 (1979), 346–59; G. Tomlinson, *Monteverdi and the End of the Renaissance*, Oxford, 1987, pp. 213–14; S. McClary, 'Excess and frame: the musical representation of madwomen', in eadem, *Feminine Endings*, Minneapolis, 1991, pp. 80–111; T. Carter, 'Resemblance and representation: towards a new aesthetic in the music of Monteverdi', in I. Fenlon and T. Carter (eds.), *'Con che soavità': Essays in Italian Opera, Song, and Dance, 1580–1740*, Oxford, 1995, pp. 118–34.

2. For the Brunelli, see P. Aldrich, *Rhythm in Seventeenth-Century Italian Monody*, London, 1966, p. 166; for the Kapsberger, see J. Whenham, *Duet and Dialogue in the Age of Monteverdi*, 2 vols., Ann Arbor, 1982, vol. II, pp. 332–3; for the Piazza, see T. Carter, '*Possente spirto*: on taming the power of music', *Early Music*, 21 (1993), 517–23. The anonymous solo-voice setting in manuscript is in Florence, Biblioteca Nazionale Centrale, Banco Rari 236 (*olim* Magliabechiano XIX.114), p. 10, which has the same music as the setting of 'Non mai più vago fiore' in Florence, Conservatorio Statale di Musica Luigi Cherubini, Codex Barbera, p. 117a. Some aspects of these settings, and also the text, are discussed in M. Ossi, 'Claudio Monteverdi's *ordine novo, bello e gustevole*: the canzonetta as dramatic module and formal archetype', *Journal of the American Musicological Society*, 45 (1992), 261–304.
3. Compare A. MacNeil, 'Weeping at the water's edge', *Early Music*, 27 (1999), 406–18.
4. For 'Non partir, ritrosetta' and its at least potential comic subversiveness (the same music appears at Seneca's death in *L'incoronazione di Poppea* and elsewhere in Monteverdi's output), see T. Carter, *Monteverdi's Musical Theatre*, New Haven and London, 2002, pp. 283–86.

11 The Venetian sacred music
1. See P. Fabbri, trans. T. Carter *Monteverdi*, Cambridge, 1994, p. 138.
2. For a study of the rich musical life of Venice in churches other than S. Marco, see E. Quaranta, *Oltre San Marco: organizzazione e prassi della musica nelle chiese di Venezia nel Rinascimento*, Florence, 1998. On music in the confraternities, see J. Glixon, *Honoring God and the City: Music at the Venetian Confraternities, 1260–1807*, Oxford, 2003.
3. See G. Rovetta, *Messa, e salmi concertati, op. 4 (1639)*, ed. L. M. Koldau, 'Recent Researches in the Music of the Baroque Era', 109–10, Middleton, WI, 2001, esp. xv, note 13, citing a rubric in F. Capello, *Motetti e dialoghi* [Venice, 1615] – 'Sanctus & Agnus breve more veneto' – and the *Avvertimento* in Ignazio Donati's *Salmi boscarecci* (Venice, 1623) – 'Il Sanctus, & l'Agnus Dei sono posti così semplici, & brevi alla Venetiana, per sbrigarsi presto, & dar loco al Concerto per l'Elevatione; & a qualche Sinfonia alla Communione'.
4. J. H. Moore, *Vespers at St. Mark's: Music of Alessandro Grandi, Giovanni Rovetta and Francesco Cavalli*, 2 vols., Ann Arbor, 1981, vol. I, pp. 151–2.
5. F. Sansovino, *Venetia città nobilissima et singolare . . . ampliata del M. R. D. Stringa, canonico della chiesa ducale di S. Marco*, Venice, Salicato, 1604, p. 340v. Further on Stringa's additions, see below, p. 212 and n. 23; for the most part, Stringa's additions are reprinted in the more accessible, 1663, edition of Sansovino's book (his comment cited here is reprinted on p. 513 of the 1663 edition). See also letter of 19 July 1620 for Monteverdi's involvement that year in the

andata to the Redentore. On the doge's *andate* in general, see above, Chapter 9.
6. Sansovino, *Venetia*, 1604, p. 338r (1663, p. 501). For an eye-witness account of the Ascension Day *andata* in 1629, see Whenham, 'The Gonzagas visit Venice', *Early Music*, 21 (1993), 525–42, at 532–4. Monteverdi mentions the solemn Mass and Vespers that he had to prepare to be sung in S. Marco on Ascension Day and the cantata in praise of the doge in his letter of 21 April 1618.
7. See D. Blazey, 'The mid-Baroque concertato Litany in northern Italy: inherited problems and borrowed solutions', in A. Colzani, A. Luppi and M. Padoan (eds.), *Tradizione e stile*, Como, 1989, pp. 125–53, at p. 126.
8. The dedication was signed 1 May 1641. On the two title-pages of the *Selva morale*, dated 1640 and 1641 respectively, see L. M. Koldau, *Die venezianische Kirchenmusik von Claudio Monteverdi*, Kassel, 2001, pp. 101–4.
9. On the 1631 Mass, see below; Huygens's description of Monteverdi directing Vespers on 2 June 1620 is quoted in Chapter 14, below. For the full context, see F. Noske, 'An unknown work by Monteverdi: the Vespers of St. John the Baptist', *Music and Letters*, 66 (1985), 118–22, and the end of this chapter.
10. Koldau, *Die venezianische Kirchenmusik*, pp. 110–16.
11. Monteverdi set a number of texts by Grillo and his *alter ego*, Livio Celiano; see Fabbri, *Monteverdi*, pp. 118–19 and 141–4.
12. For a detailed analysis, see M. Ossi, *Divining the Oracle: Monteverdi's 'Seconda Prattica'*, Chicago and London, 2003, pp. 184–8.
13. See J. H. Moore, '*Venezia favorita da Maria*: music for the Madonna Nicopeia and Santa Maria della Salute', *Journal of the American Musicological Society*, 37 (1984), 299–355. His conclusions were first questioned by Jeffrey Kurtzman in 'Monteverdi's "Mass of Thanksgiving" revisited', *Early Music*, 22 (1994), 63–84.
14. See J. Kurtzman and L. M. Koldau, '*Trombe, Trombe d'argento, Trombe squarciate, and Pifferi* in Venetian processions and ceremonies of the sixteenth and seventeenth centuries', *Journal of Seventeenth-Century Music*, 8/1 (2002) and J. Kurtzman, 'Monteverdi's Mass of thanksgiving: da capo', in *Fiori musicali: liber amicorum Alexander Silbiger*, Warren, MI: Harmonie Park Press, forthcoming.
15. Modern edition in W. Osthoff (ed.), *Claudio Monteverdi: composizioni vocali profane e sacre (inedite)*, Milan, 1958, pp. 65–105.
16. See Chapter 6, above.
17. G. Zarlino, *Le istitutioni harmoniche*, Venice, 1558, p. 268.
18. D. Bryant, 'The "cori spezzati" of St Mark's: myth and reality', *Early Music History*, 1 (1981), 165–86.
19. L. Moretti, 'Architectural spaces for music: Jacopo Sansovino and Adrian Willaert at

St Mark's', *Early Music History*, 23 (2004), 153–84; see particularly the painting of 1690 reproduced on p. 168, which shows musicians in the *pergole*.

20. Moretti, 'Architectural spaces', pp. 177–8, citing Bartolomeo Bonifacio, *Rituum ecclesiasticorum ceremoniale* (1564); details of the surviving copies of this document are given on p. 154, n. 3 of her article.

21. For the liturgy of S. Marco, see G. Cattin, *Musica e liturgia a San Marco: testi e melodie per la liturgia delle ore dal XII al XVII secolo*, 3 vols., Venice, 1990, and also Moore, *Vespers at St Mark's*.

22. The conventions governing Vespers in S. Marco are examined in depth in Moore, *Vespers at St Mark's*; see especially Chapter 5.

23. *Venetia città nobilissima*, 1604 edn. (see above, n. 5), pp. 346r-v; 1663 edn., pp. 516–17.

24. Ibid., p. 346r; 1663 edn., p. 516.

25. See J. H. Moore, 'The *Vespero delli cinque Laudate* and the role of *salmi spezzati* at St Mark's', *Journal of the American Musicological Society*, 34 (1981), 249–78, esp. p. 258 and Table 2 (260–1); also Cattin, *Musica e liturgia, passim*.

26. Moore, 'The *Vespero delli cinque Laudate*', p. 265. Cavalli's settings are edited in F. Cavalli, *Vesperi a otto voci con basso continuo: Vespero della B. V. Maria, Vespero delle Domeniche, Vespero delli Cinque Laudate (1675)*, ed. F. Bussi, Milan, 1995, pp. 243–305.

27. These are tabulated in Moore, *Vespers at St. Mark's*, pp. 214–15.

28. See E. Selfridge-Field, *Venetian Instrumental Music from Gabrieli to Vivaldi*, rev. edn., New York, 1994, pp. 21–2.

29. Sansovino, *Venetia città nobilissima*, 1604, p. 334v; 1663 edn., p. 507.

30. All the feasts can be traced through Cattin, *Musica e liturgia*, and, slightly less thoroughly, through Table V-4 of Moore, *Vespers at St Mark's*, I, pp. 216–27.

31. There is no direct evidence for the singing of motets between the psalms at Vespers at S. Marco, though the practice was sanctioned at Venice for use in the *scuole*, and observed in other churches by the German composer Paul Hainlein in 1647 (at SS Giovanni e Paolo (11 October) and at San Francesco della Vigna (13 December), both with music by Rovetta); see W. Gurlitt, 'Ein Briefwechsel zwischen Paul Hainlein und L. Friedrich Behaim aus den Jahren 1647–48', *Sammelbände der internationalen Musikgesellschaft*, 4 (1912–13), 491–9; the texts are translated in D. Stevens, 'Monteverdiana 1993', *Early Music*, 22 (1993), 571–2. I remain unconvinced that motets were sung as antiphon substitutes given the prohibition of this practice in the *Caeremonial Episcoporum*, a copy of which was owned by the basilica (see J. Whenham, *Monteverdi Vespers (1610)*, Cambridge, 1997, pp. 18–21).

32. Moore, *Vespers at St. Mark's*, p. 228, note f.

33. See J. Glixon, *Honoring God and the City: Music at the Venetian Coufraternities, 1260–1807*, Oxford, 2003, pp. 160–61 and 286–87. Although

Monteverdi claimed in a letter of 13 March 1620 that he was 'invited . . . again and again by the wardens of the confraternities', his appearances at the Scuola Grande di San Rocco in 1623 and 1627 are the only recorded examples.

34. Monteverdi states that he celebrated First Vespers on 17 July, but the Feast Day falls on 16 July, and First Vespers, thus, on the evening of 15 July.

35. See Monteverdi's letter of 17 April 1621 and, for further detail, Fabbri, *Monteverdi*, pp. 178–9. The remark of the Florentine Resident is in Archivio di Stato di Firenze, Archivio Mediceo del Principato, Filza 3007, f. 116r, despatch of 27 April 1621.

36. G. Strozzi, *Esequie fatte in Venetia dalla natione fiorentina al serenissimo d. Cosimo II quarto gran duca di Toscana il dì 25 di maggio 1621*, Venice, 1621.

37. Cited in Fabbri, *Monteverdi*, p. 179.

38. Huygens' report is quoted below, at the beginning of Chapter 14; see also Noske, 'An unknown work', at p. 119. Stevens, *Monteverdi in Venice*, p. 61, identified the church at which the Vespers were celebrated as S. Giovanni Elemosinario, near the Rialto Bridge on the grounds that Huygens's SS Giovanni e Lucia was 'an excusable phonetic rendering of "Elemosinario"'. SS Giovanni e Paolo seems a more likely, and simpler, identification.

39. Archivio di Stato di Firenze, Archivio Mediceo del Principato, Filza 3015, ff. 225r-v, and Filza 3020b, ff. 66r-v. Letter from Ippolito Buondalmenti at Venice to Andrea Cioli, First Secretary of State to the Grand Duke of Tuscany, 23 June 1629. Florentine celebrations at Venice for the Feasts of S. Giovanni Battista are noted again in Ippolito Buondalmenti's despatches for 29 June 1630, 3 July 1632 and 2 July 1633 (ASF, Archivio Mediceo del Principato, Filza 3020b, f. 90v, Filza 3018, ff. 318r-v, and Filza 3019, f. 356r, respectively).

Intermedio V: Magnificat SV 281 (1641)

1. For a reconstruction of the texts of a complete Vespers service for the Assumption of the Blessed Virgin (15 August) see J. Whenham, *Monteverdi: Vespers (1610)*, Cambridge, 1997, pp. 95–9.

2. See Chapter 11, above.

3. Monteverdi, *Selva morale e spirituale*, ed. D. Stevens, 'Claudio Monteverdi, Opera Omnia', xv, Cremona, 1998, II. 797–890; Monteverdi, *Magnificat a 8 (1640)*, reconstructed by A. Parrott, ed. C. Bartlett, Wyton, Cambs., 1992.

12 Monteverdi's late operas

1. N. Pirrotta, 'Monteverdi and the problems of opera', in *Music and Culture in Italy from the Middle Ages to the Baroque: A Collection of Essays*, Cambridge, MA, 1984, p. 248.

2. The original text is given in Rosand, *Opera in Seventeenth-Century Venice*, Berkeley and Los Angeles, 1991, pp. 16–17, n. 19. The anonymous observer may have been alluding to the composer's relationship with Benedetto Ferrari,

confirmed in a document of 28 February 1641.
See B. Glixon, 'Scenes from the life of Silvia
Gailarti Manni, a seventeenth-century virtuosa',
Early Music History, 15 (1996), 97–146, at 115.
3. The date is confirmed in a publication of 1640
by F. Malipiero, *La peripizia d'Ulisse ovvero la
casta Penelope, parte prima*, Venice, 1640. The
relevant passage is quoted in Rosand, 'Iro and the
interpretation of *Il ritorno d'Ulisse in
patria*', n. 31.
4. The text of the sonnet is given in Rosand,
Opera in Seventeenth-Century Venice, p. 408
(Appendix 1.6). Ferrari's financial responsibilities at both S. Moisé and SS Giovanni e Paolo
during the 1640/41 season are confirmed by the
document cited in note 2 above. The same source
alludes to money owed by Ferrari to Monteverdi,
possibly for the composition of *Le nozze d'Enea*.
5. This information comes from Badoaro's letter
to the composer: see note 7.
6. This information comes from *Le glorie della
musica celebrate dalla sorella poesia, rappresen-
tandosi in Bologna la Delia e l'Ulisse nel teatro de
gl'Illustriss. Guastavillani*, Bologna, 1640.
7. The full text of the letter, which prefaces the
manuscript libretto I-Vmc 564, is given in
A. Curtis (ed.), *Claudio Monteverdi, Il ritorno
d'Ulisse in patria*, London, 2002, preface.
8. Ibid.
9. Torcigliani is identified in N. Michelassi,
'Michelangelo Torcigliani è l'incognito autore
delle *Nozze di Enea con Lavinia*', *Studi secenteschi*,
48 (2007), 381–6.
10. *Argomento et scenario delle Nozze d'Enea in
Lavinia, tragedia di lieto fine. Da rappresentarsi in
Musica*, Venice, 1640, pp. 19–20. The complete
text is given in E. E. Rosand, *Monteverdi's Last
Operas: A Venetian Trilogy*, Berkeley and Los
Angeles, 2007, Appendix 2.
11. *Argomento et scenario*, p. 25.
12. The individual textual passages on which
this material is based are given in Rosand, *Opera
in Seventeenth-Century Venice*, pp. 410–11
(Appendix I. 9).
13. The facts surrounding the discovery of the
score of *Ulisse* are discussed in Rosand,
Monteverdi's Last Operas, Chapter 2. See also
A. Curtis (ed.), *Il ritorno d'Ulisse*, Preface.
14. See F. Giuntini, 'Prologo e morale nel *Ritorno
d'Ulisse in patria*', in P. Radicchi and M. Burden
(eds.), *Florilegium musicae: studi in onore di
Carolyn Gianturco*, Pisa, 2004, II, pp. 595–602.
15. See *Monteverdi's Last Operas*, Chapter 7.
16. The conversion is discussed in detail in
Rosand, *Monteverdi's Last Operas*, Chapter 4.
17. In the case of *Le nozze d'Enea*, the rearrangement was simpler: Acts I and II became the
new Act I, Acts III and IV the new Act II and Act
V became Act III.
18. For a list of these passages, see T. Carter,
Monteverdi's Musical Theatre, New Haven and
London, 2002, Table 3–1, pp. 59–60.
19. See E. Rosand, 'Monteverdi's *Il ritorno
d'Ulisse in patria* and the power of music',
Cambridge Opera Journal, 4 (1992), 75–80.

20. On dating the first performance of *Poppea* to
1643, see J. Whenham, 'Perspectives on the
chronology of the first decade of public opera at
Venice', *Il Saggiatore musicale*, 11 (2004),
253–302, at 261–2.
21. C. Ivanovich, 'Memorie teatrali di Venezia'
[app. to *Minerva al tavolino*, Venice, 1681, 2/1688],
facs. edn with intro. by N. Dubowy, Lucca, 1993.
22. Those who have questioned the existence of
the 1646 revival, and the veracity of Ivanovich,
generally, include T. Walker, 'Gli errori di
Minerva al tavolino: osservazioni sulla cronologia
delle prime opera veneziane', in *Venezia e il
melodramma nel Seicento*, ed. M. T. Muraro,
Florence, 1976, pp. 7–20, and A. Chiarelli,
'*L'incoronazione di Poppea o Il Nerone*: problemi
di filologia testuale', *Rivista italiana di musicologia*, 9 (1974), 117–51; also L. Bianconi, trans.
D. Bryant, *Music in the Seventeenth Century*,
Cambridge, 1987. J. Whenham, 'Perspectives',
reopened the case by observing the distinction in
the contemporary documents, between prose
and opera theatres.
23. See W. Osthoff, 'Filiberto Laurenzis Musik
zu *La finta savia* in Zusammenhang der frühve-
nezianischen Oper', in M. T. Muraro (ed.),
Venezia e il melodramma nel seicento, Florence,
1976, pp. 173–97; also R. Ziosi, 'I libretti di
Ascanio Pio di Savoia: un esempio di teatro
musicale a Ferrara nella prima metà del
Seicento', in P. Fabbri (ed.), *Musica in torneo
nell'Italia del Seicento*, Lucca, 1999, pp. 135–65,
at 156f.
24. See above, n. 10.
25. The questions surrounding Monteverdi's
authorship of *Poppea* have spawned an enormous bibliography; some of the main contributors to the conversation are listed above in
n. 22; an important one not mentioned there is
Alan Curtis. See, among other places, '*La
Poppea impasticciata*, or, Who wrote the music
to *L'incoronazione* (1643)?', *Journal of the
American Musicological Society*, 42 (1989),
23–54. For the most recent bibliography on
this subject, see Rosand, *Monteverdi's Last
Operas*.
26. See Osthoff, 'Laurenzi', p. 175, and Rosand,
Opera in Seventeenth-Century Venice, p. 219.
27. On the Udine libretto, see P. Fabbri, 'New
sources for *Poppea*', *Music and Letters*, 74 (1993),
16–23. Monteverdi's name appears on the first
page of the Venice score, but was clearly added
later, probably in the eighteenth century; see
Curtis, '*La Poppea impasticciata*', 26–7, and
P. Jeffery, 'The Autograph Manuscripts of
Francesco Cavalli', Ph.D. diss., Princeton
University, 1980, pp. 168–75.
28. A few of the manuscript librettos beside the
one in Udine may date from near the time of the
first performance. A complete list of sources is
found in Rosand, *Monteverdi's Last Operas*,
Chapter 3.
29. Bianconi, *Music in the Seventeenth Century*,
pp. 194–6 provides a clear summary of the
situation. See Curtis, '*La Poppea impasticciata*',

for extensive analytical evidence for the collaboration of younger composers in the scores.
30. E. Chafe, *Monteverdi's Tonal Language*, New
York, 1992, Chapter 13.

13 Monteverdi studies and 'new' musicologies
1. E. Rothstein, 'Classical view: the politics of
sharps and flats', *New York Times*, 17 November
1991.
2. S. G. Cusick, 'Gendering modern music:
thoughts on the Monteverdi–Artusi controversy', *Journal of the American Musicological
Society*, 45 (1993), 1–25. See also C. S. Brauner,
'Letter', *Journal of the American Musicological
Society*, 47 (1994), 550–4; and S. G. Cusick, 'Reply
to Charles S. Brauner', *Journal of the American
Musicological Society*, 47 (1994), 554–63.
3. G. Tomlinson, 'Madrigal, monody, and
Monteverdi's "via naturale alla immitatione"',
Journal of the American Musicological Society, 34
(1981), 60–108; and G. Tomlinson, 'Music and
the claims of text: Monteverdi, Rinuccini, and
Marino', *Critical Inquiry*, 8 (1982), 565–89.
4. N. Pirrotta, 'Monteverdi's poetic choices', in
*Music and Culture in Italy from the Middle Ages to
the Baroque: A Collection of Essays*, Cambridge,
MA, 1984, pp. 271–316.
5. On 'new criticism', see J. C. Ransom, *The New
Criticism*, New York, 1941, repr. 1979 and
J. Kerman, *Contemplating Music*, Cambridge,
MA, 1985 (published in Britain as *Musicology*).
For an example of 'new historicism', see
S. Greenblatt, *Renaissance Self-Fashioning*,
Chicago, 1980.
6. G. Tomlinson, *Monteverdi and the End of the
Renaissance*, Oxford, 1987.
7. Jeffrey Kurtzman introduced the possibility of
semiotic analysis of Monteverdi's music in
'Monteverdi's changing aesthetics: a semiotic
perspective', in *Festa Musicale: Essays in Honor of
George Buelow*, Stuyvesant, NY, 1995,
pp. 233–55. Mauro Calgano introduced analysis
by the linguistic categories of 'deictics' and
'pragmatics' in his essay '"Imitar col canto chi
parla": Monteverdi and the creation of a language for musical theater', *Journal of the
American Musicological Society*, 55 (2002),
383–431.
8. E. Rosand, 'Seneca and the interpretation of
L'incoronazione di Poppea', *Journal of the
American Musicological Society*, 38 (1985), 34–71.
9. Rosand herself applied the techniques of the
Poppea essay to *Il ritorno d'Ulisse* a few years
later, in 'Iro and the interpretation of *Il ritorno
d'Ulisse in patria*', *Journal of Musicology*,
7 (1989), 141–64. Responses to her critical
approach to both operas include I. Fenlon and
P. Miller, *The Song of the Soul: Understanding
Poppea*, RMA Monographs 5, London, 1992;
T. Carter, '"In love's harmonious consort":
Penelope and the interpretation of *Il ritorno
d'Ulisse in patria*', *Cambridge Opera Journal*,
5 (1993), 1–16; Carter, 'Re-reading *Poppea*: some
thoughts on music and meaning in Monteverdi's

last opera', *Journal of the Royal Musical
Association*, 122 (1997), 173–204; W. Heller,
'Tacitus Incognito: opera as history in
L'incoronazione di Poppea', *Journal of the
American Musicological Society*, 52 (1999), 39–96;
and M. Calcagno, 'Signifying nothing: on the
aesthetics of pure voice in early Venetian opera',
Journal of Musicology, 20 (2003), 461–97.
Calcagno's essay '"Imitar col canto chi parla"...',
cited above, represents the most significant
departure from the Rosand tradition, as
Calcagno uses linguistic theory to read
passages from both *Ulisse* and *Poppea* in terms of
subjectivity and temporality. Alan Curtis's per-
suasive argument that Monteverdi did not
write all of *Poppea* continues to trouble listeners,
students and scholars by denying the fantasy
merging of single authorship and cultural
authority; see his '*La Poppea impasticciata* or,
who wrote the music to *L'incoronazione* (1643)?',
Journal of the American Musicological Society,
42 (1989), 23–54.
10. Special issues of *Music Analysis*, 12/1 (July
1993), edited by D. Puffett, and *Early Music*, 21/4
(November 1993) and 22/1 (February 1994),
jointly edited by I. Fenlon and T. Carter, were
devoted to Monteverdian topics.
11. Puffett made this point in his 'Editorial',
Music Analysis 12 (1993), 1.
12. E. Chafe, *Monteverdi's Tonal Language*, New
York, 1992. Chafe acknowledged his methodological debt to C. Dahlhaus's
'Habilitationsschrift', which had been published
in English translation by R. Gjerdingen as *On the
Origins of Harmonic Tonality*, Princeton, 1990.
13. Carter, '"An air new and grateful to the ear"';
and G. Chew, 'The Platonic agenda of
Monteverdi's second practice: a case study',
Music Analysis, 12 (1993), 147–68.
14. S. McClary, 'The transition from modal to
tonal organization in the works of Monteverdi',
Ph.D. diss., Harvard University, 1976. McClary
revisited some of the readings in her dissertation,
showing how the gestures of mode might both
represent and enact identifiable subjectivities, in
her book *Modal Subjectivities: Self-Fashioning in
the Italian Madrigal*, Berkeley, 2004.
15. J. Kurtzman, 'A taxonomic and affective
analysis of Monteverdi's "Hor che'l ciel e la terra"',
Music Analysis, 12 (1993), 169–95. His focus on
taxonomy was inspired by reading M. Foucault,
*The Order of Things: An Archaeology of the Human
Sciences*, New York, 1971; translation of *Les Mots
et les choses*, Paris, 1966.
16. A. Pryer, 'Monteverdi, two sonnets and a
letter', *Early Music*, 25 (1997), 357–71
17. This literature, too vast to cite here, has been
a particular feature of the journal *Early Music*; see
also Chapter 14, 'Monteverdi in performance',
below. On reconstructing the original physical
space for specific performances, see Besutti's
'The "Sala degli Specchi" uncovered:
Monteverdi, the Gonzagas, and the Palazzo
Ducale, Mantua', *Early Music*, 27 (1999), 451–65.
and her Chapter 5, above.

18. R. Wistreich, "La voce è grata assai, ma …': Monteverdi on singing', *Early Music*, 22 (1994), 7–19.

19. R. Wistreich, 'Real basses, real men: *virtù* and virtuosity in the construction of noble male identity in late sixteenth-century Italy', in N. Schwindt (ed.), *Troja: Trossingen Jahrbuch zur Renaissance Musik 2: Gesang zur Laute*, Kassel and Basel, 2003, pp. 59–80; see also his monograph *Courtier, Warrior, Singer: Giulio Cesare Brancaccio and the Performance of Identity in the Late Renaissance*, Aldershot, 2007. For Butler's ideas about performativity, see her *Gender Trouble: Feminism and the Subversion of Identity*, New York, 1990 and *Bodies That Matter*, New York, 1993.

20. C. Geertz, 'Thick description', in *The interpretation of cultures*, New York, 1973; rev. New York, 2000, pp. 3–32. On the wider influence of Geertz's ideas in the humanities, see S. Greenblatt, 'The touch of the real', *Representations*, 59 (1979), special issue: *The Fate of 'Culture': Geertz and Beyond*, 14–29, and other articles in that issue.

21. G. Tomlinson, *Music and Renaissance Magic: Toward a Historiography of Others*, Chicago, 1993.

22. See ibid., pp. 33ff, especially p. 35, where he explains how archaeology differs from a history of *mentalités*; see also M. Foucault, trans. A. M. Sheridan Smith, *The Archaeology of Knowledge and the Discourse on Language*, New York, 1972.

23. See Tomlinson, *Music and Renaissance Magic*, pp. 38–40, and M. Foucault, 'Nietzsche, geneaology, history', in D. Bouchard (ed.), *Language, Counter-Memory, Practice: Selected Essays and Interviews*, Ithaca, 1977, pp. 139–64. Obviously, this view of subject formation strongly resembles feminist theories of social construction. Therefore Tomlinson's introduction of Foucauldian geneaology reinforced the power of McClary's arguments in *Feminine Endings*.

24. Foucault introduced the notion of epistemes in *The Order of Things*.

25. G. Tomlinson, *Metaphysical Song: An Essay on Opera*, Princeton, 1999.

26. Ibid, p. ix.

27. B. Glixon, 'Private lives of public women: prima donnas in mid-seventeenth-century Venice', *Music and Letters*, 76 (1995), 509–31.

28. S. G. Cusick, '"There was not one lady who failed to shed a tear": Arianna's lament and the construction of modern womanhood', *Early Music*, 22 (1994), 21–45.

29. T. Carter, 'Lamenting Ariadne?', *Early Music*, 27 (1999), 395–405.

30. MacNeil, 'Weeping at the water's edge', *Early Music*, 27 (1999), 406–18.

31. B. Gordon, 'Talking back: the female voice in *Il Ballo delle ingrate*', *Cambridge Opera Journal*, 11 (1999), 1–30.

32. R. Lewis, 'Love as persuasion in Monteverdi's *L'incoronazione di Poppea*: new

thoughts on the authorship question', *Music and Letters*, 86 (2005), 16–41.

33. T. Carter, *Monteverdi's Musical Theatre*, New Haven and London, 2002.

34. M. Ossi, *Divining the Oracle: Monteverdi's 'Seconda Prattica'*, Chicago and London, 2003.

35. W. Heller, *Emblems of Eloquence: Opera and Women's Voices in Seventeenth-Century Venice*, Berkeley, 2003.

36. B. Gordon, *Monteverdi's Unruly Women: The Power of Song in Early Modern Italy*, Cambridge, 2005.

37. A. Dell'Antonio, '"Il divino Claudio": Monteverdi and lyric nostalgia in fascist Italy' *Cambridge Opera Journal*, 8 (1996), 271–84; I. Fenlon, 'Malipiero, Monteverdi, Mussolini and musicology', in A. Latham (ed.), *Sing Ariel: Essays and Thoughts for Alexander Goehr's Seventieth Birthday*, Aldershot, 2003, pp. 241–55. I have not been able to consult a related essay, M. Tsugami, 'What incited the "Monteverdi Renaissance?"', in *Musicology and Globalization*, Tokyo, 2004, pp. 184–8.

38. For the early modern soundscape, see B. Smith, *The Acoustic World of Early Modern England: Attending to the O Factor*, Chicago, 1999; for the opacity of performance events to hermeneutics or archaeology, see C. Abbate, 'Music – drastic or gnostic?', *Critical Inquiry*, 30 (2004), 505–36. Indeed, music's use as a medium of physical torture and 'directed energy' weaponry is another sign, however disturbing, of this shift.

14 Monteverdi in performance

1. From the travel diary of the Dutch diplomat Constantijn Huygens, who visited Venice from 13 June to 5 July 1620, in Fabbri, *Monteverdi*, Cambridge, 1994, p. 176.

2. Richard Todd, review of a performance of the *Vespers* (1610) on 23 September 1998, *The Ottawa Citizen*, 25 September 1998.

3. S. Parisi, 'Acquiring musicians and instruments in the early Baroque: observations from Mantua', *The Journal of Musicology*, 14 (1996), 117–50, at 118.

4. S. Parisi, 'Ducal patronage of music in Mantua, 1587–1627: an archival study', Ph.D. diss., University of Illinois, 1989, esp. tables 3–6, pp. 28–31; Carter, 'Singing *Orfeo*: on the performers of Monteverdi's first opera', *Recercare*, 11 (1999), 75–118, at 81–2; see also Chapter 4, above.

5. See Chapters 4 and 5, for details of the various palace spaces in which these activities occurred.

6. J. H. Moore, *Vespers at St. Mark's: Music of Alessandro Grandi, Govanni Rovetta and Francesco Cavalli*, 2 vols., Ann Arbor, 1981, vol. I, pp. 80–2.

7. D. Arnold, *Monteverdi*, London, 1990, pp. 26–7; see also Chapter 9, above.

8. E. Rosand, 'Venice, 1580–1680' in C. Price (ed.), *Music and Society: The Early Baroque Era*, Englewood Cliffs, 1994, p. 78.

9. B. Blackburn and E. Lowinsky, 'Luigi Zenobi and his letter on the perfect musician', *Studi musicali*, 20 (1994), 61–107, at 103.

10. Ibid., 80, 96.

11. Pryer, 'Two sonnets and a letter', *Early Music*, 25 (1997), 357–71, at 357.

12. P. Fabbri and A. Pompilio (eds.), *Il corago*, Florence, 1983; partially translated in R. Savage and M. Sansone, '*Il Corago* and the staging of early opera: four chapters from an anonymous treatise circa 1630', *Early Music*, 17 (1989), 494–511.

13. Carter, *Monteverdi's Musical Theatre*, New Haven and London, 2002, p. 88.

14. *Orfeo*, Act V: 'Duoi Organi di legno, & duoi Chitaroni concertorno questo Canto sonando l'uno nel angolo sinistro della scena, l'altro nel destro'. See also Chapter 5, above.

15. *Il Corago*, pp. 87–90.

16. Arnold, *Monteverdi*, p. 2.

17. P. Holman, '"Col nobilissimo esercitio della vivuola": Monteverdi's string writing', *Early Music*, 21 (1993), 577–90, at 577. In 1590 Monteverdi referred in his dedication of his Second Book of Madrigals to Giacomo Ricardi, President of the Milan Senate, to having played *vivuola* in Milan; Fabbri, *Monteverdi*, Cambridge, 1994, p. 20; see also Chapter 4, above.

18. See Chapter 4, above.

19. For other singers' audition reports, see R. Wistreich, '*La voce e grata assai, ma . . .*: Monteverdi on singing', *Early Music*, 22 (1994), 7–20.

20. R. Wistreich, 'Reconstructing pre-Romantic singing technique' in J. Potter (ed), *The Cambridge Companion to Singing*, Cambridge, 2000, pp. 178–91.

21. Blackburn and Lowinsky, 'Luigi Zenobi', 101–2.

22. Wistreich, 'Reconstructing pre-Romantic singing technique', pp. 182–3; K. Schiltz, 'Church and chamber: the influence of acoustics on musical composition and performance', *Early Music*, 31 (2003), 64–80.

23. Whenham, *Monteverdi Vespers (1610)*, Cambridge, 1997, pp. 41–4.

24. Moore, *Vespers at St Mark's*, pp. 83–6.

25. *Il corago*, p. 96.

26. Savage and Sansone, '*Il corago* and the staging of early opera', 500–1; see also Carter, *Monteverdi's Musical Theatre*, especially Chapter 4, 'The art of the theatre', pp. 74–108.

27. E. Rosand, *Opera in Seventeenth Century Venice*, Berkeley and Los Angeles, 1991 pp. 227–35; see also, W. Heller, *Emblems of Eloquence: Opera and Women's Voices in Seventeenth Century Venice*, Berkeley and Los Angeles, 2003 pp. 174–7.

28. See, for example, A. Parrott, 'Monteverdi: onwards and downwards', *Early Music*, 32 (2004), 303–18, at 311 and Wistreich, 'Reconstructing pre-Romantic singing technique', pp. 181–2.

29. Parrott, 'Monteverdi: onwards and downwards', esp. pp. 306–14; see also P. Barbieri,

'*Chiavette* and modal transposition in Italian practice (*c*.1500–1837)', *Recercare*, 3 (1991), 5–69 and Chapter 8, above.

30. See Wistreich, 'Monteverdi on singing'.

31. R. Sherr, 'Gugliemo Gonzaga and the castrati', *Renaissance Quarterly*, 33 (1980), 33–56.

32. Carter, 'Singing *Orfeo*'.

33. Moore, *Vespers at St Mark's*, vol. I, p. 84.

34. Parisi, 'Ducal patronage', p. 31.

35. For example, at the Academia dei Floridi in Bologna; see T. Carter, *Music in Late Renaissance and Early Baroque Italy*, London, 1992, pp. 38–9.

36. Carter, *Monteverdi's Musical Theatre*, pp. 206–11; see also Chapter 6, above.

37. Parisi, 'Acquiring musicians', 123.

38. Letter of 28 December 1610.

39. Letter of 22 January 1611.

40. Fabbri, *Monteverdi*, pp. 145–53.

41. Carter, *Monteverdi's Musical Theatre*, pp. 93, 215–17.

42. See Rosand, *Opera in Seventeenth Century Venice*, pp. 227–35 and Chapter 12, above.

43. Carter, *Monteverdi's Musical Theatre*, pp. 200–1.

44. Letters of 7, 22, 24 May and 5 June 1627

45. Paris, 'Ducal patronage', pp. 125–6.

46. Holman, 'Monteverdi's string writing', 577.

47. Ibid., 588.

48. Parisi, 'Ducal patronage', p. 126.

49. Letter of 26 March 1611.

50. Blackburn and Lowinsky, 'Luigi Zenobi', 105.

51. Parisi, 'Ducal patronage', pp. 30–31.

52. S. Stubbs, '*L'armonia sonora*: continuo orchestration in Monteverdi's *Orfeo*', *Early Music*, 2 (1994), 86–100.

53. See A. M. Vacchelli, 'Monteverdi as a primary source for the performance of his own music', in R. Monterosso (ed.), *Proceedings of the International Congress on Performing Practice in Monteverdi's Music: The Historic-Philological Background*, Cremona, 1995, pp. 23–52.

54. Stubbs, 'Continuo orchestration'; J. Glover, 'Solving the musical problems', in J. Whenham (ed.), *Claudio Monteverdi: Orfeo*, Cambridge, 1986, pp. 138–55.

55. Holman, 'Monteverdi's string writing', 580.

56. D. Arnold, 'Performing practice', in D. Arnold and N. Fortune (eds.), *The New Monteverdi Companion*, London, 1985, pp. 329–31; L. Bianconi and T. Walker, 'Production, consumption and political function of seventeenth-century opera', *Early Music History*, 4 (1984), 209–96, at 225.

57. S. Bonta, 'The use of instruments in sacred music in Italy 1560–1700', *Early Music*, 18 (1990), 519–35, at 520; E. Selfridge-Field, 'Bassano and the orchestra of St Mark's', *Early Music* 4 (1976), 152–8.

58. C. Bartlett and P. Holman, 'Giovanni Gabrieli: a guide to the performance of his music', *Early Music*, 3 (1975), 25–32.

59. Moore, *Vespers at St Mark's*, vol. I, pp. 81–9.

60. J. Kurtzman, *The Monteverdi Vespers of 1610: Music, Context, Performance*, Oxford, 1999, pp. 358–66.

61. G. Salvetti, 'Alcuni criteri nella rielaborazione ed orchestrazione dell' "Incoronazione"', *Rivista italiana di musicologia*, 2 (1967), 332–40; see also C. Deshoulières, *L'Opéra baroque et la scène moderne*, Paris, 2000, esp. pp. 623–95.

62. Available on DVD; see Discography, below.

Bibliography

Abbate, C. 'Music: drastic or gnostic?', *Critical Inquiry*, 30 (2004), 505–36
  In Search of Opera, Princeton Studies in Opera, Princeton, 2001
Adams, K. and D. Kiel, *Claudio Monteverdi: a Guide to Research*, Composer
  Resource Manuals (New York and London, 1989)
Agee, R., *The Gardano Music Printing Firms, 1569–1611*, Rochester, NY, 1998
Arnold, D., rev. T. Carter, *Monteverdi*, London, 1990
  and N. Fortune (eds.), *The New Monteverdi Companion*, London, 1985
  Giovanni Gabrieli, Oxford, 1979
  'Music at the scuola di San Rocco', *Music and Letters*, 40 (1959), 229–41
Barbieri, P., '*Chiavette* and modal transposition in Italian practice (*c.*1500–1837)',
  Recercare, 3 (1991), 5–69
Barblan G. (ed.), *Musiche della cappella di S. Barbara in Mantova: catalogo della
  biblioteca*, Florence, 1972
Bartlett, C. and P. Holman, 'Giovanni Gabrieli: a guide to the performance of
  his music', *Early Music*, 3 (1975), 25–32
Besutti, P., 'La galleria musicale dei Gonzaga: intermediari, luoghi, musiche e
  strumenti in corte a Mantova', *Gonzaga: La celeste galeria: le raccolte,
  catalogo della mostra (Mantova, Palazzo Te, 1 settembre–8 dicembre 2002)*,
  ed. R. Morselli, Milan, 2002, pp. 407–75
  'Giostre, fuochi e naumachie a Mantova fra Cinque e Seicento', *Musica in
  torneo nell'Italia del Seicento*, ed. P. Fabbri, Lucca, 1999, pp. 3–32
  'The "Sala degli Specchi" uncovered: Monteverdi, the Gonzagas, and the
  Palazzo Ducale, Mantua', *Early Music*, 27 (1999), 451–65
  '"Ave Maris Stella": La tradizione mantovane nuovamente posta in musica da
  Monteverdi', *Claudio Monteverdi: studi e prospettive, atti del convegno
  (Mantova, 21–24 ottobre 1993)*, ed. P. Besutti, T. M. Gialdroni, and
  R. Baroncini, Florence, 1993, pp. 57–77
Biaggi, M., '*Ogni amante è guerrier*: Monteverdi and the war of love in early
  modern Italy', Ph.D. diss., Princeton University, 2006
Bianconi, L., trans. D. Bryant, *Music in the Seventeenth Century*, Cambridge, 1987
  and T. Walker, 'Production, consumption and political function of
  seventeenth-century opera', *Early Music History*, 4 (1984), 209–96
Blackburn, B. and Lowinsky, E., 'Luigi Zenobi and his letter on the perfect
  musician', *Studi musicali*, 20 (1994), 61–107
Blazey, D., 'A liturgical role for Monteverdi's Sonata sopra Sancta Maria', *Early
  Music*, 17 (1989), 175–182
  'The mid-Baroque concertato Litany in northern Italy: inherited problems and
  borrowed solutions', in A. Colzani, A. Luppi and M. Padoan (eds.), *Tradizione e
  stile*, Como, 1989, 125–53

Bonta, S., 'The use of instruments in sacred music in Italy 1560–1700', *Early Music*,
    18 (1990), 519–35
  'Liturgical problems in Monteverdi's Marian Vespers', *Journal of the American
    Musicological Society*, 20 (1967), 87–106
Bowers, R., 'Claudio Monteverdi and sacred music in the Gonzaga ducal household,
    1590–1612', forthcoming
  'An "aberration" reviewed: the reconciliation of inconsistent clef-systems in
    Monteverdi's Mass and Vespers of 1610', *Early Music*, 31 (2003), 527–38
  'Proportional notations in Monteverdi's "Orfeo"', *Music and Letters*, 76 (1995),
    149–67
Boyden, D., 'Monteverdi's "violini piccolo alla francese" and "viole da brazzo"',
    Annales Musicologiques, 6 (1958–63), 387–401
Brown, H. M., 'Emulation, competition, and homage: imitation and theories of
    imitation in the Renaissance', *Journal of the American Musicological Society*,
    35 (1982), 1–48
Bryant, D., 'The "cori spezzati" of St Mark's: myth and reality', *Early Music
    History*, 1 (1981), 165–86
Burattelli, C., *Spettacoli di corte a Mantova tra Cinque e Seicento*, Florence, 1999
Burke, P., *Popular Culture in Early Modern Europe*, London, 1978
Calcagno, M., 'Signifying nothing: on the aesthetics of pure voice in early
    Venetian opera', *Journal of Musicology*, 20 (2003), 461–97
  '"Imitar col canto chi parla": Monteverdi and the creation of a language for musical
    theatre', *Journal of the American Musicological Society*, 55 (2002), 383–431
Carpeggiani, P., *Bernardino Facciotto: Progetti cinquecenteschi per Mantova e il
    Palazzo ducale*, Milan, 1994
Carter, T., 'The first edition of Monteverdi's *Orfeo*', in *Orpheus Orfeo: Studi dedicati
    a Claudio Gallico*, Florence, forthcoming
  Monteverdi's Musical Theatre, New Haven and London, 2002
  'Two Monteverdi problems, and why they matter', *Journal of Musicology*,
    19 (2002), 417–33
  Monteverdi and his Contemporaries, Aldershot, 2000 [Carter, VARIORUM]
  'Printing the "New Music"', in K. van Orden (ed.), *Music and the Cultures of
    Print*, New York and London, 2000, pp. 3–37
  'Singing *Orfeo*: on the performers of Monteverdi's first opera', *Recercare*,
    11 (1999), 75–118
  'New light on Monteverdi's *Ballo delle ingrate* (Mantua, 1608)', *Il Saggiatore
    musicale*, 6 (1999), 63–90
  'Lamenting Ariadne?', *Early Music*, 27 (1999), 395–405
  '"Sfogava con le stelle" reconsidered: some thoughts on the analysis of Monteverdi's
    Mantuan madrigals', in P. Besutti, T. M. Gialdroni and R. Baroncini (eds.),
    *Claudio Monteverdi: studi e prospettive; atti del convegno, Mantova, 21–24 ottobre
    1993*, 'Accademia Nazionale Virgiliana di Scienze, Lettere e Arti: Miscellanea', 5,
    Florence, 1998, pp. 147–70; repr. in Carter, VARIORUM, VII
  'Re-reading *Poppea*: some thoughts on music and meaning in Monteverdi's last
    opera', *Journal of the Royal Musical Association*, 122 (1997), 173–204; repr. in
    Carter, VARIORUM, XII

'Intriguing Laments: Sigismondo d'India, Claudio Monteverdi, and Dido *alla parmigiana* (1628)', *Journal of the American Musicological Society*, 49 (1996), 32–69; repr. in Carter, VARIORUM, X

'"An air new and grateful to the ear": the concept of *aria* in late Renaissance and early Baroque Italy', *Music Analysis*, 12 (1993), 127–45; repr. in Carter, VARIORUM, V

'"In love's harmonious consort": Penelope and the interpretation of *Il ritorno d'Ulisse in patria*', *Cambridge Opera Journal*, 5 (1993), 1–16; repr. in Carter, VARIORUM, XI

'*Possente spirito:* on taming the power of music', *Early Music*, 21(1993), 517–23; repr. in Carter, VARIORUM, VIII

Music in Late Renaissance and Early Baroque Italy, London, 1992

'Artusi, Monteverdi, and the poetics of modern music', in N. Kovaleff Baker and B. Russano Hanning (eds.), *Musical Humanism and its Legacy: Essays in Honor of Claude V. Palisca*, Stuyvesant, NY, 1992, pp. 171–94; repr. in Carter, VARIORUM, VI

Cattin, G., *Musica e liturgia a San Marco: testi e melodie per la liturgia delle ore dal XII al XVII secolo*, 3 vols., Venice, 1990

Chafe, E., *Monteverdi's Tonal Language*, New York, 1992

Chew, G., 'The Platonic agenda of Monteverdi's second practice: a case study', *Music Analysis*, 12 (1993), 147–68

'The perfections of modern music: consecutive fifths and tonal coherence in Monteverdi', *Music Analysis*, 8 (1989), 247–74

Chiarelli, A., '*L'incoronazione di Poppea* o *Il Nerone*: problemi di filologia testuale', *Rivista italiana di musicologia*, 9 (1974), 117–51

Coryate, T., *Coryat's Crudities Hastily Gobled up in Five Moneths Travells in France, Savoy, Italy, Rhetia*, London, 1611

Curtis, A., '*La Poppea impasticciata* or, Who wrote the music to *L'incoronazione* (1643)?', *Journal of the American Musicological Society*, 42 (1989), 23–54

Cusick, S. G., '"There was not one lady Who failed to shed a tear": Arianna's lament and the construction of modern womanhood', *Early Music*, 22 (1994), 21–41

'Gendering modern music: thoughts on the Monteverdi–Artusi controversy', *Journal of the American Musicological Society*, 45 (1993), 1–25

Dahlhaus, C., trans. Gjerdingen, R., *Studies on the Origins of Harmonic Tonality*, Princeton, 1990

'*Ecco mormorar l'onde*: Versuch ein Monteverdi-Madrigal zu interpretieren', in H. Poos (ed.), *Chormusik und Analyse*, Mainz, 1983, pp. 139–54

Delfino, A. and M. Rosa-Barezzani (eds.), *Marc'Antonio Ingegneri e la musica a Cremona nel secondo Cinquecento*, Lucca, 1995

Dell'Antonio, A., '"Il divino Claudio": Monteverdi and lyric nostalgia in fascist Italy', *Cambridge Opera Journal*, 8 (1996), 271–84

De' Paoli, D., *Monteverdi*, Milan, 1979

Deshoulièves, C., *L'Opéra baroque et la scène moderne*, Paris, 2000

Dixon, G., 'Monteverdi's Vespers of 1610: "della Beata Vergine"?', *Early Music*, 15 (1987), 386–9

'Continuo scoring in the early Baroque: the role of bowed bass instruments', *Chelys*, 15 (1986), 38–53

Einstein, A., trans. A. H. Krappe, *et al.*, *The Italian Madrigal*, Princeton, 1949, repr. 1971

Errante, V., '"Forse che sì, forse che no": La terza spedizione del Duca Vincenzo Gonzaga in Ungheria alla guerra contro il Turco (1601) studiata su documenti inediti', *Archivio Storico Lombardo*, 42 (1915), 29–34

Fabbri, P., trans. T. Carter, *Monteverdi*, Cambridge, 1994

'New Sources for *Poppea*', *Music and Letters*, 74 (1993), 16–23

and A. Pompilio (eds.), *Il corago* (*c.*1630), Florence, 1983

Fenlon, I., 'Malipiero, Monteverdi, Mussolini and musicology', in A. Latham (ed.), *Sing Ariel: Essays and Thoughts for Alexander Goehr's Seventieth Birthday*, Aldershot, 2003, pp. 241–55

Music and Culture in Late Renaissance Italy, Oxford, 2002

Giaches de Wert: Letters and Documents, Paris, 1999

and P. Miller, *The Song of the Soul: Understanding Poppea*, RMA Monographs 5, London, 1992

Music and Patronage in Sixteenth-Century Mantua, 2 vols., Cambridge, 1980; 1982

'The Monteverdi Vespers: suggested answers to some fundamental questions', *Early Music*, 5 (1977), 380–7

Follino, F., *Compendio delle sontuose feste fatte l'anno MDCVIII nella città di Mantova per le reali nozze del serenissimo principe D. Francesco Gonzaga con la serenissima Infante Margherita di Savoia*, Mantua, 1608, facs. ed. C. Gallico and V. Rebonato, Florence, 2004

Gallico, C. and L. Volpi Ghirardini, 'Tre pittori per un *concerto* mantovano', in *Orpheus Orfeo: Studi dedicati a Claudio Gallico*, Florence, forthcoming

'Vita musicale in Sant'Andrea di Mantova', in *Sopra li fondamenti della verità: Musica italiana fra XV e XVII secolo*, Rome, 2001, pp. 195–203

'Guglielmo Gonzaga signore della musica', in *Sopra li fondamenti della verità: Musica italiana fra XV e XVII secolo*, Rome, 2001, pp. 277–350

'Emblemi strumentali negli 'Scherzi' di Monteverdi', *Rivista italiana di musicologia*, 2 (1967), 54–73

Gialdroni, T., R. Baroncini, and P. Besutti (eds.), *Claudio Monteverdi: Studi e prospettive*, Florence, 1998

Giuntini, F., 'Prologo e morale nel *Ritorno d'Ulisse in patria*', in P. Radicchi and M. Burden (eds.), *Florilegium musicae: studi in onore di Carolyn Gianturco*, Pisa, 2004, II, pp. 595–602

Glixon, B., and J. Glixon, *Inventing the Business of Opera: The Impresario and his World in Seventeenth-Century Venice*, Oxford, 2006

Glixon, B., 'Scenes from the life of Silvia Gailarti Manni, a seventeenth-century virtuosa', *Early Music History*, 15 (1996), 97–146

'Private lives of public women: prima donnas in mid seventeenth-century Venice', *Music and Letters*, 76 (1995), 509–31

Glixon, J., *Honoring God and the City: Music at the Venetian Confraternities, 1260–1807*, Oxford, 2003

'Was Monteverdi a traitor?', *Music and Letters*, 72 (1991), 404–6

'A musicians' union in sixteenth-century Venice', *Journal of the American Musicological Society*, 36 (1983), 392–421

Godt, I., 'I casi di Arianna', *Rivista italiana di musicologia*, 29 (1994), 315–405

Gordon, B., *Monteverdi's Unruly Women: The Power of Song in Early Modern Italy*, Cambridge, 2004

'Talking back: the female voice in *Il ballo delle ingrate*', *Cambridge Opera Journal*, 11 (1999), 1–30

Haar, J., 'A sixteenth-century attempt at music criticism', *Journal of the American Musicological Society*, 36 (1983), 191–209

Hanning, B. R., 'The ending of L'Orfeo: father, son, and Rinuccini', *Journal of Seventeenth-Century Music*, 9 (2003), http://sscm-jscm.press.uiuc.edu/jscm/v9no1.html

Of Poetry and Music's Power: Humanism and the Creation of Opera, Ann Arbor, 1980

Harrán, D., *Salamone Rossi: Jewish Musician in Late Renaissance Mantua*, Oxford, 1999

Hell, H., 'Zu Rhythmus und Notierung des "Vi ricorda" in Claudio Monteverdis Orfeo', *Analecta musicologica*, 15 (1975), 87–157

Heller, W., *Emblems of Eloquence: Opera and Women's Voices in Seventeenth-Century Venice*, Berkeley, 2003

'Tacitus incognito: opera as history in *L'incoronazione di Poppea*', *Journal of the American Musicological Society*, 52 (1999), 39–96

Holman, P., '"Col nobilissimo esercitio della vivuola": Monteverdi's string writing', *Early Music*, 21 (1993), 577–90

Horsley, I., 'Monteverdi's use of borrowed material in "Sfogava con le stelle"', *Music and Letters*, 49 (1978), 316–28

Holzer, R., '"Sono d'altro garbo . . . le canzonette che si cantano oggi": Pietro della Valle on music and modernity in the seventeenth century', *Studi musicali*, 21 (1992), 253–306

Ivanovich, C., 'Memorie teatrali di Venezia' [app. to *Minerva al tavolino*, Venice, 1681, 2/1688], facs. edn. with intro. by N. Dubowy, Lucca, 1993

Jeffery, P., 'The autograph manuscripts of Francesco Cavalli', PhD diss., Princeton University, 1980

Johnstone, A., '"High" clefs in composition and performance', *Early Music*, 34 (2006), 29–54

Koldau, L. M., *Die venezianische Kirchenmusik von Claudio Monteverdi*, Kassel, 2001

Kurtzman, J., 'Monteverdi's Mass of Thanksgiving: da capo', in *Fiori musicali: liber amicorum Alexander Silbiger*, Warren, MI, forthcoming

'Deconstructing gender in Monteverdi's *L'Orfeo*', *Journal of Seventeenth-Century Music*, 9/1 (2003), http://sscm-jscm.press.uiuc.edu/jscm/v9no1/Kurtzman.html

and L. M. Koldau, '*Trombe, Trombe d'argento, Trombe squarciate*, and *Pifferi* in Venetian processions and ceremonies of the sixteenth and seventeenth centuries', *Journal of Seventeenth-Century Music*, 8/1 (2002), http://sscm-jscm.press.uiuc.edu/jscm/v8no1/Kurtzman.html

The Monteverdi Vespers of 1610: Music, Context, Performance, Oxford, 1999

'Monteverdi's changing aesthetics: a semiotic perspective', in *Festa Musicale: Essays in Honor of George Buelow*, Stuyvesant, NY, 1995, pp. 233–55

'Monteverdi's 'Mass of Thanksgiving' revisited', *Early Music*, 22 (1994), 63–84

'A taxonomic and affective analysis of Monteverdi's "Hor che'l ciel e la terra"', *Music Analysis*, 12 (1993), 169–95

'An early seventeenth-century manuscript of *Canzonette e madrigaletti spirituali*', *Studi musicali*, 8 (1979), 149–71

Lapenta, S., and R. Morselli, *Le collezioni Gonzaga: La quadreria nell'elenco dei beni del 1626–1627*, Cinisello Balsamo, 2006

La Via, S., 'Monteverdi esegeta: rilettura di *Cruda Amarilli / O Mirtillo*', in M. C. Vela and R. Tibaldi (eds.), *Intorno a Monteverdi*, Lucca, 1999, pp. 77–99

Leichtentritt, M., 'Claudio Monteverdi als Madrigalkomponist', *Sammelbände der Internationalen Musikgesellschaft*, 11 (1909–10), 255–91

Leopold, S. and J. Steinheuer (eds.), *Claudio Monteverdi und die Folgen: Bericht über das Internationale Symposium Detmold 1993*, Kassel; Basel; London; New York; Prague, 1998

Leopold, S., 'Lyra Orphei', in *Claudio Monteverdi: Festschrift Reinhold Hammerstein zum 70. Geburtstag*, Laaber, 1986, pp. 337–45

Monteverdi: Music in Transition, Oxford, 1991

Die Oper im 17. Jahrhundert, Laaber, 2004

Lewis, R., 'Love as persuasion in Monteverdi's *L'incoronazione di Poppea*: new thoughts on the authorship question', *Music and Letters*, 86 (2005), 16–41

L'Occaso, S., 'Santa Croce in Corte', *Quaderni di San Lorenzo*, 3 (2005), 7–35

Lockwood, L., 'On parody as term and concept in sixteenth-century music', in *Aspects of Medieval and Renaissance Music: A Birthday Offering to Gustave Reese*, ed. Jan LaRue, New York, 1966, pp. 560–75

Lüdtke, K., *Con la sudetta sprezzatura: Tempomodifikation in der italienischen Musik der ersten Hälfte des 17. Jahrhunderts*, Kassel, 2006

Mabbett, M., 'Le connessioni stilistiche tra l'ottavo libro di Monteverdi ed il madrigale *avant-garde* a Vienna', in A. Colzani, A. Luppi, M. Padoan (eds.), *Il marigale oltre il madrigale*, Como, 1994, pp. 73–103

McClary, S., *Modal Subjectivities: Self-Fashioning in the Italian Madrigal*, Berkeley, 2004

Feminine Endings: Music, Gender and Sexuality, Minneapolis, 1991

'The transition from modal to tonal organization in the works of Monteverdi', Ph.D. diss., Harvard University, 1976

MacClintock, C., (ed.), *Readings in the History of Music in Performance*, Bloomington, 1979

MacKenney, R: 'The scuole piccole of Venice: formations and transformations', in N. Terpstra (ed.), *The Politics of Ritual Kinship: Confraternities and Social Order in Early Modern Italy*, Cambridge, 1999, pp. 172–89

'Devotional confraternities in Renaissance Venice', in W. J. Shiels and D. Wood (eds.), *Voluntary Religion*, London, 1986, pp. 85–96

MacNeil, A., *Music and Women of the Commedia dell'Arte in the Late Sixteenth Century*, Oxford, 2003

'Weeping at the water's edge', *Early Music*, 27 (1999), 407–17

Meconi, H., 'Does *Imitatio* exist?', *Journal of Musicology*, 12 (1994), 152–78

Michelassi, N., 'Michelangelo Torcigliani è l'incognito autore delle *Nozze di Enea con Lavinia*', *Studi secenteschi*, 48 (2007), 381–6

Miller, P. and I. Fenlon, *The Song of the Soul: Understanding Poppea*, London, 1992

Misurarca, P., *Carlo Gesualdo prinicipe di Venosa*, Palermo, 2000

Monterosso, R. (ed.), *Performing Practice in Monteverdi's Music*, Cremona, 1995

Monteverdi, C., *Lettere*, ed. É. Lax, Florence, 1994

    trans. and ed. D. Stevens, *The Letters of Claudio Monteverdi*, London, 1980, rev. edn. Oxford, 1995

    Songs and Madrigals in Parallel Translation, trans. D. Stevens, Ebrington, Glos., 1999

Moore, J. H., 'Venezia favorita da Maria: music for the Madonna Nicopeia and Santa Maria della Salute', *Journal of the American Musicological Society*, 37 (1984), 299–355

    Vespers at St. Mark's: Music of Alessandro Grandi, Giovanni Rovetta and Francesco Cavalli, 2 vols., Ann Arbor, 1981

    'The *Vespero delli Cinque Laudate* and the role of *Salmi Spezzati* at St Mark's', *Journal of the American Musicological Society*, 34 (1981), 249–78

Moretti, L., 'Architectural spaces for music: Jacopo Sansovino and Adrian Willaert at St Mark's', *Early Music History*, 23 (2004), 153–84

Muir, E, *Civic Ritual in Renaissance Venice*, Princeton, 1981

Murata, M., 'Image and eloquence: secular song', in T. Carter and J. Butt (eds.), *The Cambridge History of Seventeenth-Century Music*, Cambridge, 2005, pp. 378–425

Newcomb, A., *The Madrigal at Ferrara, 1579–97*, 2 vols., Princeton, 1980

Noske, F., 'An unknown work by Monteverdi: the Vespers of St. John the Baptist', *Music and Letters*, 66 (1985), 118–22

Ongaro, G, 'All work and no play?: the organization of work among musicians in late Renaissance Venice', *Journal of Medieval and Renaissance Studies*, 25 (1995), 55–72

    'Sixteenth-century patronage at St Mark's, Venice', *Early Music History*, 8 (1988), 81–115

Osthoff, W. (ed.), *Claudio Monteverdi: L'Orfeo, favola in musica*, Kassel, 1998

Ossi, M., '"Pardon me, but your teeth are in my neck": Giambattista Marino, Claudio Monteverdi, and the *bacio mordace*', *Journal of Musicology*, 21 (2004), 175–200

    Divining the Oracle: Monteverdi's 'Seconda Prattica', Chicago and London, 2003

    'Claudio Monteverdi's *ordine novo, bello et gustevole*: the canzonetta as dramatic module and formal archetype', *Journal of the American Musicological Society*, 45 (1992), 261–304

    'Claudio Monteverdi's concertato technique and its role in the development of his musical thought', Ph.D. diss., Harvard University, 1989

Paccagnini, G., *Il palazzo ducale di Mantova*, Turin, 1969

Palisca, C. V., 'The Artusi–Monteverdi controversy', in D. Arnold and N. Fortune (eds.), *The New Monteverdi Companion*, London, 1985, pp. 127–58

Parisi, S., 'The Brussels–Mantua connection: Vincenzo Gonzaga's state voyages to the Low Countries in 1599 and 1608', *Alamire Yearbook*, vol. 6/7, forthcoming

    'New documents concerning Monteverdi's relations with the Gonzagas', in P. Besutti, T. M. Gialdroni and R. Baroncini (eds.), *Claudio Monteverdi: studi e prospettive; atti del convegno, Mantova, 21–24 ottobre 1993*, 'Accademia Nazionale Virgiliana di Scienze, Lettere e Arti: Miscellanea', 5, Florence, 1998, pp. 477–511

    'Acquiring musicians and instruments in the early Baroque: observations from Mantua', *Journal of Musicology*, 14 (1996), 117–50

'Musicians at the court of Mantua during Monteverdi's time: evidence from the payrolls', in S. Gmeinwieser *et al.* (eds.), *Musicologia Humana: Studies in Honor of Warren and Ursula Kirkendale*, Florence, 1994, 183–208

'Ducal patronage of music in Mantua, 1587–1627: an archival study', Ph.D. diss., University of Illinois, 1989

'*Licenza alla Mantova*: Frescobaldi and the recruitment of musicians for Mantua, 1612–15', in A. Silbiger, ed., *Frescobaldi Studies*, Durham, NC, 1987, pp. 55–91

Parrott, A., 'Monteverdi: onwards and downwards', *Early Music*, 32 (2004), 303–18

'Getting it right (some lingering misconceptions of performance-practice in Monteverdi's "Vespers" of 1610)', *Musical Times*, 136 (1995), 531–5

'Transposition in Monteverdi's Vespers of 1610: an "aberration" defended', *Early Music*, 12 (1984), 490–516

Pigman III, G. W., 'Versions of imitation in the Renaissance', *Renaissance Quarterly*, 33 (1980), 1–32

Pirrotta, N., *Music and Culture in Italy from the Middle Ages to the Baroque: A Collection of Essays*, Cambridge, MA, 1984

and E. Povoledo, *Music and Theatre from Poliziano to Monteverdi*, trans. K. Eales, Cambridge, 1982

Pirrotta, N., 'Early opera and aria', in W. Austin (ed.), *New Looks at Italian Opera: Essays in Honor of Donald Jay Grout*, Ithaca, NY, 1968, pp. 39–107, reprinted in N. Pirrotta, *Music and Theatre from Poliziano to Monteverdi*, Cambridge, 1982

Pullan, B., *Rich and Poor in Renaissance Venice*, Oxford, 1971

Pryer, A., 'Monteverdi, two sonnets and a letter', *Early Music*, 25 (1997), 357–71

'Authentic performance, authentic experience and "Pur ti miro" from *Poppea*', in R. Monterosso (ed.), *Performing Practice in Monteverdi's Music*, Cremona, 1995, pp. 191–213

Quaranta, E., *Oltre San Marco: organizzazione e prassi della musica nelle chiese di Venezia nel Rinascimento*, Florence, 1998

Ringer, M., *Opera's First Master: The Musical Dramas of Claudio Monteverdi*, New York, 2006

Roche, J., *North Italian Church Music in the Age of Monteverdi*, Oxford, 1984

Rorke, M. A., 'Sacred contrafacta of Monteverdi madrigals and Cardinal Borromeo's Milan', *Music and Letters*, 65 (1984), 168–75

Rosand, D., *Myths of Venice: The Figuration of a State*, Chapel Hill, 2001

Rosand, E., *Monteverdi's Last Operas: A Venetian Trilogy*, Berkeley and Los Angeles, 2007

'Venice, 1580–1680', in C. Price (ed.), *Music and Society: The Early Baroque Era*, Englewood Cliffs, 1994, pp. 75–102

'Monteverdi's *Il ritorno d'Ulisse in patria* and the power of music', *Cambridge Opera Journal*, 4 (1992), 75–80

Opera in Seventeenth Century Venice, Berkeley and Los Angeles, 1991

'Iro and the interpretation of *Il ritorno d'Ulisse in patria*', *Journal of Musicology*, 7 (1989), 141–64

'Seneca and the interpretation of *L'incoronazione di Poppea*', *Journal of the American Musicological Society*, 38 (1985), 34–71

'The descending tetrachord: an emblem of lament', *Musical Quarterly*, 55 (1979), 346–59

'Music in the myth of Venice', *Renaissance Quarterly*, 30 (1977), 511–37

Rosenthal, A., 'Monteverdi's *Andromeda*: a lost libretto found', *Music and Letters*, 66 (1985), 1–8

Salvetti, G., 'Alcuni criteri nella rielaborazione ed orchestrazione dell' "Incoronazione"', *Rivista italiana di musicologia*, 2 (1967), 332–40

Sansovino, F., *Venetia città nobilissima, et singolare, descritta in XIII. Libri . . . con aggiunta di tutte le cose notabili della stessa citta, fatte, & occorse dall' anno 1580, fino al presente 1663 da D. Giustiniano Martinioni*, Venice, 1663

Sartori, C., 'Monteverdiana', *Musical Quarterly*, 38 (1952), 399–413

Saslow, J. M., *Florentine Festival as Theatrum Mundi: The Medici Wedding of 1589*, New Haven and London, 1996

Saunders, S., 'New light on the genesis of Monteverdi's Eighth Book of Madrigals', *Music and Letters*, 77 (1996), 183–93

Savage, R. and M. Sansone, '*Il Corago* and the staging of early opera: four chapters from an anonymous treatise circa 1630', *Early Music*, 17 (1989), 494–511

Schiltz, K., 'Church and chamber: the influence of acoustics on musical composition and performance', *Early Music*, 31 (2003), 64–80

Schrade, L., *Monteverdi: Creator of Modern Music*, New York, 1950

Selfridge-Field, E., *Venetian Instrumental Music from Gabrieli to Vivaldi*, 3rd rev. edn, New York, 1994

'Bassano and the orchestra of St Mark's', *Early Music*, 4 (1976), 152–8

Sherr, R., 'Gugliemo Gonzaga and the castrati', *Renaissance Quarterly*, 33 (1980), 33–56

Solerti, A., *Gli albori del melodramma*, 3 vols., Turin, 1903; facs. ed., Bologna, 1976

Stattkuss, M., *Claudio Monteverdi: Verzeichnis der erhaltenen Werke; kleine Ausgabe*, Bergkamen, 1985

Steinheuer, J., *Chamäleon und Salamander, Neue Wege der Textvertonung bei Tarquinio Merula*, Kassel, 1999

'Herzensfestungen und Luftschlösser – Zur Ikonographie militärischer Architekturen im Liebeskrieg bei Cipriano de Rore, Nicolò Fontei, Claudio Monteverdi und Barbara Strozzi', *Musiktheorie*, 21 (2006), 101–29

Sternfeld, F., *The Birth of Opera*, Oxford, 1993

Stevens, D., 'Monteverdiana 1993', *Early Music*, 22 (1993), 571–2

'*Madrigali guerrieri, et amorosi*: a reappraisal for the quatercentenary', *Musical Quarterly*, 53 (1967), 161–87

Strainchamps, E., 'The life and death of Caterina Martinelli: new light on Monteverdi's *Arianna*', *Early Music History*, 5 (1985), 155–86

Strunk, O, *Source Readings in Music History*, vol. IV, rev. M. Murata, *The Baroque Era*, New York and London, 1998

Stubbs, S., '*L'armonia sonora*: continuo orchestration in Monteverdi's *Orfeo*', *Early Music*, 2 (1994), 86–100

Szweykowski, Z. and T. Carter (eds.), *Composing Opera: from 'Dafne' to 'Ulisse Errante'*, Practica Musica 2, Kraków, 1994

Tagmann, P., 'The palace church of Santa Barbara in Mantua, and Monteverdi's relationship to its liturgy', in B. L. Karson (ed.), *Festival Essays for Pauline Alderman: a Musicological Tribute*, Provo, UT, 1976, pp. 53–60

'La cappella dei maestri cantori della basilica palatina di S. Barbara a Mantova, 1565–1630', *Civiltà Mantovana*, 4 (1970/1), 376–400

Archivalische Studien zur Musikpflege am Dom von Mantua (1500–1627), Bern and Stuttgart, 1967

Tamburini, E., 'A partire dall' *Arianna* monteverdiana pensando ai comici: Luoghi teatrali alla corte di Mantova', in P. Besutti, T. M. Gialdroni and R. Baroncini (eds.), *Claudio Monteverdi: studi e prospettive: atti del convegno, Mantova 21–24 ottobre 1993*, Florence, 1998, pp. 415–29

Tomlinson, G., *Metaphysical Song: An Essay on Opera*, Princeton, 1999

Music and Renaissance Magic: Toward a Historiography of Others, Chicago, 1993

Monteverdi and the End of the Renaissance, Oxford, 1987

'Music and the claims of text: Monteverdi, Rinuccini, and Marino', *Critical Inquiry*, 8 (1982), 565–89

'Madrigal, monody, and Monteverdi's "via naturale alla immitatione"', *Journal of the American Musicological Society*, 34 (1981), 60–108

Toscano, R., *L'edificazione di Mantova*, Padua, 1586

Tsugami, M., 'What incited the "Monteverdi Renaissance?"', in *Musicology and Globalization: Proceedings of the International Congress in Shizuoka, 2002*, Tokyo, 2004, pp. 184–8

Vacchelli, A. M., 'Monteverdi as a primary source for the performance of his own music', in R. Monterosso, (ed.), *Proceedings of the International Congress on Performing Practice in Monteverdi's Music: the Historic-Philological Background*, Cremona, 1995, pp. 23–52

Walker, T., 'Gli errori di *Minerva al tavolino*: osservazioni sulla cronologia delle prime opera veneziane', in *Venezia e il melodrama del seicento*, ed. M. T. Muraro, Florence, 1976, pp. 7–20

Watkins, G. E., and T. La May, '"Imitatio" and "Emulatio": changing concepts of originality in the madrigals of Gesualdo and Monteverdi in the 1590s', in L. Finscher (ed.), *Claudio Monteverdi: Festschrift Reinhold Hammerstein zum 70. Geburtstag*, Laaber, 1986, pp. 453–87

Whenham, J., 'Perspectives on the chronology of the first decade of public opera at Venice', *Saggiatore musicale*, 11 (2004), 253–302

'Producing Monteverdi's *Orfeo*: some fundamental considerations', in P. Gargiulo (ed.), *'Lo stupor dell'invenzione': Firenze e la nascita dell'opera*, Florence, 2001, pp. 73–86

Monteverdi Vespers (1610), Cambridge, 1997

'The Gonzagas visit Venice' *Early Music*, 21 (1993), 525–42

(ed.) *Claudio Monteverdi: Orfeo*, Cambridge, 1986

Duet and Dialogue in the Age of Monteverdi, 2 vols., Ann Arbor, 1982

Wistreich, R., 'Of Mars I sing: Monteverdi voicing virility', in I. Biddle and K. Gibson (eds.), *Men Sounding Off: Modernity, Masculinity and Western Musical Practice*, Aldershot, forthcoming

Courtier, Warrior, Singer: Giulio Cesare Brancaccio and the Performance of Identity in the Late Renaissance, Aldershot, 2007

'Real basses, real men: *virtù* and virtuosity in the construction of noble male identity in late sixteenth-century Italy', in N. Schwindt (ed.), *TroJa: Trossingen Jahrbuch fur Renaissance Musik 2: Gesang zur Laute*, Kassel and Basel, 2003, pp. 59–80

'Reconstructing pre-Romantic singing technique', in John Potter (ed.), *The Cambridge Companion to Singing*, Cambridge, 2000, pp. 178–91

'*La voce è grata assai, ma* . . .: Monteverdi on singing', *Early Music*, 22 (1994), 7–20

Wolff, C., 'Zur Frage der Instrumentalen in Monteverdis Opern', in L. Finscher (ed.), *Claudio Monteverdi: Festschrift Reinhold Hammerstein zum 70. Geburtstag*, Laaber, 1986, pp. 489–98

Zacconi, L., *Prattica di musica*, Venice, 1592

Zarlino, G., *Le istitutioni harmoniche*, Venice, 1558

Selected discography

COMPILED BY RICHARD WISTREICH

1. Madrigals

First Book of Madrigals
The Consort of Musicke, director Anthony Rooley. Virgin Veritas, 5622682 (CD1)

Second Book of Madrigals
La Venexiana, director Claudio Cavina. Glossa, GCD 920922
Concerto Italiano, director Rinaldo Alessandrini. Opus 111, OP30111
The Consort of Musicke, director Anthony Rooley. Virgin Veritas, 5622682 (CD 2)

Third Book of Madrigals
La Venexiana, director Claudio Cavina. Glossa, GCD 920910
The Consort of Musicke, director Anthony Rooley. Virgin Veritas, 5622682 (CD 3)

Fourth Book of Madrigals
La Venexiana, director Claudio Cavina. Glossa, GCD 920924
Concerto Italiano, director Rinaldo Alessandrini. Opus 111, LC 5718
The Consort of Musicke, director Anthony Rooley. Decca, L'Oiseau Lyre, 455
    719–2 (CD 1)

Fifth Book of Madrigals
Concerto Italiano, director Rinaldo Alessandrini. Opus 111, OPS 30-166
The Consort of Musicke, director Anthony Rooley. Decca, L'Oiseau Lyre, 455
    719–2 (CD 2)

Sixth Book of Madrigals
La Venexiana, director Claudio Cavina. Glossa, CD 920926
The Consort of Musicke, director Anthony Rooley. Virgin Veritas, 5622682 (CD 4)

Seventh Book of Madrigals
La Venexiana, director Claudio Cavina. Glossa, GCD 920904 (2 CDs)

Eighth Book of Madrigals
La Venexiana, director Claudio Cavina. Glossa, GCD9209283 (3 CDs)
Concerto Vocale, director Rene Jacobs. Harmonia Mundi, HMC901736.37
Concerto Italiano, director Rinaldo Alessandrini.

Volume 1: Opus 111, LC 5718
Volume 2: Opus 111, OPS 30 196
The Consort of Musicke, director Anthony Rooley. Virgin Veritas, 5622682 (CDs 5, 6, 7)

Scherzi musicali (1607, 1632)
Concerto Soave, director Jean-Marc Aymes. Harmonia Mundi, HMC901855

Selections
Chamber duets Il Complesso Barocco, director Alan Curtis. Virgin Veritas, 5624162
Madrigali concertati (madrigals from *Scherzi musicali* (1632), Seventh and Eighth Books of Madrigals). Tragicomedia, director Stephen Stubbs. Warner Classics, 2564 60710–2
Balli and Dramatic Madrigals (includes *Combattimento di Tancredi e Clorinda* and *Ballo delle ingrate*), Red Byrd and The Parley of Instruments. Hyperion, CDH55165
Addio Florida bella (selections from Fifth, Sixth and Eighth Books of Madrigals), Concerto Vocale, director Rene Jacobs. Harmonia Mundi, HMA1951084
Combattimento di Tancredi e Clorinda (madrigals from *Scherzi musicali* (1632), Sixth, Seventh and Eighth Book of Madrigals), Les Arts Florissants, director William Christie. Harmonia Mundi, HMA1951426

2. Sacred music

Vespers 1610
Taverner Consort and Players, director Andrew Parrott (liturgical reconstruction). Virgin Veritas, 5616612
The Sixteen, director Harry Christophers. 'Second Vespers for the Feast of Santa Barbara' (liturgical reconstruction). Hyperion, CDD22028
Concerto Italiano, director Rinaldo Alessandrini. Opus 111, OP30403
La Chapelle Royale, Collegium Vocale, Ghent, director Philippe Herreweghe. Harmonia Mundi, HMX2901247.48
New London Consort, director Philip Pickett. Decca, L'Oiseau Lyre, 425 823-2 (2 CDs)
Concerto Vocale, director Rene Jacobs. Harmonia Mundi, HMC901566.67
Gabrieli Consort, director Paul McCreesh. Deutsche Grammophon Archiv, 477 614–7

Selva morale e spirituale *1641*
(complete) Cantus Köln and Concerto Palatino, director Konrad Junghänel (2001). Harmonia Mundi, HMC 901718.20 (3 CDs)
(selection) Les Arts Florissants, director William Christie. Harmonia Mundi, HMA1951250

Venetian sacred music – selections

Monteverdi: The Sacred Music, The King's Consort, director Robert King. Hyperion, CDA67428, CDA67438, CDA67487, CDA67519

Venetian Vespers: 'A speculative recreation of a First Vespers of the Annunciation of the VM as it might have been celebrated in St Mark's, Venice in 1643'. The Gabrieli Consort, director Paul McCreesh. Deutsche Grammophon Archiv, 437552-2 (2 CDs)

A Mass of Thanksgiving: 'Solemn Mass for the feast of Sancta Maria delle Salute in thanksgiving for the delivery of the city of Venice from the plague, Basilica of St Mark, 21 November 1631'. The Taverner Consort, Choir and Players, director Andrew Parrott. Virgin Veritas, 3499932 (2 CDs)

From Monteverdi to Vivaldi, Taverner Consort and Players, director Andrew Parrott. Virgin Veritas, 5621672 (5 CDs): CD 1, *Venetian Vesper Music*

Venetian Church Music, Taverner Consort and Players, director Andrew Parrott. Virgin Veritas, 5691342 (2 CDs): CD1, *Monteverdi and contemporaries*

Salve regina (motets for one, two and three voices), Il Seminario Musicale and Tragicomedia, director Gerard Lesne. Virgin Veritas, 7596022

Pianto della Madonna, Motets, Concerto Soave, director Jean-Marc Aymes. Harmonia Mundi, HMC901680

Masses

The Sixteen, director Harry Christophers. Hyperion, CDH55145

Ensemble Vocale Européen, director Philippe Herreweghe. Harmonia Mundi, HMC901355

3. Operas

Orfeo

Audio

Soloists, English Baroque Soloists, director John Eliot Gardiner. Deutsche Grammophon Archiv, 419–250–2 (2 CDs)

Soloists, Chiaroscuro and London Baroque, directors Nigel Rogers, Charles Medlam. Virgin Veritas, 4820702 (2 CDs)

Soloists, New London Consort, director Philip Pickett. Decca Critics Choice, 4767213 (2 CDs)

Le Concert d'Astrée, European Voices, director Emmanuelle Haim. Virgin Veritas, 546 6422 (2 CDs)

Video

Soloists, Tragicomedia and Concerto Palatino, musical director Stephen Stubbs, stage director Pierre Audi. Opus Arte, OA0928D (2 DVDs)

Soloists, La Capella Reial de Catalunya and Le Concert des Nations, musical director Jordi Savall, stage director Gilbert Deflo. BBC Opus Arte, OA 0842 D (2 DVDs)

Il ritorno d'Ulisse in patria

Audio

Soloists, Concerto Vocale, director Rene Jacobs. Harmonia Mundi, HMC901427.29
(3 CDs)

Soloists, Les Arts Florissants, director William Christie. Virgin Classics, 4906129
(2 CDs)

Video

Soloists, Nederlands Opera Orchestra, musical director Glen Wilson, stage director
Pierre Audi. BBC Opus Arte, OA0927D (2 DVDs)

Soloists, Les Arts Florissants, musical director William Christie, stage director
Adrian Noble. Virgin Classics, 7243 4906129–2/3 (1 DVD)

Soloists, Orchestra La Scintilla of the Opera House, Zürich, musical director
Nikolaus Harnoncourt, stage director Klaus Michael Grüber. Arthaus, 100352 (1
DVD)

L'incoronazione di Poppea

Audio

Soloists, Il Complesso Barocco, director Alan Curtis. Warner Fonit, 8573 84065–2
(3 CDs)

Soloists, Concerto Vocale, director Rene Jacobs. Harmonia Mundi, HMC901330.32 I
(3 CDs)

Soloists, Monteverdi Choir and Orchestra, director: John Eliot Gardiner. Deutsche
Grammophon Archiv, 447 088-2

Video

Soloists, Les Musiciens du Louvre, musical director Marc Minkowski, stage director Klaus Michael Grüber. Bel Air Classiques, BAC 004 (2 DVDs)

Soloists, Les Musiciens du Louvre, musical director Marc Minkowski, stage director Pierre Audi. BBC Opus Arte, OA0924 D (2 DVDs)

Soloists, Concerto Köln, musical director Rene Jacobs, stage director Jose Montes-
Baquer. Arthaus Musik, 100108 (1 DVD)

The works of Monteverdi: catalogue and index

COMPILED BY JOHN WHENHAM

This guide to Monteverdi's music is constructed in three sequences. The first is a catalogue of Monteverdi's works, both surviving and lost, in as near as possible date order, followed by a list of undated manuscript sources. In the case of sources containing more than one work, the contents of the volume are listed in the order in which they appear in the earliest, or the only, source (this order is not always followed in later and modern editions – see Chapter 3, above). The second sequence is a catalogue, by short title only, of prints and manuscripts containing *contrafacta* of Monteverdi's music: that is, adaptations of his settings by a different author to texts that are usually sacred or spiritual in character (the first lines of these settings are given in the Index). The third sequence is an index of first lines and titles, which serves as an index both to the catalogue and to the discussion of individual works in the text of this book. Each work can be traced in the catalogue from the index through an identifier, which includes the date of publication or first performance, or the year(s) in which a work, now lost, is discussed in Monteverdi's letters or another source; manuscripts are identified by the *sigla* for the library in which they are located. Dates or library *sigla* followed by [CF] refer to *contrafacta*. Dates followed by a superscript number follow the convention found in *RISM* (*Répertoire international des sources musicales*, the International Inventory of Music Sources), specifically in the volume *Recueils imprimés XVIᵉ–XVIIᵉ siècles* (Munich–Duisburg, 1960). This, and the volumes of *RISM* devoted to individual composers, provides a guide to the libraries and other collections in which surviving copies of the original sources are now held; the libraries are identified by shorthand *sigla*, which are listed below.

The original sources of many of the Italian lyrics set by Monteverdi as madrigals, canzonettas and arias can be traced through *RePIM* (*Repertorio della Poesia Italiana in Musica, 1500–1700*, ed. Angelo Pompilio, www.repim.muspe.unibo.it). Spelling of the forenames of two of the most important of Monteverdi's poets – Guarini and Marino – conform to the usage in *The New Grove*, i.e. Battista Guarini (not Giovanni Battista Guarini) and Giambattista Marino (not Giovanni Battista Marino), though it is always worth trying the alternative versions in library searches.

The catalogue lists principal sources only and does not include the second and subsequent incipits of multi-section works. For a guide to the latter, see the worklist in T. Carter and G. Chew, 'Monteverdi, Claudio', *The New Grove Dictionary of Music and Musicians*, 2nd edn, ed. S. Sadie and J. Tyrrell (London, 2001), vol. XVII, pp. 45–53; and for a more complete list of sources see

SV M. H. Stattkus, *Claudio Monteverdi: Verzeichnis der erhaltenen Werke (SV): kleine Ausgabe*, Bergkamen, 1985

Each of Monteverdi's works in the catalogue below is identified by its SV number, and the place of each volume of his output (and in some cases individual works) in the principal editions of his music and the texts of his theatrical works are shown using the following abbreviations:

B   *Claudio Monteverdi: Madrigali. Opera completa*, ed. A. Bornstein, Bologna: Ut Orpheus, 1998–

DC A. Della Corte, *Drammi per musica dal Rinuccini allo Zeno*, Turin, 1958 (texts only)

F   *Claudio Monteverdi: Opera omnia*, ed. Fondazione Claudio Monteverdi, IMa, Monumenta, v, 1970–

KM King's Music. Performing editions (with English translations), ed. C. Bartlett, Wyton, Cambs.

M   *Claudio Monteverdi: Tutte le opere*, ed. G. F. Malipiero, Asolo, 1926–42, 2/ 1954–68

O   *Claudio Monteverdi: Composizioni vocali profane e sacre (inedite)*, ed. W. Osthoff, Milan, 1958

SA A. Solerti, *Gli albori del melodrama*, Milan, 1904 (mainly texts)

SM A. Solerti, *Musica, ballo e drammatica alla corte medicea dal 1600 al 1637*, Florence, 1905 (texts only)

Abbreviations

A.	Alto
arr.	arranged
Bar.	Baritone
B.	Basso
bc	basso continuo
CF	*contrafactum*
chit.	chitarrone
ed.	edited
hpd	harpsichord
insts	instruments
Mezzo	Mezzosoprano
org.	organ
perf.	performed
poss.	possibly
prob.	probably
pub.	published
rev.	revised
S.	Soprano
T.	Tenore
Tr.	Treble
trbns	trombones
vn/vns	violin/violins
vv.	voices

RISM Sigla

D-Bds	Germany, Berlin, Deutsche Staatsbibliothek
D-Dl	Germany, Dresden, Sächsische Landesbibliothek – Staats- und Universitäts-Bibliothek, Musikabteilung
D-GD	Germany, Goch-Gaesedonck, Collegium Augustinianum
D-Hs	Germany, Hamburg, Staats- und Universitätsbibliothek Carl von Ossietzky, Musiksammlung
D-Kl	Germany, Kassel, Gesamthochschul-Bibliothek
D-Lr	Germany, Lüneburg, Ratsbücherei, Musikabteilung
GB-Och	Great Britain, Oxford, Christ Church Library
GB-Lbl	Great Britain, London, British Library
I-Bc	Italy, Bologna, Civico Museo Bibliografico Musicale
I-BRq	Italy, Brescia, Biblioteca Civica Queriniana
I-Fn	Italy, Florence, Biblioteca Nazionale Centrale, Dipartimento Musica
I-MOe	Italy, Modena, Biblioteca Estense e Universitaria
I-Nf	Italy, Naples, Biblioteca Oratoriana dei Gerolamini (Filippini)
I-Vc	Italy, Venice, Conservatorio di Musica Benedetto Marcello, Biblioteca
PL-WRu	Poland, Wrocław, Uniwersytet Wrocławski, Biblioteka Uniwersytecka
S-Uu	Sweden, Uppsala, Universitetsbiblioteket

Works

On the lost theatrical works, see Carter, *Monteverdi's Musical Theatre*, particularly, though not exclusively, pp. 197–236. In the appendix to his book Carter provides a very useful guide to the sequences of letters in which Monteverdi mentions individual works.

1582   Monteverdi *Sacrae cantiunculae . . . liber primus*, 3vv., Venice, 1582 (variously cleffed). M xiv.

SV207 Lapidabant Stephanum S. A. T.
SV208 Veni sponsa Christi S. A. T.
SV209 Ego sum pastor bonus S. A. T.
SV210 Surge propera amica mea S. A. T.
SV211 Ubi duo vel tres congregati fuerint S. S. T.
SV212 Quam pulchra es et quam decora amica mea S. S. T.
SV213 Ave Maria gratia plena S. S. T.
SV214 Domine pater et Deus S. A. T.
SV215 Tu es pastor ovium S. A. T.
SV216 O magnum pietatis opus Tr. Mezzo. A.
SV217 O crux benedicta Tr. Mezzo. A.
SV218 Hodie Christus natus est Tr. Mezzo. A.
SV219 O Domine Jesu Christe adoro te Tr. Mezzo. A.
SV220 Pater venit hora clarifica filium tuum Tr. Mezzo. A.
SV221 In tua patientia possedisti animam tuam Tr. Mezzo. A.

SV222 Angelus ad pastores ait Tr. S. A.

SV223 Salve crux pretiosa S. A. T.

SV224 Quia vidisti me Thoma credidisti S. A. T.

SV225 Lauda Syon salvatorem S. S. T.

SV226 O bone Jesu illumina oculos meos S. A. T.

SV227 Surgens Jesus Dominus noster Tr. Mezzo. A.

SV228 Qui vult venire post me abneget se Tr.
    Mezzo. T.

SV229 Iusti tulerunt spolia impiorum S. A. T.

1583   Monteverdi *Madrigali spirituali*, 4vv., Brescia, 1583;
    only B. partbook survives. Texts by Fulvio Rorario,
    from *Rime spirituali*, Venice, 1581

SV179 Sacrosancta di Dio verace imago

SV180 L'aura del ciel sempre feconda spiri

SV181 Aventurosa notte, in cui risplende

SV182 D'empi martiri e un mar d'orrori varca

SV183 Mentre la stell'appar nell'oriente

SV184 Le rose lascia, gli amaranti e gigli

SV185 L'empio vestia di porpora e di bisso

SV186 L'uman discorso, quanto poc'importe

SV187 Dal sacro petto esce veloce dardo

SV188 Afflitto e scalz'ove la sacra sponda

SV189 De' miei giovenil anni era l'amore

1584   Monteverdi *Canzonette, libro primo*, 3vv. [variously
    cleffed], Venice, 1584. M x

SV1 Qual si può dir maggiore Tr. Tr. A.

SV2 Canzonette d'amore Tr. Tr. A.

SV3 La fiera vista e 'l velenoso sguardo Tr. S. A.

SV4 Raggi, dov'è il mio bene? Tr. Tr. A.

SV5 Vita de l'alma mia, cara mia vita Tr. S. A.

SV6 Il mio martir tengo celat'al cuore Tr. Tr. A.

SV7 Son questi i crespi crini e questo il viso Tr. Tr. A.

SV8 Io mi vivea com'aquila mirando Tr. Tr. A.

SV9 Su, su, che 'l giorno è fore Tr. Tr. A.

SV10 Quando sperai del mio servir mercede Tr. S. A.

SV11 Come farò, cuor mio, quando mi parto Tr. Tr. A.

SV12 Corse a la morte il povero Narciso Tr. Tr.
    Mezzo.

SV13 Tu ridi sempre mai S. S. T.

SV14 Chi vuol veder d'inverno un dolce aprile Tr. Tr. A.

SV15 Già mi credev'un sol esser in cielo Tr. Tr. A.

SV16 Godi pur del bel sen, felice pulce Tr. S. A.

SV17 Giù lí a quel petto giace un bel giardino Tr.
    Tr. Mezzo

SV18 Sì come crescon alla terra i fiori S. S. A.

SV19 Io son fenice e voi sete la fiamma Tr. Tr. Mezzo

SV55 Crudel, perché mi fuggi (Battista Guarini)

SV56 Questo specchio ti dono (Girolamo Casoni)

SV57 Non m'è grave il morire (Bartolomeo Gottifredi)

SV58 Ti spontò l'ali, Amor, la donna mia (Filippo Alberti)

SV59 Cantai un tempo, e se fu dolce il canto (Pietro Bembo)

1592   Monteverdi *Il terzo libro de madrigali*, 5vv., Venice, 1592, reissued 1594, 1600, 1604, 1607, 1611, 1615, 1621. B iii; M iii; F iv

SV60 La giovinetta pianta

SV61 O come è gran martire (Battista Guarini)

SV62 Sovra tenere erbette e bianchi fiori

SV63 O dolce anima mia, dunque è pur vero (Battista Guarini)

SV64 Stracciami pur il core (Battista Guarini)

SV65 O rossignuol che in queste verdi fronde (Pietro Bembo)

SV66 Se per estremo ardore (Battista Guarini)

SV67 Vattene pur, crudel, con quella pace (Torquato Tasso)

SV68 O primavera, gioventú dell'anno (Battista Guarini)

SV69 Perfidissimo volto (Battista Guarini)

SV70 Ch'io non t'ami, cor mio (Battista Guarini)

SV71 Occhi un tempo mia vita (Battista Guarini)

SV72 Vivrò fra i miei tormenti e le mie cure (Torquato Tasso)

SV73 Lumi, miei cari lumi (Battista Guarini)

SV74 'Rimanti in pace' a la dolente e bella (Livio Celiano = Angelo Grillo)

1594[15]   Antonio Morsolino, *Il primo libro delle canzonette a 3 voci* [variously cleffed] . . . *con alcune altre de diversi eccellenti musici*, Venice, 1594. M xvii; O

SV309 Io ardo sì, ma 'l fuoco è di tal sorte Tr. Tr. Bar.

SV314 Occhi miei, se mirar più non debb'io Tr. Tr. Bar

SV324 Quante son stelle in ciel e in mar arene (Scipione Cerreto) S. S. B.

SV331 Se non mi date aita Tr. S. Bar.

1597[13]   *Fiori del giardino di diversi eccellentissimi autori* 4–9vv., Nuremberg, 1597

SV75 Ah dolente partita (Battista Guarini), 5vv.; also published in Monteverdi *Quarto libro*, 1603; B iv; M iv; F v

1603   Monteverdi *Il quarto libro de madrigali*, 5vv., Venice, 1603, reissued 1605, 1607, 1611, 1615 (twice), 1622, 1644. B iv; M iv; F v

SV75 Ah dolente partita (Battista Guarini); first pub.
    in 1597[13]

SV76 Cor mio, mentre vi miro (Battista Guarini)

SV77 Cor mio, non mori? E mori

SV78 Sfogava con le stelle (?Ottavio Rinuccini)

SV79 Volgea l'anima mia soavemente (Battista
    Guarini)

SV80 Anima mia, perdona (Battista Guarini)

SV81 Luci serene e chiare (Ridolfo Arlotti)

SV82 La piaga c'ho nel core (Alessandro Gatti)

SV83 Voi pur da me partite, anima dura (Battista
    Guarini)

SV84 A un giro sol de bell'occhi lucenti (Battista
    Guarini)

SV85 Ohimé, se tanto amate (Battista Guarini)

SV86 Io mi son giovinetta (Battista Guarini)

SV87 Quell'augellin che canta (Battista Guarini)

SV88 Non più guerra, pietate (Battista Guarini)

SV89 Sì ch'io vorrei morire (Maurizio Moro)

SV90 Anima dolorosa che vivendo (Battista Guarini)

SV91 Anima del cor mio

SV92 Longe da te, cor mio

SV93 Piagne e sospira, e quando i caldi raggi
    (Torquato Tasso)

perf. prob.
  Carnival 1604–5
	[*Endimione (ballo)*]. First perf. prob. Mantua; see letter
	  of December 1604. Music and text lost

1605[12]	Amante Franzoni, *Il nuovi fioretti a 3 voci . . . co 'l suo* *basso generale* (Venice, 1605)
	SV322 Prima vedrò ch'in questi prati nascano, S. S. B. bc; M xvii; O

1605	Monteverdi *Il quinto libro de madrigali*, Venice, 1605,
	  reissued 1606, 1608, 1610, 1611, 1613, 1615 (twice),
	  1620, 1643. B v; M v; F vi.; K. Jacobsen and J. P.
	  Jacobsen (eds.), *Claudio Monteverdi: Il quinto libro*
	  de madrigali, Egtved, 1985

    SV94 Cruda Amarilli, che col nome ancora (Battista
      Guarini), 5vv., bc ad lib; (arr. [S.] S. B./bc in GB-Lbl
      Add. 31440 (B. only), GB-Och 878 (S.2 only, GB-Och
      880 (bc only))

    SV95 O Mirtillo, Mirtillo anima mia (Battista Guarini),
      5vv., bc ad lib

    SV96 Era l'anima mia (Battista Guarini), 5vv.,
      bc ad lib

    SV97 Ecco, Silvio, colei che in odio hai tanto
      (Battista Guarini), 5vv., bc ad lib; (arr. S. S. bc, GB-
      Lbl Add. 31440)

SV98 Ch'io t'ami, e t'ami più della mia vita (Battista
Guarini) 5vv., bc ad lib (arr. S. S. bc in GB-Lbl Add.
31440)

SV99 Che dar più vi poss'io? 5vv., bc ad lib

SV100 M'è più dolce il penar per Amarilli (Battista
Guarini) 5vv., bc ad lib

SV101 Ahi, come a un vago sol cortese giro (Battista
Guarini) 5vv., bc; (arr. S. S. bc in GB-Och 878, 880)

SV102 Troppo ben può questo tiranno Amore (Battista
Guarini) 5vv., bc

SV103 Amor, se giusto sei 5vv., bc

SV104 'T'amo, mia vita' la mia cara vita (Battista
Guarini) 5vv., bc; (arr. [S.] S. bc in GB-Och 878, 880)

SV105 E così a poco a poco (Battista Guarini) 5vv., bc

SV106 Questi vaghi concenti 9vv., 9 insts, bc

perf. 24 Feb 1607   SV318 *Orfeo* (*favola in musica*). Text by Alessandro
Striggio Jr. pub. Mantua, 1607 (twice); SA iii, DC i.
First perf. Mantua, ducal palace, before members of the
Accademia degli Invaghiti, and repeated there 1 March
1607. Score pub. Venice, 1609, reissued 1615. M xi; ed.
E.H. Tarr, Paris, 1974; ed. Clifford Bartlett, with
English trans., KM

pub. 1607[21]   SV245 'De la bellezza le dovute lodi' (*balletto*). Text
?Ferdinando Gonzaga/?Alessandro Striggio Published
in *Scherzi musicali*, Venice, 1607; reissued 1609, 1615,
1619, 1628. M x

1607[21]   Monteverdi *Scherzi musicali . . . raccolti da Giulio Cesare
Monteverde suo fratello*, 3vv. [variously cleffed], 2vn, bc
Venice, 1607. M x

SV230 I bei legami (Gabriello Chiabrera) Tr. Tr. B.

SV231 Amarilli onde m'assale (Gabriello Chiabrera) Tr.
Tr. B.

SV232 Fugge il verno dei dolori (?Gabriello Chiabrera)
S. S. B.

SV233 Quando l'alba in oriente (Gabriello Chiabrera)
S. S. B.

SV234 Non così tost'io miro (Gabriello Chiabrera)
Tr. S. B.

SV235 Damigella tutta bella (Gabriello Chiabrera) Tr. S. B.

SV236 La pastorella mia spietata e rigida (Jacopo
Sannazaro) Tr. S. B.

SV237 O rosetta che rossetta (Gabriello Chiabrera)
Tr. S. B.

SV238 Amorosa pupilletta (Ansaldo Cebà) Tr. S. B.

SV239 Vaghi rai di cigli ardenti (Gabriello Chiabrera) Tr. S. B.

SV240 La vïoletta (Gabriello Chiabrera) Tr. S. B.

SV241 Giovinetta, ritrosetta (Ansaldo Cebà) Tr. Tr. B.;
(arr. S. bc in I-MOe Mus.G.239)

SV242 Dolci miei sospiri (Gabriello Chiabrera) S. S. B.

SV243 Clori amorosa (?Gabriello Chiabrera) S. S. B.

SV244 Lidia spina del mio core (Ansaldo Cebà) S. S. B.

SV245 De la bellezza le dovute lodi (*balletto*) (Text
?Ferdinando Gonzaga/?Alessandro Striggio) S. S. B.

perf. 28 May 1608 SV291 *Arianna* (*tragedia in musica*). Text by Ottavio
Rinuccini pub. Florence, Mantua, Venice, 1608; also
in Federico Follino, *Compendio delle sontuose feste fatto
l'anno M.D.C.VIII*, Mantua, 1608. First perf. Mantua,
ducal palace, as part of the wedding festivities for
Francesco Gonzaga and Margherita of Savoy. Music lost
except for the *Lamento d'Arianna* (Arianna's lament);
SV22 monodic version of the lament in 5 sections pub.
Venice, 1623 (M xi), also pub. in 1623[8] and in MS in
I-Moe Mus. G. 239 and I-Vc Torrefranca 28600, copied
by Francesco Maria Fucci; SV22a MS version in 9 sections
in GB-Lbl Add. 30491 (copied by or for Luigi Rossi,
perhaps in 1617) and I-Fn B.R. 238 (Magl. XIX.114),
the latter pub. in SA i. between pp. 96 and 97); SV288
sacred *contrafacum* of first 4 sections as 'Iam moriar mi
Fili' (*Pianto della Madonna*), in Monteverdi, *Selva
morale* (Venice, 1641; M xv). SV107 first 4 sections of
lament arr. for 5vv. in 1610 by Monteverdi (see Fabbri
Monteverdi, p. 109) and published in his *Sesto libro de'
madrigali* (Venice, 1614; B vi, M vi); for the *contrafactum*
of Arianna's lament as the *Pianto della Maddalena*, see
below, *La Maddalena* (perf. March 1617). Revised version
of the opera perf. Venice, Carnival 1639–40 (before 21
Feb), poss. Teatro S. Moisé (see Whenham, 'Perspectives',
pp. 262–4, 288–9)

perf. 2 June 1608 Prologue (= Intermedio I) ('Ha cento lustri con etereo
giri'), text by Gabriello Chiabrera (pub. in Follino,
Compendio (1608); SA iii), to performance of Battista
Guarini, *L'idropica*. First perf. Mantua, ducal palace, as
part of the wedding festivities for Francesco Gonzaga
and Margherita of Savoy. Music lost

perf. 4 June 1608 SV167 *Mascherata dell'ingrate* ([*ballo*]). Text by Ottavio
Rinuccini, pub. Mantua, 1608; also in Federico Follino,
Compendio delle sontuose feste fatto l'anno M.D.C.VIII,
(Mantua, 1608; SA ii). First perf. Mantua, ducal palace, as
part of the wedding festivities for Francesco Gonzaga and
Margherita of Savoy.

Text and poss. music rev. as *Ballo delle ingrate* in
Monteverdi, *Madrigali guerrieri, et amorosi* (1638); this

version poss. perf. at the Viennese court in 1636. B viii,
KM, M viii

Wert 1608   G. de Wert *Il duodecimo libro de madrigali*, 4–7vv., Venice,
1608; only B. partbook survives)

SV319 Pensier aspro e crudele

SV329 Sdegno la fiamma estinse (Orsina Cavaletta)

1610   Monteverdi, *Sanctissimae Virgini missa senis vocibus ad
ecclesiarum choros ac vesperae pluribus decantandae cum
nonnullis sacris concentibus, ad sacella sive principum
cubicula accommodata*, 1–3, 6–8, 10vv., insts, bc, Venice,
1610. M xiv; Vespers music also ed. Bartlett (KM, 1990),
Roche (Eulenburg, 1994), Kurtzman (Oxford, 1999)

SV205 Missa da capella 6vv. bc (also in MS I-Rvat
Cappella Sistina 107)

SV206:1 [Deus in adiutorium] Domine ad adiuvandum
6vv. 12 insts bc; also in Georg Ruber (ed.) *Reliquiae
sacrorum concentuum Giovan Gabrielis, Iohan-Leonis
Hasleri, utriusque praestantissimi musici*, Nuremburg,
1615 (= 1615^2)

SV206:2 Dixit Dominus 6vv. 6 insts ad lib. bc; rev.
in 1615^2

SV206:3 Nigra sum T. bc

SV206:4 Laudate pueri Dominum 8vv. org.

SV206:5 Pulchra es S. S. bc

SV206:6 Laetatus sum 6vv. bc

SV206:7 Duo seraphim T. T. T. bc

SV206:8 Nisi Dominus 10vv. (2 choirs) bc

SV206:9 Audi coelum verba mea T. 6vv. bc

SV206:10 Lauda Jerusalem 7vv. bc

SV206:11 Sonata sopra 'Sancta Maria, ora pro nobis' S. 8
insts bc

SV206:12 Ave maris stella 10vv. (2 choirs) 5 insts bc

SV206:13 Magnificat 7vv. 12 insts org.

SV206a:12 Magnificat 6vv. org.

1611 (letter   The following works, mentioned in Monteverdi's letter,
of 26 March)   do not appear to have survived

Dixit Dominus for eight voices

Motet for the Elevation (2 vv.)

Motet to the Blessed Virgin (5 vv.)

1614   Monteverdi *Il sesto libro de madrigali*, 5vv. . . . *con uno
dialogo*, 7vv. Venice, 1614; reissued 1615, 1620, 1639.
5vv., bc except final dialogue, 7vv., bc. B vi; M vi; F x

SV107 Lasciatemi morire (*Lamento d'Arianna*) (Ottavio
Rinuccini); first 4 sections of the lament arr. for 5 vv.
See above, *Arianna* (perf. 28 May 1608)

SV108 Zefiro torna e 'l bel tempo rimena (Petrarch)

SV109 Una donna fra l'altre onesta e bella

SV110 A Dio, Florida bella, il cor piagato (Giambattista Marino)

SV111 Incenerite spoglie, avara tomba (*Sestina: Lagrime d'amante al sepolcro dell'amata*) (Scipione Agnelli)

SV112 Ohimé il bel viso, ohimé il soave sguardo (Petrarch)

SV113 Qui rise, o Tirsi, e qui ver me rivolse (Giambattista Marino)

SV114 Misero Alceo, dal caro albergo fore (Giambattista Marino)(early variants in D-Kl 2° MS Mus.57f)

SV115 Batto, qui pianse Ergasto; ecco la riva (Giambattista Marino)

SV116 Presso a un fiume tranquillo (dialogue) (Giambattista Marino) (variants in D-Kl 2° MS Mus.57f); M vi, 113; F x, 211

1615¹³   Giovanni Battista Bonometti (ed.), *Parnassus musicus Ferdinandeus in quo musici nobilissimi qua suavitate, qua arte prorsus admirabili, & divina ludunt*, 1–5vv., [?org.], Venice, 1615

SV292 Cantate Domino canticum novum S. S./T. T. bc. M xvi

perf. prob. Jan 1616   SV145 *Tirsi e Clori* (*ballo*). First perf. Mantua, ducal palace; on probable date of performance see Carter, *Monteverdi's Musical Theatre*, p. 159. Pub. in Monteverdi, *Settimo libro de' madrigali* (1619). KM, M vii. (On performance practice, see Monteverdi, letter of 21 November 1615)

1616–1617   *Le nozze di Tetide* (*favola marittima*). Text by Scipione Agnelli. For performance at Mantua. Intended as part of the wedding festivities for Duke Ferdinando Gonzaga and Caterina de' Medici (married 7 February 1617). Known only from Monteverdi's letters 9 December 1616–14 Jan 1617. Project cancelled; music lost

perf. March 1617   SV333 Prologue ('Su le penne de' venti il ciel varcando') to *La Maddalena* (*sacra rappresentazione*). Text by Giovanni Battista Andreini. First perf. Mantua, ducal palace as part of the wedding festivities for Duke Ferdinando Gonzaga and Caterina de' Medici (married 7 February 1617). Music pub. in *Musiche. . .per La Maddalena* (Venice, 1617³); M xi

Revived Vienna 1629, poss. with *contrafactum* of *Lamento d'Arianna* as *Lamento della Maddalena* (in I-Bc Q43[CF])

1618	G.B. Ala *Primo libro delli concerti ecclesiastici*, 1–4vv., org., Milan, 1618
	SV328 Sancta Maria succurre miseris S. S. bc. M xvi; KM
1619	Monteverdi *Concerto: settimo libro de madrigali, con altri generi de canti*, 1–4, 6vv., Venice, 1619, reissued 1622, 1623, 1628, 1641. M vii
	SV117 Tempro la cetra, e per cantar gli onori (Giambattista Marino) T. 5 insts, bc. KM
	SV118 Non è di gentil core S. S. bc
	SV119 A quest'olmo, a quest'ombre et a quest'onde (Giambattista Marino) 6vv., 2 vns, 2 recorders/fifare, bc
	SV120 O come sei gentile (Battista Guarini) S. S. bc
	SV121 Io son pur vezzosetta pastorella (Incolto Accademico Immaturo) S. S. bc
	SV122 O viva fiamma, o miei sospiri ardenti (Giovanni Andrea Gesualdo) S. S. bc
	SV123 Vorrei baciarti, o Filli (Giambattista Marino) A. A. bc
	SV124 Dice la mia bellissima Licori (Battista Guarini) T. B. bc
	SV125 Ah che non si conviene T. T. bc
	SV126 Non vedrò mai le stelle T. T. bc
	SV127 Ecco vicine, o bella tigre, l'ore (Claudio Achillini) T. T. bc
	SV128 Perché fuggi tra' salci, ritrosetta (Giambattista Marino) T. T. bc
	SV129 Tornate, o cari baci (Giambattista Marino) T. T. bc
	SV130 Soave libertate (Gabriello Chiabrera) T. T. bc
	SV131 Se 'l vostro cor, madonna (Battista Guarini) T. B. bc
	SV132 Interrotte speranze, eterna fede (Battista Guarini) T. T. bc
	SV133 Augellin che la voce al canto spieghi T. T. B. bc
	SV134 Vaga su spina ascosa (Gabriello Chiabrera) T. T. B. bc
	SV135 Eccomi pronta ai baci (Giambattista Marino) T. T. B. bc
	SV136 Parlo, miser, o taccio? (Battista Guarini) S. S. B. bc
	SV137 Tu dormi, ah crudo core 4vv., bc
	SV138 Al lume delle stelle (Torquato Tasso) 4vv., bc
	SV139 Con che soavità, labbra odorate (Battista Guarini), S. 12 insts
	SV140 Ohimé, dov'è il mio ben, dov'è il mio core? (*romanesca*) (Bernardo Tasso) S. S. bc
	SV141 Se i languidi miei sguardi (*Lettera amorosa in genere rapresentativo*) (Claudio Achillini) S. bc (also pub. 1623)

SV142 Se pur destina e vole (*Partenza Amorosa . . . in genere rapresentativo*) (?Ottavio Rinuccini) T. bc (also pub. 1623)

SV143 Chiome d'oro (*Canzonetta*), S. S. 2 vns, chit./spinet. KM

SV144 Amor, che deggio far? (*Canzonetta*) 4vv., 2 vns, chit./spinet

SV145 *Tirsi e Clori* (*ballo*) S. T. 5vv., and insts, bc (first perf. prob. Jan. 1616; on performance practice, see Monteverdi, letter of 21 November 1615). KM

perf. between 1 and 3 March 1620(a)
Andromeda (*favola in musica*). Text by Ercole Marigliani, pub. Mantua 1620. First perf. Mantua, ducal palace. Music lost

perf. between 1 and 3 March 1620(b)
Apollo (*ballo*). Text Alessandro Striggio. Known from Monteverdi's letters 9 Feb. 1619–24 July 1620. First perf. Mantua, prob. ducal palace; revived Mantua, July 1620. Text and music lost

1620³
Giulio Cesare Bianchi *Libro primo de motetti in lode d'Iddio nostro Signore, 1–5, 8 vv . . . con un altro a 5, e 3 a 6 del sig. Claudio Monteverde*, Venice, 1620

SV293 Cantate Domino canticum novum 6vv., bc. M xvi; KM

SV294 Christe adoramus te 5vv., bc. M xvi; KM

SV298 Domine ne in furore tuo 6vv., bc. M xvi; KM

SV289 Adoramus te Christe 6vv., bc. M xvi; KM

1620⁴
Giulio Cesare Bianchi *Libro secondo de motetti. In lode della gloriosissima Vergine Maria Nostra Signora, 1–5 vv, & una messa, à 4, con il basso general. . . con le letanie à 6 voci del Sig. Claudio Monteverde*, Venice, 1620

SV204 Laetaniae della Beata Vergine 6vv., bc; also published in 1626³, and 1650. M xvi; F xviii

perf. 25 May 1621
Requiem for Grand Duke Cosimo II of Tuscany (Venice, SS. Giovanni e Paolo). Music lost

O vos omnes

Requiem aeternam (uncertain)

Dies irae

De profundis

Subvenite, sancti Dei

Qui Lazarum

Domine, quando veneris

Ne recorderis

Libera me, Domine

1621⁴
Lorenzo Calvi (ed.), *Symbolae diversorum musicorum 2–5 vocibus cantandae. Unacum basso ad organum*, Venice, 1621

SV305 Fuge anima mea mundum S. A. vn bc. M xvi

SV312 O beatae viae S.S./T.T. bc. M xvi

perf. 18 Jan. 1622   *La contesa di Amore e Cupido*; prologue, four *intermedi* and *licenza*, texts by Ercole Marigliani (pub. Mantua, 1622), for Marigliani's play *Le tre costanti*. Performed Mantua, ducal palace, as part of wedding festivities for Eleonora Gonzaga and Emperor Ferdinand II. Monteverdi contributed (?parts of) the third *intermedio* and the *licenza*. See letters 5 March 1621–27 Nov. 1621

1622[2]   Johann Donfried (ed.), *Promptuarii musici concentus ecclesiasticos 2–4 vv cum basso continuo & generali, organo applicato, e diversis, iisque illustrissimis et musica laude praestentissimis hujus aetatis authoribus, collectos exhibentis. Pars prima*, Strasburg, 1622

SV313 O bone Jesu, o piissime Jesu S. S. bc. M xvi

1623[8]   Giovanni Battista Rocchigiani (ed.) *Il maggio fiorito arie, sonetti, e madrigali . . . de diversi autori*, 1–3vv. (Orvieto, 1623)

SV22 Lasciatemi morire (*Lamento d'Arianna*) (Ottavio Rinuccini) S. bc; see also *Arianna* (perf. 28 May 1608); version in 5 sections

1623   Monteverdi *Lamento d'Arianna . . . con due lettere amorose in genere rapresentativo*, Venice, 1623

SV22 Lasciatemi morire (*Lamento d'Arianna*) (Ottavio Rinuccini) S. bc; see also *Arianna* (perf. 28 May 1608); M xi

SV141 Se i languidi miei sguardi (*Lettera amorosa in genere rapresentativo*) (Claudio Achillini) S. bc (first pub. 1619); M vii

SV142 Se pur destina e vole (*Partenza Amorosa . . . in genere rapresentativo*) (?Ottavio Rinuccini) T. bc (first pub. 1619); M vii

Camarella ?1623   G.B. Camarella *Madrigali et arie*, Venice, ?1623 (date not clearly legible); now lost; formerly in D-Bds. On the dating, see above, Chapter 10, n. 2

SV249 Ecco di dolci raggi il sol armato, T, bc; also pub. in 1632; M x, 81

1624[2]   Lorenzo Calvi (ed.), *Seconda raccolta de' sacri canti a 1–4 vv de diversi eccellentissimi autori*, org., Venice, 1624

SV301 Ego flos campi A. bc. M xvi; KM

SV335 Venite sitientes ad aquas S. S. bc. M xvi

SV326 Salve o regina T./S. bc. M xvi

perf. Carnival 1624   SV153 *Combattimento di Tancredi e Clorinda* (*opuscolo in*
(?= 1624–1625)   *genere rappresentativo*). Text drawn from Torquato Tasso, *Gerusalemme liberata*, xii, with readings from *Gerusalemme conquistata*, xv. First perf. Palazzo

Dandolo (now the Danieli Hotel), Venice, home of
Monteverdi's patron Girolamo Mocenigo. Pub. in
Monteverdi, *Madrigali guerrieri, et amorosi* (1638).
B viii; KM; M viii

1624[11]   *Madrigali del signor cavaliero Anselmi nobile di Treviso posti
in musica da diversi eccellentissimi spiriti*, 2–5vv., bc,
Venice, 1624

SV315 O come vaghi, o come (Giovanni Battista Anselmi)
T. T. bc; M ix

SV334 Taci, Armelin, deh taci (Giovanni Battista Anselmi)
A. T. bc; M ix

Milanuzzi 1624   Carlo Milanuzzi, *Quarto scherzo delle ariose vaghezze . . .
con una cantata, & altre arie del Signor Monteverde, e del
Sig. Francesco suo figliolo*, 1v., bc, Venice 1624 [reissue
(date of first publication unknown); formerly in D-Hs,
now lost]

SV316 Ohimé ch'io cado, ohimé S. bc; M ix

SV310 La mia turca che d'amor S. bc; M ix

SV332 Sì dolce è l tormento. S. bc; M ix

1625[1]   Francesco Sammaruco (ed.), *Sacri affetti contesti da
diversi eccellentissimi autori . . . a 2–4 vv e aggiunti nel fine
le letanie della B.V.*, Rome, 1625

SV300 Ego dormio et cor meum vigilat S. B. bc. M xvi

1625[2]   Leonardo Simonetti (ed.), *Ghirlanda sacra scielta da
diversi eccellentissimi compositori de varii motteti à voce
sola. Libro primo*, Venice, 1625. M xvi

SV317 O quam pulchra es anima mea T. bc. M xvi; KM

SV297 Currite populi, psallite timpanis T. bc. M xvi; KM.

SV299 Ecce sacrum paratum convivium T. bc. M xvi.
(Ornamented version in Böddecker, 1651)

SV327 Salve Regina T. bc. M xvi; KM

1626[3]   Lorenzo Calvi (ed.), *Rosarium litanarium beatae V. Mariae
3–8 vocibus concinendarum una cum basso ad organum*,
Venice, 1626

SV204 Laetaniae della Beata Vergine 6vv., bc;
first published in 1620[4]; also published in 1650.
M xvi; F xviii

1626(?)–1627   *Armida abbandonata*. Text drawn from Torquato Tasso,
Gerusalemme liberata, xvi and perhaps similar in
conception to *Combattimento*. Music lost; known only
from Monteverdi's letters, 1 May 1627–4 Feb. 1628

1627   *La finta pazza Licori* [opera]. Text by Giulio Strozzi.
Known only from Monteverdi's letters 1 May 1627–18
Sept. 1627 (to Alessandro Striggio). Monteverdi may,
in fact, have completed little of the musical setting

1627[4]	Giovanni Maria Sabino da Turi, *Psalmi de vespere a 4vv* (Naples, 1627)
	SV295 Confitebor tibi Domine 4vv., bc; also in D-Kl 2° MS Mus.51v. O
perf. (?5) March 1628	*Gli Argonauti* (*mascherata*). Text by Claudio Achillini Known only from a letter of Francesco Guitti (Parma, 3 March 1628); see Fabbri, *Monteverdi*, p. 217
perf. 8 April 1628	La Garda impoverir di pesci egregi (*I cinque fratelli*), sonnet cycle, 2vv., ?bc (Giulio Strozzi); music lost. Performed at a banquet at the Arsenale, Venice, given in honour of the visit to Venice of the Grand Duke of Tuscany
perf. 13 Dec. 1628	*Teti e Flora*, etc. Prologue (text by Claudio Achillini) and 5 *intermedi* (texts by Ascanio Pio di Savoia) for Torquato Tasso, *Aminta*. First perf. Parma, courtyard of S. Pietro Martire as part of the wedding festivities for Duke Odoardo Farnese and Margherita de' Medici. Texts pub. Parma, 1629. Music lost. See letters 10 Sept. 1627 (to Enzo Bentivoglio) through to 9 March 1630
perf. 21 Dec. 1628	*Mercurio e Marte* [tournament]. Text by Claudio Achillini (Parma, 1629). First perf. Parma, Teatro Farnese as part of the wedding festivities for Duke Odoardo Farnese and Margherita de' Medici. Music lost. See letters 18 Sept. 1627 (to Enzo Bentivoglio) through to 4 Feb. 1628
1629[5]	Lorenzo Calvi (ed.), *Quarta raccolta de sacri canti 1–4 vv de diversi eccellentissimi autori*, Venice, 1629
	SV303 Exulta filia Sion S. bc. M xvii; O; KM
	SV304 Exultent coeli et gaudeant angeli ('Questa cantada . . . si puol radoppiare, cioè ricopiarla, & farla sonare da gli istromenti, & cantare insieme con le voci'), 5vv., 5 insts ad lib, bc. M xvii; O; KM.
	SV285 Salve [o] Regina A. T./S. B. bc; also in 1641. M xv; F xv
perf. 16 April 1630	SV323 *Proserpina rapita* (*anatopismo*). Text by Giulio Strozzi (pub. Venice, 1630). First perf. in upper solar of Palazzo Dandolo (now the Danieli Hotel), Venice, home of Monteverdi's patron Girolamo Mocenigo as part of wedding festivities for Giustiniana Mocenigo and Lorenzo Giustiniani. Music lost except for the canzonetta for SSS bc 'Come dolce oggi l'auretta' (described in the libretto as *Canzonetta Parthenia cantata dalle tre ninfe con armonia Lidia, cioè di suono molle, & a' fanciulli convenevole*) pub. in Monteverdi, *Madrigali e canzonette. . .libro nono* (Venice, 1651)

1632	Monteverdi *Scherzi musicali cioè arie, & madrigali in stil recitativo, con una ciaccona . . . raccolti da Bartholomeo Magni*, 1, 2vv., bc, Venice, 1632
	SV150 Armato il cor d'adamantina fede T. T. bc; also pub. in Monteverdi 1638, 1651; M ix; F xix
	SV246 Maledetto S. bc; M x
	SV247 Quel sguardo sdegnosetto S. bc; M x
	SV248 Eri già tutta mia S. bc; M x
	SV249 Ecco di dolci raggi il sol armato T. bc; first pub. in G. B. Camarella *Madrigali et arie*, Venice, ?1623; M x
	SV250 Et è pur dunque vero S. 1 inst. bc; M x
	SV251 Zefiro torna e di soavi accenti, 'ciaccona' (Ottavio Rinuccini) T. T. bc; also pub. 1651; M ix; F xix; KM
1634[7]	Alessandro Vincenti (ed.), *Arie di diversi*, Venice, 1634
	SV320 Perché, se m'odiavi S. bc; M xvii
	SV321 Più lieto il guardo S. bc; M xvii
1636(?)	SV154 'Volgendo il ciel per l'immortal sentiero' – 'Movete al mio bel suon le piante snelle' (*ballo per l'imperatore Ferdinando III*). Text by Ottavio Rinuccini. Seemingly intended for Vienna following election of Ferdinand III in Dec. 1636. Pub. in Monteverdi, *Madrigali guerrieri, et amorosi* (Venice, 1638); B viii, M viii
1637	SVA1 *Ballo del Monte Verde*, in P. Milioni and L. Monte *Vero e facil modo d'imparare a sonare, et accordare da se medesimo la chitarra spagnuola* (Rome and Macerata, 1637)
1638	Monteverdi *Madrigali guerrieri, et amorosi con alcuni opuscoli in genere rappresentativo, che saranno per brevi episodii frà i canti senza gesto. Libro ottavo*, 1–8vv., insts, bc, Venice, 1638. B viii (M and F as shown for individual works)
	SV146 Altri canti d'Amor, tenero arciero 6vv. 6 insts bc; M viii; KM
	SV147 Or che 'l cielo e la terra e 'l vento tace (Petrarch) 6vv. 2 vns bc; M viii; KM
	SV148 Gira il nemico insidioso Amore (Giulio Strozzi) A. T. B. bc; M viii
	SV149 Se vittorie sì belle (Fulvio Testi) T. T. bc; also pub. 1651; M ix; F xix
	SV150 Armato il cor d'adamantina fede T. T. bc; also pub. in Monteverdi 1651; M ix; F xix
	SV151 Ogni amante è guerrier: nel suo gran regno (Ottavio Rinuccini) T. T. B. bc; M viii
	SV152 Ardo, avvampo, mi struggo, ardo: accorrete 8vv., 2 vns, bc; M viii
	SV153 *Combattimento di Tancredi e Clorinda* (*in genere rappresentativo*) (Torquato Tasso) S. T. T. 5 insts, bc (perf. Carnival 1624 (?= 1624–5); M viii; KM

SV154 'Volgendo il ciel per l'immortal sentiero' – 'Movete al mio bel suon le piante snelle' (*Ballo*) (Ottavio Rinuccini) T. 5vv., 2vns, bc; perf. 1636(?); M viii; KM

SV155 Altri canti di Marte e di sua schiera (Giambattista Marino) 6vv., 2 vns, bc. M viii; KM.

SV156 Vago augelletto che cantando vai (Petrarch) 7vv., 2 vn, contrabasso, bc, 1638. M viii; KM

SV157 Mentre vaga angioletta (Battista Guarini), T. T. bc; M viii

SV158 Ardo e scoprir, ahi lasso, io non ardisco T. T. bc; also pub. 1651; M ix; F xix

SV159 O sia tranquillo il mare, o pien d'orgoglio T. T. bc; also pub. 1651; M ix; F xix

SV160 Ninfa che scalza il piede e sciolto il crine T. T. B. bc. M viii; KM

SV161 Dolcissimo uscignolo ('cantato à voce piena, alla francese') (Battista Guarini) 5vv., bc; M viii

SV162 Chi vol aver felice e lieto il core, ('cantato à voce piena, alla francese') (Battista Guarini) 5vv., bc; M viii

SV163 Non avea Febo ancora (the second section is headed *Lamento della ninfa . . . rappresentativo*) (Ottavio Rinuccini) S. [nymph] T. T. B. bc. M viii; KM

SV164 Perché te 'n fuggi, o Fillide? (Ottavio Rinuccini) A. T. B. bc; M viii

SV165 Non partir, ritrosetta A. A. B. bc; M viii

SV166 Su, su, su, pastorelli vezzosi S. S. A. bc. M viii; KM

SV167 *Ballo delle ingrate* (*in genere rapresentativo*); see also *Mascherata dell'ingrate* (perf. 4 June 1608), above; this version, with text and poss. music revised, may have been performed at the Viennese court in 1636. M VIII; KM

Perf. Carnival 1639–40   SV291 *Arianna* (first perf. 28 May 1608; see above); Venice, poss. Teatro S. Moisè, before 21 February 1640

perf. 1640, before 22 Feb. [= Ash Wednesday]   SV154 *Il ritorno d'Ulisse in patria* [opera]. Text (in 5 acts) by Giacomo Badoaro (survives only in manuscript). First perf. prob. Teatro SS Giovanni e Paolo, Venice. The opera was revived in Bologna in 1640, and in Venice, prob at SS Giovanni e Paolo, in Carnival 1640–41. The music for a three-act version survives in Vienna, Österreichische Nationalbibliothek, MS 18763. M xii; also ed. Alan Curtis, with English translation (London: Novello, 2002)

perf. Carnival 1640–1641   *Le nozze d'Enea e Lavinia* [opera]. Text by Michelangelo Torcigliani (text survives only in manuscript). First perf., following the revival of *Il ritorno d'Ulisse*, prob. at the Teatro SS Giovanni e Paolo, Venice. Music lost

perf. 7 Feb. 1641	*Vittoria d'Amore* (*balletto*). Text by Bernardo Morando (description by Morando pub. Piacenza, n.d.). First performed Piacenza to celebrate the birth of the seventh child of Duke Odoardo Farnese. Music lost
1641	Monteverdi *Selva morale e spirituale*, Venice, 1640–41 (some of the part-books carry the date 1640, but the dedication is dated 1 May 1641). M xv; F xv

SV252 O ciechi, il tanto affaticar che giova? (*madrigale morale*) (Petrarch) 5vv., 2 vn, bc

SV253 Voi ch'ascoltate in rime sparse il suono (*madrigale morale*) (Petrarch) 5vv., 2 vn, bc; (= Haec dicit Dominus in 1642[4])

SV254 È questa vita un lampo (Angelo Grillo) 5vv., bc

SV255 Spuntava il dí (*canzonetta morale*) (Francesco Balducci) A. T. B. bc

SV256 Chi vol che m'innamori (*canzon morale*) A. T. B. 2 vns, bc

SV257 Messa . . . da cappella 4vv., bc; for alternative settings of Crucifixus, Et resurrexit, Et iterum venturus est, see below

SV258 Gloria in excelsis Deo (*concertata*) 7vv., 2 vns, 4 viole da braccio/trbns (the latter ad lib) bc. KM

SV259 Crucifixus (*concertato*) 4vv., bc; can also be used to replace the corresponding section in the Messa . . . da cappella, above

SV260 Et resurrexit S. S./T. T. 2 vns; can also be used to replace the corresponding section in the Messa . . . da cappella, above

SV261 Et iterum venturus est A. A. B. 4 trbns/viole da braccio ad lib bc; can also be used to replace the corresponding section in the Messa . . . da cappella, above

SV262 Ab aeterno ordinata sum (*motetto*) B. bc

SV263 Dixit Dominus I (*concertato*) 8vv., 2 vns, 4 viole da braccio/trbns ad lib, bc

SV264 Dixit Dominus II (*concertato*) 8vv., 2 vns, 4 viole da braccio/trbns ad lib, bc

SV265 Confitebor tibi Domine I A. T. B. 5vv., bc

SV266 Confitebor tibi Domine II (*concertato*) S. T. B. 2 vns, bc

SV267 Confitebor tibi Domine III (*stile alla franzese*) 5vv (or S. 4 viole da braccio) bc. KM

SV268 Beatus vir I (*concertato*) 6vv., 2 vns, 3 viole da braccio/trbns ad lib, bc. KM

SV269 Beatus vir II ('si puo cantare ridoppiato & forte o come piacerà') 5vv., bc

SV270 Laudate pueri Dominum I (*concertato*) 5vv., 2 vns, bc

SV271 Laudate pueri Dominum II ('con instrumenti')
5vv., bc

SV272 Laudate Dominum omnes gentes I (*concertato*) 5vv.,
chorus 4vv. ad lib, 4 viole da braccio/trbns ad lib, bc

SV273 Laudate Dominum omnes gentes II 8vv., 2 vns, bc

SV274 Laudate Dominum omnes gentes III 8vv., bc

SV275 Credidi propter quod locutus sum ('del quarto
tuono', 'da capella') 8vv. (2 choirs), bc

SV276 [Memento Domine David] et omnis mansuetudinis
('quarti toni', 'da capella') 8vv. (2 choirs), bc

SV277 Sanctorum meritis I ('Primo himnus comune
plurimorum martirum', 'sopra alla qual aria si potranno
cantare anco altri hinni pero che sijno dello stesso
metro') S. 2 vns, bc

SV278 Sanctorum meritis II ('Plurimorum martirum &
confessorum', 'sopra a la qual aria si puo cantare anco
altri hinni delo stesso metro') T. 2 vns, bc

SV278a Deus tuorum militum [I] ('Himnus sopra ad una
medesima aria commune unius martyris'); same music
as 'Sanctorum merritis I' and 'Iste confessor' [I]

SV278b Iste confessor [I] ('Himnus sopra ad una
medesima aria commune confessorum'); same
music as 'Sanctorum meritis I' and 'Deus tuorum
militum' [I]

SV279 Iste confessor [II] ('Himnus comune confessorum',
'sopra alla qual aria si puo cantare parimente Ut queant
laxis di S. Gio. Batt. et simili') S. S. 2 vns, bc

SV279a Ut queant laxis ('Himnus Sancti Ioannis') S. S. 2
vns, bc; same music as 'Iste confessor' [II]. KM

SV280 Deus tuorum militum [II] ('Himnus unius martiris',
'Sopra la stessa aria si potranno cantare ancora Iesu
corona Virginum, Christe Redemptor omnium, &
altri del medesimo metro') T. T. B. 2 vns, bc

SV281 Magnificat I 8vv. (2 choirs), 2 vns, 4 viole da braccio/
trbns ad lib, bc. KM.

SV282 Magnificat II ('Primo tuono', 'in genere da capella')
4vv., bc

SV283 Salve Regina I [begins with words 'Audi coelum']
('in ecco *concertata*') T. T. 2 vns, bc

SV284 Salve Regina II T. T./S. S. bc. KM

SV285 Salve [o] Regina A. T./S. B. bc; first pub. in 1629[5]

SV286 Jubilet tota civitas ('motetto . . . in dialogo') S. bc

SV287 Laudate Dominum in sanctis eius S./T. bc. KM

SV288 Iam moriar mi fili (*Pianto della Madonna*)
(*contrafactum* of *Lamento d'Arianna*, sections 1–4;
S bc; also in 1642[4] [CF]

perf. 1643, late Jan./
early Feb. to before
18 Feb. [= Ash
Wednesday]

SV308 *L'incoronazione* [*La coronatione*] *di Poppea* / *Il Nerone*
(*opera reggia*). Text by Giovanni Francesco Busenello
(pub. 1656 in the collected edition of Busenello's work).
Scenario (Venice, 1643). Music survives in two
manuscripts (I-Vnm, MS 9963 (It. IV.439) and I-Nc, Rari
6.4.1) both dating probably from after 1650. M xiii; also
ed. Alan Curtis with English trans., London: Novello,
1989, and by Clifford Bartlett, with Engish trans, KM

The opera was revived in Paris early in 1647, and in
Naples in 1651

On the dating of the first performance to 1643, see
Whenham, 'Perspectives', 261–2

1645³

*Motetti a voce sola de diversi eccellentissimi autori. . .Libro
primo*, Venice, 1645

SV336 Venite videte martirem S. bc. M xvii

1650

Monteverdi *Messa, 4vv, et salmi, 1–8vv, concertati, e parte
da cappella, & con le Letanie della B.V.*, Venice, 1650.
M xvi; F xviii

SV190 Messa . . . da capella 4vv., bc

SV191 Dixit Dominus I 8vv. (2 choirs), bc. KM

SV192 Dixit Dominus II ('alla breve') 8vv. (2 choirs),
bc. KM

SV193 Confitebor tibi Domine I S. 2 vns/viole da
braccio, bc

SV194 Confitebor tibi Domine II S. T. 2 vns, bc

SV195 Beatus vir 7vv., 2 vns, bc

SV196 Laudate pueri Dominum ('alla quarta bassa. Da
capella') 5vv., bc. KM

SV197 Laudate Dominum omnes gentes B. bc;
ornamented version in 1651². KM

SV198 Laetatus sum I 6vv., 2 vns, 2 trbns, bassoon. KM

SV199 Laetatus sum II 5vv., bc

SV200 Nisi Dominus I S. T. B. 2 vns, bc. KM

SV201 Nisi Dominus II 6vv., bc. KM

SV202 Lauda Jerusalem I A. T. B. bc

SV203 Lauda Jerusalem II 5vv., bc. KM

SV204 Laetaniae della Beata Vergine 6vv., bc; first
published in 1620⁴; also published in 1626³. KM

1651

Monteverdi *Madrigali e canzonette . . . Libro nono*, 2, 3vv.,
Venice, 1651; M ix; F xix

SV168 Bel pastor dal cui bel sguardo (Ottavio Rinuccini)
S. T. bc

SV251 Zefiro torna e di soavi accenti, 'ciaccona' (Ottavio
Rinuccini) T. T. bc; first pub. 1632

SV149 Se vittorie sì belle (Fulvio Testi) T. T. bc; first pub. 1638

SV150 Armato il cor d'adamantina fede T. T. bc; first pub.
in Monteverdi 1632; also pub. in Monteverdi 1638

SV158 Ardo e scoprir, ahi lasso, io non ardisco T. T. bc;
first pub. 1638

SV159 O sia tranquillo il mare, o pien d'orgoglio T. T. bc;
first pub. 1638

SV169 Alcun non mi consigli A. T. B. bc

SV170 Di far sempre gioire A. T. B. bc

SV171 Quando dentro al tuo seno T. T. B. bc

SV172 Non voglio amare T. T. B. bc

SV173 Come dolce oggi l'auretta (Giulio Strozzi, from
Proserpina rapita (perf. 16 April 1630)) S. S. S. bc

SV174 Alle danze, alle gioie, ai diletti T. T. B. bc

SV175 Perché, se m'odiavi T. T. B. bc

SV176 Sì, sì, ch'io v'amo T. T. T. bc

SV177 Su, su, su, pastorelli vezzosi T. T. B. bc

SV178 O mio bene, o mia vita. T. T. B. bc

1651[2]	*Raccolta di motetti a 1–3 vv di Gasparo Casati et de diversi altri eccellentissimi autori*, Venice, 1651

SV197 Laudate Dominum omnes gentes B. bc;
ornamented version of the psalm first published in
1650). M xvi; F xviii

SV302 En gratulemur hodie T. 2 vns, bc. M xvi

Böddecker 1651	P.F. Böddecker *Sacra partitura*, 1v., Strasburg, 1651

SV299 Ecce sacrum paratum convivium T. bc; ornamented
version of the motet published in 1625[2]

Manuscripts

D-Kl MS 2° MS Mus. 51v	SV311 Laudate pueri Dominum 6vv., bc; ed. D. Arnold (London, 1982)
	SV295 Confitebor tibi Domine 4vv., bc; pub. in 1627[4]; O
D-Kl 2° MS Mus. 57f	SV114a Misero Alceo, dal caro albergo fore (Giambattista Marino) (variant of madrigal pub. in 1614)
	SV116a Presso a un fiume tranquillo, dialogue (Giambattista Marino) (variant of madrigal pub. in 1614)
GB-Lbl Add. 30491	SV22a Lasciatemi morire (*Lamento d'Arianna*; see above, *Arianna* (perf. 28 May 1608); version in 9 sections copied by or for Luigi Rossi, perhaps in 1617
	SVA2 Voglio, voglio morir, voglio morire (*Lamento d'Olimpia*) S., bc [doubtful atttribution]; also in GB-Lbm Add. 31440. O
GB-Lbl Add. 31440	Only the arrangements of Monteverdi's madrigals probably by Angelo Notari, together with the

Lamento d'Olimpia (a doubtful attribution) are listed here; see Ian Spink, 'Notari, Angelo', *New Grove*, vol. XVIII, pp. 72–3

SV98 Ch'io t'ami, e t'ami più della mia vita (Battista Guarini) arr. S. S. bc; original version 5vv., bc ad lib, pub. 1605

SV94 Cruda Amarilli, che col nome ancora (Battista Guarini) arr. [S]. S. B/bc, (B only), original version 5vv., bc ad lib, 1605; see also GB-Och, 878, 880

SV 97 Ecco, Silvio, colei che in odio hai tanto (Battista Guarini) arr. S. S. bc; original version 5vv., bc ad lib, 1605

SVA2 Voglio, voglio morir, voglio morire (*Lamento d'Olimpia*), S. bc [doubtful atttribution]; also in GB-Lbm Add. 30491. O

GB-Och 878, 880 | See the bibliographical note to GB-Lbl Add. 31440, above.

SV101 Ahi come a un vago sol cortese giro (Battista Guarini) arr. S. S. bc; original version 5vv., bc, pub. 1605

SV94 Cruda Amarilli, che col nome ancora (Battista Guarini) arr. [S.], S. B./bc, Lbl Add.31440 (B. only), Och 878 (S.2 only), 880 (bc only); original version 5vv., bc ad lib, pub. 1605

SV104 'T'amo, mia vita' la mia cara vita (Battista Guarini) arr. [S.], S. bc; original version 5vv., bc pub. 1605

I-BRq L.IV.99 | (Canto part-book dated 1610); see J. Kurtzman, 'An early 17th-century manuscript of *Canzonette e madrigaletti spirituali*', *Studi musicali*, 8 (1979), 149–71

SV306 Fuggi, fuggi, cor, fuggi a tutte l'or

SV244 Dolce spina del mio core (= 'Lidia spina del mio core', pub. 1607[21]); [CF]

SV235 Su fanciullo (= ' Damigella tutta bella', pub. 1607[21]) [CF]

SV237 O rosetta che rossetta (= 'O rosetta che rossetta', pub. 1607[21])

SV330 Se d'un angel il bel viso

I-Fn B.R. 238 (Magl. XIX.114) | SV22a Lasciatemi morire (*Lamento d'Arianna*; see above, *Arianna* (perf. 28 May 1608); version in 9 sections; the reading of this MS pub. in SA, i)

I-MOe α.K.6.31 | SV290 Ahi, che si parte il mio bel sol adorno S. S. T.; M xvii

I-MOe Mus.G.239 | SV22 Lasciatemi morire (*Lamento d'Arianna*; see above, *Arianna* (perf. 28 May 1608); version in 5 sections

	SV241 Giovinetta, ritrosetta (Ansaldo Cebà) arr. S. bc; original version 3vv., 2 vns, bc, pub. in 1607[21]
I-Nf 473.1 (olim IV–2–23a)	SV307 Gloria in excelsis Deo 8vv. (2 choirs) bc; O.
I-Nf 473.2 (olim IV–2–23b)	SV337 Voglio di vita uscir, voglio che cadano S. bc; O
I-Vc Torrefranca 28600	SV22 Lasciatemi morire (*Lamento d'Arianna*; see above, *Arianna* (perf. 28 May 1608); version in 5 sections
S-Uu Vok.mus.i hs. 29:22 and 79:10	SV296 Confitebor tibi Domine S. 5 insts, org., bc, doubtful attribution (probably by J. Rosenmüller); ed. A. Watty (Wolfenbüttel and Zürich, 1986)

Contrafacta of Monteverdi's Works [CF]

Literature

Sabine Ehrmann-Herfort, '"Ad Religionem ergò referatur Musica": Monteverdi-Kontrafakturen bei Aquilino Coppini', *Claudio Monteverdi und die Folgen*, ed. Silke Leopold and Joachim Steinheuer, Kassel, 1998, pp. 325–38

Margaret Ann Rorke, 'Sacred contrafacta of Monteverdi madrigals and Cardinal Borromeo's Milan', *Music and Letters*, 65 (1984), 168–75

K. M. Sponheim, 'The anthologies of Ambrosius Profe (1589–1661) and the transmission of Italian music in Germany', Ph.D. thesis, Yale University, 1995

1607[20][CF]   Aquilino Coppini (ed.), *Musica tolta da i madrigali di Claudio Monteverdi, e d'altri autori, e fatta spirituale*, 5, 6vv., Milan, 1607

1608[CF]   Aquilino Coppini (ed.), *Il secondo libro della musica di Claudio Monteverdi e d'altri autori fatta spirituale*, 5vv., Milan, 1608

1609[CF]   Aquilino Coppini (ed.), *Il terzo libro della musica di Claudio Monteverdi, fatta spirituale*, 5vv., Milan, 1609

1623[CF]   P. Lappi (ed.), *Concerti sacri, libro secondo*, 1–7vv., bc, Venice, 1623

1633[CF]   J. Staden *Geistliche Music-Klang*, Nuremberg, 1633

1641[2][CF]   Ambrosius Profe (ed.), *Erster Theil geistlicher Concerten und Harmonien*, 1–7vv., 2 vn, org., Breslau, 1641

1641[3][CF]   Ambrosius Profe (ed.), *Ander Theil geistlicher Concerten und Harmonien*, 1–7vv., 2 vn, org., Leipzig, 1641

1642[4][CF]   Ambrosius Profe (ed.), *Dritter Theil geistlicher Concerten und Harmonien*, 1–5vv., 2 vn, org., Leipzig, 1642

1649[6][CF]   Ambrosius Profe, ed., *Corollarum geistlicher collectaneorum* (Leipzig, 1649)

1654[CF]   *Cantiones natalitiae*, Antwerp, 1654; ed. R. Rasch, Exempla musica neerlandica, xii–xiii (Amsterdam, 1981)

Manuscripts of contrafacta

D-Dl MS Mus.Pi.8 [CF]
D-Kl 2° MS Mus.58j [CF]

D-GD, MS Cath. q.28 [CF]

D-Lr MS Mus. Ant. Pract. K.N.206 [CF]

I-Bc Q27 [CF] [incomplete, lacks Canto 2]. The compiler of this manuscript altered the original text of Monteverdi's canzonets only when the original could not be read, ambiguously, as a spiritual text (see Fabbri, *Monteverdi*, trans. Carter, pp. 29–30)

I-Bc Q43[CF]. *Lamento della Maddalena*; see above, *Arianna* (perf. 28 May 1608) and *La Maddalena* (perf. March 1617)

PL-WRu[CF] (un-named MS now lost (see SV, H78)

Malta, Mdina, Cathedral Museum, MS 47 [CF]

Index of titles and first lines

(Dates in parenthesis can be used to locate the works in the Catalogue of Monteverdi's works, above)

Index of Names and Subjects

Cambridge Companions to Music

Topics

The Cambridge Companion to Blues and
Gospel Music
Edited by Allan Moore

The Cambridge Companion to Conducting
Edited by José Antonio Bowen

The Cambridge Companion to Electronic Music
Edited by Nick Collins and Julio d'Escrivan

The Cambridge Companion to Grand Opera
Edited by David Charlton

The Cambridge Companion to Jazz
Edited by Mervyn Cooke and David Horn

The Cambridge Companion to the Lied
Edited by James Parsons

The Cambridge Companion to the Musical
Edited by William Everett and Paul Laird

The Cambridge Companion to the Orchestra
Edited by Colin Lawson

The Cambridge Companion to Pop and Rock
Edited by Simon Frith, Will Straw and
John Street

The Cambridge Companion to the String
Quartet
Edited by Robin Stowell

Composers

The Cambridge Companion to Bach
Edited by John Butt

The Cambridge Companion to Bartók
Edited by Amanda Bayley

The Cambridge Companion to Beethoven
Edited by Glenn Stanley

The Cambridge Companion to Berg
Edited by Anthony Pople

The Cambridge Companion to Berlioz
Edited by Peter Bloom

The Cambridge Companion to Brahms
Edited by Michael Musgrave

The Cambridge Companion to Benjamin Britten
Edited by Mervyn Cooke

The Cambridge Companion to Bruckner
Edited by John Williamson

The Cambridge Companion to John Cage
Edited by David Nicholls

The Cambridge Companion to Chopin
Edited by Jim Samson

The Cambridge Companion to Debussy
Edited by Simon Trezise

The Cambridge Companion to Elgar
Edited by Daniel M. Grimley and Julian Rushton

The Cambridge Companion to Handel
Edited by Donald Burrows

The Cambridge Companion to Liszt
Edited by Kenneth Hamilton

The Cambridge Companion to Mahler
Edited by Jeremy Barham

The Cambridge Companion to Mendelssohn
Edited by Peter Mercer-Taylor

The Cambridge Companion to Monteverdi
Edited by John Whenham and Richard Wistreich

The Cambridge Companion to Mozart
Edited by Simon P. Keefe

The Cambridge Companion to Ravel
Edited by Deborah Mawer

The Cambridge Companion to Rossini
Edited by Emanuele Senici

The Cambridge Companion to Schubert
Edited by Christopher Gibbs

The Cambridge Companion to Sibelius
Edited by Daniel M. Grimley

The Cambridge Companion to Stravinsky
Edited by Jonathan Cross

The Cambridge Companion to Verdi
Edited by Scott L. Balthazar

Instruments

The Cambridge Companion to Brass
Instruments
Edited by Trevor Herbert and John Wallace

The Cambridge Companion to the Cello
Edited by Robin Stowell

The Cambridge Companion to the Clarinet
Edited by Colin Lawson

The Cambridge Companion to the Guitar
Edited by Victor Coelho

The Cambridge Companion to the Organ
Edited by Nicholas Thistlethwaite and
Geoffrey Webber

The Cambridge Companion to the Piano
Edited by David Rowland

The Cambridge Companion to the Recorder
Edited by John Mansfield Thomson

The Cambridge Companion to the Saxophone
Edited by Richard Ingham

The Cambridge Companion to Singing
Edited by John Potter

The Cambridge Companion to the Violin
Edited by Robin Stowell